The Antebellum Era

The Antebellum Era

Primary Documents on Events from 1820 to 1860

David A. Copeland

Debating Historical Issues in the Media of the Time

GREENWOOD PRESS
Westport, Connecticut • London

Library of Congress Cataloging-in-Publication Data

The Antebellum era : primary documents on events from 1820 to 1860 / [compiled by] David A. Copeland.
p. cm.—(Debating historical issues in the media of the time, ISSN 1542-8079)
Includes bibliographical references and index.
ISBN 0-313-32079-9 (alk. paper)
1. United States—History—1783-1865—Sources. I. Copeland, David A., 1951- II. Series.
E301.D43 2003
973.5—dc21 2002192776

British Library Cataloguing in Publication Data is available.

Library of Congress Catalog Card Number: 2002192776
ISBN: 0-313-32079-9
ISSN: 1542-8079

First published in 2003

Greenwood Press, 88 Post Road West, Westport, CT 06881
An imprint of Greenwood Publishing Group, Inc.
www.greenwood.com

Printed in the United States of America

The paper used in this book complies with the Permanent Paper Standard issued by the National Information Standards Organization (Z39.48-1984).

10 9 8 7 6 5 4 3 2 1

Contents

Series Foreword

As the eighteenth century was giving way to the nineteenth, the *Columbian Centinel* of Boston, quoting a wise judge in its January 1, 1799, issue said, "Give to any set men the command of the press, and you give them the command of the country, for you give them the command of public opinion, which commands everything." One month later, Thomas Jefferson wrote to James Madison with a similar insight. "We are sensible," Jefferson said of the efforts it would take to put their party—the Republicans—in power, "'The engine is the press."

Both writers were correct in their assessment of the role the press would play in American life in the years ahead. The press was already helping to shape the opinions and direction of America. It had been doing so for decades, but its influence would erupt following the Revolutionary War and would continue into the 1920s and farther. From less than forty newspapers in 1783—each with circulations of around 500—the number of papers greatly increased in the United States. By 1860, newspaper circulation exceeded 1 million, and in 1898, Joseph Pulitzer's *World* alone had a daily circulation of 1.3 million. By the beginning of World War I, about 16,600 daily and weekly newspapers were published, and circulation figures surpassed 22.5 million copies per day, with no slowdown in circulation in sight. Magazines grew even more impressively. From around five at the end of the Revolution, journalism historian Frank Luther Mott counted 600 in 1860, and a phenomenal 3,300 by 1885. Some circulations surpassed 1 million, and the number of magazines continued to grow into the twentieth century.

The amazing growth of the press happened because the printed page of periodicals assumed a critical role in the United States. Newspapers and magazines became the place where Americans discussed and debated the issues that affected them. Newspapers, editors, and citizens took sides, and they used the press as the conduit for discussion. The *Debating Historical Issues in the Media of the Time* series offers a glimpse into how the press was used by Americans to shape and influence the major events and issues facing the nation during different periods of its development. Each volume is based on the documents, that is, the writings that appeared in the press of the time. Each volume presents articles, essays, and editorials that support opposing interests on the events and issues; and each provides readers with background and explanation of the events, issues, and, if possible, the people who wrote the articles that have been selected. Each volume also includes a chronology of events and a selected bibliography. Books in the *Debating Historical Issues in the Media of the Time* series cover the following periods: the Revolution and the young republic, the Federalist era, the antebellum period, the Civil War, Reconstruction, the progressive era, and World War I.

This volume on the antebellum period focuses upon the issues that affected the nation from 1820 to 1860 and that ultimately led to the Civil War. The papers of this period were highly political in their content, and they usually aligned themselves with political parties. As one might suspect, slavery increasingly became the main focus of this period, and in some ways helped to shape much that happened and that was debated in the press.

Acknowledgments

A number of people helped in the completion of this book. Carol Sue Humphrey of Oklahoma Baptist University, John Coward of Tulsa University, and Bernell Tripp of the University of Florida shared their knowledge and information about the 1820s, Native Americans, and the black press respectively. Dale Broadhurst of Hilo, Hawaii, has done extensive research into coverage of Mormons in the antebellum period. His research and conversations greatly aided in preparation of the chapter on Joseph Smith. In addition, Scott H. Faulring of the Fielding Smith Institute for Latter-day Saint History at Brigham Young University aided in the search for documents. Shannon Martin of the University of Maine tracked down elusive newspaper reports from Maine. Lloyd Benson at Furman University has done considerable research into the events of the 1850s. It was a great help in completing some chapters in this book. Laura West and Lynn Melchor of the Carol Grotnes Belk Library at Elon University worked to locate materials. Frederick Merck's work on Manifest Destiny was also an indispensable asset in producing this work, especially his extensive use of primary documents.

The School of Communications at Elon University supported this project with a schedule conducive to research and constant encouragement, and Margaret Blanchard of the University of North Carolina continued in her effort to keep me excited about writing and research. Finally, as always, my family served as my greatest supporters. To Robin Copeland, who went to bed too many nights with lights blazing in her eyes and keyboard tapping in her ears, I thank you for all that you mean to me.

Chronology of Events

1820	Missouri Compromise; first steam engine pulls train cars
1821	Mexico gains independence from Spain; First American move into Texas; Boston opens first public secondary school; Sante Fe trail
1822	First free black Americans arrive in Liberia; Denmark Vesey conspiracy
1823	Monroe Doctrine
1824	Congress raises tariff duties
1825	Erie Canal opens; House elects John Quincy Adams president
1826	American Society for the Promotion of Temperance formed; James Fenimore Cooper's *Last of the Mohicans*
1827	Cherokee nation adopts written constitution; *Freedom's Journal*, first African American newspaper, begins in New York; Massachusetts Public School Act
1828	Andrew Jackson elected president; John C. Calhoun's *South Carolina Exposition and Protest*; Tariff of Abominations
1829	*Walker's Appeal to the Colored Citizens of the World* published; typewriter invented
1830	Baltimore and Ohio Railroad begins passenger service; Indian Removal Act; Church of Jesus Christ of Latter-day Saints formed; U.S. population nears 13 million; Webster–Hayne Debate
1831	Abolitionist paper the *Liberator* begins in Boston; Nat Turner rebellion; McCormick's mechanical wheat reaper; *Cherokee Nation v. Georgia*; Alexis de Tocqueville visits America
1832	*Worcester v. Georgia*; Jackson vetoes Bank of the United

	States recharter; Jackson re-elected; New England Anti-Slavery Society organized
1833	Penny Press begins in New York; 1,200 newspapers printed in America
1834	Whig party organized
1835	Osceola leads Seminole War
1836	Van Buren elected president; Battle of the Alamo; Texas wins independence from Mexico; Second Bank of the United States dissolved; Ralph Waldo Emerson's *Nature*
1837	Economic panic sends nation into depression; Samuel Morse invents telegraph
1838	Trail of Tears
1839	Daguerreotype invented; *Amistad* lands in America
1840	Harrison elected president; Edgar Allan Poe's *Tales of the Grotesque and Arabesque*; the moral war
1841	Harrison dies, and Tyler becomes president; Dorothea Dix begins crusade against insane asylums; Brook Farm founded; *United States v. Amistad*
1842	Dorr Rebellion in Rhode Island; Webster–Ashburton Treaty
1843	Dorothea Dix reports on treatment of the insane
1844	Telegraph perfected; Polk elected president; Joseph Smith killed in Illinois
1845	Texas joins the Union; Manifest Destiny coined; Baptists divide over slavery
1846	Mexican War; Buchanan–Pakenham treaty decides Oregon issue; Wilmot Proviso introduced
1848	Gold discovered in California; Taylor elected president; First Women's Rights Convention
1849	Gold rush begins
1850	Fugitive Slave Act; Compromise of 1850; Nathaniel Hawthorne's *The Scarlet Letter*
1851	*Uncle Tom's Cabin* published in serial form in the *National Era*; Singer sewing machine; Herman Melville's *Moby-Dick*
1852	*Uncle Tom's Cabin* as a book is published; Pierce elected president
1853	Gadsden Purchase; Commodore Matthew Perry arrives in Japan
1854	Kansas–Nebraska Act; Republican Party formed; Henry David Thoreau's *Walden*
1855	Walt Whitman's *Leaves of Grass*

1856	Buchanan elected president; caning of Charles Sumner; Pottawatomie massacre
1857	Economic panic and depression; *Dred Scott* decision
1858	Lincoln–Douglas debates; washing machine patented
1859	John Brown's raid
1860	Lincoln elected president; South Carolina secedes from Union; U.S. population surpasses 31.4 million; newspaper circulation exceeds 1 million; 600 magazines published in America; Charles Darwin's *Origin of Species*

Introduction: Newspapers and Antebellum America

On May 6, 1835, James Gordon Bennett published the first issue of the New York *Herald*. In it, he predicted, "This is the age of the Daily Press, inspired with the accumulated wisdom of past ages, enriched with the spoils of history, and looking forward to a millennium of a thousand years, the happiest and most splendid ever yet known in the measured span of eternity!" Bennett's *Herald* had entered the competitive world of the "Penny Press," where newspapers—selling for one penny—found a large and eager audience among tens of thousands of Americans who had never before been able to afford a newspaper. Bennett was correct in saying the period was the age of the press. Newspaper publication erupted in the nineteenth century. In 1820, 512 newspapers were published regularly in America with a circulation of less than 300,000. By 1860, about 3,000 newspapers were regularly published, with circulation reaching nearly 1.5 million. Magazines grew at an even more phenomenal rate. A dozen magazines were published in 1800. By 1860, that number grew to 1,000.[1] Visitors to the United States observed the power of the press. Alexis de Tocqueville explained its power when he wrote, following his early 1831–32 tour of the nation, that the press "causes political life to circulate through all the parts of that vast country. . . . It rallies the interests of the community round certain principles and draws up the creed of every party."[2] Newspapers in the first half of the nineteenth century fueled public dialogue as never before in America.

However, Bennett was wrong when he claimed that the times would be "the happiest and most splendid ever yet known in the measured span of eternity!" The antebellum period, the name given to the decades preceding the Civil War (1820–1860), saw America splinter into political factions and regions that would end with the bloodiest war in terms of American casualties that the nation has seen. America, less than fifty years after fighting for independence from Great Britain and struggling to establish a new form of government, faced a host of problems. Slavery, moral and social reform, women's rights, burgeoning immigration, economic depression, a move toward urbanization, public education, westward expansion, and the desire by some to hold onto an agrarian lifestyle combined to create a nation more disjointed than unified. America's problems may have been solvable had it not been for one issue– slavery. Ultimately, this "peculiar institution" led many to the conclusion that the North and South "are better apart."[3]

As the United States approached the 1820s, Americans found themselves in a period called "the era of good feelings," a term coined by Boston newspaper editor Benjamin Russell.[4] The political battles that had raged from the beginning of the century between the Federalists and the Republicans ceased. James Monroe won the 1816 presidential election in a landslide, and he ran unopposed in 1820 as the Federalist party faded away. Good feelings soon gave way to sectional bickering, however, and the nation found itself embroiled in argument again, with slavery at its heart. Controversy surrounding slavery was not new to America. The delegates to the Constitutional Convention had grappled with the issue. They had agreed that five slaves would equal three free people as a means of determining states' populations, and that slaves could continue to be imported into the nation until 1808.[5] The balance of power between slave and nonslave states kept the issue of slavery somewhat out of the national political arena. The number of free and slave states in 1819 was the same, eleven each, but that was about to change. In that year, Missouri sought admission to the Union as a slave state. This would mean that the slave states would hold the balance of power in Congress.

After the ratification of the Constitution, Congress had accepted the conditions of the Northwest Ordinance of 1787, which disallowed slavery in the territory that would become Ohio, Indiana, Illinois, Michigan, and Wisconsin, but Missouri was not part of that land acquisition. It was part of the Louisiana Purchase, and most of Missouri's settlers came from Kentucky and Tennessee, slave states. Slavery suddenly became a major issue in the United States. The practice, which had been attacked in American writings as early as 1700, now became the focus of debate in Congress. In order to maintain harmony, Congress agreed to a compromise. Missouri would be allowed to enter the Union as a slave state. Maine, which had been a part of Massachusetts, would enter as a free state. With regard to the rest of the nation's western territory, Congress agreed that slavery would be prohibited from all lands north of latitude 36 degrees, 30 minutes. Slavery would be allowed in the territory below that latitude, if so chosen by the territory's inhabitants when the region applied for statehood. The antebellum period, Latin for "before the war," had begun.

The antebellum period was one of tremendous growth in the United States. The nation began the period with twenty-two states. By 1860, there were thirty-three. Even more dramatic was the growth of the nation's population, which increased by more than 210 percent. In 1820, America's population was slightly more than 10 million. By 1860, the population surpassed 31 million. Despite efforts to limit slavery through the Missouri Compromise, the Compromise of 1850, the Kansas-Nebraska Act of 1854, and other legislation, the number of slaves grew, too. In 1820, census figures placed the slave population at more than 1.5 million. By 1860, it had swelled to nearly 4 million, an increase of more than 158 percent. Free African Americans by 1860, however, numbered less than 500,000.[6] Immigration, in part, fueled America's population explosion after 1840. More than 1.7 million people entered America in the 1840s, and in the 1850s, that number jumped to more than 2.5 million.[7] Most immigrants came from Europe. The large influx of people produced a movement against immigrants that was called nativism. This movement was driven by a dislike of Catholicism and American workers' fear of job loss.

As America's population grew in the East, people pushed into lands west of the Mississippi River. Americans began to see it as their birthright to inhabit what would soon become the continental United States. An 1845 editorial in the *United States Magazine and Democratic Review* explained the concept best–and coined a term for it–when it stated, "Our manifest destiny is to overspread the continent allotted by Providence for the free development of our yearly multiplying millions."[8] By 1848, the United States completed its manifest destiny, controlling the lands between the Atlantic and Pacific oceans. First, in 1845, America annexed Texas. Texas had operated as an independent nation since 1836 when Americans, invited to settle there by the Mexican government, rebelled. Although the Americans were defeated at the Alamo, this event became the rallying point for other Americans in Texas. They defeated General Santa Ana and earned independence. Mexico, however, did not acknowledge Texas as an independent state, and America's annexation of Texas started the Mexican War. The United States defeated its southern neighbor and, with the Treaty of Guadalupe-Hidalgo in 1848, America obtained New Mexico and California from Mexico. The treaty also established the Rio Grande River as the boundary between the two nations. In two years, California became a state, and Oregon followed nine years later.

America's new territory only intensified the problems that had previously existed in the nation. The debate concerning slavery in the territories increased with the introduction of the Wilmot Proviso in 1846, a move to exclude slavery from all western lands acquired from Mexico after the war. Attacks against slavery in territories ultimately became attacks on the way of life in the South. Many Southern leaders began to advocate the idea of states' rights. Under the concept of states' rights, the powers of the federal government were limited solely to what was explicit in the Constitution. All other powers were reserved for the states. This meant that all states and all territories had the right to choose whether or not their citizens could own slaves. The argument would not be decided until the Civil War.

Newspapers played an important role in American events during the antebellum period. Even though the total number of newspapers and their circulation was rather small at the beginning of the period, their impact on society was much greater. In 1825, Virginian David Roper proposed a new publication for Richmond and noted that "A thirst for newspaper reading prevails among all ranks of society throughout our country."[9] By 1830, more than half of all American families subscribed to a newspaper.[10] People shared their newspapers with others, and newspapers were available in taverns and places of lodging for public reading and debate, making their impact on American society extremely forceful. Tocqueville observed on his tour of America that newspapers "drop the same thought into a thousand minds at the same moment."[11]

Numbers tell an important story in discovering the importance of newspapers in the antebellum period. Typically, between 10 and 15 percent of eligible voters actually voted during the first years of the American nation.[12] As the number of newspapers grew and more people had access to them, voting percentages rose. Approximately 44 percent of eligible voters participated in the 1832 election, an increase of more than 190 percent. [13] At the same time, about half of all households subscribed to a paper. The correlation of the two–voting and newspaper subscription–is not a coincidence. Martin Van Buren, who was elected president in 1836, realized the importance of newspapers to politics. After moving into the White House, he said, "Without a paper, we may hang our harps on the willows."[14] Van Buren meant that what was said in newspapers had an effect on the way Americans voted. Without newspaper support, candidates on any level would have a difficult time being elected.

President John Quincy Adams learned first-hand what negative newspaper exposure could do. Adams and Andrew Jackson outdistanced the two other presidential candidates in the 1824 election; neither received enough electoral votes to win the presidency. However, Jackson, a political newcomer, won fifteen more electoral votes than his Massachusetts counterpart and easily surpassed Adams in the popular vote. The House of Representatives decided the election and sent Adams to the White House. After that, many Americans turned to newspapers to ensure that the governmental power play that elected Adams would not be repeated. One newspaper declared that "public opinion will eventually be respected by the election of the General."[15] The public outcry intensified, and Jackson handily won the 1828 election. Jackson wisely read the papers and realized what people wanted; he complied. "The recent demonstration of public sentiment in-

GROUP OF PORTRAITS OF THE PRESIDENTS OF THE UNITED STATES

Gleason's Pictorial View of the Presidents. *Illustrated newspapers and magazines often ran images of political figures. The printed media provided the only way many would ever know what famous Americans looked like. This woodcut illustration appeared in the July 16, 1853, issue of Boston's* Gleason's Pictorial Newspaper.

scribes on the list of Executive duties, in characters too legible to be overlooked, the task of reform," Jackson said in his 1829 inaugural address, in direct reference to public opinion as voiced in newspapers.[16] That sentiment helped set the agenda for Jackson's presidency.

The press's role in American politics during the antebellum period was one of partisanship and patronage. American newspapers developed their partisan nature before the Revolution. As colonial America pulled away from Great Britain, newspapers divided into Patriot and Tory factions. The Tory faction was never large, and Americans who favored independence coerced Tory printers into silence. The lives of the printers of the *Boston Chronicle* and *New- York Gazetteer* were threatened. Both John Mein and James Rivington returned to the safety of England. Following the Revolution, as America worked to formulate its new government, politicians divided into Federalists and Republicans. Politicians realized the power of public opinion as created by newspapers and decided to harness that power. "We are sensible," Thomas Jefferson wrote to James Madison on the verge of the pivotal presidential election of 1800, "The engine is the press."[17] The Republican leaders were correct, and their party captured the presidency.

Newspapers began to support and promote the ideologies of parties and their chief spokesmen. The resulting partisan press, while not specifically owned by the political parties, advocated and promoted what their respective party leaders said. The political system of the day ensured that the party in power could reward its loyal editors by granting them government printing contracts and political office. Patronage meant considerable income for the newspaperman—John Fenno, for example, received up to $2,500 a year as printer to the Senate—so it was unlikely that his newspaper would ever make negative comments about the party granting favoritism. The same privileges were granted on all levels in America, from the presidency to local councils.[18] Patronage did not officially end in the United States until 1846, when Congress voted to solicit bids on federal printing. The debate on this reached its peak, though, with the second Adams–Jackson election. Giving editors who supported a specific political view government contracts and fat pay checks grew so prevalent in the 1820s that North Carolina Senator Nathaniel Macon remarked in 1827, "Let the executive patronage be increased and every president will appoint his successor."[19] Even though political patronage died out, party politics did not, and newspapers throughout the antebellum period advocated one political ideology while vehemently attacking others. Often, one could tell the political preference of a newspaper by its name, such as the Richmond *Whig*, the Nashville *Republican*, or the Philadelphia *Democratic Press*.

Publications did not limit their discussion during the antebellum period to politics. A great number of moral and ideological issues arose, and the press offered the perfect venue for discussion. Some—like slavery—combined the political with the moral. In 1821, Benjamin Lundy started a newspaper, *Genius of Universal Emancipation,* to address specifically the issue of slavery. The most ardent of abolitionist editors, however, was William Lloyd Garrison, who, in 1831, began publication of the *Liberator* in Boston. In his first issue, Garrison declared, in reference to the ills of slavery, "I am in earnest—I will not equivocate—I will not excuse—I will not retreat a single inch—AND I WILL BE HEARD"[20] By 1835, more than 1 million antislavery publications were produced in New York City alone.[21] Free blacks used the press, too, to fight against slavery and other social injustices. Before the Civil War, about forty black newspapers were begun. Often, they were started by African American ministers and educators, like Samuel Cornish and John Russworm, who published the first black-run newspaper, *Freedom's Journal,* beginning in 1827. Black newspapers railed against slavery, but they fought for civil rights, pride, education, and progress for African Americans even more.[22]

Religious groups used the press, too. Early in the antebellum period, a religious press grew and competed successfully with secular papers.[23] Religious newspapers looked like their secular counterparts, and they published the same news. They also discussed theology and morality, along with group-specific subject matter. The 1850 Census listed 191 religious newspapers or periodicals in America,[24] and religious journalism, according to one source, may have accounted for three-fourths of America's reading material in 1840.[25] The press soon provided a voice for nearly every cause or occupation in America. The Industrial Revolution provided America with a new job market, and labor newspapers began to address the circumstances of factory workers. These publications soon expanded to cover the needs of various professions, from bankers to miners. Agricultural newspapers sought ways to help farmers. Other specialized publications addressed inventions and discoveries aimed at making life easier.[26]

During the antebellum period, magazines joined newspapers as important publications. Most magazines initially looked like newspapers, but they soon took on an appearance more like today's tabloids. Early in the nineteenth century, magazines were expensive, and few people could afford a subscription. Improved and cheaper printing processes reduced cost and made a wider audience possible. Magazine subject matter, as a result, varied. Two of the more successful magazines were the *American Turf Register and Sporting Magazine,* which dealt with "veterinary subjects" and "various rural sports,"[27] and *Niles' Weekly Register,* a news magazine begun in Baltimore by Hezekiah Niles but read in every state because of its thorough coverage of issues. Perhaps the greatest development of the magazine press, though, was magazines for women. Sara Josepha Hale began the first magazine for women, the *Ladies Magazine,* in 1828. Numerous other titles followed, but *Godey's Lady's Book,* founded in Philadelphia in 1830, was the most widely read. It had a circulation of 150,000 before the Civil War.[28] *Godey's Lady's Book* and other women's magazines included a wealth of information on domestic life. This included sheet music, patterns for clothes and needlework, short stories, recipes, and carefully colored fold-out sheets of the latest fashions.

When the antebellum period began, newspaper and magazine production did not vary greatly from printing methods used since the beginning of newspaper production in America more than a century earlier. Type was handset with lead letters for each page. Letters were slid into a "stick," which held the lines of type. Once the lettering for the page was completed, printers locked it into an iron frame that was then fastened to the press. In America, the printing press was still manual in 1820, but some press operations, especially the successful ones in New York City, did not use the hand-operated screw press but one operated by levers. In either case, a worker, using a dauber, inked the letters while another placed the paper onto the press. The impression in the frame was then transferred to the paper. It was removed and placed on hanging wires to dry as the process was repeated. Creating newspapers was labor intensive, and producing more than about 250 impressions per hour on a hand-cranked press was difficult. In addition, paper was made of cloth and was not always easy to obtain. Newspapers, out of necessity, were expensive.

In the 1820s, inventors began applying technology to the printing press. Cylinders were the first improvement. The cylinders revolved and pressed the paper against the type, which was held on a flatbed. The addition of steam power, however, truly revolutionized printing. Steam-driven presses produced thousands of pages per hour instead of several hundred as produced on manual presses. The Koenig press, invented by the German Friedrich Koenig, employed a moveable bed that allowed easy inking of the frame between impressions. Koenig also affixed an additional cylinder to the press. This made it possible to print both sides of the paper at once. Richard Hoe built the new presses in America, and by 1830, the new steam cylinder presses could produce 4,000 newspapers per hour. Hoe continued to find ways to improve the steam press. In 1840, R. Hoe & Company introduced a revolving press that printed eight pages at a time. Typeset pages were attached to the cylinders, not a flatbed, and an automated process applied ink to type. The press produced 19,000 papers per hour. Steam presses were able to print large numbers of newspapers per hour, too, because of the invention of an automatic papermaking machine. The cost of newsprint dropped by 25 percent.[29]

HARPER'S WEEKLY.
A JOURNAL OF CIVILIZATION.

VOL. I.—No. 23.] NEW YORK, SATURDAY, JUNE 6, 1857. [PRICE FIVE CENTS.

PUBLISHERS' NOTICES.

OUR readers will be glad to hear that SIR EDWARD BULWER LYTTON is writing a new story, which he compares to the "Caxtons" and "My Novel." We have made arrangements with him for publishing it in the columns of this journal. The first number will appear in the course of next month, and it will be continued till it is completed, each number appearing here simultaneously with its publication in England. We congratulate our readers on the prospect. A new work by Bulwer is perhaps the noblest intellectual treat that can be offered to a person of refined and cultivated taste.

HARPER'S WEEKLY has already reached a regular issue of more than *Sixty Thousand Copies*, and the editions printed are steadily increasing.

The proprietors beg to say that they will be happy to receive sketches or photographic pictures of striking scenes, important events, and leading men from artists in every part of the world, and to pay liberally for such as they may use.

TWO NOBLE WOMEN.

WE are fortunate enough to be enabled to present our readers with portraits of two of the noblest women of the present day—Miss Florence Nightingale and Miss Annie M. Andrews.

The former—be it said without disparagement to her eminent qualities and her paramount claims on the world for fame and on her countrymen for gratitude—enjoyed a remarkable advantage over our countrywoman in respect of the publicity of her noble deeds: she won her laurels in the blaze of day, when thousands of voices and pens were eager to proclaim her mission of mercy and her meed of fame; and if they were won at less personal risk than those of Miss Andrews, they involved, perhaps, a bolder character and less shrinking from the public gaze.

FLORENCE NIGHTINGALE.

The two women differed in age, and somewhat in position. Miss Nightingale is a lady of some forty odd years of age; Miss Andrews was barely twenty when she embarked on her mission. Miss Nightingale is a lady of fortune and high social rank; when she announced her intention of proceeding to the East, a staff of officers offered her an escort, and a cohort of ladies of the best families of England solicited the privilege of being allowed to serve under her orders. Miss Andrews, though, we believe, a lady of some independent means, was living with an uncle at Syracuse when the terrible news from Norfolk roused her energy; she proceeded to the scene of her labors by railway alone and unnoticed.

MEDAL PRESENTED TO MISS ANDREWS BY THE HOWARD ASSOCIATION OF NORFOLK.

But the contrast will be best discovered by a somewhat more detailed biography of Miss Andrews.

The father of Miss Andrews, a self-made man, a native of New York, realized a fortune by the practice of the medical profession in the South, and now resides on a plantation of his own in the vicinity of New Orleans. His daughter, the subject of this sketch, was not indebted to her parents for her education. At an early age she was placed with an aunt, to whom she owed a sound religious and moral training. While quite a child, her fondness for visiting the sick was remarked among her young companions. She seems to have been born a nurse. When the fever at Norfolk broke out, she was living with her uncle, Judge Hall, of Syracuse, New York; she instantly announced her desire to go and offer her services as nurse. The need of nurses was so pressing, it will be remembered, that the most enormous prices were paid for very sorry attendants; still, the danger was so obvious that Miss Andrews's relations were much opposed to the scheme. By much entreaty she prevailed on them to allow her to write to the Mayor of Norfolk, tendering her services; they consented—mainly from the persuasion that the Mayor would decline the offer.

He, like a prudent man, neither declined nor accepted. He stated the pressing want of nurses, and described the terrible suffering of the people, but gave no opinion on Miss Andrews's application.—His description of the destitution of the poor sufferers was enough for her; she stipulated that she was to pay her own expenses, and departed alone. For two days and nights she traveled alone by rail. On approaching Norfolk she met three Sisters of Charity, bent on the same errand as herself; in their company she reported herself to the Mayor, and received permission to serve as nurse. It was late in *the evening* when this formality was fulfilled: the Sisters of Charity, with professional experience, prudently retired for the night; Miss Andrews went directly to the hospital, and waited on the sick that night.

Previous to the outbreak of fever, Norfolk had no hospital; an old race-stand was temporarily converted into an infirmary and baptized the Julappi Hospital. It was a miserable building; through the roof the rain poured in bad weather; every moment Miss Andrews could steal from her duties as nurse was devoted to calking the seams in the building. Though courage sustained her frame under trials that were indeed terrible to bear, her duties involved inconveniences over which her feelings had no control. Her tender hands and feet, unused to work, suffered severely, and even, at times, stood in need of surgical assistance; and at last, finding the repeated annoyance too troublesome, she bathed both hands and feet daily in strong salt and water to harden them; succeeding, indeed, in her immediate aim, but at the cost of what every young lady prizes—her hands are wrinkled and discolored, like those of a much older person.

Those who have had experience of a yellow fever hospital can alone appreciate the danger and the discomfort of Miss Andrews's position. It has often been said that of all patients the most unpleasant to nurse are sufferers from gun-shot wounds; the effluvia from the wound impart a poisonous taint to the air. But experienced nurses aver that not only is the air around the bed of a person dying of yellow fever sickening to breathe, but it is absolutely loaded with a poison which is likely to be fatal to one of every two persons who inhale it. Our own history contains many instances of persons dying of yellow fever without a human being near them—so repulsive is their death-bed. Miss Andrews shrank from no trial of the kind. Many and many a poor sufferer, in his last delirious moments, was recalled to consciousness by feeling her cool hand on his fevered forehead, and by hearing gentle words of a future life uttered by her kind voice.

The patients, as we all know, far outnumbered the capacity of the hospital; the nurses were far too few. Miss Andrews was frequently in attendance at several death-beds at the same time. A visitor to Norfolk has preserved an account of one night during the height of the pestilence, when she was on duty in a private house. Two persons, one of whom was a physician, were dying of fever in the house. The physician was delirious; he ranted, and raved, and sang snatches of some old familiar tune. The other dying man had passed the crisis of the malady, and was quietly sinking into death. His companion's cries distracted him. Miss Andrews rose from his bedside, and approached the physician. She laid her small soft hand on his brow, and looked at him. The cool pressure roused him; he looked up, started at seeing this fair girl beside him, and muttered—"Who is this?" Kind womanly words of sympathy and consolation taught him that the intruder was a friend; he was subdued and quiet. His nurse hastened to return to the dying man in the adjacent room. His agony had come. Her task was now to support the dying head during the minutes which life had yet to endure. Midnight was long past; she was alone; the physician, relapsing into delirium, had begun to scream and to sing again. What nerve that young girl must have had! A brief space released her from her care of one patient; he died with his head resting on her arm. Then she hastened to the poor physician. At the first sound of her gentle voice his paroxysm ended; calm was restored to his wandering spirit; he was enabled to listen consciously to the pious exhortation of his last friend. He had a wife—but she was far away; it was Miss Andrews who, in that dreadful hour, stood in stead to him of mother, sister, and wife, and soothed the moments which preceded his final dissolution. Gray morning dawned as he died. What a night!

Even death did not limit the cares which her self-imposed mission devolved upon Miss Andrews. When patients died of yellow fever, it was almost impossible to find persons to lay them out for burial; this also fell to her lot; and when the number of corpses made it necessary for her to hire assistance, she paid for the services of a negro out of her own funds.

It only remains to say that the Howard Association of Norfolk, grateful as well for the eminent services of Miss Andrews as for the noble example she set, have presented her with the gold medal usually awarded to physicians. Impressions were

ANNIE M. ANDREWS.—[FROM AN AMBROTYPE BY BRADY.]

Harper's Weekly. *The proliferation of the press in antebellum America led to a new type of publication, the illustrated weekly. Part magazine, part newspaper, the illustrated prints relied heavily on woodcut engravings.* Harper's Weekly *increased the number of illustrations it carried as the years passed. This issue features the heroics of women, here Florence Nightingale and Annie M. Andrews. Magazines increasingly targeted women readers in the middle of the nineteenth century.*

Bigger, faster, stronger. *Until the 1820s, newspaper production in America was done on printing presses that differed little from that invented by Johannes Gutenberg in 1455. Steam was added as a power source instead of a manual crank. Rotating cylinders increased the speed of production. Pictured is the Hoe revolving press, circa 1855. It produced up to 20,000 pages per hour and allowed newspapers to be printed on sheets three feet by five feet if desired. These large newspapers were called blanket sheets.*

The ability to print quickly and cheaply was accompanied by a change in the size of newspapers. In colonial America, newspapers varied in size but were generally the size of today's supermarket tabloids or smaller. In the 1790s, printers began to produce papers similar in size to the typical broadsheet used by most newspapers. Cylinder and roller presses allowed printers to use larger paper, and editors began to think that larger was better. Some newspapers of the antebellum period, known appropriately as blanket sheets, were three feet by five feet in size and contained eleven, three-inch-wide columns per page. One Boston newspaper in 1859 printed editions that were more than four feet by eight feet. A New York newspaper in 1835 noted that one of its competitor's papers was so large "that it will require two boys, at least to hold it for perusal."[30]

At the beginning of the antebellum period, news moved slowly and in the ways it had for a century. Newspapers traveled by mail and on ships. It took weeks for news to circulate from New England to states like Alabama and Mississippi. As has been seen, political leaders such as Jefferson and Madison realized in the 1790s how important newspapers were to setting national agenda, so Madison championed the Post Office Act of 1792. The act allowed printers and editors to send each other newspapers gratis through the nation's mail system. The legislation allowed editors to gather news from throughout the nation to share with local patrons. Nearly 20 percent of newspapers in 1810, for example, were delivered by mail to regions outside of the area of publication.[31] Newspaper postage was cheap for those who had to pay. In 1825, it cost one and one-half cents to deliver a newspaper of any size to any place in America, and the nation had more post offices than any other country. The same rate applied for the next twenty years.[32]

The post remained vital to the dissemination of information throughout the antebellum period, but one invention radicalized information gathering. That invention was the telegraph. The first message sent via Samuel F.B. Morse's invention sped along lines from the nation's capital to Baltimore in 1844. The press had continually sought ways to speed up the dissemination and gathering of news. The railroad helped, as did a pony express system. Some editors even used carrier pigeons and news boats in efforts to cut down on the time between events and the sharing of news about them. The telegraph ensured that information could travel almost instantaneously throughout the United States, provided telegraph lines were in place. Access to the telegraph stimulated circulation wars among New York City newspapers and led to news associations, groups of newspapers that joined together to collect news. In 1848, papers in the New York area created what would become the New York Associated Press, the precursor to the Associated Press. Other press associations followed. By the 1850s, the telegraph reached all major American cities with one exception. Lines did not reach San Francisco until 1861.

The innovations in printing and changes in America itself combined in the 1830s to produce a revolutionary product–the penny paper. By 1830, presses could print 4,000 newspapers per hour on paper that was cheaper than any previously available. The nation's population was increasing, and literacy was expanding. The partisan nature of the press and its use by political leaders made papers the principal venue of debate. People had a thirst for information, as witnessed by the increase in the number of newspapers and the rapid expansion of magazines. But newspapers were still expensive, six cents per copy with subscription rates of ten dollars per year, which was more than a week's wages for the average worker. The daily circulation of newspapers averaged around 1,000. Into this environment, Benjamin Day introduced the New York *Sun* on September 3, 1833, for a penny an issue. "The object of this paper," Day said in that first issue, "is to lay before the public, at a price within the means of every one, ALL THE NEWS OF THE DAY, and at the same time offer an advantageous medium for advertisements." A month later, he said in the *Sun* that "the penny press, by diffusing useful knowledge among the operative classes of society, is effecting the march of independence to a greater degree than any other mode of instruction."[33]

PROFESSOR MORSE, THE INVENTOR OF THE TELEGRAPH.

made to flow through considerable lengths of wire.

1746.—Winckler at Leipsic, and Le Monnier at Paris, experimented on the same subject of the transmission of the electric current through conducting bodies.

1747.—Dr. Watson, in England, repeated and extended these experiments, sending a current through two miles of wire and two of earth; sending shocks across the Thames and the New River. Dr. Franklin in 1748, and De Luc in 1749, repeated many of these experiments. In addition, experiments, bearing more or less on the subject of electric telegraphy, were made by Lesage in 1774, and incontinuous in its action, and, from its small quantity, devoid of energetic force.

1809.—Sömmering made a step forward by his application of galvanism to the purposes of telegraphing. He constructed, at Munich, a telegraphic apparatus, using thirty-five wires. The signals were made by the decomposition of water in thirty-five tubes, which were in connection with the thirty-five wires of the line.

1816.—Francis Ronalds, of Hammersmith, England, constructed a telegraph of eight miles in length. This telegraph was one of the best that had then been invented, and was capable of transmitting intelligence with considerable rapidity.

THE RELAY MAGNET OF THE MORSE INSTRUMENT.

The telegraph. *In 1844, Samuel Morse perfected the telegraph and sent a message from Baltimore to Washington. In the September 4, 1858, edition of* Harper's Weekly, *Morse and his invention were featured following the sending of the first transatlantic message.*

Day's hunch paid off. Within six months, the *Sun*'s circulation reached nearly 8,000. Within three years, its circulation was nearly 30,000. Other New York publishers followed Day's lead and either changed their publications to penny papers or started them. Penny papers began to appear in other cities, too, although not all newspapers in America followed suit. The success and price of penny papers made it nearly impossible for publishers to charge the previous high prices for their papers, though, or to ignore the content and success of the penny papers.

Day's newspaper did not look at all like the blanket-sheet newspapers. It was about the size of a piece of notebook paper and four pages in length. It contained news attuned more to everyday Americans, rather than to social elites. The penny papers did not abandon opinion or partisanship in their content. They did, however, include human interest stories, police reports, graphic descriptions of crime, and stories similar to those found in today's supermarket tabloids such as the *Sun*'s "moon hoax," which claimed an astronomer in South Africa had discovered life on the moon—humans with batlike wings. As editors of penny papers were able to afford it, they added visual images to their products, images of events and people created by engravers. The engravers used sketches to create woodcuts. The woodcut was a block of wood that had an image carved into it. The highlights were inked and became the image in the paper, while the recessed areas in the woodcut became the white areas in the newspaper. Woodcut engravings for images were the standard method of creating visuals in America until the introduction of the halftone process in the late 1870s, which allowed newspapers to run photographs.

The penny papers made other important changes, especially in the economic function of the press. First, newsboys hawked papers on the streets. Before this, newspapers were sold by subscription. Now, anyone could purchase a paper at any time. Second, and most important, the penny papers turned to advertising revenue as their principal means of financial support. Advertising revenue meant that publications were not dependent on political patronage or on subscription revenue, which often never came since Americans notoriously did not pay for their newspaper subscriptions. Penny press publishers used their large circulation numbers to prove to potential advertisers the extent to which penny papers reached the public. When it came to advertising, the penny papers approached the products they advertised much as they did the news: anything goes. One penny paper explained its advertising policy by saying:

> Our advertising columns are open to the "public, the whole public, and nothing but the public." We admit any advertisements of any thing or any opinion, from any persons who will pay the price. . . . Our advertising is our

Creating woodcuts for illustrations. *The August 2, 1856, issue of* Frank Leslie's Illustrated Newspaper *contained a feature on the making of woodcuts used to create the illustrations readers saw in it and other publications. The spread discussed everything from the artist, the engraver, and the engraver's tools, to how the woodblocks were fastened together to form one- and two-page illustrations.*

> revenue, and in a paper involving so many expenses as a penny paper . . . the only source of revenue.[34]

The success of the penny papers changed other facets of journalism, too. Penny papers did not remain four-page issues for long, and their physical size increased as well. Editors needed copy and began to hire reporters to cover "beats," specialized areas of information such as police reports and sports, to fill the pages. They also honed the editorial during this period. News of moon men and gruesome murders was good for circulation, but so, too, were opinion pieces. Editors of the penny papers used their newspapers for platforms on the nation's political and social agendas, as did editors of more traditional newspapers. Perhaps the greatest editorial voice of the era was that of Horace Greeley, publisher of the New York *Tribune,* but nearly all newspapers allowed their columns to serve as platforms for opinion and debate, even those in the years before the advent of the penny press.

The very nature of American society made publications of the antebellum period the place in which society discussed and debated issues. Following American tradition that dated back to the colonial era, citizens turned to newspapers to voice their concerns. The growing moral, social, and political issues of the antebellum period, combined with the rapid growth in the numbers of newspapers and their circulations, produced the ideal avenue for public debate, often called the public sphere. More people sought ways to insert themselves into public discussions, especially as more trade and industry created a more influential middle class. They discovered that the press was the best way to do this.[35] Newspapers principally, but also magazines, served as the catalyst for public deliberations in settings ranging from public gathering spots to homes, from public ceremony and oration to private conversations.[36] The printed and disseminated word became a storehouse for all types of information that was of value.

This book presents the debates on issues of importance in antebellum America as they were discussed in newspapers and magazines. Each chapter focuses upon a specific event or issue during the period from 1820 to 1860. Each chapter presents writings on both sides of an issue, as editors, reporters, and citizens used the press to sway public opinion. During the antebellum period, headlines did not accompany all articles in newspapers. In this book, stories are given heads regardless, but, in most cases, the explanation states that the story or editorial appeared initially without a headline. In addition, authors still, at times, used pseudonyms, a practice dating back to colonial America and to seventeenth-century England. Editorials, too, were not generally accompanied by a name. In the selections of writings, names are attributed to unsigned editorials, letters, and articles when it is possible to do so. If the author's identity is uncertain, the piece will be labeled with "an anonymous report."

All of America's publications during this period became potential sources for chapter selections, but newspapers located in the larger cities are often central to chapter selections. Increasingly during the antebellum period, New York became the center for print news and for publications. Newspapers in the North were much more prevalent than those in other regions, especially the South. The North had about three newspapers for every one in the South, and their circulation was much greater. The New York *Tribune,* for example, had a daily circulation of 77,000 compared to 8,000 for the South's largest paper, the Richmond *Enquirer.*[37] Still, the *Enquirer* was a highly influential news sheet whose pages were often copied and reprinted throughout America.

The selection of events and issues for such a book is subjective to a certain extent but also limited by newspaper content. Major events of the antebellum period are arranged chronologically. Issues to be discussed, such as women's rights, are based, wherever possible, on events. In the case of women's rights—an ongoing issue—the event is the 1848 Seneca Falls meeting of the Female Moral Reform Society. Wherever possible, letters, editorials, and articles are included in their entirety, but in many cases doing this is

FRANK LESLIE'S ILLUSTRATED NEWSPAPER

No. 1.—VOL. I.] NEW YORK, SATURDAY, DEC. 15, 1855. {WITH SUPPLEMENT GRATIS} PRICE TEN CENTS.

JOHN BULL'S LAST GASCONADE.

THE *mal-entendu* between this country and Great Britain would be regarded as a farce were it not for the gravity of the consequences involved in it. It presents the two nations in a somewhat ridiculous light, their quarrel resembling that of a couple of Gascons, who, after lashing themselves into a fury, and venting their passion in ugly epithets, finally fall into each other's arms with a slobbering acknowledgment of the folly of their dispute. As far as the two Governments are concerned, their share in the matter has been very much exaggerated. It was the press on both sides that gave to the quarrel all its importance. The truculent articles of the London *Times*, and of two or three other journals, supposed to be the organs of the Palmerston cabinet, naturally aroused a strong feeling of indignation at this side. We could not forget that the subject-matter of complaint which had excited the ire of these journals—the letters of Mr. Cushing—had been created by the misconduct of the British Government itself; and American journals could not, consequently, be expected to treat, in any very lenient fashion, the abuse so lavishly heaped on their country. Their resentment was aggravated by the consciousness that everything had been done by our Government to maintain the strict letter of the neutrality laws, as regarded all the belligerents. The steps taken in the case of the bark "Maury," showed that it had no disposition to deal more favorably with Russian than with British interests. It was rather too bad, after the impartiality observed, that offence should be taken at a legitimate retaliation for the aggressions

Frank Leslie's Illustrated Newspaper. *On December 15, 1855, the first issue of* Frank Leslie's Illustrated Newspaper *appeared. Although it was called a newspaper, the pictorial periodical was more like a magazine. It was filled with images, and it carried many stories that had nothing to do with the politics of the day. Leslie's real name was Henry Carver, but he changed it because his father did not approve of his work as an artist and engraver. His first issue of the* Illustrated Newspaper *featured an engraving and a story about Arctic explorers.*

impossible. Because of the large size of antebellum newspapers and their use of extremely small type, some newspaper articles could equal twenty pages of double-spaced, twelve-point type. Each chapter offers multiple readings on each side of the event it discusses to give readers better perspective. Twenty-nine issues of concern during the antebellum period are included. Each issue concludes with questions for discussion, and the book includes a time line of the antebellum period and a selected bibliography for further research.

NOTES

1. Numbers are based on Alfred McClung Lee, *The Daily Newspaper in America* (New York: Macmillan, 1937); Edward Connery Lathem, comp., *Chronological Tables of American Newspapers, 1690–1820* (Barre, Mass.: American Antiquarian Society & Barre Publishers, 1972); Carol Sue Humphrey, *The Press of the Young Republic, 1783–1833* (Westport, Conn.: Greenwood Press, 1996); Wm. David Sloan and James D. Startt, *The Media in America: A History,* 4th ed. (North Port, Ala.: Vision Press, 1999), 250; and William E. Huntzicker, *The Popular Press, 1833–1865* (Westport, Conn.: Greenwood Press, 1999), 170.

2. Alexis de Tocqueville, *Democracy in America,* 2 vols. (New York: Alfred A. Knopf, 1946), 1:187–88.

3. *Bee* (New Orleans), 14 December 1860.

4. *Columbian Centinel* (Boston), 12 July 1817.

5. *Constitution,* Article I, Section 2; Article I, Section 9.

6. Study 00003: "Historical Demographic, Economic, and Social Data: U.S., 1790–1970." Ann Arbor: Inter-University Consortium for Political and Social Research. Access to the census records is available at a number of on-line sources including: http://www.icpsr.umich.edu/ *and* http://fisher.lib.virginia.edu/census/.

7. John M. Blum, et al., *The National Experience,* 2 vols., 6th ed. (San Diego: Harcourt Brace Jovanovich, 1985), 1:310.

8. "Annexation," *United States Magazine and Democratic Review* 17:85 (July and August 1845). Scholars now dispute whether the editor of the *Democratic Review,* John Louis O'Sullivan or one of his writers, Jane McManus Storm Cazneau, wrote the editorial. For views on the latter, see Linda S. Hudson, *Mistress of Manifest Destiny: A Biography of Jane McManus Storm Cazneau, 1807–1878* (Austin: Texas State Historical Association, 2001).

9. Prospectus for *Christian Journal* (Richmond), published in *Family Visitor* (Richmond), 8 October 1825.

10. William J. Gilmore, *Reading Becomes a Necessity of Life: Material and Cultural Life in Rural New England, 1780–1835* (Knoxville: University of Tennessee Press, 1989), 193–94.

11. Tocqueville, *Democracy in America,* 2:111.

12. Michael Schudson, "Was There Ever a Public Sphere? If So, When? Reflec-

tions on the American Case," *Habermas and the Public Sphere,* ed. Craig Calhoun (Cambridge: The MIT Press, 1992), 149.

13. Gilmore, *Reading Becomes a Necessity of Life,* 193–94; Walter Dean Burnham, *The Current Crisis in American Politics* (New York: Oxford University Press, 1982), 129.

14. Quoted in Culver H. Smith, *The Press, Politics, and Patronage: The American Government's Use of Newspapers 1789–1875* (Athens: University of Georgia Press, 1977), 56.

15. *Aurora* (Philadelphia), 2 February 1825.

16. Andrew Jackson, *The Correspondence of Andrew Jackson,* 7 vols., ed. John Spencer Bassett (Washington, D.C., 1926–35), 4:19.

17. Jefferson to Madison, 5 February 1799, in Paul L. Ford, *The Works of Thomas Jefferson* (New York, 1892–1899), 7:344.

18. David A. Copeland, "America, 1750–1820." *The Press and the Public Sphere: Politics and Social Change in Late Eighteenth- and Early Nineteenth-Century Europe and America,* ed. Hannah Barker and Simon Burrows (Cambridge: Cambridge University Press, 2002), 210.

19. Quoted in Smith, *The Press, Politics, and Patronage,* 73.

20. *Liberator* (Boston), 1 January 1831.

21. Thomas Leonard, *News for All: America's Coming-of-Age with the Press* (New York: Oxford University Press, 1995), 67.

22. See "The Abolitionist Press," in Wm David Sloan and David A. Copeland, *Mass Media: A Documentary History* (Northport, Ala.: Vision Press, forthcoming).

23. Frank Luther Mott, *American Journalism. A History: 1690–1960.* 3rd ed. (New York: The Macmillan Company, 1962), 206.

24. Frank Luther Mott, *A History of American Magazines, 1741–1850* (Cambridge: Harvard University Press, 1966), 342.

25. Benjamin P. Browne, *Christian Journalism for Today* (Philadelphia: The Judson Press, 1952), 14.

26. Huntzicker, *The Popular Press,* 56–60.

27. *American Turf Register and Sporting Magazine* (Baltimore), September 1829.

28. Mott, *American Journalism,* 320.

29. Information on printing comes from David A. Copeland, *Debating the Issues in Colonial Newspapers* (Westport, Conn.: Greenwood Press, 2000), vii-x; Mott, *American Journalism,* 203- 04; Michael Emery and Edwin Emery, *The Press and America: An Interpretive History of the Mass Media,* 6th ed. (Englewood Cliffs, N.J.: Prentice Hall, 1988), 112–14; and Sidney Kobre, *Development of American Journalism* (Dubuque, Iowa: Wm. C. Brown, 1969), 216–17, 219.

30. *Mirror* (New York), 32 May 1835, quoted in Mott, *American Journalism,* 294.

31. William A. Dill, *Growth of Newspapers in the United States* (Lawrence: University of Kansas, 1928), 11.

32. Richard B. Kielbowicz, *News in the Mail: The Press, Post Office, and Public Information, 1700–1860s* (Westport, Conn.: Greenwood Press, 1989), 57–58.

33. *Sun* (New York), 9 November 1833.

34. *Public Ledger* (Philadelphia), quoted in Lee, *The Daily Newspaper in America*, 181.

35. Jürgen Habermas, *The Structural Transformation of the Public Sphere: A Structural Transformation of Bourgeois Society*, tran. Thomas Burger and Frederick Lawrence (Cambridge: The MIT Press, 1989), 29.

36. Richard D. Brown, *Knowledge Is Power: The Diffusion of Information in Early America, 1700–1865* (New York and London: Oxford University Press, 1989), 292. See also David Waldstreicher, *In the Midst of Perpetual Fetes: The Making of American Nationalism, 1776- 1820* (Chapel Hill: University of North Carolina Press, 1997). David S. Shields, *Civil Tongues & Polite Letters in British America* (Chapel Hill: University of North Carolina Press, 1997).

37. Sloan and Startt, *The Media in America*, 153.

CHAPTER 1

The Missouri Compromise, 1820

In 1819, Congress entered into a battle that would end in war forty years later. Even at this time, some Americans were talking of disunion. The subject of the debate in 1819 and 1820 was whether to allow slavery in American territory west of the Mississippi River–more specifically in Missouri. The Missouri territory applied for statehood in 1819; many of its residents owned slaves. Suddenly, the issue of slavery took center stage in American life and produced a series of questions for Americans that needed answers. The political question for the nation centered on the fact that the country was balanced evenly between free states and those that allowed slavery; there were eleven of each. Missouri, as a slave state, would tip the balance of power. The ethical question focused on the morality of slavery. Increasingly, many Americans in Northern states advocated an end to slavery in the United States. The constitutional question dealt with the legality of slavery. The Constitution legitimated slavery in the nation.[1] To keep slavery out of the territories west of the Mississippi, slavery advocates argued, violated the principles of the Constitution.

The idea that slavery should not be allowed in Missouri did not develop solely from abolitionist sentiment that involuntary servitude needed to cease. Under the Articles of Confederation, America adopted the Ordinance of 1787. The United States incorporated its principles in 1789. Basically, the ordinance kept slavery out of the Northwest Territory, the area that would become Ohio, Indiana, Illinois, Michigan, and Wisconsin. The Ohio River became the unofficial but recognized boundary between slave and free states west of the Appalachian Mountains, just as Mason's and Dixon's line did in the original states.[2] The Missouri territory was above the point where the Ohio flowed into the Mississippi. The debate was on.

On the political issue of balance of power, many New Englanders already felt they were losing strength in Congress. One more slave state would simply exacerbate the situation. "The increased relative power which the slave holding states possess over those in which slavery is prohibited, is so completely demonstrated," one Boston writer said on admitting Missouri to the Union, "as to preclude all hesitation from the mind of a correct Statesman of the course which, as individuals, and as a State, we ought to pursue on this all important question."[3] The balance of power between free and slave states was removed from the debate, however, when Maine applied for statehood. If Maine, which had been a part of Massachusetts, could be admitted as a free state, the slave and free state balance would remain intact. Congress agreed to this, but admission of the two was separated. Maine became a state before Missouri.

The issue of keeping slavery out of Missouri quickly became entwined with the constitutional issue of slavery. After adjourning in March 1819 without resolving the issue, Congress took up the argument again in December. In January 1820, Rufus King of New York pointed out that, legally, Congress could keep slavery out of American territories and subsequently any states that came out of them. King said, "it has been established in the States north-west of the river Ohio."[4] The slave states turned first to the Louisiana Purchase agreement. One Virginia resident noted that in it, "'The inhabitants of the ceded territory shall be incorporated in the Union of the United States . . .to the enjoyment of *all the rights,* advantages and immunities" of American citizens.[5] That meant, since the Constitution allowed for slavery, that people living in territories could own slaves, and those territories could become slave states if they so chose when they applied for admission to the Union. Abolitionists both in and out of Congress added to the argument. Slavery was "an abomination in the sight of God,"[6] and it was irreconcilable with a major American premise, "*We hold this truth to be self-evident, that all men are born* FREE *and* EQUAL."[7]

Into this volatile situation, Illinois Senator Jesse Thomas offered a compromise. Let Missouri enter the Union as a slave state but establish a new line of demarcation between slave and free in the territory west of the Mississippi. The line would run along the 36 degree, 30 minute latitude, roughly the boundary between Virginia and North Carolina, Kentucky and Tennessee, and Missouri and the Arkansas territory. In 1820, that line stopped at the beginning of Spanish possessions in North America, which included what would become the states of Texas, Colorado, Utah, Arizona, New Mexico, Nevada, and California, so Americans never considered that the issue of slavery in the territories would erupt again. Even though people in the South and in North had opposite opinions on slavery, many agreed on one thing: the Missouri Compromise was bad law. Southerners opposed it because it limited slavery in territory. Northerners opposed it because it allowed slavery in Missouri. Still, compromise seemed to be the only solution to the impasse, and on March 2, the House of Representatives accepted, by a margin of three votes, Thomas's compromise, which had already been passed by the Senate.[8] The slavery issue in the territories may have been settled for the moment, but most Americans were unhappy with the results.

The chapter's readings begin with those that supported the Missouri Compromise. The first comes from the *National Intelligencer,* a pair of reports from the last day of February and the first of March 1820. The next is from Pennsylvania and says that the compromise outwitted the Southerners. The third is the official record of debate in Congress over the compromise. The final, from North Carolina Senator Montford Stokes, explains why he voted for the compromise. It should be noted that newspapers discussed extensively why slavery should be allowed or prohibited in Missouri, but they did not discuss the compromise to any great degree.

The readings that oppose the compromise come from the South and the North. Both regions thought the compromise should not become law, but for different reasons. The first, from Philadelphia, notes that it is time to call for an amendment outlawing slavery, not for approving a compromise that spreads it. The second selection predicts trouble for the nation if the compromise is passed. The next readings are reactions from the South and North to passage of the compromise. The last reading predicts the nation will never rid itself of slavery because of the compromise.

Support for the Compromise

Joseph Gales and W. W. Seaton: "Missouri Question Settled"

Gales and Seaton published the National Intelligencer, *and it served as the official voice of the administration of James Monroe. Here, the pair praise the Missouri Compromise. Reports on the compromise are given from back-to-back issues of the* Intelligencer; *the editors have hope for the compromise's passage and for the good that it is doing in Washington.*

National Intelligencer (Washington, D.C.), 28 February 1820

The Missouri Question, it appears, is happily settled in Congress; the resolution which has passed the House of Representatives, having been ordered to a third reading in the Senate, by such a majority as leaves no doubt of its final passage in that body, when it will want only the signature of the President to give it effect. We trust it will never again, in any shape, make its appearance in the Councils of the Nation.

***National Intelligencer* (Washington, D.C.), 1 March 1820**

The effect of the settlement of the Missouri question is already perceptible, in the comparatively rapid progress which has been since made in the dispatch of the business before the Congress. The resolution for the admission of Missouri into the Union has finally passed both Houses. Several measures have already passed in review, which never would have been taken into consideration during the suspension of that question. . . .

Chester Miner: "Missouri"

Miner, the editor of the Village Record, *felt the Missouri Compromise was a masterful political move against the South. Though it allowed slavery in Missouri, it kept it from most of America's territory.*

***Village Record*, or *Chester (Pa.) and Delaware Federalist*, 7 March 1820**

We announce, with unfeigned satisfaction, that the 'perplexing question'—the 'disheartening question'—the 'all-engrossing question'—of the admission of Missouri, is decided. . . . Never was a subject managed with more wisdom than this—never did statesmen exhibit more political sagacity and firmness than were shewn by our friends throughout this very delicate, and trying discussion. For once the South has been completely out-generaled; and forced to do right, in spite of all their pride and prejudices, and all their preconceived opinions and resolutions.

An Anonymous Report: "The Missouri Bill"

Newspapers went to great lengths to discuss the pros and cons of extending slavery to Missouri, but they talked little about the actual compromise proposed by Senator Jesse Thomas of Illinois. Instead, most simply recorded the actions of the Senate and the House of Representatives in reaching the compromise. Here is the Congressional record followed by a simple statement by Newport Mercury *editor J.H. Barber, which appeared on the same page of the paper.*

***Newport (R.I.) Mercury*, 11 March 1820**

This bill was received from the House of Representatives, and, on motion of Mr. Barbour, was immediately read twice, and referred to a Committee of the whole.

Mr. Barbour, then moved to strike out of the bill the provision for the interdiction of Slavery and added that he thought it unnecessary to say any thing on a subject which had been so full discussed.

Mr. King, of N.Y. concurred in the sentiment; and the question was immediately put, and decided. . . .

Mr. Thomas then proposed to insert a section, declaring the inhibition of Slavery in the Territories of the United States North of 36_30' North Latitude.—[*The same which was previously proposed to be added to the Maine bill.*]

This motion was agreed to without debate.

These amendments were then reported, and the first of them, [*to strike out the restriction*] was concurred in without a division.

The second [*inhibiting Slavery in the Territories*] Mr. Trimble offered an amendment, to extend the territory in which Slavery should be inhibited: But it was negatived, without debate, 30 to 12.

Mr. Thomas' amendment was then concurred in. The bill was then ordered to be engrossed; afterwards it was read a third time, passed, and sent to the House of Representatives, requesting their concurrence in the amendments. . . .

"MISSOURI QUESTION"

This important question is at length decided in favor of admitting Missouri without any restriction of Slavery. . . . Thus amended, the Bill was returned to the House, and the amendment was adopted by a majority of *four*. . . .

Montford Stokes: "Missouri Question"

Montford Stokes was one of North Carolina's senators. In this letter to the Register, *he discusses the debate on allowing Missouri to enter the Union and the pressure to prohibit slavery from it if it is to become a state. Stokes believes such a limit is a constitutional violation, and his letter reflects discussions that led to the Missouri Compromise. Still, the senator favors the compromise as a way to settle the issue.*

***Raleigh Register, and North-Carolina Gazette,* 17 March 1820**

"*My dear Sir,*

"The question of compelling the free people of Missouri territory to form their Constitution so as forever thereafter to prevent the introduction of Slaves into that State when admitted into the Union, has occupied both Houses of Congress for several weeks, and has not yet been settled. You have seen, and will see volumes of speeches on the subject most of which, (not having been listened to in either House,) are intended for *home consumption.* As I differ from my honorable colleague upon some propositions for accommodating and settling for years to come, this all important contest, which is agitating the people of the United States in a great degree every where; but which in some of the Northern States has produced and delirium and phrenzy approaching to madness; I have thought it proper to state the grounds upon which my conduct has been. . . . Those who are opposed to this unconstitutional restriction . . . expect that Missouri will be admitted into the Union without the restriction unless some concession or agreement shall take place excluding slavery from a portion of the extensive territory beyond the Mississippi. This is not mere matter of opinion: it has been ascertained by several votes in the House of Representatives, that a considerable majority of that body are in favor of restriction as to all the territory purchased from France under the name Louisiana. It is useless to examine at this time, whether this is a correct principle or not. The majority have satisfied their own minds upon the subject and are disposed to enforce the restraint. All that we from the slave-holding States can do at present, is to rescue from the rapacious grasp of these misguided fanatics a considerable portion of the Louisiana purchase, including all the inhabited parts of that extensive country. I can see no means, either now or hereafter, of accomplishing this desirable object, but by consenting that slavery may be prohibited in the Northern portion of the Louisiana purchase. I believe that by agreeing to this regulation, we may secure the remaining portion of that purchase as an asylum for Slaves already too numerous to be comfortably supported in some of the Southern States. With this view, I have consented that Slavery may be excluded by an act of Congress from the territory lying west of the contemplated State of Missouri, and north of the parallel of thirty-six degrees thirty minutes north latitude. I do not think the Constitution violated by the terms of this act, inasmuch as Congress are only legislating upon a territory in which there is not one citizen of the United States settled at this time. By this prudent and proper concession, we shall quiet the minds of many people who have already been excited by bad men to commit the most daring acts of injustice and outrage. . . .

"I have thus taken the liberty, my dear sirs, of writing to you, that it may be recorded as my deliberate opinion, and referred to in case of misrepresentation hereafter. . . .

"M. STOKES."

Opposition to the Compromise

An Anonymous Report: "Slavery"

The debate over the Missouri Compromise created definite sides among Americans. This article, which American Daily Advertiser *editor Zachariah Poulson reprinted from the* Salem Gazette, *calls for a constitutional amendment prohibiting slavery in any new state.*

American Daily Advertiser (Philadelphia), 29 November 1819

The great question which now agitates the people of the United States—Whether a State should be incorporated and admitted into the Union, with the detestable privilege of holding Slaves, is a practice repugnant to the spirit of liberty which effected our revolution, and was the basis of our national fabric. It is indeed to be regretted, that this should be at all a Congressional question, and depend upon a legislative act. It ought to be settled "by the constitution itself," and an amendment now made, agreeable to the common sense and feeling and principle of the country, that no new State should be formed or admitted without an express prohibition of slavery. At the present period, we trust, there would be no difficulty in affecting such an amendment.

An Anonymous Report: "Evils We Cannot Contemplate"

As the debate that produced the Missouri Compromise intensified, a number of Americans realized that the subject of the debate—slavery—had the potential to destroy the Union. This untitled selection originally appeared in the Eastern Argus *of Portland, Maine. Here it is reprinted by the* Register *in Raleigh, North Carolina, whose editor, Joseph Gales, supported no restrictions on slavery in the territories and, therefore, opposed the compromise. The* Argus*'s editorial predicts that if the compromise is accepted, the nation is headed for horrible times because it will have divided itself, not along political party lines, but as slave versus free.*

Raleigh Register, and North-Carolina Gazette, 3 March 1820

The following are the remarks of the Eastern Argus, a standard Republican Journal, printed at Portland, in the District of Maine, on the subject lately before the Senate, and now before the House of Representatives. It is gratifying to find in that paper, the Boston Patriot, and one or two other Eastern prints of high character, just sentiments, and a proper temper, on this subject. The concluding words of the Argus cannot be too emphatically marked:

Mr. Thomas, of Illinois, in the Senate, has moved an amendment, providing "that slavery and involuntary servitude shall be excluded from all that tract of country ceded by France to the United Stated under the name of Louisiana, which lies north of 36 degrees and a half of north latitude, excepting only such parts as is included within the limits of the State contemplated by the bill under consideration."

Should this amendment or something of the kind succeed in the Senate, and the House yield so far as to accept it as a compromise, the question which has produced so much excitement, may be settled amicably. If otherwise, it is not easy to foresee what the consequences may be.

This is the first question that has *distinctly marked out the country in to parties, divided by lines of latitude and longitude.* IF PUSHED TO SUCH AN EXTREME AS TO RENDER THE DISTINCTION PERMANENT, IT WILL LEAD TO EVILS WHICH WE CANNOT CONTEMPLATE WITHOUT HORROR.

Theodore Dwight: "Slavery"

Theodore Dwight was the editor of the Daily Advertiser *and found the Missouri Compromise just as repulsive as many Southern editors. His reasons were different; he believed the spread of slavery should be stopped and that the compromise perpetuated the practice. His terminology here is that of an angry person, embarrassed by his country's actions, and his sentiments were echoed in many New England newspapers.*

Daily Advertiser **(New York), 7 March 1820**

We had yesterday the mortification of publishing the result of the *winter's debate,* in the House of Representatives of the United States, on the subject of restricting slavery in the new state of Missouri—a result, we hesitate not to say, as unexpected, and as unpalatable, to the people in this part of the country, as any that has ever been experienced in the course of our political history. By this decision, SLAVERY, that abomination in the sight of God, that foul reproach to a Christian nation, is fastened upon this land, and will probably never be exterminated, unless in blood. For the mere selfish gratification of those who are too indolent to labour, but who prefer spending their lives in the indulgences of wealth and luxury, in the exercise of lordly domination, and the gratifications of despotic tyranny over abject bondsmen, the national legislature have sanctioned a measure, which will stamp indelible and perpetual disgrace upon our national character. In vain shall we, hereafter appeal to our Constitution, our laws, and our moral and religious pretensions, as evidence that we are a free just and humane nation.—Our conduct gives the lie to our professions; our acts proclaim us to be political hypocrites. . . .

The freedom of our country has been sacrificed in the house of its friends.

Thomas Ritchie: "Missouri Question—Settled!"

Thomas Ritchie loudly proclaimed opposition to the Missouri Compromise. Here he acknowledges the compromise is accepted, but it limits Americans' rights while guaranteeing them to the people of Missouri.

Enquirer (Richmond), 7 March 1820

The National Intelligencer informs us, that the Question is settled. We presume it is so. He congratulates the country upon the settlement–we regret our inability to echo back the gratulation. "Those who win, say the proverb, may laugh." . . . We cannot join him in the sentiment. Instead of joy, we scarcely ever recollect to have tasted of a bitterer cup. We cannot chuckle over the prospect which *this* compromise presents to *our* comprehension. A constitution warped from its legitimate bearings, and an immense region of territory closed for ever against the Southern and Western people–such is the "sorry sight" which rises to *our* view. . . .

We cannot compromise with the constitution. Under that constitution as it now stands, no such measure as this ought to be adopted. . . .

The *fact* is, whatever may be the *law,* that the door is *for ever* shut against us, in that immensely vast region which stretches north of 361/2. . . .

But the deed is done–The treaty is signed, sealed and delivered. . . . But with all our disquietude and regrets, there is intermingled one pleasurable emotion, that the high minded citizens of Missouri have succeeded in their wishes; and are about to enter the Union, "unshorn of their beams"–free, sovereign–*on an equal footing with the original states.*

An Anonymous Report: "Missouri Question"

Joseph Gales of the Register *opposed the Missouri Compromise, and he ran this unsigned letter in his paper to support his position. The writer begins by discussing talk of disunion and the importance of the United States. He closes with the same thoughts. In between, he reveals why the compromise should be illegal. He also points out the inequity of the debate to make it illegal to have slaves in Missouri. The article ran over two weeks, and the closing paragraph that appears here was in the 17 March issue.*

Raleigh Register, and North-Carolina Gazette, 10 March 1820

Mr. MACON, of North-Carolina, said, he agreed in opinion with the gentleman who had declared this to be the greatest question ever debated in the Senate, and that it ought to be discussed in the most calm and cool manner; without attempting to excite passion or prejudice. . . .

The public mind was then greatly excited, and men in whom the people properly placed the utmost confidence, were divided. There was then no whisper about disunion: every one considered the union as absolutely necessary for the good of all. But, to day we have been told, by the hon. gentleman from Pennsylvania, (Mr. Lowrie) that he would prefer disunion, rather than slaves should be carried west of the Mississippi. . . . Get clear of this

Union and this Constitution, and it will be found vastly more difficult to unite again and form another than it was to form this. . . . When we are told disunion rather than slaves be carried over the Mississippi, it ought not to be forgotten that the union of the people and the confederation carried us through the Revolutionary War; a war, of which no man can wish to see the like again in this country; but as soon as peace came, it was found to be entirely unfit for that, so unfit, that it was given up for the present constitution: Destroy it, and what may be the condition of the country, no man, not the most sagacious, can even imagine. . . . A majority of them want things right. Leave them to form their own opinions, without the aid of inflammatory speeches at town meetings, and they will always form them correctly. . . . It is more easy to inflame the public mind, than to quiet it when inflamed. A child may set the woods on fire, but it requires great exertions to extinguish it. This now very great question, was but a spark the last session.

All the states now have equal rights, and all are content. Deprive one of the least right which it now enjoys in common with the others, and it will no longer be content. So, if government had an unlimited power to put whatever it pleased on the admission of a new state into the Union, a state admitted with a condition unknown to the others, would not be content, no matter what might be the character of the condition, even though it was, not to steal or commit murder. The difference in the terms of admission would not be acceptable. All the new states have the same rights that the old have and why make Missouri an exception? She has not done a single act to deserve it; and why depart, in her case, from the great American principle, that the people can govern themselves? No reason has been assigned for the attempt at the departure, nor can one be assigned, which would not apply as strong to Louisiana. In every free country that ever existed, the first violations of the principles of the government were indiscreet, and not well understood, or supported with great zeal, by a part of the people.

All the country west of the Mississippi was acquired by the same treaty, and on the same terms, and the people in every part have the same rights; but if the amendment be adopted, Missouri will not have the same rights which Louisiana now enjoys. She has been admitted into the Union as a full sister, but her twin sister Missouri, under the proposed amendment, is to be admitted as a sister of the half blood, or rather a step daughter, under an unjust step-mother: for what? Because she, as well as Louisiana, performed well her part during the late war; and because she has never given the General Government any trouble. The operation of the amendment is unjust, as it relates to the people who have moved there from the other states. They carried with them the property which was common in the states they left, secured to them by the constitution and laws of the United States, as well as by the treaty. There they purchased public lands and settled with their slaves, without a single objection to their owning and carrying them; but now, unfortunately for them, it is discovered that they ought not to have been permitted to have carried a single one. What a pity it is, the discovery had not been made before they sold their land in the old states and moved. . . . The country was bought with the money of all, slave-holders as well as those who are not so; and every one knew, when he bought land and moved with his property, he had a perfect right to do so. And no one, till last session, ever said to the contrary, or moved the restriction about slaves. . . .

If the decision be in favor of the amendment, it may ruin us and our children after us; if against it, no injury will result to any part of the U.S. Let it be what it may, my prayer to God shall be, that it may benefit the nation and promote the happiness of the people, and that the Union of these states and the constitution, may be as lasting as the Allegany.

An Anonymous Report: "Missouri"

The Advertiser, *better known as the* Aurora, *opposed the Missouri Compromise. Slavery was viewed as a disease that the nation inherited but one that needed to be cured. The Missouri Compromise allowed the disease and permitted a practice that the paper's editor William Duane—who probably wrote this article—considered contrary to the laws of God and man to be extended.*

General Advertiser (Philadelphia), 23 December 1820

On the foundation of independence, the country found itself burdened with an evil, which admitted of no immediate, adequate, and safe remedy: in a situation which compelled an acquiescence in the existence of an inveterate disease, adverse to the very life of liberty, and a contradiction of the sacred declaration, upon which was established resistance to tyranny, emancipation from subjection; and the assertion of the equal rights of all mankind.—Society found itself infected with a leprosy, which could not be washed off in a bath; but which must be cured by the slow process of a salutary medicament: which to touch hardly was to hazard civil and social life. . . . The rights of the free people of this union, are already sacrificed—and wrested from them—in proportion to the number of three fifths of "all other persons"—that is of human slaves— . . . and it is proposed to be extended over Missouri; and thence by an accumulating series of extensions; the free people who disdain slavery and deprecate its very existence as contrary alike to the laws of God and man, are not only now so governed, but the design is to extend and perpetuate this detestable and horrible subjection for ever.

Questions

1. What is Stokes's rationale for compromise on the Missouri issue?
2. Often laws are repugnant, but they are upheld as parts of people's rights. One example would be the legality of flag burning as a form of free expression. How would you argue that slavery was a right of the people, or argue that it was a violation of rights?
3. How is it possible that those who supported slavery and those who wanted slavery abolished could be on the same side of the Missouri issue? Was there any resolution to their dispute short of the Missouri Compromise?

Notes

1. *Constitution,* Article I, Section 2; Article I, Section 9.
2. David M. Potter, *The Impending Crisis, 1848–1861* (New York: Harper & Row, 1976), 54–55.
3. *Columbian Centinel* (Boston), 25 December 1819.
4. *Columbian Centinel* (Boston), 22 January 1820.
5. *Enquirer* (Richmond), 6 January 1820.
6. *Daily Advertiser* (New York), 7 March 1820.
7. *Columbian Centinel* (Boston), 11 March 1820.
8. *Evening Post* (New York), 7 March 1820.

CHAPTER 2

The Back-to-Africa Movement, 1822

In the spring of 1822, a group from America landed on the shore of West Africa. Twenty years earlier, Americans landing there might have been looking for Africans to enslave. This time, however, the intent was different. Those on board were coming to Africa to live as the first citizens of the country of Liberia. They were free blacks from the United States who accepted the offer of the American Colonization Society to "return" to their homeland to create a better life than any believed they could ever obtain in America. The emigration from America, sponsored by the society, helped more than 15,000 black Americans return to Africa in the nineteenth century.[1]

The idea for the repatriation of free blacks grew out of the religious revival that affected much of America at the beginning of the nineteenth century. Christians should, those affected by the revivalism of the Second Great Awakening believed, work to make the lives of their fellow humans better. As a result, a number of benevolent societies began. One person greatly affected by revivalism was Robert Finley, a Presbyterian minister from New Jersey, who voiced his idea to start a society that would create an African colony for free blacks in 1816. He took his plans to Washington, and there advertised that a meeting would be held for colonizing free blacks.[2] Finley believed that allowing free blacks to begin a new life in Africa would remove blacks from America, would allow Africa to have a more civilized and Christian population, and would give blacks a better situation than what they experienced in America.

Finley's call was answered by a number of prominent Americans, including Francis Scott Key, author of the *Star-Spangled Banner;* Henry Clay, the skilled politician from Kentucky; and numerous other influential politicians who were mostly Southerners. To reinforce colonization, Finley published a pamphlet titled *Thoughts on Colonization.* The seed for the American Colonization Society was planted, and numerous groups endorsed it, including the Virginia legislature and various church groups. In order to accomplish its objectives, the ACS would need financial backing, and Congress was the likely source. But Congress never gave its blessings monetarily to the proposal, even though President James Monroe strongly supported the effort. The society began to organize cells in various cities and states, and by 1821, it had raised enough money to buy a piece of land in West Africa. The new nation was named Liberia, Latin for freemen, and its capital was to be called Monrovia, named in honor of the president.

The idea of colonization did not meet with universal approval among abolitionists or free blacks. Most black Americans felt that colonization was just a way to remove them from America; they considered America their home, not Africa. Among abolitionists, many believed the same thing, and the attack against the American Colonization Society was headed by the nation's most vocal abolitionist, William Lloyd Garrison (see Chapter 8). Garrison said that rather than being a friend to black Americans, the ACS was really a "conspiracy against human rights."[3] Garrison pointed out that the society's sole purpose was sending free blacks back to Africa. It never intended to work toward freeing slaves. Slavery had to be ended, Garrison and many others believed; sending free blacks to live in Africa did nothing to help this cause. The American Colonization Society, of course, agreed that slavery needed to end, but it never denied that manumission was not a part of its purpose. As a result, the ACS and groups such as the American Anti-Slavery Society were constantly at odds, and the efforts by the Anti-Slavery Society to halt colonization cut significantly into the funds raised by the ACS and helped create conflict within the ACS.

This chapter looks at the arguments surrounding the back-to-Africa movement in America and the controversy caused by the American Colonization Society, which was synonymous with the colonization movement. The first section contains readings supporting colonization and begins with a letter written in 1817 by Robert Harper, a Maryland politician, that talks of the benefits of colonization for blacks and whites. The next article is by John Russwurm, co-editor of America's first black-run newspaper. Russwurm slowly concluded that colonization was good and emigrated to Liberia in 1830. This is followed by a letter from a ship's captain describing the wonderful conditions in Liberia. The last entry in this section comes from the 1832 annual report of the American Colonization Society.

The readings that oppose colonization start with a *Freedom's Journal* letter that claims the society is forcing blacks to leave America. The next article is an attack on the society leveled in Garrison's newspaper, the *Liberator*. The next readings attack the society's stance of not fighting for manumission of slaves. The final reading comes from *Frederick Douglass' Newspaper* and points out all the lies and misinformation promoted by the ACS.

For Colonization

Robert G. Harper: "Colonization of the Blacks"

Robert Goodloe Harper had been actively involved in the politics and activities of America since the late eighteenth century. Shortly after the formation of the American Colonization Society, the Maryland congressman wrote this letter to it. He praises what the society aims to do, but notice Harper's opinion of Africans in general. The back-to-Africa concept for him was as much a benefit to whites as to blacks. He also intends to send all Africans back to Africa, not just free blacks.

Columbian Centinel (Boston), 13 November 1819

"I MAY, perhaps, on some future occasion, develope a plan, on which I have long meditated, for colonizing gradually, and with the consent of their owners, and of themselves where free, the whole colored population, slaves and all. But this is not the proper place for such an explanation, for which, indeed, I have not time now. But it is an essential part of the plan, and of every such plan, to prepare the way for its adoption and execution, by commencing a colony of blacks, in a suitable situation, and under proper management. This is what your Society propose to accomplish. Their project, therefore, if rightly formed and well conducted, will open the way for this more extensive and beneficial plan, of removing gradually and imperceptibly, but certainly, the whole colored population from the country, and leaving its place to be imperceptibly supplied, as it would necessarily be, by a class of free white cultivators. . . .

"This great end is to be attained in no other way, than by a plan of universal colonization, founded on the consent of the slave holders, and of the colonists themselves. For such a plan that of the present Colonization Society opens and prepares the way, by exploring the ground, selecting a proper situation, and planting a Colony, which may serve as a receptacle, a nursery, and a school, for those who are to follow. . . .

"The advantages of this undertaking, to which I have hitherto adverted, are continued to ourselves. They consist of ridding us of color, and preparing the way for getting rid of the free people of the slaves and of slavery. In these points of view they are undoubtedly very great. But there are advantages to the free blacks themselves, to the slaves, and to the immense population of middle and southern Africa, which no less recommend this undertaking to our cordial and zealous support.

"To the free blacks themselves the benefits are the most obvious, and will be the most immediate. Here they are condemned to a state of hopeless inferiority, and consequent degradation. As they cannot emerge from this state, they lose, by degrees, the hope at last the desire of emerging. . . . Transplanted to a colony composed of themselves alone, they would enjoy real equality; in other words real freedom. They would become proprietors of land, master mechanics, ship owners, navigators, and merchants, and by degrees, school masters, justices of the peace, militia officers, ministers of religion, judges and legislators. There would be no white population to remind them of and to perpetuate their original inferiority; but enjoying all the privileges of freedom, they would soon enjoy all its advantages, and all its dignity. . . .

"To the slaves the advantages, though not so obvious and immediate, are yet certain and great.

"In the first place, they would be greatly benefitted by the removal of the free blacks, who now corrupt them and render them discontented; thus exposing them to harsher treatment and greater privations. In the next place, this measure would open the way to their more frequent manumission: for many persons who are now restrained from manumitting their slaves, by the conviction that they generally become a nuisance when manumitted in the country, would gladly give them freedom. . . .

"The greatest benefit, however, to be hoped from this enterprize, that which in contemplation most delights the philanthropic mind, still remains to be unfolded. It is the benefit to Africa herself, from this return of her sons to her bosom, bearing with them arts, knowledge, and civilization, to which she has hitherto been a stranger. . . .

"Ages, indeed, may be required, for the full attainment of these objects. Untoward events or unforeseen difficulties may retard or defeat them: But the prospect however remote or uncertain, is still animating, and the hope of success seems sufficient to stimulate us to the utmost exertion. How vast and sublime a career does this undertaking open to a generous ambition, aspiring to deathless fame by great and useful actions! Who can count the millions, that in future times shall know and bless the names of those by whom this magnificent scheme of beneficence and philanthrophy has been conceived and shall be carried into execution? Throughout the widely extended regions of middle and southern Africa, then filled with populous and polished nations, their memories shall be cherished and their praises sung. . . ."

John Russwurm: "Liberia"

Freedom's Journal, *America's first newspaper published by African Americans, initially opposed the American Colonization Society. In this editorial by one of the paper's two editors, John Russwurm says that he is gradually changing his mind about Liberia. Within a year, Russworm moved to Liberia, began a short-lived newspaper and assumed a position in government.*

Freedom's Journal **(New York), 21 February 1829**

LIBERIA.–Of late, we have thought, that the principal objections, which the mass of our brethren, have against colonization, arise from ignorance of the designs and progress of the Society. We confess, as a man of colour, that we have hitherto viewed the members of the society with jealousy–to all their labors, we have imputed wrong motives–but are we, the only one, who have formed our opinions after this manner? . . .

The American Colonization Society have met with much opposition from us, but the mist which completely darkened our vision, having been dispelled, we now stand before the community a feeble advocate of the society. We have generally wrong ideas of the society, and the members thereof. It cannot be denied that our brethren mostly, believe that Southern interest completely guide the plans of the society–that all their movements tend to fetter more closely the chains of the enslaved–and that the removal of the free from among their slaves, is the ultimatum of their wishes. And further, so ignorant are many of our people, that they are even afraid to trust themselves under the protection of the society, from fear of being carried into foreign lands, and sold into bondage. We have also wrong ideas upon what the society have reflected & what they are now doing in our behalf. Everyone who will give these objections the least examination, will perceive, that to answer them, the society need but point to the flourishing colony of Liberia, as an unanswerable argument in its favour, against all that can be brought forward.

We have wrong conceptions of the plans of the society; than which nothing can be more simple, namely, the removal of those among the free coloured population of the United States, who are anxious to emigrate to Africa. We ask every man of colour can any thing be more simple; here, is a land in which we cannot enjoy the privileges of citizen, for certain reasons known and felt daily; but there, is one where we may enjoy all the rights of freemen; where every thing will tend to call forth our best and most generous feelings. . . .

As the work of emancipation has thus commenced under the immediate auspices of the society, we cannot consider it out of the natural course of things to conclude, that as the means and patronage of the society extend, this great and glorious work will also advance in the same ratio, until the blessed period come, so ardently desired by the Friends when the soil of this happy land shall not be watered by the tears of poor Africa's sons and daughters.

William Abels: "Colony of Liberia"

William Abels was a ship captain, and he wrote this letter to describe what he observed of the conditions in Liberia, the home of recolonization efforts, when his ship stopped there. Abels makes the African colony sound like paradise, affirming the American Colonization Society's efforts.

Connecticut Courant **(Hartford), 21 February 1832**

Dear Sir: Having just arrived in the United States from the Colony of Liberia, to which place I went as master of the schooner Margaret Mercer, and where I remained thirteen days, during which time I was daily on shore, and carefully observed the state of affairs, and inquired into the condition of the people, I venture to state some facts in regard to the circumstances and prospects of the Colony. On the 14th December I arrived, and on the 15th went on shore, and was received in the most polite and friendly manner by the Governor, Dr. MECHLIN, who introduced me to the ministers and principal inhabitants. All the colonists appeared to be in good health. All my expectations in regard to the aspect of things, the health, harmony, order, contentment, industry, and general prosperity of the settlers, were more than realized. There are about two hundred buildings in the town of Monrovia.... Most of these are good substantial houses and stores ...and some of them handsome, spacious, painted, and with Venetian blinds. Nothing struck me as more remarkable than the great superiority, in intelligence, manners, conversation, dress, and general appearance in every respect, of the people over their colored brethren in America. So much was I pleased with what I saw, that I observed to the people, should I make a true report it would hardly be credited in the United States. Among all that I conversed with, *I did not find a discontented person,* or hear one express a desire to return to America. I saw no intemperance, nor did I hear a profane word uttered by any one. Being a Minister of the Gospel, on Christmas day I preached both in the Methodist and Baptist Church, to full and attentive congregations of from three to four hundred persons in each. I know of no place where the Sabbath appears to be more respected than in Monrovia. I was glad to see that the Colonial Agent or governor is a constant attendant, and appears desirous of promoting the moral and religious welfare of the people. Most of the settlers appear to be rapidly acquiring property; and I have no doubt they are doing better for themselves and their children in Liberia, than they could do in any other part of the world. Could the free people of color in this country but see the real condition of their brethren who have settled in Africa, I am persuaded they would require no other motive to induce them to emigrate. This is my decided and deliberate judgment....

WILLIAM ABELS.

Managers, American Colonization Society: "Address"

Newspapers in Connecticut and other New England states began printing abolitionist literature well before the Revolutionary War, and they continued to support the cause of manumission until it was achieved in America. Each year from its formation, the American Colonization Society prepared an address to the nation that promoted its activities. Here, that address is presented by the Connecticut Courant.

Connecticut Courant (Hartford), 31 July 1832

The practicability of colonizing in Africa, any number of the Free People of Colour of the United States, that may choose to emigrate, being demonstrated; the Managers of the American Colonization Society, address their fellow-citizens, under a deep conviction, that this whole nation is now summoned to aid the work, by the most weighty considerations of interest, duty, and charity. . . . Of the success of the plan, they can now speak not merely with hope, but with confidence.—A Colony of more than two thousand persons, firmly established, well-ordered and well-governed; prosperous in trade; moral and religious in character; with schools and churches; courts of justice, and a periodical press; enlarging its territory, and growing in strength; respected by all who have visited it from Europe, and exerting a salutary and extensive influence over the native tribes, now offers an asylum for our free coloured population, and to our citizens, every means and motive for conferring freedom on those who enjoy it not, and imparting civilization and christianity to Africa.

Though the Managers regard the scheme of the Society, as essentially connected with the unity and stability of our political institutions, and the glory of our national character, yet it is rather in its benevolent aspect towards a long afflicted and degraded people, in the midst of us, and their more wretched brethren in Africa, that they would commend it to the patronage of the public.—That there are causes operating to retard the improvement and depress the minds of the free people of colour in the United States, which no benevolence nor even Religion, can for ages, if ever remove; and that the elevation, to any great degree, of our coloured population generally, depends upon their settlement as a distinct community, in some country beyond the reach of those embarrassing circumstances, from which, neither humanity nor legislation can relieve them here. . . .

But while the Society would confer upon free men of colour unspeakable blessings, it offers the best asylum for slaves manumitted from regard to interest, humanity or conscience. Who does not know that in many States, the right of emancipation has been denied to the master, on the ground, that the exercise of such right would be inconsistent with the public good? . . . The Society adhering closely to its original design and principles, and exerting no influence upon slavery, except a moral influence, through the will of the master; gives freedom to that will. . . .

And who can doubt that to this Nation *the interests of the African race are, by Providence, especially entrusted.* The means by which our high and solemn duty to her is to be discharged, is evident. Her exiled children in the midst of us, are waiting to return to her, not as they came, ignorant and enslaved barbarians, but free and instructed christians, capable with the aid that we can give them, of founding upon her shores civilized institutions, of becoming teachers and guides to her people, of inculcating among them, those lessons of wisdom, which men with few advantages are not always the last to learn, that the duty of man is never at war with his interest, and that happiness is the handmaid of virtue. Already in the vicinity of Liberia are they abandoning the traffic in slaves, for a more peaceful commerce and the humane arts of life, and numerous tribes have sought the protection and adopted as their own, the laws of the Colony. . . .

Let every Editor in the country, feel himself responsible to make known throughout the limits of his influence, the views, operations and success of The Society; and that which it has been attempting in weakness will be done with power, that which private charity has so well commenced, be completed by the bounty of the States and the Nation.

In concluding this, perhaps too protracted address, the Managers beg leave to say, that not less than one thousand emigrants are now seeking a passage to Liberia; that the Colony is prepared to receive them, that funds only are wanting to enable the Society to prosecute its enterprise on a large scale, and that all which can appeal to our interests, encourage our hopes, or move our hearts to charity, now commends the cause of African Colonization to the affection and liberality of our countrymen. . . .

Against Colonization

An Anonymous Report: "American Colonization Society"

Samuel Cornish and John Russwurm, editors of Freedom's Journal, *opposed colonization initially. Russwurm changed his mind, but not Cornish. In this article, reprinted from the* Genius of Universal Emancipation, *the writer talks about how the ACS was forcing its colonization on blacks.*

Freedom's Journal **(New York), 11 July 1828**

Editor: It is a fact not to be denied that every man has a right to choose whom he will to represent his sentiments & interests. . . . What then would you think of any man, or set of men, who would, to accomplish their own purposes, take upon themselves to represent, prejudicially the interest of thousands who had never delegated them any such power, and whose interests, according to the account of the representatives themselves, were conflicting with their own? Would you not think such a course of procedure a most unwarrantable assumption of power? Would you not think such men deserving the execration of all whom they had misrepresented and injured? I anticipate your answer. But introduction aside and now to the point. Does not the American Colonization Society bear, precisely, the same relation to the free coloured people of the United States, as the latter of the two preceding relations of constituent and representative? Have the members of that society ever come among us for the purpose of eliciting our true sentiments relative to colonization in Africa? . . . "To colonize upon the coast of Africa, with their own consent, the free people of Colour, (all, I suppose) of the United States, and such others as may be emancipated by individual humanity or the laws of the States." This description of the object of that Society, is not only too concise but entirely too vague. If any person wishes to become thoroughly acquainted with the object of that society, let him peruse its numerous publications issued from time to time. . . . After such an examination, if they still incline to the pretensions of that society, let them appeal again to their consciences and ask, if they have done all for the Coloured portion of their congregations that they might and ought to have done. If the "clergy of all denominations in our city and throughout the United States" will condescend to such a course of examination I am led to believe, they will find that justice and humanity require the improvement of our condition in this land of civilization and gospel light. . . .

A Colored Baltimorean: "To the Editor"

William Lloyd Garrison, the editor of the Liberator, *met William Watkins—the writer of this letter—when Garrison worked for Benjamin Lundy's* Genius of Universal Emancipation *in Baltimore in 1829. Watkins used that paper and Garrison's to voice his strong complaints against the American Colonization Society and African colonization efforts. In this letter, Watkins refers to anticolonization resolutions. After meeting Garrison, Watkins urged him to put together a pamphlet opposing colonization, which Garrison did and titled* Thoughts on African Colonization.

Liberator (Boston), 4 June 1831

MR. EDITOR: I have just found time to notice a few very exceptionable features of a communication. . . . The writer is unquestionably entitled to the credit of being a thorough-going colonizationist. He writes in the *true spirit* of the cause. He seems to be under an excitement produced by the publication of our anti-colonization resolutions. This being the case, it is not to be expected that he would, throughout his communication, avail himself of the guarded, accommodating, and conciliating language usual with colonization writers and declaimers. . . . [H]e says, "I would propose then that Maryland should colonize her own free blacks." He does not add the usual qualification, "*with their own consent:*" he knows this will never be obtained. He therefore says: "I earnestly *hope* that the time *is now* come when our state will wake up to all the importance of this subject, and will instantly commence a *system of measures* imperatively demanded by the *sternest* principles . . . of *sound* policy." We would tell this precocious statesman that we are not to be intimidated into colonization "*measures*" by the angry effusions of his illiberal soul; that we rather die in Maryland under the pressure of unrighteous and cruel laws than be driven, like cattle, to the pestilential clime of Liberia, where grievous privation, inevitable disease, and premature death, await us in all their horrors. . . . The unmerited abuse, that has been so unsparingly heaped upon us by colonizationists for expressing our opinions of their project as connected with our happiness, their manifest determination to effectuate their object regardless of our consent, abundantly corroborate the opinion we have long since entertained. We turn, however, from the contemplation of the persecution and oppression, which, it seems, are in reserve for us, to notice, briefly, the moving cause of this virulent and relentless attack upon our rights and happiness. "The *census just taken . . . admonishes patriotic,* the *benevolent,* the *christian,* principle, by which the colonization societies, throughout our land, are actuated." This is the selfish policy of which we complain, and which should be execrated by all *true* patriots, philanthropists, and christians. Our increase is represented as an "*alarming evil—an evil*" said one of our colonization orators in the pulpit, not long since, "which *threatens* our very *existence.*" . . .He who is for us, is stronger than all that are against us. "The rulers" of the land may "take counsel together," and some of the professed ministers of Jesus may "come into their secret," but "He that sitteth in the heavens shall laugh; the Lord shall have them in derision." Fear not then, my colored countrymen, but press forward, with a laudable ambition, for all that heaven has intended for you and your children, remembering that the path of duty is the path of safety, and that "righteousness" alone "exalteth a nation."

A Colored Baltimorean

An Anonymous Report: "New Jersey"

Though several thousand free blacks returned to Africa through the work of the American Colonization Society, most free blacks opposed the move. In this anonymous letter, the writer—who was probably white—warns of the dangers the society brings. The writer believes the ACS is simply attempting to remove all people of color from the United States. The "school of the prophets" referred to is Princeton College.

The Colored American (New York), 1 September 1838

Hydra-headed colonization has fixed its strong hold in the, hitherto, peaceful state of New Jersey. Always like itself, and true to its first principles, it has excited and is carrying on the most unrelenting persecution of the colored people of that State, and that, too, in connection with the basest attempts to lower the true friends of the colored man in the estimation of the public, and by the most foul and wicked calumny and misrepresentation, which the ingenuity of man, aided by the father of lies, can possibly invent.

This *anti-christian and inhuman crusade* against the defenceless and unoffending colored citizens, commenced with the adoption, promulgation, and embodying in the constitution of the State Society, as one of its articles, the following resolution:

"*Resolved,* That the objects of this society shall be to circulate information among the inhabitants of this State, on the subject of Colonization—and to secure for the people of color in New Jersey, if they prefer it, a distinct settlement in Liberia under the control of the American Colonization Society." . . .

These christian men and wise politicians, in the year of our Lord 1838, and within ten miles of the great seat of science, and "school of the prophets," had the hardihood to pass the above resolution, and make it an article in their constitution, for themselves, and all whom they may have influence to enlist in the unholy crusade, to act under—while at the same time, we hesitate not in saying, *every man of them knew* that there was not a single *colored man, woman, nor child,* in the state of New Jersey, willing to go to Liberia. They further knew, that the only hope of getting them willing, was in cruel proscription and unrelenting persecution.—No argument nor persuasion being capable of effecting it. . . .

Such is the influence of these men, and such the "dying struggles" of the Society, after resuscitation . . . that colored men in New Jersey are more persecuted and more brutally treated, than the slaves of some of the slaveholding States.—And, alas! this persecution is rather than otherwise peculiar to professors. It is in the church that its most prominent features are seen. There it is organized and practiced by system—and such is the proficiency of ministers and members, in the maintenance and management of an unholy hatred of the colored man. . . . And here, by the way, we are proud to state, that while there are some *little souls,* who are ever ready to insult a colored man, there are many *native Americans,* and a host of *noble English, Scotch and*

Irishmen, who despise the mean principle of estimating men, by *country or color.*–It is truly good to live among such, especially at the present dry [*sic*] of excited agitation.–But while we make this exception, we warn our brethren against Jersey *colonization screws and snares.*

The churches, the schools, the steamboats, the railroads, the stage coaches, the public houses, and the highways–the priests and the people–all, all are apparatus of torture, *set in motion,* to drive colored Americans to Liberia.

Gamaliel Bailey: "Candid"

One of the complaints by abolitionists who did not support the American Colonization Society was the society's policy of leaving the slave population of America alone. It wanted only to send free blacks to Africa or those manumitted. Of course the society said it longed for the abolition of slavery, but working toward that purpose was not the goal of the society. Here Gamaliel Bailey, an abolitionist editor, chastises the ACS for this policy.

National Era (Washington, D.C.), 7 August 1851

The *African Repository* for July, the national organ of the American Colonization Society, says:

"We repeat, with the institution of slavery we have nothing to do the operations of our society having reference to *free* colored persons only; nor have we any sympathy with the wild fanaticism of ultra Abolitionists."

This may be regarded as an official announcement. The American Colonization Society has nothing to do with Slavery it has no sympathy with the slave in his sufferings it makes no efforts to elevate his condition above that of the brute, and has no word of censure for a system which debases humanity, and crushes beneath its iron heel the nobler instincts of an entire race. The Colonization Society is strongly commended to the favor and support of the Christian church. It may be that the Saviour came into the world to inculcate such Christianity as this, but we do not so understand his teachings.

An Anonymous Report: "The African Colony at Liberia"

Frederick Douglass always opposed African colonization. This letter speaks of the misrepresentations of the American Colonization Society of its Liberian colony.

Frederick Douglass' Paper (Rochester, New York), 20 April 1855

Mr. Editor:–We have heard various conjectures respecting the African Colony at Liberia, and the scheme of colonizing the free blacks of America;

but never before have we been so thoroughly convinced of its utter futileness, as we have by . . . letters. These letters exhibit the fact, that the colored people of America are not prepared for direct colonization. . . .

Samuel Williams, one of the company, . . . sought to return to the United States; but before he was permitted to leave, he, as his letter states, had to resort to gross deception in order to obtain a passport. Thus we learn, that the Colonization Society uses deception in this country, to get the colored people to Africa; and after they arrive there force them to stay.

Now, sir, what we wish to say is, that the colonization of colored people in any country, under the patronage of the American Colonization Society, never can succeed in bettering the condition of the African race, for this reason the whole scheme is not natural; it is the bastard spawn of prejudice. . . .

Again: How can you form a prosperous government, when the will of the governed is not in it? Such a government is not natural, and must fail. Can you take the slave the untutored slave, who knows not the value of land, houses, commerce, nor association, much less civil government, thrown on the shores of heathen Africa with the expectation of developing the man and the nation, when the man himself has no more mind to it than the rude African among whom his lot is cast? It cannot be done; and the American statesman who would advance such a doctrine, denies the cardinal principles of his own government.

The American Colonization Society can never succeed. . . . There is no place so unsuitable to the growth of man, as where the mind does not take hold on the soil. How can the roots extend, or the branches spread, if a people be dwarfed and stunted by being forced against their will? It never can be done, try it who may; it is not natural.

"If this be the truth," says proud America, "what are we to do with the Negroes?" I say, educate them. Admit them to all the rights of citizens of this country. Do not cramp their limbs, nor dwarf their minds. Teach them the value of association; the value of civil government; of wealth, arts, commerce, &c., and they will solve the vexed problem of the destiny of the colored race, both here and in Africa. Christian Recorder.

QUESTIONS

1. What are the reasons given in the writings for colonization to promote the back-to-Africa movement?
2. Why might free blacks and abolitionists such as William Lloyd Garrison believe emancipation of slaves is more important than sending free blacks to Africa?

3. According to the readings, why did free black Americans so detest colonization? Why did John Russwurm change his mind?

Notes

1. *Liberia Bulletin* (February 1900): 28.

2. Information on the formation of the American Colonization Society and its activities comes from P.J. Staudenraus, *The African Colonization Movement, 1816–1865* (New York: Columbia University Press, 1961), 15–67.

3. *Liberator* (Boston), 23 April 1831.

CHAPTER 3

The Monroe Doctrine, 1823

When James Monroe moved into the White House following his election to the presidency in 1816, the United States, as a nation operating under the Constitution, was nearly thirty years old. Americans had spent much of that time working out their new form of republican government. Americans had an interest in the French Revolution of 1798 and had fought and won a "second war of independence" from Great Britain in 1812, but the nation had been more concerned with its own survival than with world politics in both cases. Now, with the nation entering what one Boston editor called "the era of good feelings," the unified nation began to look beyond its own borders.

The United States had not ignored the events of the world, though. In fact, the country took advantage of revolution and war in Europe to double its size through the Louisiana Purchase of 1803. By 1813, America annexed West Florida, a Spanish possession, and did the same with East Florida in 1818. Spain did not recognize the annexations, and America officially paid Spain for Florida in 1819. The United States was able to seize control of Florida and then force its sale, in part, because Spain, just like much of Europe, had been involved first with the Napoleonic wars and then with internal conflict. Nearly all of Spain's vast colonial territory in Latin America subsequently declared independence. Portuguese territories such as Brazil did the same thing for the same reasons. Most Americans applauded the efforts of Latin Americans to establish nations independent of Europe.

Europe, however, sought normalcy following the Napoleonic wars, and its nations convened a congress in Vienna in 1814. Its purpose was to restore Europe's pre-French Revolution political situation. As part of the plan, the nations agreed that Ferdinand VII should be returned to power in Spain, and the constitutional movement in that country halted. Many Americans believed such a move to restore the Spanish monarchy would be accompanied by efforts to assist the Spanish in retaking control of their colonies in the New World. One way to make such moves more difficult, some thought, was to have America recognize the independent governments of the newly established Latin American nations. "[N]o nation has yet recognized their independence," one editor said of the former Spanish possessions, "and there are undoubtedly good reasons why the U. States should be the first to adopt that measure."[1]

The United States recognized the sovereignty of the former Spanish and Portuguese colonies of Latin America in 1822, but that did little to stop European plans for recolonization. The United States needed a strong ally, and it found one in Great Britain. British ships could keep the Spanish—who would receive assistance from other European nations—out of the Americas. America and Great Britain agreed in principle to issuing a joint statement against European intervention in the Americas, but Monroe's Secretary of State, John Quincy Adams, persuaded the president to issue a statement for America alone. On December 2, 1823, speaking to a joint session of Congress, Monroe declared "that the American continents, by the free and independent condition which they have assumed and maintain, are henceforth not to be considered as subjects for future colonization by any European powers." He said that the United States had not meddled in the affairs of Europe and would continue not to do so. He advised European nations to consider the same policy toward the Americas and warned, "We owe it, therefore, to candor and to the amicable relations existing between the United States and those powers to declare that we should consider any attempt on their part to extend their system to any portion of this hemisphere as dangerous to our peace and safety."[2]

Monroe's declaration to the annual assembly of Congress was not adopted as United States policy in 1823; it simply developed into America's personal statement of sovereignty and that of the Western Hemisphere over time. Americans did not begin calling the statement the Monroe Doctrine until 1852, but its principles were used, in part, to justify America's annexation of Texas and other lands from Mexico in the 1840s and 1850s. In reality, the United States did not have the means to enforce the doctrine when Monroe uttered it, and European nations did not officially respond to the president's words.[3]

Two readings supporting the Monroe Doctrine are included. The first by Thomas Ritchie of the Richmond *Enquirer* explains the doctrine in terms of the events that precipitated it. In the second, by George Goodwin of the *Connecticut Courant*, the editor explains why the doctrine is good for America. The readings opposing the doctrine begin with an extended anonymous article by Crantor. Without mentioning the Monroe Doctrine, it warns of intervention in the affairs of other nations that has no direct bearing on the United States. The final entry is a brief comment about the doctrine on the floor of Great Britain's House of Commons.

Support for the Doctrine

Thomas Ritchie: "The President's Message"

Editor Thomas Ritchie did not think much of most of President James Monroe's State of the Union Address upon his initial reading of it. The Richmond editor did, however, like what his fellow Virginian had to say about United States involvement in world affairs. Ritchie saved his praise for what would become known as the Monroe Doctrine for the end of this lengthy editorial.

Enquirer **(Richmond), 6 December 1823**

We confess that this document completely disappointed us. We took it up without any high expectations of interesting matters: but very different were the feelings with which we laid it down. Its high tone soon struck our attention. We saw that propositions had been made to foreign nations, which were as interesting as they were unexpected. The conclusion of the Message will rivet every one's attention. The policy chalked out towards South America breathes a generous and lofty spirit, which is worthy of the Chief Magistrate of the Nation. . . .

We approach the last topic of the Message–the view which it takes of the present struggles of the world. He rejoices in the success of the Greeks–he deprecates the interference of France with the affairs of Spain. He does not pretend to mingle our politics with those of Europe–but when he intimates an intention on the part of the Holy Allies to extend their principles to S. America, it is then the President employs a bold and decided tune. He intimates that Spain may re-conquer if she can, her former colonies, (and by parity of reasoning, Portugal may re-conquer the Brazils,) but that if the *Allied Powers* should interfere, we must consider it "as the manifestation of an unfriendly disposition towards the U States"–and that we could not "behold such interposition in any form, with indifference."

This strong language induces us to believe, that the President is actuated to use it, at this time, by some extraordinary information which he has received.–Let us suppose such a case–and then let us judge of the propriety of his declarations. Let us suppose, that the President has received information, on which he can rely, that the Allied Powers are bent on restoring the reign of legitimacy to South America; that they are determined to reconquer the free states, whose independence we have recognised: to extinguish their republican principles, and reduce them under the yoke of Spain:–Let us suppose, that they are not only bent on this design, but that Great Britain, the great constitutional nation of Europe, is equally resolute in preventing it; that she has intimated this determination to our government, and proposed for the sake of free principles, to co-operate with the U. States in staying the hand of despotism from this quarter of the globe. Suppose the President to believe that it was high time to take our stand, lest South America, being overrun, we should be the next to be devoured, what was a conscientious magistrate to do? To bury this information in his own bosom? to give no warning? to sound no tocsin? to employ no tome calculated to recall the powers of Europe to a sense of their injustice?—For our own parts, we think it was time to speak; time to remonstrate with the powers of Europe; time to arouse our slumbering people.

What, in fact, does the last intelligence from Europe, following so immediately upon the heels of this Message, tell us? That "it is not against the principles of freedom in Europe alone, that the Holy Alliance intend to limit their operations; but every effort, according to the advices received this day from Paris, is also to be made to put down, what these legitimates call, Revolution in America, and in conformity with this vast and gigantic resolution, the Emperor Alexander has recalled all his accredited agents from the Brazils, and an expedition is forthwith to be forwarded from Spain under the flag of that nation, against the *Republic of Columbia.*" And what is said of England? That she "makes a stand against any farther extension of power of Russia in the East of Europe, and any attack on the new, American states, except by Spain or Portugal, *dependent solely on their own resources.*" It was time then for the President to declare what he thought of the decisions of the Allied Powers.

George Goodwin: "President's Message"

Just like Thomas Ritchie of the Richmond Enquirer, *George Goodwin of the* Courant *served as an editor of a newspaper for decades. And, just like Ritchie, Goodwin believed President Monroe's statement on European intervention in the Western Hemisphere was greatly needed. Goodwin said he felt most Americans would second the president's statement, and he was correct.*

Connecticut Courant **(Hartford), 9 December 1823**

We lay before our readers this week the president's message. Although it is something longer and more minute in detail than common, yet it will be found interesting, embracing a great variety of important topics. Among them . . . a negociation to prevent the further colonization by European powers [of] the western part of this continent . . . the suppression of piracies off the Island of Cuba . . . and lastly, the cause of the South American Republics, on which he observes that we should consider any attempts on the part of the European powers for the purpose of oppressing or controlling the destiny of those governments whose independence we have acknowledged, in any other light than a manifestation of an unfriendly disposition towards the United States. To what extent such interposition may be carried upon the principle on which they have acted in Europe. all other governments are deeply interested. It is impossible therefore that we should view such interposition in any form with indifference. We have thus stated concisely the prominent parts of the president's message. The last topic mentioned is most interesting to our feelings and interests, and we believe the almost unanimous voice of this nation will respond in unison with the sentiments expressed by the president. It is impossible for the European governments to attempt the subjugation of the southern republics upon any principle that would not wrest from us our independence. We have recognized them free and independent as our own, and if European Powers are afraid of the contagion of Republics in their hemisphere, from a parity of reason we should dread the contagion of monarchies in our vicinage. If they have the right to declare among themselves that no government is legitimate but what emanates from Kings, we have in our hemisphere the same right to declare no government has any claims to legitimacy, but what flows from the free choice of the people.

Opposition to the Doctrine

Crantor: "Maintaining Our Own Rights"

In this untitled article from the American Daily Advertiser *that appeared in the* Connecticut Courant, *the anonymous Crantor delicately questions the rationale behind the Monroe Doctrine as it may pertain to American involvement in South America. While never actually mentioning the president or his warning to European powers, Crantor notes that we need not become involved in the struggles of other nations when they have no direct bearing on the United States. He uses a quote from George Washington to make his point. Crantor also says that Americans do not really know the situation in South America, and to be so bold might harm American interests in the long run. The "Allied Powers" to which Crantor refers are France, Spain, and Portugal, the European nations looking to regain territory in South America.*

Connecticut Courant (Hartford), 20 January 1824

The People of the United States feel a lively and disinterested concern in the liberties and happiness of other nations. Possessing in the highest perfection the blessings of free Institutions, and all the means of political and social happiness, they rejoice to see these benefits extended in whatever degree to the people of other countries. The friends of liberty throughout the world receive the cheering and animating applause of this people, while its enemies are arraigned and their conduct condemned and reprobated by every mouth and from every press. The opinion of this country expressed with freedom and without reserve has already been strongly felt abroad, and will hereafter be still more so in the political agitations of the world.

This commanding situation, this high moral influence depends upon two circumstances. In the first place upon our own perfect safety, and in the next place upon the dignified impartiality of our government towards Foreign Powers.

Our own security is beyond question. The remote situation of this country—the number and spirit of the people—their power invincible in self-defence—the total absence of any party or faction among us, favourable to arbitrary government or to any change—in short, the unanimous attachment of the people to their political institutions—render every idea of the subjugation of this country, or an attempt to force another government upon us, chimerical and absurd in the last degree. Add to these considerations, the want of motive in any power or confederacy of powers to make so desperate an attempt, and the facility of counteracting it by forming temporary alliances with other rival powers in aid of our resources.

Our character and influence as a nation will depend then upon our conduct towards others. The policy of this Country is peace. It is in Peace that our Institutions are matured and perfected, that our population increases in a ratio far beyond that of other Countries, and that all the other means of strength and consistency are improved. Maintaining our own rights, we can have no inducement to violate those of others.—To extend our Territory; to acquire foreign possessions, the usual objects of conquests; these acquisitions would be useless and worse than useless to us. We have indeed, no motive for war but self-defence, and while we cherish our own resources and maintain a fair and strict neutrality with respect to other Nations, we are not likely to be disturbed in our peaceful course.

Why should we capriciously throw away these advantages? Why quit our own to stand upon foreign ground? Why involve ourselves in wasteful contest for imaginary interests, or still more fanciful predilections. Must we always have our friends and our enemies, and by what rule shall we select them? Shall we make the despots of the earth our enemies, and the Republics our friends? Alas! experience proves the fallacy of such a plan, and that similarity of institutions forms no tie which will not be broken by any of the ordinary causes of dispute and difference between nations. The despotisms of France and Spain assisted us in establishing our Independence.

With the Republic of France, short-lived as it was, we had a war to maintain, and the History of the Ancient Republics is the History of constant and sanguinary conflicts with each other. All are governed by their views of interest, and projects of ambition are not confined to any particular form of Government.

Reflections of this kind are so obvious that one is surprised to hear the opinions expressed by many at the present time. We meet with persons who think it our duty to go forth, the champions of liberty, to fight its enemies wherever we can encounter them without regard to consequences.—Who are disposed imitate the enthusiastic madness of revolutionary France, when her republicans proffered their services, to every people, and to any portion of the people friendly to liberty: though the consequence of that misguided zeal was, as might have been expected, their own ruin, and that of their friends. Such politicians are far too generous and benevolent to be patriotic and think the interest of their own country a secondary consideration. There are some who gravely argue that we have a right to join in any war for the purpose of doing justice between the combatants, though we have no interest of our own in the contest and having such a right, what shall prevent us from exercising it. There are some, I fear, who, feeling irksomeness of a long exile from power are anxious to return into popular favor, and are therefore led to join in circulating opinions which their own better judgments must condemn.

From such visionary and pernicious notions, it is a relief to turn to those sound maxims left for our instruction by the Father of his country, in his farewell address. The whole is worthy of an attentive perusal at the present time, but I shall merely extract a few sentences which have a particular application to our subject.

"The Nation which indulges towards another an habitual hatred or an habitual fondness, is in some degree a slave. It is a slave to its animosity or to its affection, either of which is sufficient to lead it astray from its duty and its interest."

"A passionate attachment of one nation for another produces a variety of evils. Sympathy for the favourite nation, facilitating the *illusion of an imaginary common interest in cases where no real interest exists,* and infusing into one the enmities of the other, betrays the former in a participation in the quarrels and wars of the latter, without adequate inducements or justification." "There can be no greater error than to expect or calculate upon real favours from nation to nation. It is an illusion which experience must cure, which a just pride ought to discard." "The duty of holding a neutral conduct may be inferred, without any thing more, from the objection which justice and humanity impose on every nation, in cases in which it is free to act, to maintain, inviolate the relations of peace and amity towards other nations."

In relation to the South American contest, which has drawn forth these remarks, we are still without any authentic information as to the alleged interference of the Allied Powers, nor is there any intelligence respecting it upon which we can rely. If any attempt of the kind should be made, it will most probably be opposed by England, from her jealously of those powers, and as interring with her commercial views. England wages no wars for the liberation of other people. Her rule of conduct is her own interest, and this we know even without the avowal of Mr. Canning. She did not consider the conduct of the Allies in assisting the king of Spain to establish a government upon the principles adverse to those of the British, as a cause for entering into the war. Though possessed of an immense disposable force, always ready for action, she reserves her power for cases of real interest. Such she deems her commerce with South America, and the prevention of other European powers from acquiring any portion of that country. She will be well pleased to persuade us, for the love of liberty, to join her in the contest, though she laughs at our motives, and will no doubt treat herself with the lion's share of the spoil. For myself, I unite, most cordially, in the general sentiment in favour of the Souther Americans, and believe that they will triumph. Their rivalships of the European powers will prevent any combination strong enough to overwhelm them, and their own efforts will rise with the occasion.

In no event of the contest, however, is our peace or safety endangered, nor have we any motive to depart from our neutrality.

CRANTOR.

An Anonymous Report: "House of Commons"

Even though European nations ignored Monroe's pronouncement, the administration and Britain were involved in negotiations to stop interference in South America by Spain, Portugal, and France. Monroe tended to undermine those negotiations with his message. Here, a member of Parliament notes his displeasure with Monroe's remarks but says nothing else.

Connecticut Courant **(Hartford), 16 March 1824**

After the speech had been read, Mr. Hill moved, and Mr. J. Daly seconded an Address in answer.

After the address was read Mr. Brougham, in answer to Mr. J. Daly, observed, that he had not any objection to the first part of the address, but protested against the concluding part. . . .

Alluding to the President's Message, he said, "the House would recollect, that its doctrines and principles were to be found in the State Papers of

England. He went the whole way with the United States, that no foreign power had a right to interfere and assist Spain, in the recovery of her Colonies. But he was not prepared to admit, that the Mother Country had waived the right of reconquering those provinces. . . .

Questions

1. Should one nation interfere in the affairs of others over matters of principle? What was Crantor's view on this?
2. What was the rationale behind support of Monroe's Doctrine for Thomas Ritchie and George Goodwin?

Notes

1. *Old Colony Reporter* (Tauton, Mass.), 20 March 1822, quoted in Carol Sue Humphrey, *The Press and the Young Republic, 1783–1833* (Westport, Conn.: Greenwood Press, 1996), 105.

2. Monroe Doctrine, in Dexter Perkins, *A History of the Monroe Doctrine* (Boston: Little, Brown and Company, 1941), 391–93.

3. George Brown Tindall, *America: A Narrative History,* 2 vols. (New York: W.W. Norton, 1984), 1:380–81.

CHAPTER 4

The Elections of 1824 and 1828

The election of 1824 was unlike any the United States had known or would know again. When James Monroe was elected president for his second term in 1820, he ran unopposed. Monroe followed the two-term policy established by George Washington and did not seek a third. The two-party political system had vanished for a time, and four candidates—all Democratic-Republican—had aspirations to be in the White House. Even though the four candidates claimed the same political affiliation, they differed in philosophies, and they came from different regions of the expanding nation. For the first time, viable candidates from America's states beyond the Appalachian Mountains sought the office that had been held solely by the nation's founding fathers—four from Virginia, one from Massachusetts—since the first presidential election. And, after the vote, no candidate captured enough votes to win the election outright in the Electoral College. The House of Representatives would decide the nation's next president.

Another factor entered the presidential contest of 1824—newspapers. Each of the four candidates—John Quincy Adams, William Crawford, Henry Clay, and Andrew Jackson—sought and received support from influential newspaper editors. The system of political patronage, which granted to supportive newspaper printers lucrative governmental printing, had been a part of the political scene since Thomas Jefferson and James Madison devised a scheme to use the press to win the 1800 election.[1] In 1824, however, there were three times as many printing offices to produce newspapers as there had been just fifteen years earlier,[2] and the penetration of newspapers throughout society was greater than it had ever been. Newspapers wielded considerable influence, and each of the candidates garnered support from them. Indeed, the power of the press to effect political change in America grew greatly because of the 1824 election. Following the election, many editors worked overtly to correct what they and many Americans believed to be a stolen election. One newspaper, the *United States Telegraph* of Washington, D.C., adopted the motto, "Power is always stealing from the many to the few," as its editor, Duff Green, worked to make sure the results of the 1824 election were corrected.[3]

What happened in 1824? First, there were no real issues dividing the country. The slave issue in the territories had for the moment been decided by the Missouri Compromise. Second, Monroe failed to endorse any candidate, a diversion from the policy of most of his predecessors. Third, three of the four candidates running for office held important positions in government. Adams was Monroe's vice president and a favorite son of New England. Crawford was the secretary of the treasury, a native of Virginia who now lived in Georgia, and the one candidate who could continue the Virginia presidential legacy. Clay was speaker of the house and a representative of Kentucky. Only the fourth, Andrew Jackson–the hero of the Battle of New Orleans and the War of 1812–was a relative political newcomer, but Jackson was a folk hero among many Americans, especially those who did not consider themselves to be among the affluent part of society or who were from west of the Appalachians.

When the results of the election were tallied, no candidate had enough electoral votes to win the election. Amendment XII to the Constitution called for the president in such cases to be selected by the House of Representatives. Jackson won the popular vote, and Adams finished second. That did not mean, however, that the voting would follow the popular vote, and it did not. Crawford, who finished third by strength of his carrying Virginia, was never really an option since he was afflicted with an unknown illness that left him partially paralyzed and partially blind in 1823. Clay, who believed his own political career would be in jeopardy if Jackson were elected, knew he could never win the election in the House because of his fourth-place finish. He accepted, therefore, an offer from Adams to be secretary of state in exchange for the Kentuckian's support. The combination was enough to push Adams past Jackson in the one-state-one-vote election in the House.[4]

Many Americans were livid at the dealings, and newspapers quickly chose sides. The battle for the White House and the 1828 election began almost as soon as the House voted on February 9, 1825, to make Adams the sixth president. Though Jackson had his detractors, the bulk of newspapers supported the general. Jackson acknowledged the role public opinion, as found in newspapers, played in his election and in what would become the policy of his administration. In his inaugural address. he said, "The recent demonstration of public sentiment inscribes on the list of Executive duties, in characters too legible to be overlooked, the task of reform."[5]

This chapter looks at how the press supported Jackson's presidential bids in both 1824 and 1828. The readings begin with those that address the 1824 election. In the first entry, Jackson's role as an American hero are evident, as are opinions that Jackson would favor the rights of the people. The next deals with the fact that many felt the election of Adams over Jackson in 1824 was a miscarriage of election principles. The final entry in this section equates Jackson with Thomas Jefferson.

The readings opposing Jackson begin with an editorial attacking Jackson's 1824 position on tariffs. The second selection is typical of the period, as it lays out why people should vote for one candidate and not the other. In this case, Henry Clay is the preferred candidate. The next article is a short note that attacks Jackson's lineage, calling him the son of a prostitute. The final chapter selection comes from 1832. It is included to show how controversial Jackson remained as a president.

Support for Jackson

Richard Penn Smith: "The Hero of Orleans"

As the election of 1824 approached, the popularity of Andrew Jackson grew in many areas of the nation. Jackson's popularity as the hero of the War of 1812 and of the "common man" made him the candidate most unlike the other three running for the office. In this news report, the Aurora *(as the* General Advertiser *was commonly called) editor Richard Penn Smith discusses that growing popularity and predicts Jackson will create a truly American party. Even though Smith spoke in positive terms about Jackson, he threw his support to Henry Clay (see opposition section below).*

General Advertiser (Philadelphia), 13 April 1824

The mails daily bring us, from all quarters of the Union, some evidence of the increasing popularity of this distinguished personage. . . . We have expressed an opinion, that the election of the Hero of Orleans, will give rise to a purely American party, and become a rallying point for those who have retired from the political ranks, disgusted with party zeal. There are thousands of young men, who now for the first time, come forward to exercise their right of suffrage—who have declared a predilection in favour of neither of the old parties, and of course feel little interest in the worn out dispute between Democracy and Federalism; but who as Americans, are resolved to support a candidate whose political principles are based upon our republican form of government and is so far removed from the influence of professed politicians, as to be enabled to look upon all parties, as citizens of the same country, and consequently bearing an equal affection towards their native land. It is time that the ultra Federalism, which lately prevailed in the New England states, was shipped across the Atlantic; and on the other hand, the radical democracy, which is shouted forth in anathemas by certain bigotted Caucusites, should descend to the Tomb of the Capulets; for the reasonable class of all parties, turn with aversion from the one, and will not tolerate the violence of the other. We repeat it, the election of Jackson, will change the features of affairs, and create a purely American party.

John Norvell: "A Violation of Principle"

Though Jackson won the popular vote and the electoral vote, the lack of a majority of electoral votes sent the presidential election to the House of Representatives. In this editorial, Norvall, the paper's publisher, rails against representatives who voted in the House contrary to the votes of their respective states' populations. He predicts a rousing victory for Jackson in the next election, demonstrating the fact that the 1828 election was already on the minds of many Americans before the sixth president was ever in office.

Aurora and Franklin Gazette **(Philadelphia), 16 February 1825**

Speaking , then, our own opinions, and those we believe of nine-tenths of the community, the majority of the representatives of the states of North Carolina, Maryland, Kentucky, Ohio, Illinois, Louisiana and Missouri, did, in voting against General JACKSON, in contravention of the manifest wishes of their constituents as, expressed at the polls, or since, in various forms, violate one of the most sacred principles of free republican government. That principle is, that in the selection of their rulers, the will and opinions of the people, or the larger portion of the people, should decide the choice; and if, according to the constitution, an election cannot be made by them at the polls, then their representatives, when the decision of the question devolves upon them, are bound faithfully to respect and follow their wishes in deciding it. By this principle the members from Pennsylvania, from every party, were governed in voting for General Jackson. In the violation of this principle, the members from other states, who disregarded the voice of the people, have aimed a much more fatal blow at our liberties and "the permanence of our institutions," than they could have directed at them if they had contributed "to the election of a military chieftain," in conformity to the expressed or known will of their constituents. If, in this early stage of our political existence, congress may constitute itself into an independent college of cardinals, and choose a President without reference to the will of the nation who are to suffer or to be benefited by selection, then, in time, we fear, an injured and indignant people, in a moment of unreflecting feeling or deep despair, may be impelled to resort to a "military chieftain," to create a dictator, for the redress of their grievances and the punishment of their unfaithful representatives . . . as they are the representatives of other states, and not of Pennsylvania, it is for the people of other states to call them to account for their actions. "Our" representatives having done their duty, we see no occasion, no justification, for town meetings, at which we can only exhaust our energies in vain complaints and protests. It remains, therefore, for the discreet and intelligent friends of General JACKSON here to imitate his own magnanimous example, to discard all "murmurings and feelings of complaint," and cheerfully to acquiesce in that result, which, by the constitution and the law, has placed the subject for the present beyond their control. When the time again arrives for the exercise of their suffrages upon the question of chief magistrate, the rights of the people, the purity of republican principles, grossly violated against General JACKSON, may be triumphantly vindicated in his person and in his favor.

Cimber: "To the People of Virginia"

As the 1828 election approached, newspapers throughout the nation ran editorials and letters in support of the candidates. The Richmond Enquirer *offers a good example. In the weeks before the November 3 election, dozens of writings in support of the paper's candidate—Andrew Jackson—appeared. In this letter, the anonymous Cimber says that the re-election of John Quincy Adams or the election of Henry Clay would mean an end to American liberties. The writer plays on the memories and sympathies of Virginians as he equates Jackson with one of the Commonwealth's greatest citizens, Thomas Jefferson.*

Enquirer (Richmond), 30 September 1828

"*The cry is still—they come! they come!*"

People of Virginia! the crisis of your liberties is at hand. The last pillar of the constitution trembles on its base; and if you love yourselves, if you love your posterity, if you love your country, if you love mankind, you will rush to its support. . . .

Men of Virginia—my countrymen—charge, as you have charged with the immortal Jefferson at your head, and the detestable Adams can no more withstand the terrible collision, than did his Father and predecessor, when that great apostle of liberty at the head of the republican armies came down upon the tyrant.

If I could speak, as with the power convulsed elements, I would thunder this exhortation in the ears of every man in the country. I would say: "You, Sir, you are the very man whose freedom is the awful stake. It is your own beloved Virginia—your country—the loveliest country that the Sun shines upon—whose honour and glory are in peril. She has always marched in the front rank—(the front rank is her own proud and proper station) of the republican host: and in this tremendous crisis the eyes of mankind are upon her. They expect her to do her duty. . . .

If Adams should be re-elected—which God of his infinite mercy avert!—he will have been self-elected, & so will be his successors Mr. Clay; &c. to the end of the list, and to the end of time. By voting for Jackson you will assert the right of the people to self government; you will contribute to hurl from the high places of the State, an administration that has disgraced them by its stupidity, and polluted them by its corruption, and elevate to office a man who has at least a reputation to maintain, and a capacity for affairs. What say you, my countryman, for Jackson, or for Adams!—Can you doubt? Impossible! . . .

For honour of the country & the salvation of the constitution, we are required to make such a manifestation of power, that opposition shall fly from before it, as from the aspect of death. Let every man then plunge his dagger deep into the bosom of the foe, and brandish aloft its dripping point to shew his comrades the he has performed his duty, to stimulate them to imitate the example.

Friends of Jackson and Reform! let no man believe that the great work can be accomplished without his personal presence and assistance at the polls. Let every man be there. We must conquer, but we should annihilate the enemy.

CIMBER.

Opposition to Jackson

Thomas Ritchie: "Gen. Jackson—The Tariff"

In 1824, Thomas Ritchie and the Enquirer *strongly opposed the election of Andrew Jackson, specifically because of his position on tariffs, the subject of this editorial. Other writers to Ritchie's newspaper complained about Jackson's character and the way he knowingly disobeyed the law when he invaded Florida to fight Indians and in New Orleans at the conclusion of the War of 1812. Ritchie and the* Enquirer, *however, joined the Jackson campaign by the 1828 election, as seen in the section above. Two weeks before that election, Ritchie published an* Enquirer–Extra *that told Virginians why they needed to elect Jackson. Ritchie, the editor, was also Ritchie, the Democratic committee member, for this handbill.*

Enquirer **(Richmond), 22 June 1824**

The friends of Gen. Jackson in the two Carolinas were *thrown all aback* by his strong propensity to the new Tariff. . . . How was he to steer? At first it was reported, that he was against the Tariff. New rumours, however, began to circulate that he had thought better of the subject; and would come out in its favor.

We object to the character which has been given of this paper, by some of his Southern friends. They would have us believe, that Gen. J. is in favor of the Tariff, simply as the means of promoting *national defence* (in time of war) or of discharging the *public debt.* In these points of view, they attempt to justify the letter. But, unfortunately for their argument, the General goes farther. He says "Beyond this, I look to the tariff with an eye to the *proper distribution of labour, and to revenue,*" &c. Again—he says emphatically, "and last, *though not least, give a proper distribution to our labor,* which must prove beneficial to the happiness, independence and *wealth* of the community." He is, therefore, in favor of a judicious revision of the tariff for these objects. . . .

But, perhaps, the states which grow tobacco, cotton, rice and sugar, have in these times of pecuniary distress made money faster than the western and other tariff states; and it is right, therefore, according to the political morality of Gen. Jackson and the other tariffites, to check our prosperity *by law,* to drain off a part of our earnings and bestow them on those citizens, who have been less fortunate in their vocations. Mark, we pray you, the words of Gen. Jackson himself. "It is therefore my opinion, that a careful and judicious tariff is much wanted to pay our national debt" *(or rather to throw the payment of it on the non-manufacturing states)* "and afford us the means of that defence within ourselves, on which the safety of our country and liberty depends, and last, though not least, give a proper distribution to our labor, which must prove beneficial to the happiness, independence and wealth of the community." . . .

That Gen. Jackson, entertaining these opinions, should be supported for the Presidency by any of the non-manufacturing States, is to us passing strange. . . .

Gen. Jackson sins against the best lights of the age. Whilst the wisest economists of Europe are attempting to knock off the shackles which have so long fettered the industry of the people, and are getting back to the system of free-trade and unshackled labour, Gen. J. is for taking up their cast off fetters, and binding them on the young and growing limbs of our infant Republic. While they are leaving human labour to regulate itself, and exerting its own lynx-eyed vigilance to discern its most productive employments, he is calling upon the bungling machinery of government to regulate it for us.—He says common sense points out the remedy! Whose common sense? That of the President, and members of Congress? Or, that of the people themselves—each one of whom tries to study his own interest and to better his own condition. If too much labour is now devoted to agriculture and too little manufactures take my word for it, the people interested are likely to find out as soon as Gen. J. and of their own accord to remedy the evils by its proper distribution.

Richard Penn Smith: "The Election of 1824"

The General Advertiser *in the weeks before the 1824 election presented the reasons that its readers should support the candidacy of Henry Clay of Kentucky. In his editorial, Smith gives all the reasons to support Clay and not to support the other candidates. Concerning Andrew Jackson, Smith noted that he lacked civility; Jackson's arbitrary actions in Florida and Louisiana supported this conclusion, even though Smith had praised Jackson a few months earlier (see editorial above). This is a typically lengthy editorial of the era that goes into detail about the positive and negative aspects of candidates.*

General Advertiser (Philadelphia), 29 October 1824

This is the important day upon which Electors of President are to be chosen by the people. We regret to perceive the apathy which pervades a respectable portion of the community upon this subject. The office of Chief Magistrate of the United States, is the most exalted in the world, and from the important duties connected with it, requires of its possessor, talents and qualifications of no common nature. To place in that station a man calculated to reflect honour on the nation, and to serve us according to best interests, ought to be the anxious and active endeavour of every freeman. We have reflected long and frequently upon the subject, with the sincere desire of coming to a right conclusion, and the result has been a deep conviction, that the fittest man of the four candidates, is

HENRY CLAY.

We support him because he is the only honest and consistent democrat of them all; the man who has never given a vote in opposition to the principles of true republicanism; We support him because he supported the rights and honour of our country against foreign aggression, and maintained our cause with a zeal and ability displayed by no other of the candidates: we support him because he has advocated with energy and eloquence and constancy the true interests of this country; the interests of agriculture, commerce and manufactures: We support him because he is the father and champion of the AMERICAN SYSTEM, by which domestic, and not foreign industry is encouraged, by which our own honest artisans are fed and clothed, and not the profligate monarchs and priests of Europe; and by which the internal communication of our country–the roads, canals and bridges are constructed; We support him because he has on all occasions upheld the interests of the merchants and traders; because he supported the navy, the bankrupt law and other measures by which commerce would be benefited: in fine we support him because he is an honest and able AMERICAN PATRIOT, of suitable age, talents and acquirements; a true republican, and an enemy of slavery and oppression every where. We prefer him to

ANDREW JACKSON.

Because although we respect the military talents of the latter, we do not consider them enough to qualify him for the Presidency; because we fear lest he may govern at Washington in the same arbitrary manner that he acted in Florida and Louisiana: because he has never displayed the necessary requisites for civil life, although he has been in Congress twice, and was a judge, &c. in Tennessee, and above all, because we have no assurance that he is disposed and able to maintain the system of protecting American industry, but on the contrary, his votes against the duty on woolens, &c. at the last session of Congress, show that he wants either wisdom or strength of mind sufficient to pursue the true policy of the country.—We have besides, no reason to believe that he is favourable to the protection of commerce. We oppose

WILLIAM H. CRAWFORD.

Because he was nominated by an illegal caucus of congressmen; because he is an enemy to the manufactures of the country and because he is hostile to internal improvements. In a word because we think he has neither talents nor a political system to fit him for the office. We oppose

JOHN Q. ADAMS.

Because we have no faith in his republicanism; because we fear he will imitate the weak and arbitrary measures of his father's administration; because as far as his opinions are known he is believed to be an enemy to domestic manufactures and internal improvements. And because he has never declared himself to be a friend to trade and commerce. He may be a good ambassador at a foreign court, but we want no such President.

Such are our reasons for supporting HENRY CLAY. And for withholding our support from Andrew Jackson, Wm. H. Crawford, and John Q. Adams. Firmly persuaded that with the election of Henry Clay the true interests of every section of our country and of every class of our community are vitally involved, we call upon our fellow citizens to come forward on this occasion, and manifest their sensibility to the country's welfare, by voting the electoral ticket which has been prepared for his support.

To the MERCHANTS AND TRADERS of Philadelphia we would say, HENRY CLAY has never been unmindful of your interests but has on all occasions been your friend and advocate. Which of the candidates has proved himself the friend of the navy but HENRY CLAY? Has John Q. Adams ever shown a regard for it? Has Ge. Jackson? Did not Wm. H. Crawford declare it was a 'fungus' on the body politic? Which of the other candidates has avowed himself friendly to a bankrupt bill? Did not Henry Clay advocate that bill with all his talents and energy? Do not be deceived by the assertions of the Adams presses in relation to his wish to favour one branch of public industry at the expense of another, but examine for yourselves. Look at his public conduct in relation to the Bank of the U. States, the South American question, the restriction system of the British West Indies, the appropriations for light houses and other public works in the Atlantic States, and ask whether HENRY CLAY can be considered in any other light than as a decided friend of commerce.

MANUFACTURERS AND MECHANICS, in HENRY CLAY, you have always found an honest friend and steady champion. He has supported your interests every where, and at all times. "He has never flinched for fear of losing popularity in any quarter."—He thought it better that you and your wives and children should be encouraged to obtain a living in a respectable way, than that the money of this country should go abroad to fatten foreigners, and thinking so he has never hesitated to avow the opinion and to act upon it in Congress. He has lost a great many friends in the southern states in consequence of this system of policy.—Shall he not find friends in you? You have been told that Gen. Jackson is equally the friend of your interests. IT IS NOT SO. There is no proof of it. He has done nothing more all his life than give a silent vote last winter in favor of some of the provisions of the Tariff. While on the other hand his vote against the duty on woolens and on cotton bagging, shews conclusively that he is not the friend of the system. Supposing then that their merits in other respects were equal, Henry Clay is entitled to your preference because he is a steady and determined friend. But in fact, Fellow Citizens, the merits of the two are not equal. Henry Clay possesses every qualification of mind, temper, disposition and education. Andrew Jackson possesses little more than the merit of a brave General. Under such circumstances you cannot hesitate. Come then to the polls, and record your gratitude for his services and your opinion of his policy by voting the electoral ticket headed by LANGDON CHEVES. Should you be told that your vote will be thrown away if given to Henry Clay, disbelieve the suggestion. "It is a trick of the enemy," which has often been exposed. The fact is, that the prospects of Henry Clay are at this moment better than those of any other candidate, but should he not get Pennsylvania, he will nevertheless be elected.—"Your vote can never be thrown away, if given to a man who deserves it better than the others, and who will receive a sufficient support from other states."

An Anonymous Report: "Son of a Prostitute"

Comments about candidates did not have to be true in the 1820s. This sentence printed two months before the November 3, 1828, election is an example.

National Journal **(Washington, D.C.), 4 September 1828**

General Jackson's mother was a COMMON PROSTITUTE, brought to this country by the British soldiers! She afterward married a MULATTO

MAN, with whom she had several children, of which number General JACKSON IS ONE!!!

Ambrose Spencer: "A Note of Alarm"

Even though the elections of 1824 and 1828 involving Andrew Jackson were controversial, the general's ability to draw either affections or ire did not diminish with the 1832 election. This letter from Judge Ambrose Spencer demonstrates that Jackson's first term actions did not allow people to remain neutral about him. This letter was first published in the Green County Advocate *but presented to a wider audience in the state's larger paper, the* Connecticut Courant.

Connecticut Courant (Hartford), 16 October 1832

If ought I said can influence an individual to oppose the re-election of Gen. Jackson, it would afford me sincere gratification. I appeal to the searcher of hearts when I say, that I advanced nothing that I did not most conscientiously believe. IT APPEARS WONDERFUL TO ME THAT ANY INTELLIGENT BEING CAN READ THE LAST VETO MESSAGE WITHOUT A CONVICTION THAT GEN. JACKSON ADVANCES DOCTRINES, WHICH IF CARRIED OUT. LEAD TO ANARCHY AND RUIN. He denies that the decisions of the Supreme Court of the United States are binding on Congress, the Executive, or any other officer of the Government–and he denounces the Tariff, a protecting system of the United States, as an abandonment of the true principles of legislation and as improvident.

He has refused obedience to the act of Congress of 1802, regulating intercourse with the Indians–in effect pronouncing it unconstitutional. HE HAS DENIED THE VALIDITY OF ALL TREATIES WITH THE INDIAN TRIBES, ENTERED INTO BY WASHINGTON AND ALL HIS PREDECESSORS. In short, he has done all that lay in his power to derange the policy uniformly pursued by all who went before him, and bring contempt on the Government. AND IT IS MY DEEP AND ABIDING CONVICTION THAT SHOULD HE BE RE-ELECTED, OUR INSTITUTIONS WILL BE SUBVERTED, AND OUR NATIONAL GLORY BE DESTROYED.

Questions

1. What legitimate arguments are offered against Jackson's election in 1824 and 1828? Do they differ?
2. Why did the *General Advertiser* support Henry Clay over the other candidates?

3. What were the reasons offered for supporting Jackson's presidential bids? Which were based in sound reasoning, and which were appeals to emotion?

Notes

1. David Copeland, "America, 1750–1820," *The Press and the Public Sphere: Politics and Social Change in Late Eighteenth- and Early Nineteenth-Century Europe and America,* ed. Hannah Barker and Simon Burrows (Cambridge: Cambridge University Press, 2002), 153.

2. Michael Emery and Edwin Emery, *The Press and America: An Interpretive History of the Mass Media,* 6th ed. (Englewood Cliffs, N.J.: Prentice Hall, 1988), 103.

3. Quoted in Carol Sue Humphrey, *The Press of the Young Republic, 1783–1833* (Westport, Conn.: Greenwood Press, 1996), 120.

4. Culver H. Smith, *The Press, Politics, and Patronage: The American Government's Use of Newspapers 1789–1875* (Athens: University of Georgia Press, 1977), 59.

5. Andrew Jackson, *The Correspondence of Andrew Jackson,* 7 vols., ed. John Spencer Bassett (Washington, D.C., 1926–35), 4:19.

CHAPTER 5

The Massachusetts Public School Act, 1827

Early in 1827, the Commonwealth of Massachusetts passed a law requiring towns to provide schools and teachers. The first section of the nineteen-section codicil to existing laws stated:

> Each town or district of 50 families must have a teacher of orthography, geography, reading, writing, English grammar, arithmetic and good behavior at least 6 months in a year. If of 100 families, there must be teachers to equal 18 months in a year. If 500 families must equal 24 months in a year and must add the History of the United States, bookkeeping by single entry, geometry, surveying, and algebra and must have a Master for Latin and Greek.[1]

Massachusetts' new law applied to the education of females and males. Later in the year, the state went further and set up a fund to provide schools designed specifically to train teachers.[2]

The idea of providing education in America was not new. Shortly after British colonization efforts began in the seventeenth century, Massachusetts established Harvard in 1636 to train ministers; Virginia did the same with William and Mary in 1693. Individuals and individual colonies also provided schools for young people. New England, however, led efforts at education in America. In 1635, for example, Boston sought a person "for the teaching and nurturing of children with us."[3] Later, Americans viewed the knowledge education imparted as part of what allowed them liberty and freedom. "Knowledge among a People makes them free, enterprizing and dauntless," New York lawyer William Livingston wrote in 1753, "but Ignorance enslaves, emasculates and depresses them."[4] Livingston's ideas became an important part of the move toward public education in America.

Despite what we may think today, Americans of the eighteenth century and through the antebellum period of the nineteenth would have considered a strong understanding of religion—specifically Christianity—vital to being a "free, enterprizing and dauntless" people. As a result, religious instruction was central in many educational situations. In the nineteenth century, church schools or Sunday schools remained a principal means of educating young people. Samuel Bowles wrote in the *Springfield Republican* in 1827 "that 200,000 children in this country receive the benefits of Sabbath Schools."[5] The Sunday schools were not part of a public school system, but they still provided a key ingredient in American education.

In the United States, the push for tax-supported schools that were free and compulsory coincided with the reform movements of the antebellum period. Religious revival initiated reform efforts in a number of areas of American life (see Chapter 2, for example), and reading and writing for the sake of understanding the Bible were important, but Sunday schools could not provide enough education to meet the needs of Northern society that was quickly turning away from agriculture and toward industrialization. As a result, people such as Horace Mann began to push for common schools, that is, schools that offered a common educational experience to all. Mann believed the common school could "become the most effective and benignant of all the forces of civilization."[6] Mann helped to create a state board of education in Massachusetts to ensure that all children would have an adequate education. The Massachusetts Public School Act of 1827 was but one step in the process, and the idea caught on in the states above the Mason-Dixon line. Even in the South, though, where few large cities existed, agrarian lifestyles lent themselves less to education and more to labor, and slavery meant that a sizeable portion of the population could not legally be educated, private schools flourished for both males and females. Even schools for free blacks existed. The South, however, did not follow the move to common schools that were supported by tax dollars until after the Civil War.[7]

One of the key ingredients in education in antebellum America was the press. Newspapers and magazines provided Americans with the bulk of their knowledge on every subject. Newspapers such as New York's the *New World* and magazines such as *Godey's Lady's Book*, printed novels, plays, and poems in each edition. The Washington *Globe* regularly printed the proceedings of Congress, and the other newspapers, which numbered 1,200 in 1833, provided and guided the politics of the day. New York publisher James Gordon Bennett even believed, "A newspaper can send more souls to Heaven, and save more from Hell, than all the churches or chapels in New York"[8] The cheap penny papers that sprang up after Benjamin Day's *Sun* in 1833 provided a cost-effective way for people to obtain information, but even the more expensive newspapers did the same. The proliferation of newspapers and reading materials and the development of common schools went hand in hand.

This chapter looks at public reaction to the push toward compulsory education through common school systems. It also provides readings on female education and attempts to keep slaves from learning to read and write. Support for schools begins with a letter that points out how important education is in order to vote and watch the government. The second discusses the value of church schools, one of the places some Americans learned to read and write. The next entry calls for quality education for all children, not just the wealthy. It is followed by a request for better normal schools, that is, those that train teachers. The final selection discusses the growth in female education.

The section that opposes education contains two articles. The first is a lengthy attack on universal education in America. The writer claims providing equal education for all children will slow the educational process for gifted students. The last entry discusses the sentencing of a Virginia woman for teaching blacks to read and write. Following the 1831 Nat Turner rebellion, many Southern states passed laws making it illegal to educate blacks.

SUPPORT FOR SCHOOLS

An Anonymous Report: "Importance of Education"

In the antebellum period, Americans' interest in politics may have grown to be greater than it was at any other time in the nation's history. Less than 27 percent of Americans able to vote did so in 1824, but close to 60 percent voted in the next election, and more than 80 percent did in 1840. The election of 1824, in which the most popular candidate–Andrew Jackson–lost in the House of Representatives, no doubt helped increase voter interest. This anonymous piece appeared originally in the Nashville Whig, *hometown newspaper of Jackson. The election was the impetus for its author.*

Newport (R. I) Mercury, 4 December 1824

It is too true, we fear, that, in many parts of the country, education, instead of advancing as we have been accustomed to flatter ourselves, is on the decline. We do not speak of College learning, of course because the facilities for acquiring that description of education are rapidly multiplying and extending themselves over the country. We speak of a common school education–including a knowledge of reading, writing, arithmetick, a general idea of geography and history, some notion of the government in general, and especially of our own government, and of the duty of a good citizen, &c. Unless instruction in these matters be better attended to, we fear that in the parts of our country more remote from its centre, the people will, in time, begin to imbibe very confused notions of legal and political rights, duties, and obligations. Nay, we have already seen considerable approaches, in avowals of political sentiment, to the conclusion that all government is a nuisance, all law and restraint on the principles of nature, and all Judges, in particular . . . whom it is quite amusing, and very patriotick withal, to hunt down. . . .

Samuel Bowles: "The Sabbath Schools"

The education of American youth came in many variations. Americans often followed the lead of Great Britain, and church schools were no different. The concept began in England. The church schools were precursors to the common schools and continued after the common school movement began. Although children were taught to read only from the Bible and read only scripture, they still learned to read, something Bowles believed was imperative.

***Springfield (Mass.) Republican*, 27 January 1827**

It is now 45 years since Robert Raikes first commenced a little Sabbath School in the city of Gloucester. His benevolent heart thought only of doing a service to a few poor children in a provincial town; but in less than half a century the rich fruits of his labors are extended directly to more than one million, two hundred thousand individuals and their influence is felt in every Protestant country on the globe. It is estimated that 200,000 children in this country receive the benefits of Sabbath Schools and a million in other parts of the world.

Friends of Equal Education: "Education in Pennsylvania"

Concerned citizens throughout America evaluated education during the antebellum period. This report, published by a group called Friends of Equal Education in Philadelphia, first appeared in that city's Mechanic's Free Press. *It was reprinted elsewhere, this version appearing in George H. Evan's* Working Man's Advocate *of New York. Both newspapers were labor right's publications, and education was seen as imperative for workers in Northern and Western states during the antebellum period as a way to improve their situation in society.*

***Working Man's Advocate* (New York), 6 March 1830**

Of the Joint Committees of the City and County of Philadelphia, appointed September, 1829, to ascertain the state of public instruction in Pennsylvania, and to digest and propose such improvements in education as may be deemed essential to the intellectual and moral prosperity of the people. . . .

With the exception of this city and county, the city and incorporated borough of Lancaster, and the city of Pittsburgh, erected into "school districts" since 1818, it appears that the entire state is destitute of any provisions for public instruction, except those furnished by the enactment of 1809. This law requires the assessors of the several counties to ascertain and return the number of children whose parents are unable, through poverty, to educate them; and such children are permitted to be instructed at the most convenient schools at the expense of their respective counties.

The provisions of this act, however, are incomplete and frequently inoperative. . . .

The elementary schools throughout the state are irresponsible institutions, established by individuals, from mere motives of private speculation or gain, who are sometimes destitute of character, and frequently, of the requisite attainments and abilities. . . .

From this view of the public instruction in Pennsylvania, it is manifest that, even to "*the school districts,*" to say nothing of the remainder of the state, a very large proportion of youth are either partially or entirely destitute of education. . . .

The original element of *despotism* is a MONOPOLY OF TALENT, which consigns the multitude to comparative ignorance, and secures the balance of knowledge on the side of the rich and the rulers. If then the healthy existence of a free government be, as the committee believe, rooted in the WILL of the American people, it follows as a necessary consequence, of a government based upon that *will,* that this monopoly should be broken up, and that the means of equal knowledge, (the only security for equal liberty) should be rendered, by legal provision, the common property of all classes. . . .

It appears, therefore, to the committees that there can be no real liberty without a wide diffusion of real intelligence; that the members of a republic, should all be alike instructed in the nature and character of their equal rights and duties, as human beings, and as citizens; and that education, instead of being our public poor schools, to a simple acquaintance with words and cyphers, should tend, as far as possible, to the production of a just disposition, virtuous habits, and a rational self governing character. . . .

The committees, therefore, believe, that one school, at least should be established in each county, in which some principle should be adopted, calculated to obviate the defects that have been alluded to, and by which the children of all who desire it, may be enabled to procure, at their own expense, a liberal and scientific education. They are of the opinion that a principle fully calculated to secure this object, will be found in a union of agricultural and mechanical with literary and scientific instruction; and they have therefore, in addition to a plan of common elementary schools, the substance of a bill providing for the establishment of high schools, or model schools, based upon this principle, which they also present for public deliberation. . . .

Patriotism: "Normal School"

Even though Massachusetts supported public schools, Patriotism, the anonymous writer of this letter to the Massachusetts Spy, *lamented the condition of the normal school in Barre because it was not providing the best for those who attended it. The writer notes how well the universities and seminaries are funded, but they are not the ones providing teachers for the public schools. Education, Patriotism says, can never improve unless the quality of education for teachers improves.*

Massachusetts Spy **(Worcester), 21 July 1841**

To the Citizens of Worcester County:—You have within the limits of your County one of the most important institutions in the country; yet, permit me to say you seem profoundly indifferent as to its prosperity and fate, although some of the dearest hopes of the patriot are suspended upon its yet doubtful success. This institution is the Normal School, or School for Teachers at Barre. If the public mind can be brought to consider this subject, in all its momentous bearings, with suitable care and adequate interest, I am certain that the present languishing and inefficient condition of the School will be succeeded by one of vigorous and extensive usefulness.

The State bestowed its support directly and largely for many years upon the higher institutions of learning, academies, medical schools, and colleges. Undoubtedly the leading object in these appropriations was the good and advancement of the entire community. The Legislature expected that these seminaries would send forth graduates of highly cultivated minds, who should imbue society with some leaven of their own refinement and knowledge, and be fitted to occupy, to general advantage, the important and controlling stations among the people. But, in the establishment of schools for teachers, Massachusetts acted directly and derisively for the benefit of all, but especially of the middling and poorer classes. The rich can provide for the education of their children, and are generally sagacious enough to procure the best instruction cost what it may. . . .

It might, indeed, be demonstrated, and is clear, that the establishment of Normal Schools, and all influences going to improve the ignorant in knowledge and the vicious in virtue, tend directly to the security of property and the increase of its value, and are, therefore, for the advantage of the rich as well as the poor. Still, the Normal Schools are directly and emphatically the poor man's schools. They reap the best harvest. For it has generally been the case that the common district schools have been taught by whomever the prudential committee or school agent might chance to employ. . . .

When, therefore, the State undertakes to elevate the qualifications of teachers, it is in fact, legislating in the wisest, most benevolent, and most efficient way for the improvement of the minds and hearts of the children of our population. It is conferring an infinitely higher obligation upon the coming generation than to provide, by law, a handsome property for each child on coming of age. Now it is to this majestic enterprize of imparting a superior education to the children of Massachusetts, of giving a larger and better development to their intellect and affections; it is to this wise and magnificent plan to which, it seems to me, people of Worcester, that you are so thoroughly indifferent. There is too little interest felt in this subject, to be sure, all over Massachusetts; and it would be well for the Normal Schools, but better still for us and for the State, if a wholesome earnestness pervaded our population, in behalf of this great practical undertaking for the immediate and prospective benefit of our children.

PATRIOTISM.

New Bernian: "Female Education"

Increasingly, Americans realized that all needed to be educated. This letter from North Carolina touts the increasing number of public schools.

Weekly Raleigh Register, and North Carolina Gazette, 16 February 1848

One of the most interesting and promising signs of the advancement of sound principle, solid morals and intelligence in the present age, is the growing interest felt throughout the breadth of our country, for Female Education. And we are happy in the belief that the Old North State is taking hold of this matter in good earnest. The best security which a people can have for whatever is elevated intellect, morals, manners, courage, enterprise, benevolence or patriotism in the rising generation, next to the general diffusion of the principles of our holy christianity, is in the thorough cultivation of the *female mind.* The day was when woman held a degraded and humble position beneath man; but christianity brought her up from that debasement, not to lord it over him, but to be his equal; and now education comes in to mould and fit her for that high station. Strange is it, that it was left almost entirely to the enterprise of the nineteenth century to strike out those high schemes of intellectual improvement, which are now esteemed essential to the prouder and full development of the female mind. Happy for us that we live in such an age! and right glad are we that North Carolina is putting forth a strong arm in this work. . . .

One would think . . . that we believe in the Ladies. Well, we do. . . . *'I have great faith in women; and I have but little faith in that man who has not!'*

New Bernian.

Opposition to Schools

Robert Walsh: "No Confidence in Compulsory Equalization"

The Daily National Gazette *was one of America's more influential newspapers in the first two decades of the antebellum period. In this editorial, Walsh does not deny the value of education, but he does say that forcing mandatory education funded by the public would make it requisite for the education of the poor to be funded by others, a way to have government more involved in the lives and decisions of people. In addition, those less prepared for schooling would "slow down" the education of those more suited to school.*

Daily National Gazette (Philadelphia), 19 August 1830

. . . [T]he scheme of Universal Equal Education at the expense of the State is virtually "Agrarianism." It would be a compulsory application of the means of the richer, for the direct use of the poorer classes; and so far *an arbitrary division of property among them.* The declared object is to procure the opportunity of instruction for the child or children of every citizen; to elevate the standard of the education of the working classes; or *equalize the standard for all classes;* which would, doubtless, be to lower or narrow that which the rich may now compass. But the most sensible and reflecting possessors of property sufficient to enable them to educate their children in the most liberal and efficacious way, and upon the broadest scale, would prefer to share their means for any other purpose, or in any other mode than such as would injuriously affect or circumscribe the proficiency of their offspring. . . .

Thus, a direct tax for "the equal means of obtaining useful learning" is not deemed improbable, and it is admitted that the amount which would be paid by the wealthy would be "far greater" than that paid by their "less eligibly situated fellow citizens." Here, we contend, would be the action, if not the name, of the Agrarian system. Authority—that is, the State—is to force the more eligibly situated citizens to contribute a part (which might be very considerable) of their means, for the accommodation of the rest; and this is equivalent to the idea of an actual compulsory partition of their substance. The more thriving members of the "mechanical and working classes" would themselves feel the evil of the direct taxation;—they would find that they had toiled for the benefit of other families than their own. One of the chief excitements to industry, among those classes, is the hope of earning the means of educating their children respectably or liberally; that incentive would be removed, and the scheme of State and equal education be thus a premium of comparative idleness, to be taken out of the pockets of the laborious and conscientious. . . . Similar advantages might be pleaded for a more direct comprehensive Agrarian project; indeed, we have seen the general distribution of the means of the rich,—the total destruction of what is called the aristocracy,—argued, in some of the New York publications, upon the same grounds for beneficial consequence—additional strength to our republican institutions, and so forth.

We have no confidence in any compulsory equalizations; it has been well observed that they pull down what is above, but never much raise what is below, and often "depress high and low together beneath the level at what was originally the lowest." By no possibility could a perfect equality be procured. A scheme of universal equal education, attempted in reality, would be an unexampled *bed of Procrustes* for the understandings of our youth; and in fact, could not be used with any degree of equality or profit, unless the dispositions and circumstances of parents and children were nearly the same to accomplish which phenomenon, in a nation of many millions, engaged in a great variety of pursuits, would be beyond human power. For the original, prodigious, and splendid conceptions of his modern philosophers, Swift chose an island,—the far-famed Laputa—of only ten thousand acres of surface. No one of his professors in the school of political projectors, in the Grand Academy of Lagado, even imagined any thing more difficult than what is now seriously proposed to the working classes of the United States.

We have thrown out the foregoing remarks cursorily, and as it were accidentally,—without meaning to develope now a question which may be made,—advantageously for the public mind,—to embrace a consideration of the nature of our political institutions. . . . It is a fundamental part of the Republican system to yield no power to *government* or to state except what is necessary—to leave as much as possible to individual enterprise and individual discretion;—to interfere only from imperative motives and for public ends of the highest and clearest utility, with the direction of private industry and the disposal of private fortune. Upon all this, the idea of committing to the State the regulation and care of the education of all citizens, with a uniform plan, is a broad encroachment,—a bold and momentous innovation. A number of the soundest and most patriotic thinkers, among us, might chose [*sic*] rather to assign to the State a general control over private property for any other object; or a multitude of parents would be glad to escape to any other land,—whatever might be the designation of its government,—where they could enjoy at least freedom of choice as to the tuition of their children. . . .

An Anonymous Report: "Mrs. Margaret Douglass"

Though Massachusetts would desegregate its schools before the Civil War and schools for free blacks could be found both North and South, the Nat Turner rebellion on August 21, 1831, sent alarms through the Southern community (see Chapter 9). As a result, many Southern legislatures passed laws that made it illegal to teach slaves to read or write. Turner, who had been taught to read by his first owner Benjamin Turner, read the Bible and preached to other slaves. He ultimately saw religious signs that led to his rebellion. The article below describes the punishment of Margaret Douglass, who was convicted of teaching Virginia slaves to read and write. Though her jury sentence was light, the judge overruled the punishment and sent Douglass to jail. As can be seen from this report, education of blacks was directly tied to abolition, states' rights, and any number of other issues that divided the nation at this time.

Daily Southern Argus **(Norfolk), 9 February 1854**

We publish to-day the judgment of Hon. Judge Baker in the case of Mrs. Douglass, which has much excited our citizens. The first time within the passage of the act forbidding the teaching of slave or free colored persons to read or write, has a case of this description come under the jurisdiction of our Court, and it was singular that this case should be a woman. The jury found a verdict of guilty, and the law had to be sustained. Sympathy was aroused for Mrs. Douglass. It was revolting to the citizens to have a woman imprisoned in our jail, and every inducement was offered Mrs. Douglass to escape punishment. The Court obliged to adjourn its judgment over, and although a copias was awarded, yet it was the hope and wish of every one that she would leave the city. But no; "a martyr" she "should be to the cause of benevolence"; and to cap the climax, she brought her daughter, a maiden of some seventeen summers, who had obeyed the injunctions of her mother as a child should, to try the stern realities of the laws, and to use her own language in defending her cause, "to glory in works of benevolence and charity to a race downtrodden" Then sympathy departed, and in the breast of every one rose a righteous indignation towards a person who would throw contempt in the face of our laws, and brave the imprisonment for "the cause of humanity."

The decision of Judge Baker is cogent and pungent, and will be read with interest. The laws must be upheld. It is not for the Judge to set upon the constitutionality or just of the law; it is for him a sacred duty to impose the punishment meted out in the code. Virginia must keep in restraint the wire-workings of abolition sentiments. We have in this town suffered much from the agression of Northern foes, and a strong cordon must encircle our domestic institutions.

We must preserve from discord and angry passions our firesides and homesteads. We must preserve inviolate the majority of laws necessary for the protection of our rights; and there is no one of intelligence and foresight who will pronounce the judgment unrighteous.

Mrs. Douglass' time will run out this week, and we have heard it stated from good authority that her imprisonment will be a pecuniary reward to her. We hope that our citizens will prevent by all possible means any attempt to aid this woman, but let her depart hence with only one wish, that her presence will never be intruded upon us again. Let her seek her associates at the North, and with them commingle, but let us put a check to such mischievous views as fell from her lips last November, sentiments unworthy a resident of the state, and in direct rebellion against our Constitution.

Questions

1. What was Robert Walsh's basic argument against the common or public school? Is there any validity to his argument? Explain.
2. What are the complaints lodged against the common schools?
3. What were normal schools, and why were they so important?

Notes

1. *Springfield (Mass.) Republican,* 27 March 1827.

2. *Springfield (Mass.) Republican,* 2 May 1827.

3. *Second Report of the Record Commissioners of the City of Boston; Containing the Boston Records, 1634–1660, and the Book of Possessions,* quoted in Lawrence A. Cremin, *American Education: The Colonial Experience, 1607–1783* (New York: Harper & Row, 1970), 180.

4. *Independent Reflector* (New York), 8 November 1753.

5. *Springfield (Mass.) Republican,* 27 January 1827.

6. James W. Fraser, *The School in the United States* (Boston: McGraw-Hill, 2001), 48–49.

7. Fraser, *The School in the United States,* 49.

8. *Herald* (New York), 19 August 1836.

CHAPTER 6

The South Carolina Tariff Conflict, 1828

What else can the government do to us, was, no doubt, how many South Carolina farmers and planters in the Tidewater region felt in 1828. From the colonial period into the nineteenth century, they had experienced great financial success by growing indigo, rice, and cotton. Things had not been so good, however, for the last ten years. First, the price of cotton fell by more than 56 percent in the British market, the principal buyer of South Carolina's cotton. The price had risen drastically during the century up to that point, and South Carolinians had borrowed heavily to purchase more slaves and land to grow the crop. Now, the government was set to pass another tariff act that would protect manufactured goods–produced principally in the North–while hurting Southern imports–principally obtained from foreign countries. The tariff also applied a high tax on cotton sold in Europe.

Opposition to the tariffs of the 1820s in South Carolina was obviously based on economic interests, but it was part of a larger movement in the United States toward states' rights. American nationalism swelled following the War of 1812, and it continued into a period called the era of good feelings that began in 1816 when James Monroe handily won the presidential election. The national two-party political system collapsed. Economically, the nation was in good shape, and all sections appeared to be working in harmony. Events beginning in 1819, however, changed the nation's mood. First, there was the economic depression that killed cotton prices in South Carolina and other parts of the South. Next, sectional strife arose around the Missouri Compromise and slavery (see Chapter 1). Sectional differences could also be seen in the directions that North and South were taking. The North was turning more toward industrialization and commerce. The South remained agrarian. The national government increasingly worked to protect commercial interests and increasingly injected itself more into everyday life–tariffs, the national bank, and nationalist rulings by the Supreme Court are some examples.

While other parts of the nation—including the more rural areas of the North—advocated states' rights, South Carolina's most influential citizens and politicians increasingly believed that federal interference was at the root of all their problems. As a result, the state became the primary battleground over tariffs, federal power over the states, and the concept of states' rights. Despite strong arguments by the state's Washington delegation against tariffs in 1827 and 1828, Congress passed and President John Quincy Adams signed into law the Tariff of 1828 in May, commonly referred to as the Tariff of Abominations by South Carolinians.

For one South Carolinian, Vice President John C. Calhoun, the states' rights movement offered profound repercussions. Calhoun had been one of the nation's principal architects of the national movement in the teens and early 1820s. He had supported tariffs in 1816 and in 1824. Now, even though he was vice president and would likely continue to be because of his close affiliation with Andrew Jackson and the Democratic party, he faced opposition in his home state. At this time, Calhoun began to rethink his nationalist position and initiated a dramatic shift toward states' rights. As a result, Calhoun wrote the *South Carolina Exposition and Protest.* The South Carolina legislature adopted the *Exposition* as part of its rebuttal of the Tariff of Abominations, though the *Exposition* was presented as an anonymous document and only later was it revealed that Calhoun was its author.[1]

Calhoun developed a theory of nullification in his writing. Calhoun did not seek to tear apart the Union; he sought a way to protect the rights of the minority where the vote of the majority established law. Calhoun believed that the United States was a covenant between sovereign states. Therefore, if a state objected to a particular federal law, it could reject the law through a state convention. If that happened, two options remained for the federal government. It could repeal the law, or it could propose the law as an amendment to the Constitution. If the law became part of the Constitution, the state could then accept the law or—as an action of last resort—remove itself from the Union, the latter being something Calhoun hoped would not happen. But many in South Carolina believed secession was the state's proper course, and that set up a confrontation between the state and Jackson, who said before the 1828 election, "There is nothing I shudder at more than the idea of a separation of the Union."[2] That confrontation came to a head in 1832 when South Carolina voted to nullify the Tariff of 1828, and Jackson threatened to send federal troops into the state (see Chapter 10). Though the sides reached a compromise, it was never satisfactory to many South Carolinians, and secession from the Union would become the only solution.

The battle over the tariff and nullification in 1828 in South Carolina, however, was not one with a united front. South Carolinians disagreed over the harm of the tariff and over nullification. People throughout America did the same, but the argument was most intense in South Carolina. This chapter looks at how those opposed to the tariff and those who supported it presented their cause. It focuses primarily on writings from South Carolina publications and begins with writings that oppose the tariff. All of the readings come from the *Mercury* of Charleston with the exception of the second, which appeared in a Maine newspaper.

Articles supporting the tariff begin with three that appeared in South Carolina papers. Not all South Carolinians opposed the tariff or supported Calhoun's views. The last entry appeared in *Niles' Weekly Register* and voices approval for the tariff for a group in Baltimore.

In Opposition to the Tariff

Brutus: "The Crisis—No. I"

Robert J. Turnbull, a lowcountry planter, was one of South Carolina's most adamant proponents of nullification. In 1827, he wrote a series of essays that appeared in the Charleston Mercury. *For Turnbull and many other planters in South Carolina's tidewater, slavery was a principal concern, and many of them equated that concern with federal tariffs. In this first essay, Turnbull sets the stage for the nullification argument as he talks about "Southern interests and Southern safety" versus an overbearing federal government. Turnbull believes it will make no difference who is president; states' rights will gradually be eroded in favor of national power. With this essay, Turnbull set the stage for the arguments for nullification that followed.*

Mercury (Charleston), 17 August 1827

It is amongst the invaluable privileges of the citizen, as secured to him by the Constitution, that he has the right at all times to address his fellow citizens, and to speak with freedom of the measures of government, when such measures affect their rights, their interests, or their safety. It is a right which has been freely exercised since the foundation of the government; and it is no trifling eulogy on the Constitution itself. . . .

The present is an era amongst us, in which we are all satisfied to forget and forgive our old bitter dissentions as Federalists and Republicans, and to regard merit and long services, as the only legitimate claim to the favor and patronage of the people.

It is in this delightful and comparatively calm state of the public feeling . . . when each State has every motive to attend to its own local concerns, and when men are more disposed to look rationally and dispassionately into every subject connected with the welfare of the State; it is this period which I seize to address you on subjects of most vital importance to you as citizens of South-Carolina, and to arouse you to a just and lively sense of the dangers that threaten your temporal prosperity and your domestic quiet.... They come from a period more distant than the recent era of his [John Quincy Adams] inauguration into power. They are dangers which will approach nearer and nearer to us, under every future Administration, and unless we take some decisive measures to shield ourselves, they must, in due time, bring us to overwhelming ruin. In my remarks on this subject, I shall fearlessly speak the truth and the whole truth—I have no motive beyond my country's good. I never did, nor do I now, seek office or honors. My feelings, I confess, are more *sectional* than they are *national*. "Not that I love Cæsar *less* but that I love Rome *more*." Not, because I am insensible to the glory and the proud distinction of the American name, but because I believe that to the predominance of these feelings, above all others, we are in future to look for the preservation of Southern interests and Southern safety.

BRUTUS.

An Anonymous Report: "The Tariff Bill Has Passed"

While South Carolinians and many other Southerners may have been the most contentious about the Tariff of 1828, they were not alone in opposing it. Rural areas of New England and New York, especially, lobbied against the tariff. This notice on the tariff's passage comes from Portland, Maine. The basic difference between this and responses from South Carolina is in the acceptance that now that the bill has been passed, it is law and must be obeyed.

***Eastern Argus* (Portland), 23 May 1828**

The Tariff Bill has finally passed both Houses of Congress, and has now become, we presume, a law. We had never entirely abandoned the hope that this bill would be defeated.... It was manifest that the public mind, up to the last hour, was unprepared for the news. When it was at last ascertained that it had prevailed, the news cast a gloom over the town, such as has not been witnessed in this place for years. It sounded upon our ears like the warning of some deep public calamity, and there is but one opinion here, and that is, that it will be felt as such. It will not wholly destroy, but it deranges, interrupts, and throws into confusion all the business of the town. The vessels in our harbour, which were preparing for sea, have stopped the taking in of their cargoes.... No state in the union will probably be so deeply injured by this ill omened law as Maine, and no place in this state so much as this town....

The news was received with no tumultuous or disorderly expression of feeling, though it occasioned some which in other countries might be called seditious. The next morning the bells were tolled, the flags of the shipping were put half mast high, and processions were formed, and marched through the town. . . .

What gives peculiar bitterness and point to our feelings, is the fact, for it is confidently stated to be a fact, that there was a majority in the Senate certainly, if not in the House, who were *opposed to the bill* on its own merits, and were finally brought over to support it by the force of party alone. . . .

Leonidas: "No. 1"

In the summer of 1828, a number of writers selected pseudonyms and wrote for and against the South Carolina position on the tariff. One of those writers chose the name Leonidas, the king of Sparta who led his troops into battle against the Persians. Many of the writers in this controversy on both sides wrote a series of letters concerning the tariff. This is Leonidas' first letter, and it speaks of a collective Southern opposition to tyranny and love of freedom.

Mercury (Charleston), 14 July 1828

It requires no skill in Eastern astrology or in Scottish second sight, to perceive the rising spirit of discontent, that daily manifests itself more and more amongst us, to the Tariff Bill now in operation, by the usurped powers of the Congress of the United States. . . . The man who has owned slaves can never be made a slave. You may give his dwelling to the flames, his children to slaughter;–you may ride him down by dragoons, or strangle him upon the gallows–the spirit, the free spirit that has arisen from his habits of command, and the privileged superiority, is beyond the grasp of human torture. In the Northern States, liberty is a principle–a noble principle: with us, it is a *right* or, a *passion,* and a principle. In the northern States oppression is rather hated because it injures, because it degrades.

This is the genius of the Southern people. Devastation–inexorable–inexpressible detestation of tyranny and oppression. Difficult indeed to arouse–because their generosity makes them slow to suspect, and their relaxing sun inspires patience under suffering. But awake the slaveholders to stern activity, by an invasion of his rights–ask of him tribute-money, and as if oppression simply may not be speedy enough in its operation. Heap scorn and contumely upon his once proud head, and there never sprang forth from the jungles of India a fiercer foe to man, than an armed slaveholder, to the tyrant and oppressing. . . .

Such is the genius of the Southern States; and such, the principles upon which this coming contest must depend. Who can doubt the result? Not he who has studied our institutions, and has perceived, that free will and opinion, not force, has preserved and can alone keep this Union together. Not he, who understands the vast, the overwhelming importance of the Southern States to the confederacy. Not he, who knows the unequal strength that nerves the oppressed and the oppressor's arm, and has felt his spirit lifted high by the tales of his father's wrongs and liberty avenged. Not he who can lay his hand upon his bible, and by all the pure principles it contains, before the altar of his country, can–

"Swear for her to live, with her to die."

LEONIDAS.

Sidney: "For the Mercury"

The anonymous Sidney believed that the very nature of constitutional government granted rights to the minority that the majority had to respect. For him, checks and balances and the division of political power between the federal government and the states meant that South Carolina had a right to nullify the tariff.

Mercury (Charleston), 16 July 1828

We are so situated by Nature as to trade under the greatest advantages, of any people on earth, if it were not for the odious Interference of government.... I love the Union, but I love my State too. Let us all take a firm stand together under the sovereignty of our States, and on the principles of the constitution and we may yet preserve our rights and the Union also. There is no course that can produce disunion sooner, than a tame temporising policy. We must proceed upon the principle, that the minority have a right to check the majority. That they have a right to say that, when a law tends to our ruin, it shall be inoperative on us. The majority have power, and that power acts on us; but they are not responsible to us, and of course we have no protection there. Where else then is power placed? In the state governments of the minority, as well as the majority. And why is it there, I emphatically ask, if it is not for our protections? And this is not the end of the union. It only forces the general government to consult the interests of the whole. It compels that power to move only on general interests, and not local affairs. It forces it to look to the good of the whole. Without this right in all the interests to political protection, they can have no liberty....

And what idea does our own general government have in its division of powers, but that they may check by their veto each other, and thus protect the interest of the whole? And why is there another location of power in the

States, but they may check the operation of other powers, to protect their local interests? This is the theory and truth of the constitution, or it has no meaning. And this right, which all interests and minorities have to protect themselves, is one of the everlasting principles of liberty. This does not make our government a weak one. On the contrary, it makes it a strong one, because it forces it from the nature of things, to act only for the interests of the whole, and thus to unite all to support it....

SIDNEY.

An Anonymous Report: "A Beautiful Scheme"

Hezekiah Niles's Weekly Register *of Baltimore provided one of the more balanced accounts of American political events in the mid-nineteenth century. Niles personally opposed South Carolina's nullification position, but he still presented both sides of the issue. In this article, Niles lifts excerpts from writings in a July issue of the Charleston* Mercury, *referring to South Carolina's plan as a "beautiful scheme," about which Niles said not much had been written that was "more hostile to* republican principles *and the* union." *He followed this article with a renunciation of South Carolina's actions at a Maryland meeting. That resolution is included with the readings that support the tariff.*

Niles' Weekly Register **(Baltimore), 16 August 1828**

The following *beautiful* scheme of operations has been projected, and thrown out to the public, through the Charleston "Mercury." We give it as a further specimen, and in preparation of a large collection of like articles which we intend to record....

Let congress here be distinctly told, that either the general government must recede from its pretensions to inordinate power, or the state must recede from the compact; and should that government resolutely persist in the scheme of subverting our prosperity and sovereignty to its very foundations, let the governor be directed, by proclamation, to open our ports for the reception of the vessels of all nations, not excepting even those of our northern friends or enemies!...All this may be done without the spilling of one drop of blood! There will be no necessity for firing a gun. Let the United States' government fire the first shot, if it chooses! Better it would be, "that it had been born with a mill-stone around its neck," than to try this! *We* must take care not to be the aggressors in the shedding of blood! Let us stand on the defensive!...By such a course as this, the people of the north may be made to reflect on a subject which they have never yet considered *fully*, if they have considered it at all! Instead of despising us, as they now do, as vain boasters, they will begin to respect us—they will, by degrees, as they inquire into the powers of the general government, see the justice of our cause; and by a timely change of rulers, congress may be probably brought to its senses, the constitution explained and expounded anew, the union preserved, and the sovereignty of the states and civil liberty hereafter placed on such an immoveable basis....

Support of the Tariff

An Anonymous Report: "From the Savannah *Mercury*"

In its effort to counter the move toward nullification that arose with the 1828 tariff, the Courier*'s editor, A.S. Willington, printed numerous reports from other papers that opposed what was being proposed in South Carolina. This article comes from the June 9 Savannah* Mercury, *and it points out that the true burden of the tariff will be on foreign manufacturers, not Southern planters.*

Courier (Charleston), 12 June 1828

Our politicians were equally clamourous against the Tariff of 1824, as they are now, against that of 1828. It was asserted that the price of all articles upon which it operated, would be enhanced; that the planter would be oppressed by its operation, and that *Southern interests,* would be entirely destroyed, &c. Now time and experience, those infallible tests of truth, have proved the fallacy of those assertions in the one case, as we presume they will in the other....

If we had no manufacturers in our own country—if we depended solely and entirely upon foreign supply, then a duty on any article would raise its price to market, and consequently be a tax on the consumer. But while we have home manufactories, nearly adequate to the supply of all our wants, the foreigner cannot raise on his articles, because in that case, the domestic manufacturer would undersell him. Consequently the duty comes out of the foreign manufacturer, and not out of the consumer. That such has been the operation of the Tariff of 1824, we appeal to the experience of the last four years.

Carolinian: "For the Courier"

The anonymous Carolinian believed that those opposing the 1828 tariff did so for their own purposes, political and otherwise. In this letter, Carolinian points out the value of being a part of the United States for South

Carolina and insists that those who would tear the Union apart will be guilty of treason.

Courier (Charleston), 19 July 1828

IT is indeed time to calculate the value of our happy union, when resistance and disunion has become the theme of every political demagogue, and the subject for every public harangue, until the political horizon of our State, in all her glory, has been darkened by repeated threats and imprudent speeches, as fuel to fire, to increase the excitement that has been created by those whose zeal and imagination have been more fertile in exciting the feelings and fears of others, than their judgment or their justice has been, to allay and correct the errors of their creating.

To please their fancy, public meetings must be called, that their lofty and patriotic sentiments may be known and resounded; to proclaim the dark spirit of the times, by which we are threatened with disunion, under the frightful shadow of an overwhelming Tariff. . . .

Is it just, or is it generous, that infatuated zeal should bias our judgment to such a degree, as to have reason and truth shrouded in the darkness of mysterious midnight, and bid defiance to argument and facts to produce conviction. . . . How is it that our politicians have become infallible in their opinions, and gifted with such foresight; when the majority in Congress are charged with cupidity, without any other proof than broad assertion, supported by implication, reiterated until it becomes an assumed fact, at the sacrifice of reason and evidence. Let the people look to motives that govern actions, and decide for themselves. . . .

It may be well to calculate the value of this Union; not by the sordid standard of gold, or selfish opinions of disappointed ambition; but, as the truest pledge to our safety and happiness; and, by the more liberal and philanthropic compact of '75—which pledged the lives, the fortunes and sacred honor of our citizens, and State; to protect and defend the rights of all; or the safety of each, and the bulwark of our independence. Shall we forget these most sacred pledges? *Forbid it Justice* . . . .

Can it be possible, that the proud and patriotic State of South Carolina, should, by the indiscretion of a few of her clamorous sons, sacrifice her fair name upon the shrine of prejudice and popular excitement; and be the first to raise the standard of rebellion, and to draw the sword, in opposition to the constitutional acts of Government, under the liberal construction of the majority. Believe it not, ye patriots of the Revolution, who yet survive to witness the inglorious threats of some of proud Carolina's sons, who would dare advise resistance and disunion.

It cannot be, that the beautiful structure of our republican form of Government, cemented by the blood of the living and departed heroes, that flowed from north to south, in mutual defence of our rights, should be so unstable as to be shaken by internal commotion. That Government, which bade defiance to monarchy and unjust oppression, will spurn the attempts of treason, to undermine her institutions and her power.

Words flow smoothly form the lips of the over anxious politician, who has an electioneering purpose to serve; while his influence may mislead many of our most worthy citizens, to sanction by their countenance, the popular harrangue, suited to every company and all occasions.

To all this, the patriot may listen, and even suffer his feelings, after being highly excited by designing individuals, to mislead his judgment; but there is too much of a redeeming spirit of independence among the people, to be always lead by faction, and the would-be aristocracy of the State.

CAROLINIAN.

An Anonymous Report: "Traitors"

Most South Carolina disunionists were wealthy planters from the Tidewater region. There, large plantations produced most of the state's cotton and other crops. The inland regions of the state, where farms were much smaller, opposed the concept of leaving the Union. This anonymous letter in the Greenville Republican *called the disunionists traitors who could expect a backlash against their politics.*

Republican **(Greenville), 19 July 1828**

The traitors who have been urging disunion, begin to haul in their horns. As robbers, before they venture out to steal, reconnoitre the road, which, if they find well guarded, they skulk back to their hiding places; so these wretches, having felt the pulse of the people, and finding that the thing will not do—that all attempts to dissolve the Union are regarded with horror and disgust, and that the people will not listen to them, they change their note, and affect never to have desired disunion. . . .

As for the *stuff* that comes from some part of the low country, we, the people of Greenville, we, the people of the mountains and back country, we, who could produce three fighting men for every one the lowlanders can show—we tell the low country people we are not with them—we will not go along with them, and if they could succeed in separating South Carolina from the Union, we will separate from South Carolina. . . .

Union and disunion will be made the question on which our elections to Congress and the State Legislature will turn. Then it will be seen how the people of the back country feel on this subject. There is too much blood of the Revolution alive in Greenville to tolerate the word disunion—we have expunged it from our political vocabulary.

"A Resolution: Punish Treason and Suppress Rebellion"

Some states, such as Maryland, were torn concerning the issue of the tariff. Maryland's congressional delegation voted three for the tariff and four against it. Many, including Revolutionary patriot James H. McCulloch, detested South Carolina's position. The short resolution below was included in Niles' Weekly Register *following an insert from the Charleston* Mercury, *which is included above. Those supporting the resolution considered South Carolina's actions treason.*

Niles' Weekly Register **(Baltimore), 16 August 1828**

Resolved, as we love the UNION—the constitution which binds it, and the sacred memory of those whose blood and treasure were drained to establish the *independence* upon which THAT UNION was founded, WE WILL SUPPORT IT TO THE LAST, and *assist with our lives and fortunes the general government, whenever it shall be come necessary* TO PUNISH TREASON AND SUPPRESS REBELLION.

QUESTIONS

1. Why might South Carolinians believe in 1828, more so than we do today, that the United States was a compact of states that could be deserted?
2. Why might some Americans believe that the talk coming out of South Carolina was treason and rebellion?
3. Writers to newspapers and magazines offered reasons to support South Carolina's *Exposition* and why it should be opposed. Weigh their arguments and determine which is more credible.

NOTES

1. To understand the issues surrounding South Carolina, John C. Calhoun, and nullification, see John Niven, *John C. Calhoun and the Price of Union: A Biography*

(Baton Rouge: Louisiana State University Press, 1988); Richard E. Ellis, *The Union at Risk: Jacksonian Democracy, States' Rights, and the Nullification Crisis* (New York: Oxford University Press, 1987); William W. Freehling, *Prelude to Civil War: The Nullification Controversy in South Carolina 1816–1836* (New York: Harper & Row, 1966); Chauncey Samuel Boucher, *The Nullification Controversy in South Carolina* (Chicago: University of Chicago Press, 1916).

2. Quoted in Ellis, *The Union at Risk*, 48.

CHAPTER 7

The Indian Removal Act, 1830

The relationship between white Americans and Native Americans in the United States' colonial period was one of mixed messages. Throughout the American Revolution, colonials actively sought alliances with Native American nations for trade and protection. America looked to the Cherokee in the South and the Six Nations in the North as allies in both the French and Indian War and the Revolution. At the same time, Americans viewed Indians as a group to be feared, removed, or destroyed.[1] The latter generally became American sentiment in the nineteenth century, as the white population mushroomed in the states along the Atlantic seaboard and pushed into territory west of the Appalachian Mountains and along the coast of the Gulf of Mexico.

Even before the end of the Revolution, however, Americans were thinking that removal of Indians from the Eastern seaboard was a good idea. Georgia, in particular, wanted the lands that Native nations occupied in its western territory. At the same time, the United States wanted land claimed by Georgia through its original charter with Great Britain–territory that would eventually become Alabama and Mississippi. Georgia and the federal government struck a deal. Georgia agreed to give up claims to its western territory. The United States agreed to nullify all Indian land claims within the borders of the now-existing state. The resulting deal between the state and the administration of Thomas Jefferson led to the Indian Removal Act of 1830.

Most Americans liked the idea of moving Native Americans west, especially after the United States obtained the Louisiana territory from France in 1803. Most white Americans did not envision, at the beginning of the nineteenth century, that they would move any farther west than the Mississippi River. Western land would be the perfect place for Native Americans, and Congress agreed. It passed an act in 1804 that allowed the president to exchange any lands claimed by Native Americans east of the Mississippi for property west of the river that was part of the Louisiana Purchase.[2]

In the 1820s, Georgia began to pressure the federal government to uphold its end of the 1802 agreement and to negate Indian land claims. James Monroe, in one of his last acts as president in January 1825, put the wheels in motion to repeal Indian claims in Georgia and elsewhere in the Eastern United States. Monroe said in his address to Congress that removal of Indian tribes from the existing states and territories "is of very high importance to our Union. . . . For the removal of the tribes within the State of Georgia, the motive has been peculiarly strong." The president adopted a common rationale of the time that Native Americans would never fit into the "American" way of life. Removal, therefore, was in the best interest of Indians and of whites, who would eventually have their safety jeopardized by the other group. Monroe said of Indians that "it is impossible to incorporate them, in such masses, in any form whatever, into our system," and that "their degradation and extermination will be inevitable."[3]

Even though Monroe called for Indian removal, the election of Andrew Jackson in 1828 was the catalyst that put removal into motion. Jackson, the hero of the War of 1812 and a Southerner, believed agreements between the United States and Native Americans were preposterous. "I have long viewed treaties with the Indians an absurdity not to be reconciled to the principles of our government," Jackson said in 1817 in the midst of battles he led against the Creek in Alabama and the Seminole in Florida. "The Indians are subjects of the United States, inhabiting its territory and acknowledging its sovereignty, then is it not absurd for the sovereign to negotiate by treaty with the subject?"[4]

Jackson pushed for passage of an Indian removal bill by Congress and got his wish on May 26, 1830. The bill authorized the forced removal of the Cherokee, Choctaw, Creek, Chickasaw, and Seminole—the "Five Civilized Tribes"—to lands west of the Mississippi River. The largest and most organized of the nations, the Cherokee, mounted a legal response. Since they no longer had legal standing in Georgia, the nation appealed to the Supreme Court. In *Cherokee Nation v. Georgia*,[5] the Cherokee looked to stop not only the Indian Removal Act, but, more importantly, Georgia legislation that stripped them of political rights and power. The Court sided with Georgia. Although Indian removal did not begin immediately, the fate of the Cherokee and the other "Civilized Tribes" was sealed in the Southern states. Beginning in 1836 and culminating in 1838, the Cherokee and other nations were gathered together and marched to Oklahoma along three different routes, known collectively as the Trail of Tears (see Chapter 14).

This chapter looks at the debate that occurred in newspapers surrounding Indian removal and the congressional act that legislated it. According to newspaper scholar John Coward, part of the argument centered on Indian character. Was the Native American a noble individual or a savage?[6] Native

Americans had long found cohabitation with whites difficult. In fact, European diseases claimed most Indians who came into contact with the first white American settlers, and war between Indians and whites occurred regularly in the seventeenth and eighteenth centuries. But the Cherokee, following a war from 1759–1761 with colonists, principally in South Carolina, had sought to coexist peacefully with whites.[7] They and many other members of the "Civilized Tribes" simply wanted to live their lives in harmony on lands in the South that had always belonged to their people.

The chapter begins with a selection of pieces advocating Indian removal. These readings center on the correspondence of George Gilmer, Governor of Georgia, and William Wirt, former attorney general and counsel for the Cherokee in their legal dispute with Georgia. Gilmer's reply to Wirt opens the section along with the *Georgia Journal*'s abrasive comments on national meddling in Georgia's affairs. It is followed by the comments of two others on the dispute. The first places the argument within the states' rights controversy of the day. The other deals with the law suit to stop Cherokee removal as a money-making scheme that overlooks what is best for most Cherokees. The last reading from the *Arkansas Gazette* makes it look as if the Cherokees support their transplantation to the West.

The readings in the chapter that deal with support of Native Americans center on the writings of Jeremiah Evarts, a Vermont lawyer who became an editor of religious publications and champion of the Indian cause. Evarts, using the pseudonym William Penn, wrote a series of letters and essays denouncing Indian removal and the general treatment of Native Americans. His writings appeared first in the *National Intelligencer* of Washington, D.C., but they were reprinted widely in America. Also included is a selection by Elias Boudinot, editor of the *Cherokee Phoenix*, the newspaper of the Cherokee nation that was published in New Echota, Georgia. Editors also reprinted writings from the *Phoenix*. Although the first section refers to letters written by William Wirt in support of legal action to aid the Cherokees, those writings are not included because Evart and Boudinot portray the Cherokee situation in more detail and with more specifics.

Support for Indian Removal

George Gilmer: "Cherokee Removal"

Georgia Governor George Gilmer advocated the removal of the Cherokees. In the debate over the Indian Removal Act, numerous people became involved in the discussion. William Wirt, a Maryland lawyer who had served as the nation's attorney general, took up the Cherokees' cause and wrote on the Indians' behalf to Gilmer. He suggested that neither the state nor federal governments had the power to remove the Cherokees and that the issue should be settled by the Supreme Court, the first case being Cherokee Nation v. Georgia, *which ruled in favor of Georgia in 1831. The letters were first published in the* Georgia Journal *in Milledgeville on August 28, but Hezekiah Niles reprinted them for a national audience, as did dozens of editors in America. This selection comes from the preface the* Journal *printed concerning the letters and Gilmer's letter where he advocates removal of the Cherokees as an act done in the Indians' best interests.*

Niles' Weekly Register (Baltimore), 18 September 1830

. . . Has it come to this, that a sovereign and independent state is to be insulted by being asked to become a party, before the supreme court, with a few savages, residing on her own territory!!!—Unparalleled impudence.

As we suggest . . . we verily expect that the next movement will be an attempt on the part of the Cherokee nation to extend the Indian laws over the people of Georgia. . . .

Sir.—Your communication addressed to the governor of Georgia has been received, informing him of your employment by the Cherokee Indians to defend them against the operation of the laws of the states, and proposing a reference of what you have thought proper to call the dispute between the Cherokee nation and the state of Georgia, to the supreme court of the United States. . . . It is known that the extent of the jurisdiction of Georgia, and the policy of removing the Cherokees and other Indians to the west of the Mississippi have become party questions. It is not therefore surprising that those who engage in the struggle for power, should find usurpation and faithlessness in the measures of the government, accordingly as the loss of office, or the hope of its acquisition may enlighten their understandings. . . .

There are no fears felt in Georgia of Indian violence, altho' it is highly probably that your efforts will be productive of some mischief.—It is believed that the Cherokees in Georgia had determined to unite with that portion of their tribe who had removed to the west of the Mississippi if the policy of the president, were sustained by congress. . . . It was not known however until the receipt of your letter that the spirit of resistance to the laws of the state and views of the United States which have of late been evident among the Indians, had in any manner been occasioned by your advice. . . .

You have thought proper to give the governor of Georgia an account of the civilization of the Cherokees, describing those whom you do not know, to be polished gentlemen, and those whom you do not know, to have ceased to be savages. What you say of the intelligence of the members of the Cherokee tribe who were in Washington last winter is partly true, and equally descriptive of many others. They are not Indians however, but the children of white men, whose corrupt habits or vile passion led him into connection with the Cherokee tribe. It is not surprising that the white man and the children of white men have availed themselves of the easy means of acquiring wealth which the Cherokee territory has present for thirty or forty years; nor that intelligence and spirited activity should increase with their increased wealth, nor that when wealth, intelligence and industry are confined to the whites and the children of white men that the power over the tribe should be centered in the same hands. But that these causes were calculated to produce similar effects upon the Indians, the real aborigines, is disproved by every example among the thousands which the experience of the two last centuries has furnished in every part of this continent. The Cherokees have lost all that was valuable in their Indian character, have become spiritless, dependent and depraved; as the whites and their children have become wealthy, intelligent and powerful. . . . It was the power of the whites and their children among the Cherokees, that destroyed the ancient laws, customs, and authority of the tribe, and subjected the natives to the rule of that most oppressive of governments, an oligarchy. . . . It was this state of things that rendered it obligatory upon the state of Georgia, to vindicate the rights of her sovereignty by abolishing all Cherokee government within its limits. Whether intelligent or ignorant the state of Georgia has passed no laws violative of the liberty, personal security, or private property of any Indian. It has been the object of humanity and wisdom, to separate the two classes among them, giving the rights of citizenship to those who are capable of performing its duties and property estimating its privileges, and increasing the enjoyment, and the probability of future improvements to the ignorant and idle, by removing them to a situation where the inducements to action will be more in accordance with the character of the Cherokee people. . . .

It is hoped that the efforts of the general government to execute its contract with Georgia to secure the continuance and advance the happiness of the Indian tribes, and to give quiet to the country may be so effectually successful as to prevent the necessity of any further intercourse upon this subject.

Yours &c.

GEORGE C. GILMER.

Thomas Ritchie: "The Cherokees"

As the correspondence between Gilmer and Wirt appeared in print across America, some editors commented on them. Thomas Ritchie of the Richmond Enquirer *was as outspoken as any editor of the period. In this editorial preface to the Gilmer-Wirt letters, Ritchie supports the idea that Indian removal will be good for the Cherokees while saying that all the legal wrangling surrounding the federal bill is only to make certain "mixt Breeds" wealthy.*

Enquirer (Richmond), 10 September 1830

We lay before our Readers the correspondence between Mr. Wirt and the Governor of Georgia. The reply of the latter is spicy and piquant enough.—We understand the following to be facts; and we state them at this time, because they serve to explain particular allusions in these letters.—We understand then that the Cherokees are governed by a Council of about thirty; most, if not all of whom, are not Indians, but mixt Breeds—and that they govern the tribe in most cases with an almost arbitrary will. . . . These men, who enjoy most of the benefits of the Oligarchy, are of course opposed to Emigration, and are the most active in enlisting Counsel, and carrying up the case to the Supreme Court of the U. States. These are the "polished gentlemen" to whom Mr. Wirt alludes. Ross, the Chief of the Tribe, is himself one of the mixed breeds, with probably not more than 15th or 16th of Indian blood in his veins—with little or none of the copper colour on his skin. Others of the Council are also mixt—and of different proportions of Indian blood. These are the people who clamour against Removal—seeing lawyers and seeking injunctions. But the great body of the Indians are poor and miserable—wretched in their appearance—and profiting little, or nothing, by the annuties [*sic*] of the U. States—These facts furnish a key to most of the ensuing Correspondence, and to the various Views of the Chiefs of the Cherokee tribe. . . .

Such are the Men, whom Mr. Wirt speaks of as *Indians* who rule the Cherokees—in fact, profit by the annuity of the United States, contest the right of jurisdiction of Georgia over her own soil, and prevent the great body of the poor and wretched Indians from bettering their condition to the West of the Mississippi.

An Anonymous Report: "Indian Sovereignty"

As should be expected, the issues of the time did not stand in isolation. The question of the removal of the Cherokee in Georgia was entwined with nullification and states' rights issues. In this article, reprinted in the Richmond Enquirer *from the Baltimore* Republican, *the issue of states' rights is the concern of the author. The question of Indian removal is no question here because the author, as did many others, accepted President Jackson's view that Indian removal was for the good of Native Americans.*

Enquirer (Richmond), 24 September 1830

We give to-day the correspondence between Mr. Wirt and Gov. Gilmer of Georgia. . . .

How Mr. Wirt and his clients can bring their cause into the Supreme Court, we cannot see; nor is Georgia likely to allow the question to be tried with her consent or to meet this tribe of savages on equal terms, to debate their right, to dismember her territory, and to erect a foreign government within her limits, thus abrogating her constitution at will, and partitioning her soil. The agitators of this controversy, those who have labored to defeat all the beneficent intentions and peaceful measures of the Federal government in this matter, by encouraging the Indians to make such extravagant assumptions, and counseling them to disobey the laws of the state, must meet the question without blinking the consequences, and be prepared to sustain them to their full extent, to the assertion by the general government of supreme unlimited power over state laws, and indeed, over the existence of state governments.

In what manner the decrees of the general government, for dismembering & partitioning the state of Georgia, are to be carried into effect, and how far the safety of the Union will be compromised, are also matters of serious reflection for those who are making up the dreadful issue.

We believe the claims of the Indians to sovereignty within a state, to be untenable, and we look upon the relations between them and Georgia in that particular, as purely municipal concerns, in which the United States have no more right to interfere than in any other domestic relation. We can conceive no case in which the Federal government has a right to abrogate state laws, not *individually* repugnant to the United States Constitution. . . .

An Anonymous Report: "The Cherokees"

In order to make the removal of the Five Civilized Tribes more palatable, Native American acknowledgment that the move would benefit them often appeared in the press. In this paragraph from the Arkansas Gazette, *an unknown writer tells of a conversation with a Cherokee who says that the territory west of the Mississippi River is superior to the land on which he and other Cherokees live in the "Old Nation."*

Arkansas Gazette (Little Rock), 26 November 1830

The alarm from the Indian news, has in a good degree subsided. I have lately seen an intelligent Cherokee from the nation east of the Mississippi, who (I am privately informed) has been sent to look at the country west of us, and ascertain what the prospects are for the Old Nation, provided they should cede their lands in Tennessee and Georgia. I am gratified to learn that he is agreeably disappointed in the country now possessed by the Cherokees. He is highly pleased with it in many respects, and was likewise well pleased with the accounts which he received of the vacant section of country lying west of the Missouri, and adjoining the Cherokee lands on the north. He says he is anxious to reach home again in order to prepare for removing, and to inform his red brethren of the flattering prospects that await them in the west.

Opposition to Indian Removal

William Penn: "No. I. Present Crisis in the Condition of the American Indian"

Jeremiah Evarts was a Vermont lawyer who became editor of the Panoplist, *a New England monthly publication that promoted foreign missions. The* Panoplist *became the* Missionary Herald *in 1821. Evarts studied the legal rights of Native Americans, especially the Cherokee in Georgia. From August through December of 1829, Evarts wrote a series of twenty-four letters to the editor of the* National Intelligencer. *The letters were more like essays and were often quite lengthy. Evarts's pseudonym "William Penn" was based on the Pennsylvania founder whom Evarts considered an honest and philanthropic person. The Indian Removal Act, which the president strongly supported and lobbied for, was a closer vote than imagined because of Evarts's efforts on the part of the Five Civilized Tribes.*[8] *In the end, however, Jackson signed the act into law on May 28, 1830. Evarts continued to push for Indian rights even after the bill's passage.*

National Intelligencer **(Washington, D.C.), 5 August 1829**

Every careful observer of public affairs must have seen, that a crisis has been rapidly approaching, for several years past, in reference to the condition, relations, and prospects, of the Indian tribes, in the southwestern parts of the United States. The attention of many of our most intelligent citizens has been fixed upon the subject with great interest. . . .

Still, however, the mass of the community possess but very little information on the subject; and, even among the best informed, scarcely a man can be found, who is thoroughly acquainted with the questions at issue. . . . Some persons think, that the Indians have a perfect right to the lands which they occupy. . . . Others pretend, that Indians have no other right to their lands, than that of *a tenant at will*; that is, the right of remaining where they are, till the *owners of the land* shall require them to remove. . . .

The questions have forced themselves upon us, as a nation:—*What is to become of the Indians? Have they any rights?* If they have, *What are these rights? and how are they to be secured?* . . .

It should be remembered, by our rulers as well as others, that this controversy . . . will be well understood by the whole civilized world. No subject, not even war, slavery, nor the nature of free institutions, will be more thoroughly canvassed. . . . Any course of measures, in regard to the Indians, which is manifestly fair, and generous, and benevolent, will command the warm and decided approbation of intelligent men, not only in the present age, but in all succeeding times. . . .

The simple question is: *Have the Indian tribes, residing as separate communities in the neighborhood of the whites, a permanent title to the territory, which they inherited from their fathers, which they have neither forfeited nor sold, and which they now occupy?* . . .

The government of the United States alleges . . . that Great Britain, previous to the revolution, "*claimed* entire sovereignty within the limits of what constituted the thirteen United States;" that 'all the rights of sovereignty which Great Britain had within said States became vested in said States respectively, as a consequence of the declaration of independence, and the treaty of 1783; that the Cherokees were merely 'permitted' to reside on their lands by the United States; that this permission is not to be construed so as to deny to Georgia the exercise of sovereignty; and that the Unites States has no power to guarantee any thing more than a right of possession, till the State of Georgia should see fit to legislate for the Cherokees, and dispose of them as she should judge expedient, without any control from the general government.

William Penn: "No. XXIV. Plan for Removal of the Indians"

In this essay, Evarts concludes his arguments on the ills of removing the Cherokee and other Southern Indian nations.

National Intelligencer (Washington, D.C.), 29 December 1829

I have now arrived at my closing number; in which I propose to examine the plan for the removal of the Indians beyond the Mississippi. . . .

It is a suspicious circumstance, that the wishes and supposed interests of the whites, and not the benefit of the Indians, afford all the impulse, under which Georgia and her advocates appear to act. The Indians are in the way of the whites; they must be removed for the gratification of the whites; and this is at the bottom of the plan. . . . A very intelligent member of Congress from the west declared to the writer of these numbers, that the design of the parties most interested was, to destroy the Indians, and not to save them. I do not vouch for the accuracy of this opinion to one, or two, or twenty, of our public men. At any rate there is no uncharitableness in saying, that Georgia is actuated by *a desire to not get the lands of the Cherokees*, for she openly avows it. As little can it be doubted, that the plan in question is suited to accomplish her desires. . . .

The Indians assert, that there is not a sufficient quantity of good land, in the contemplated tract, to accommodate half their present numbers; to say nothing of the other tribes to be thrust into their company. Even the agents of the United States, who have been employed with a special view to make the scheme popular, admit that there is a deficiency of wood and water. Without wood for fences and buildings, and for shelter against the furious northwestern blasts of winter, the Indians cannot be comfortable. Without running streams, they can never keep live stock; nor could they easily dig wells and cisterns for the use of their families. The vast prairies of the west will ultimately be inhabited. But it would require all the wealth, the enterprize, and the energy, of Anglo-Americans, to make a prosperous settlement upon them. . . . The good land, including all that could be brought into use by partially civilized men, is stated to be comparatively small. . . .

If the Indians are removed, let it be said, in an open and manly tone, that they are removed because we have the power to remove them, and there is a political reason for doing it; and that they will be removed again, whenever the whites demand their removal, in a style sufficiently clamorous and imperious to make trouble for the government. . . .

The constrained migration of 60,000 souls, men, women and children, most of them in circumstances of deep poverty, must be attended with much suffering. . . .

A dead and mournful silence will reign; for the Indian communities will have been blotted out forever. Individuals will remain to feel that they are vassals, and to sink unheeded to despondency, despair, and extinction.

But the memory of these transactions will not be forgotten. A bitter roll will be unfolded, on which *Mourning, Lamentation, and Woe to the People of the United States* will be seen written in characters, which no eye can refuse to see. . . .

Elias Boudinot: "A Challenge for Georgia"

Following the passage of the Indian Removal Act, the Cherokees in Georgia mounted a legal challenge to it, but more specifically to an 1829 Georgia law that gave the state jurisdiction over the nation as it stripped Cherokees of their legal rights. Since the Cherokees no longer had any legal rights in

Georgia, they were forced to take their case to the United States Supreme Court. Elias Boudinot started a newspaper principally for the Cherokees in 1828, calling it the Cherokee Phoenix. *It was published in New Echota, Georgia. Boudinot's real name was Buck Watie, but he changed it to Boudinot, the name of a hero of the American Revolution. The newspaper printed articles in English and in Cherokee through an alphabet developed in 1809 by Sequoya. In this untitled column, Boudinot explains the trust the Cherokees placed in the American judicial system to protect Native American rights, a trust that was crushed with the 1831 Court decision* Cherokee Nation v. Georgia.

Cherokee Phoenix (New Echota), 24 July 1830

Every man must know, who has watched the progress of the Indian question during the last six months, & who has been familiar with the doings of the Congress of the United States respecting the Cherokees and other tribes, and the proceedings of the state of Georgia, that, by the refusal of the former to protect, and the extension of the jurisdiction of the latter over them, they are placed under new and very trying circumstances, and that their views, feelings, and the course they have determined to pursue should be speedily made known to the world. . . . If we are removed . . .we wish to leave in the records of her judicial tribunals, for future generations to read, when we are gone, ample testimony that she acted *justly* or *unjustly*. The reasonableness of this determination must appear evident to every mind.

The Cherokees think they have rights, secured to them under their various treaties and the laws of the United States.–This opinion has never been shaken by all that the general Government has done, and the proceedings and oppressive laws of the state of Georgia. . . . Surely the Supreme Court of the United States is the proper tribunal where the great question at issue must be settled. To this tribunal the Cherokees will freely refer their case.

William Penn: "What Are the People of the United States Bound to Do in Regard to the Indian Question?"

Jeremiah Evarts, writing under the pseudonym William Penn, did not stop his efforts to assist the Civilized Tribes even after the passage of the Indian Removal Act. In this letter, which was the second of two written to the Intelligencer *in November, Evarts points out what is owed to Native Americans as human beings and as residents of the United States.*

National Intelligencer (Washington, D.C.), 27 November 1830

TO THE EDITORS OF THE NATIONAL INTELLIGENCER. . . .

Let it be borne in mind, that the evil apprehended is no less than this: *That the people of the U. States will deliberately, for a small temptation, commit a wanton and flagitious violation of the public faith; that, in doing this, they will oppress weak and dependent allies; and that they will thus bring upon themselves great disgrace and guilt, and upon the country never ending reproach and shame.* This is the evil to be averted. . . .

The people of the United States are bound to regard the Cherokees and other Indians, as *men*; as human beings, entitled to receive the same treatment as Englishmen, Frenchmen, or ourselves, would be entitled to receive in the same circumstances. Here is the only weak place in their cause. They are not treated as men; and if they are finally ejected from their patrimonial inheritance by arbitrary and unrighteous power, the people of the United States will be impeached and condemned for treating the Indians, not as men, but as animals. . . .

Why should not the Cherokees, Creeks, and Choctaws, be treated as men? Their ancestors were thus treated, when Oglethorpe landed at Savannah; and when he begged them, as the rightful sovereigns of the territory, to spare him a little land on which to settle, and promised them everlasting friendship and good neighborhood. . . . The Cherokees and Choctaws were treated as men, during the last war, when they fought by the side of the commander who is now President of the United States, and were praised for their bravery, their fidelity, and their devotedness to the cause of their great ally. . . .

The Indian Bill leaves almost every thing to the discretion of the President; and this makes it peculiarly proper to address him personally. Caution and delay cannot injure the United States, or the rightful claims of any State; but haste may destroy the Indians, and inflict tremendous evils upon ourselves. . . .

The people of the United States are bound to oppose the contemplated measures, in every legal and constitutional way. . . . No people ever had a better opportunity to obtain a durable name for justice and benevolence toward acknowledged inferiors, (to whom we are yet under great obligations,) than the people of the United States have at the present moment. . . .

WILLIAM PENN.

QUESTIONS

1. For more than a century before the Indian Removal Act, Americans dealt alternately with Native Americans as enemies and as members of sover-

eign nations and allies. From the readings, what do you think were the underlying issues for support of Indian removal?

2. What are Jeremiah Evart's main points in support of the Indians?
3. Why do you think so many editors discussed Indian removal as beneficial for Native Americans? What do you think could have been advantages of moving west? What were the advantages of remaining in the East?

Notes

1. David A. Copeland, *Debating the Issues in Colonial Newspapers* (Westport, Conn.: Greenwood Press, 2000), 180–82.

2. John M. Coward, *The Newspaper Indian: Native American Identity in the Press, 1820–1860* (Urbana: University of Illinois Press, 1999), 67.

3. Monroe Message to Congress, 25 January 1825, quoted in Henry R. Schoolcraft, *Historical and Statistical Information Respecting the History, Conditions and Prospects of the Indian Tribes of the United States,* 6 vols. (Philadelphia: Lippincott, 1851–1857), 6:407; and in Edward H. Spicer, *A Short History of the Indians of the United States* (New York: D. Van Nostrand, 1969), 229.

4. Andrew Jackson to James Monroe, 1817, in Spicer, *A Short History of the Indians of the United States,* 228.

5. *Cherokee Nation v. Georgia,* 1831, U.S. Supreme Court *Reports,* 5 Peters, 15–18.

6. Coward, *The Newspaper Indian,* 68.

7. See David A. Copeland, *Colonial American Newspapers: Character and Content* (Newark: University of Delaware Press, 1997).

8. Francis Paul Prucha, "Introduction," Jeremiah Evarts, *Cherokee Removal: The "William Penn" Essays and Other Writings* (Knoxville: University of Tennessee Press, 1981), 6–17.

CHAPTER 8

William Lloyd Garrison and the Abolitionist Movement, 1831

On January 1, 1831, a former printer's apprentice from Newburyport, Massachusetts, declared in the newspaper he had just begun, "I am in earnest—I will not equivocate—I will not excuse—I will not retreat a single inch—AND I WILL BE HEARD." Twenty-five-year-old William Lloyd Garrison promised to be heard on the evils of slavery in America, and he continued to advocate manumission for slaves for the next thirty-four years in his Boston-based newspaper, the *Liberator*, until the end of the Civil War.

Garrison's was not the first voice in America to speak out on the evils of slavery, though he may well be the best known abolitionist of antebellum America. As early as 1700, Americans were writing and printing documents that called for the end of slavery and the manumission of those held in captivity.[1] In the 1770s, many newspapers—mostly in New England—began to print lengthy articles on the evils of slavery, but convincing people in America that slavery was wrong would not be an easy task because slavery had been a part of the British-American experience from the failed settlement attempts at Roanoke Island onward.[2] And, people throughout America owned slaves. "The colony will never thrive untill we gett," a letter to Massachusetts Bay Governor John Winthrop declared in 1645, "a stock of slaves sufficient to doe all our business."[3]

Slavery was central to the debate to ratify the Constitution, which allowed slaves to be counted as three-fifths of a person when tallying a state's population. The Constitution also addressed slave trade, declaring the United States would no longer deal in it from 1808 on. In 1775, Rhode Island became the first state to outlaw slavery, and by 1804 six other Northern states joined them. Efforts to end slavery received a boost about this time as religious revival swept across America. Many of those affected by the Second Great Revival believed it was their duty to God to make life better for all. This "Benevolent Empire" worked in many areas of social reform—temperance, education, penal rights, women's rights, and the abolition of slavery.[4] The antislavery movement was the most controversial of all reform

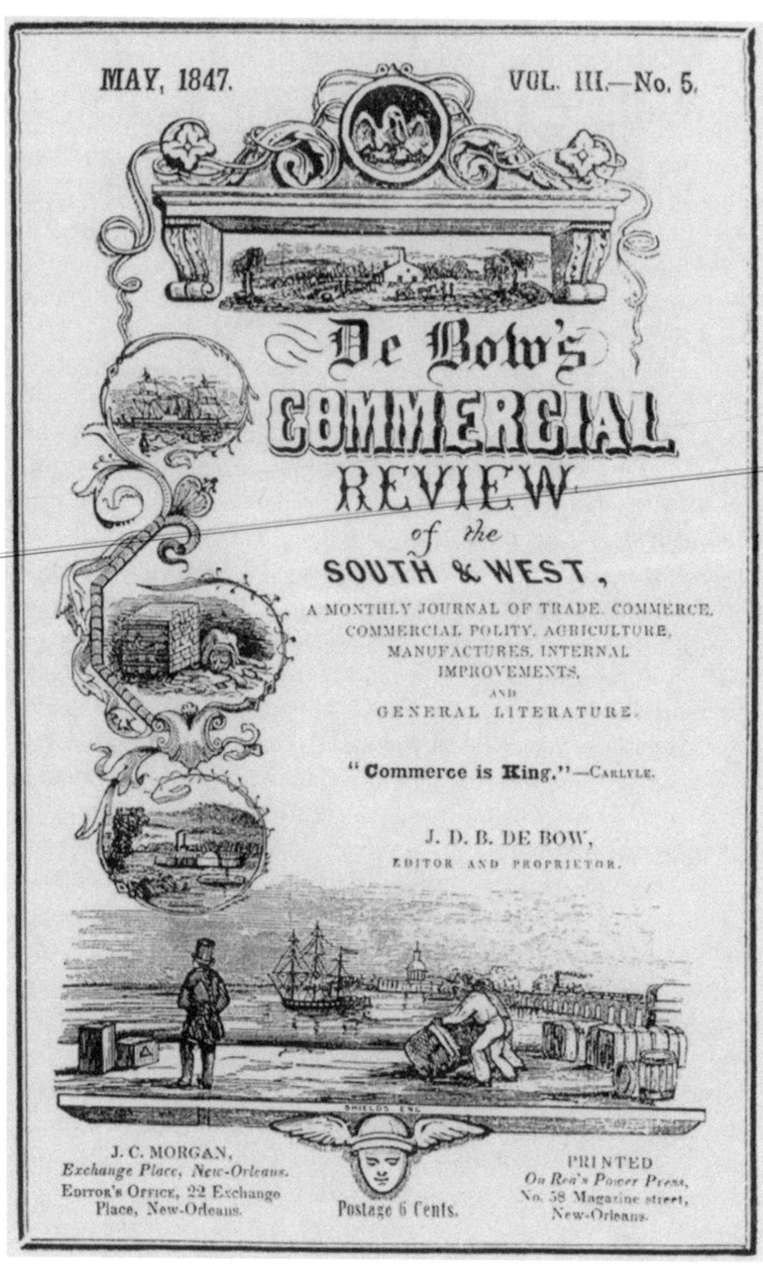

MAY, 1847. VOL. III.—No. 5.

De Bow's
COMMERCIAL
REVIEW
of the
SOUTH & WEST,

A MONTHLY JOURNAL OF TRADE, COMMERCE, COMMERCIAL POLITY, AGRICULTURE, MANUFACTURES, INTERNAL IMPROVEMENTS, AND GENERAL LITERATURE.

"Commerce is King."—CARLYLE.

J. D. B. DE BOW,
EDITOR AND PROPRIETOR.

J. C. MORGAN,
Exchange Place, New-Orleans.
EDITOR'S OFFICE, 22 Exchange Place, New-Orleans.

Postage 6 Cents.

PRINTED
On Rea's Power Press,
No. 58 Magazine street,
New-Orleans.

De Bow's Review. *James De Bow of New Orleans began his* Review *in 1846. He was one of the South's most vocal editors in the fight to protect slavery. In addition to editorial opinion, De Bow ran stories about trade and commerce. He also ran agricultural information and assorted informational pieces about the South and other areas.*

efforts. Even in states that forbade slavery, not all citizens could agree that slavery should be outlawed and was immoral. Those on both sides of the issue often based their arguments pro or con on the same subject matter. Biblical teachings were often used as a basis for slavery's legitimacy and for its illegitimacy, but by the 1830s, most arguments on slavery discussed the morality of slavery, the welfare of slaves, the agrarian way of life it supported in the South, and the legality involved when the federal government denied states' citizens the right to own or not own slaves.

Abolition of slaves was but one part of the argument over slavery that appeared in the antebellum press. Slavery ultimately consumed nearly all debate in public print as America moved closer to disunion, and William Lloyd Garrison was but one player–although a key one–in keeping the issue of slavery in the national spotlight. Garrison got his start as an abolitionist journalist by working for Benjamin Lundy's abolitionist newspaper in Baltimore, Maryland, in 1828. Gamaliel Bailey edited the *National Era* in Washington, D.C., for the same purpose. Arthur Tappan began the *Journal of Commerce* in New York. It became a mouthpiece for abolitionist causes with Tappan's brother, Lewis, being a principal contributor. Both Tappans, however, worked ceaselessly to end slavery. African Americans began their own publications to further not only abolition but rights for free blacks. Samuel Cornish and John Russwurm started the *Freedman's Journal* in 1827 for this purpose, and Frederick Douglass became the best-known black journalist before the Civil War.

While all of these people and their publications furthered the cause of slaves and blacks in America, Garrison was the chief target of most opponents of the abolitionists. At an antislavery rally in Boston, they tied a rope "under his arms and about his neck" and led Garrison "into State street."[5] America's postmaster general allowed Southern postmasters to halt delivery of the *Liberator* in the South. Georgia offered a $5,000 reward for Garrison's arrest shortly after the *Liberator* started publication, and South Carolina offered $1,500 to anyone who could provide information that could lead to the arrest of anyone distributing the *Liberator* within the state. People attacked Garrison in public,[6] and as late as 1859, a writer to the *New-York Times* said that the North must let the people of the South know that the Garrisons and other radical abolitionists "have no extensive influence" in the North.[7]

This chapter looks at writings that support abolition and those that support slavery. The abolitionist section begins with a piece from Benjamin Lundy's *Genius of Universal Emancipation*. It is followed by two writings by Garrison. The first is his rationale for beginning the *Liberator*. The second explains why slavery is acceptable to so many Americans. The next entry comes from Horace Greeley's New York *Tribune*. Greeley was as outspoken as any American editor who published a traditional newspaper. In this article, a Southern slave auction is described in detail.

The section supporting slavery begins with Amos Kendall's decree that Southern postmasters may halt distribution of the *Liberator*. It is followed by a derogatory and demeaning account of an American Foreign Anti-slavery Society meeting taken from James Gordon Bennett's New York *Herald*. Bennett was supportive of the South and slavery. The last two chapter selections present the Southern rationale that slavery was good for Africans. The first, from *De Bow's Review* of New Orleans addresses how Southern slaves are better off than Northern freedmen. The second, from the Charleston, South Carolina, *Mercury*, discusses the plight of blacks in Africa.

Support for Abolitionism

Benjamin Lundy: "Equality"

Lundy's publication, which he began in 1821, set the tone for the abolitionist press in America. He moved his newspaper to Jonesborough, Tennessee, in 1822 because he wanted to publish his abolitionist paper in a state that condoned slavery. In this editorial, Lundy bases his argument on the Declaration of Independence, something done by many who believed slavery was wrong.

Genius of Universal Emancipation **(Baltimore), 9 August 1828**

"'Hail Columbia! Happy Land! We hold these truths to be self-evident' – what truths?–that all men are created equal!' what?–created how?–'EQUAL'–pooh! it's all stuff and nonsense! created equal indeed!–Ask the lawmakers, lawyers, judges and jailors, of Delaware, Maryland, Virginia, N. Carolina, S. Carolina, Georgia, Alabama, Mississippi, Louisiana, Tennessee, Kentucky, Missouri, Arkansas, and the District of Columbia, if there's a word of truth in it.–Ask the 'highly polished' newspapers of our 'happy' country–in which we find so many pleasing articles headed 'Taken up'–'Cash in Market'–'Committed to Jail'–'Ran Away'–'Money for Negroes', &c. &c. &c. &c. We say, ask the editors of the papers in which we find so many striking evidences of the 'Christian' and 'Republican' purity of our government, if 'all men are created equal?' and see if they don't tell you it's a lie invented by Washington, Jefferson, Adams, &c., with the malignant design of interfering with the 'gentlemanly pursuits' and 'avocations' of our countrymen! What could have induced the old enthusiastic dunces to gabble so foolishly about the 'equality' of 'all men,' when every part and particle of our 'inclination, conduct' and character, give them a 'clear, unequivocal,' and 'conclusive contradiction.' Why have not the American people congregated themselves together by the 'great ones' among them, to witness a solemn burning of the Declaration of Independence, long ago! Why is the old musty thing suffered to defile our dusty book shelves any longer? But to be serious. We ask the reader's attention. . . . "

William Lloyd Garrison: "To the Public"

When William Lloyd Garrison published the first issue of the Liberator *in 1831, he was a veteran of the abolitionist effort, having begun writing for Benjamin Lundy's* Genius of Universal Emancipation *in 1829 and having spent time in jail on charges of libel because of his attacks on slavery. In the first issue of the* Liberator, *Garrison explained why he chose Boston for his newspaper's home. He also promised to have his views on slavery heard, basing his hatred of the institution, in part, on the Declaration of Independence.*

Liberator (Boston), 1 January 1831

In the month of August, I issued proposals for publishing "The Liberator" in Washington City; but the enterprise, though hailed in different sections of the country, was palsied by public indifference. Since that time, the removal of the *Genius of Universal Emancipation* to the Seat of Government has rendered less imperious the establishment of a similar periodical in that quarter.

During my recent tour for the purpose of exciting the minds of the people by a series of discourses on the subject of slavery, every place that I visited gave fresh evidence of the fact, that a greater revolution in public sentiment was to be effected in the free States—*and particularly in New-England*—than at the South. I found contempt more bitter, opposition more active, detraction more relentless, prejudice more stubborn, and apathy more frozen, than among slave-owners themselves. Of course, there were individual exceptions to the contrary. This state of things afflicted, but did not dishearten me. I determined, at every hazard, to lift up the standard of emancipation in the eyes of the nation, *within sight of Bunker Hill and in the birthplace of liberty.* That standard is now unfurled; and long may it float, unhurt by the spoliations of time or the missiles of a desperate foe—yea, till every chain be broken, and every bondman set free! Let Southern oppressors tremble—let their secret abettors tremble—let their Northern apologists tremble—let all the enemies of the persecuted blacks tremble. . . .

Assenting to the "self-evident truth" maintained in the American Declaration of Independence, "that all men are created equal, and endowed by their Creator with certain inalienable rights—among which are life, liberty and the pursuit of happiness," I shall strenuously contend for the immediate enfranchisement of our slave population. . . . I seize this moment to make a full and unequivocal recantation, and thus publicly to ask pardon of my God, of my country, and of my brethren the poor slaves, for having uttered a sentiment so full of timidity, injustice, and absurdity. . . .

I am aware that many object to the severity of my language; but is there not cause for severity? I will be as harsh as truth, and as uncompromising as justice. On this subject, I do not wish to think, or to speak, or write, with moderation. No! no! Tell a man whose house is on fire to give a moderate alarm; tell him to moderately rescue his wife from the hands of the ravisher; tell the mother to gradually extricate her babe from the fire into which it has fallen;—but urge me not to use moderation in a cause like the present. I am in earnest—I will not equivocate—I will not excuse—I will not retreat a single inch—AND I WILL BE HEARD. . . .

William Lloyd Garrison: "A Short Catechism Adapted to All Parts of the United States"

For Garrison, the reason that slavery was so acceptable in America was based in racial bias and hatred. He also believed that the silence of America's religious institutions also contributed to the continuance of slavery.

Liberator (Boston), 17 November 1837

1. Why is American slaveholding in all cases not sinful?
   Because its victims are *black*.
2. Why is gradual emancipation right?
   Because the slaves are *black*.
3. Why is immediate emancipation wrong and dangerous?
   Because the slaves are *black*.
4. Why ought one-sixth portion of the American population to be exiled from their native soil?
   Because they are *black*.
5. Why would the slaves if emancipated, cut the throats of their masters?
   Because they are *black*.
6. Why are our slaves not fit for freedom?
   Because they are *black*.
7. Why are American slaveholders not thieves, tyrants and men-stealers ?
   Because their victims are *black*.

8. Why does the Bible justify American slavery?
   Because its victims are *black.*
9. Why ought not the Priest and the Levite, 'passing by on the other side,' to be sternly rebuked ?
   Because the man who has fallen among thieves, and lies weltering in his blood, is *black.*
10. Why are abolitionists fanatics, madmen and incendiaries?
    Because those for whom they plead are *black.*
11. Why are they wrong in their principles and measures?
    Because the slaves are *black.*
12. Why is all the prudence, moderation, judiciousness, philanthropy and piety on the side of their opponents ?
    Because the slaves are *black.*
13. Why ought not the free discussion of slavery to be tolerated ?
    Because its victims are *black.*
14. Why is Lynch law, as applied to abolitionists, better than common law?
    Because the slaves, whom they seek to emancipate, are *black.*
15. Why are the slaves contented and happy?
    Because they are *black!*
16. Why don't they want to be free?
    Because they are *black!*
17. Why are they not created in the image of God?
    Because their skin is *black.*
18. Why are they not cruelly treated, but enjoy unusual comforts and privileges?
    Because they are *black*
19. Why are they not our brethren and countrymen?
    Because they are *black.*
20. Why is it unconstitutional to pity and defend them?
    Because they are *black.*
21. Why is it a violation of the national compact to rebuke their masters?
    Because they are *black.*
22. Why will they be lazy, improvident, and worthless, if set free?
    Because their skin is *black.*
23. Why will the whites wish to amalgamate with them in a state of freedom?
    Because they are *black.*
24. Why must the Union be dissolved, should Congress abolish slavery in the District of Columbia?
    Because the slaves in that District are *black.*

25. Why are abolitionists justly treated as outlaws in one half of the Union?
Because those whose cause they espouse are *black*.
26. Why is slavery 'the corner-stone of our republican edifice?'
Because its victims are *black*.

We have thus given twenty-six replies to those who assail our principles and measures—that is, one reply, unanswerable and all-comprehensive, to all the cavils, complaints, criticisms, objections and difficulties which swarm in each State in the Union, against our holy enterprise. The victims are BLACK! 'That alters the case!' There is not an individual in all this country, who is not conscious before God, that if the slaves at the South should be to-day miraculously transformed into men of white complexions, to-morrow the abolitionists would be recognised and cheered as the best friends of their race; their principles would be eulogised as sound and incontrovertible, and their measures as rational and indispensable! Then, indeed, immediate emancipation would be the right of the slaves, and the duty of the masters! . . .

An Anonymous Report: "A Great Slave Auction"

The Tribune*'s description of a Georgia slave auction attempts to give readers insight into what editor Horace Greeley considered a most inhuman activity. Greeley probably did not write this article, instead sending a reporter to cover it.*

Tribune **(New York), 9 March 1859**

The largest sale of human chattels that has been made in Star-Spangled America for several years took place on Wednesday and Thursday of last week, at the race course near the city of Savannah, Georgia. The lot consisted of four hundred and thirty-six men, women, children, and infants. . . .

The sale had been advertised largely for many weeks, and as the Negroes were known to be a choice lot and very desirable property, the attendance of buyers was large. . . . For several days before the sale every hotel in Savannah was crowded with Negro speculators from North and South Carolina, Virginia, Georgia, Alabama, Louisiana, who had been attracted hither by the prospects of making good bargains. Nothing was heard for days, in the bar-rooms and public rooms, but talk of the great sale . . . and speculations as to the probable prices the stock would bring. . . .

The slaves remained at the race course, some of them for more than a week and all of them for four days before the sale. They were brought in thus early that buyers who desired to inspect them might enjoy that privilege, although none of them were sold at private sale. For these preliminary days their shed was constantly visited by speculators. The Negroes were examined with as little consideration as if they had been brutes indeed; the buyers pulling their mouths open to see their teeth, pinching their limbs to find how muscular they were, walking them up and down to detect any signs of lameness, making them stoop and bend in different ways that they might be certain there was no concealed rupture or wound; and, in addition to all this treatment, asking them scores of questions relative to their qualifications and accomplishments. All these humiliations were submitted to without a murmur, and in some instances with good-natured cheerfulness—where the slave liked the appearance of the proposed buyer and fancied that he might prove a kind "mas'r."

The following curiously sad scene is the type of a score of others that were there enacted:

"Elisha," chattel No. 5 in the catalogue, had taken a fancy to a benevolent-looking middle-aged gentleman who was inspecting the stock, and thus used his powers of persuasion to induce the benevolent man to purchase him, with his wife, boy, and girl, Molly, Israel, and Sevanda, chattels Nos. 6, 7, and 8. The earnestness with which the poor fellow pressed his suit, knowing, as he did, that perhaps the happiness of his whole life depended on his success, was interesting, and the arguments he used were most pathetic. He made no appeal to the feelings of the buyer; he rested no hope on his charity and kindness, but only strove to show how well worth his dollars were the bone and blood he was entreating him to buy.

"Look at me, mas'r; am prime rice planter: sho' you won't find a better man den me; no better on de whole plantation; not a bit old yet; do mo' work den ever; do carpenter work, too, little; better buy me, mas'r; I'se be good servant, mas'r. Molly, too, my wife, Sa, fus'-rate rice hand; mos' as good as me. Stan' out yer, Molly, and let the gen'lem'n see."

Molly advances, with her hands crossed on her bosom, and makes a quick short curtsy, and stands mute, looking appealingly in the benevolent man's face. But Elisha talks all the faster.

"Show mas'r yer arm, Molly—good arm dat, mas'r—she do a heap of work mo' with dat arm yet. Let good mas'r see yer teeth, Molly—see dat, mas'r. Teeth all reg'lar, all good—she'm young gal yet. Come out yer, Israel, walk aroun' an' let the gen'lem'n see how spry you be."

Then, pointing to the three-year-old girl who stood with her chubby hand to her mouth, holding onto her mother's dress, and uncertain what to make of the strange scene:

"Little Vandy's on'y a chile yet; make prime gal by-and-by. Better buy us, mas'r, we'm fus'-rate bargain"—and so on. But the benevolent gentleman found where he could drive a closer bargain and so bought somebody else. . . .

The buyers, who were present to the number of about two hundred, clustered around the platform; while the Negroes, who were not likely to be immediately wanted, gathered into sad groups in the background to watch the progress of the selling in which they were so sorrowfully interested. The wind howled outside, and through the open side of the building the driving rain came pouring in; the bar down stairs ceased for a short time its brisk trade; the buyers lit fresh cigars, got ready their catalogues and pencils, and the first lot of human chattels are led upon the stand, not by a white man, but by a sleek mulatto, himself a slave, and who seems to regard the selling of his brethren, in which he so glibly assists, as a capital joke. It had been announced that the Negroes would be sold in "families," that is to say, a man would not be parted from his wife, or a mother from a very young child. There is perhaps as much policy as humanity in this arrangement, for thereby many aged and unserviceable people are disposed of, who otherwise would not find a ready sale. . . .

The auctioneer brought up . . . Molly and family. He announced that Molly insisted that she was lame in her left foot and perversely would walk lame, although, for his part, he did not believe a word of it. He had caused her to be examined by an eminent physician in Savannah, which medical light had declared that Joshua's Molly was not lame, but was only shamming. However, the gentlemen must judge for themselves and bid accordingly. So Molly was put through her paces, and compelled to trot up and down along the stage, to go up and down the stage, to go up and down steps, and to exercise her feet in various ways, but always with the same result, the left foot *would* be lame. She was finally sold for $695.

Whether she really was lame or not, no one knows but herself, but it must be remembered that to a slave a lameness, or anything that decreases his market value, is a thing to be rejoiced over. A man in the prime of life, worth $1,600 or thereabouts, can have little savings of his own, to purchase his liberty. But let him have a rupture, or lose a limb, or sustain any other injury that renders him of much less service to his owner, and reduces his value to $300 or $400, and he may hope to accumulate that sum, and eventually to purchase his liberty. Freedom without health is infinitely sweeter than health without freedom.

And so the Great Sale went on for two long days, during which time there were sold 429 men, women, and children. There were 436 announced to be sold, but a few were detained on the plantations by sickness.

The total amount of the sale foots up to $303,850—the proceeds of the first day being $161,480, and of the second day $142,370.

Leaving the race buildings, where the scenes we have described took place, a crowd of Negroes were seen gathered eagerly about a man in their midst. That man was Mr. Pierce M. Butler of the free city of Philadelphia, who was solacing the wounded hearts of the people he had sold from their firesides and their homes, by dolling out to them small change at the rate of a dollar a head. To every Negro he had sold, who presented his claim for the paltry pittance, he gave the munificent stipend of one whole dollar in specie; he being provided with two canvas bags of twenty-five-cent pieces, fresh from the mint, to give an additional glitter to his munificent generosity.

Opposition to Abolitionism

Amos Kendall: "Abolitionists Want to Destroy the South"

Amos Kendall was the postmaster general of the United States and a former newspaperman. He did not, however, think that the wholesale shipping of abolitionist newspapers to the South was a good thing. In this letter, Kendall says that using power to stop lawless activity—such as inciting slaves to revolt—was not wrong.

New York Times, 22 August 1835

From the specimens I have seen of anti-slavery publications, and the concurrent testimony of every class of citizens except the abolitionists, they tend directly to produce in the south, evils and horrors surpassing those usually resulting from foreign invasion or ordinary insurrection. From their revolting pictures and fervid appeals addressed to the senses and passions of the blacks they are calculated to fill every family with assassins and produce at no distant day an exterminating servile war. So aggravated is the character of those papers that the people of the southern states with an unanimity never witnessed except in cases of extreme danger, have evinced, in public meetings and by other demonstrations, a determination to seek defence and safety in putting an end to their circulation by any means, and at any hazard. Lawless power is to be resisted; but power which is exerted in palpable self-defence, is not lawless. That such is the power whose elements are now agitating the south, the united people of that section religiously believe; and so long as that shall be their impression, it will require the array of armies to carry the mails in safety through their territories, if they continue to be used as the instrument of those who are supposed to seek their destruction. . . .

Now, have these people a legal right to do by the mail carriers and postmasters of the United States, acts, which if done by themselves or their agents, would lawfully subject them to the punishment due to felons of the deepest dye? Are the officers of the United States compelled by the constitution and laws, to become the instruments and accomplices of those who design to baffle and make nugatory the constitutional laws of the states—to fill them with sedition, murder and insurrection—to overthrow those institutions which are recognised and guaranteed by the constitution itself? . . .

An Anonymous Report: "American Foreign Anti-Slavery Society Annual Meeting"

James Gordon Bennett's Herald *became the ultimate Penny Press newspaper with its sensational reporting. Others even mounted attacks against Bennett and his policies (see Chapter 12). In this article by an unnamed reporter, the paper pokes fun at abolitionists. It uses derogatory language to describe blacks and abolitionist leaders like William Lloyd Garrison and Arthur and Lewis Tappan.*

Morning Herald (New York), 12 May 1841

The society met last night, at the church corner of Houston and Thompson streets. It is the genuine, legitimate, Simon Pure abolition society, and all others claiming to be national, are but inerlopers and bastards. Garrison and his white and nigger burden, who claim to be *the society, par excellence,* are mere marplots and disorganizers, who must have their own way, come what may come, and who are determined to rule or ruin. Mr. Tappan and his worthy coadjutors, who constitute the genuine society, manage matters with great propriety, and are ready to do all the mischief possible with the utmost decorum. They are a little aristocratic, and do not inhale the odor of coffee with so much gusto as Garrison & Co. The consequence is, that very few negroes honor their meetings with their presence.

When the services commenced last evening, there were in the gallery on the right of the desk, two gentlemen of color, and one in whose composition milk and molasses seems to have been used in about equal portions—seven or eight sisters varying in hue from jet black to brunette—and one picaninny, so black that he looked as if he might have been dipped twice after the color was set. On the left of the desk was a very rum lot of yellow girls, a handsome yellow boy, and three or four greasy wenches, big enough to yield half a barrel of oil a piece. In the body of the church was a big black booby, towards whom the eyes of many of the ladies were directed, as if wondering what the devil he had to do there. Lewis Tappan was running about, eyeing the colored brethren and sister, and thinking, apparently, what a fine chance to raise wool. Arthur Tappan, the president of the society was in the chair. After a prayer by the Rev. Mr. Workham, Lewis Tappan rose and said—

"Some explanation may be expected of the circumstances that caused the meeting of the society at this place, and some may enquire why we had not met at the Tabernacle. We would not interfere with any other society, either in or out of the house. We could have had the option of any afternoon this week; but all the forenoons had been previously engaged, and we concluded to hold the meeting this evening. It had been agreed on Sunday that the meeting should be held at the church corner of Madison and Catharine streets. We had understood that a majority of the trustees had consented that we should occupy the house; but there was some misunderstanding about it and a majority of the church voted that we should not meet there, and we were constrained to hold our anniversary here."

By this time the body of the church had got quite full, and numbers were standing in the aisles. Some dozen or twenty blacks entered with others, and one fellow, as black as a thunder cloud, with unctuous lips an inch thick, marched up and took a seat on the pulpit stairs along side of Lewis Tappan. That gentleman edged off as fast as possible, but he bore the infliction with considerable fortitude.

Mr. Leavitt then read the annual report. The circumstances under which the society was formed a year ago, were too well know to require repetition. Three hundred members of the old society were unjustly driven off by the overbearing and intolerant spirit of some of the members of the society. Most of the officers of the society entered into this, and although the meeting was the first in form, in point of fact, it was the eighth. They had separated rather than to live in contests. . . .

James De Bow: "The Blessings of Slavery"

James De Bow began his publication in 1846 and became one of the leading apologists for slavery. In this article, DeBow considers slavery a "blessing" for Africans because it provides so much for them that could not be obtained either in Africa or as a free citizen of the North.

De Bow's Review (New Orleans), July 1855

Divine Providence, for its own high and inscrutable purposes, has rescued more than three millions of human beings from the hardships of a savage state, and placed them in a condition of greater comfort than any other laboring class in the world. . . .

Between the Southern master and his slave there is a fellow-feeling in sorrow and in joy, a mutual dependence and affection, which calls into play all the finer feelings of man's nature. What of all this is there between the Northern capitalist and his day-laborer? They have not known each other from infancy, nor been partners through good and evil fortune. Perhaps the tide of emigration brought them together yesterday and will hurry them apart tomorrow. The laborer does not look to his employer as his natural protector against the injustice of the powerful, or as his refuge in sickness or in old age. He must find that in the almshouse. If the laborer is a factory operative—perhaps a girl, or even a child, for in manufacturing societies the children of the poor never know the plays or freedom of childhood—he is regarded as but a part of the loom he attends to. Factory labor becomes more and more divided, the employments more and more monotonous, with each improvement in machinery. There is none of that variety of occupation and those frequent calls upon the discretion and intelligence of the laborer, which make the work upon a plantation in the South at once the most improving, the healthiest, and the most delightful species of manual labor. The factory operative, on the contrary, is chained to some single minute employment, which must be repeated thousands of times without the least variation. Nothing worse for the intellect can be imagined.

Idiocy and insanity multiply under their influences. In 1840, the proportion of idiots and insane to the whole population was 1 in 1,100 in the slave States, it was 1 in 900 in all the free States, and as much as 1 in 630 in New England alone. The effects of factory life on health are quite as bad. The cotton factories, the dyeing and bleaching factories, are hotbeds of consumption and disease of the lungs. At Sheffield a dry-grinder, no matter how vigorous his constitution, is never known to live beyond the fated age of thirty-five. In Massachusetts, according to her own statistics, factories shorten the life of the operative one-third! According to the evidence taken before the committee of the House of Commons it has taken but thirty-two years to change the operatives of Manchester from a race more vigorous than those of New England now are—a well-fed, well-clothed, moral population—into demoralized, enervated, feeble beings. As one of the witnesses says, "their life has been passed in turning the mule jenny; their minds have been weakened and withered like a tree." How many years will it require to produce these effects in the North, when the span of man's life is already so much shortened? . . .

In what regard is such a condition of labor superior to Southern slavery? . . .

Clayton Banner: "Negroes in Africa"

Comparing the conditions of African slaves in the South to conditions in Africa became a popular means to counter abolitionist arguments of the cruelty and inhumanity of slavery. In this letter to the Mercury, *Clayton*

Banner draws on a letter by a Boston naval officer who had visited Africa and described slavery and conditions there. Banner points out that the unnamed believed Southern slaves were fortunate to be in America and that Southern slave owners should be thanked by all Christians for what they had and were doing for Africans by making them slaves.

Mercury (Charleston), 3 March 1857

"As I live, I do not believe there is one negro in one thousand upon the coast of Africa, who is as well off, morally, physically, or socially, as the worst-abused slave in the United States. Slavery here is slavery indeed, and of the most horrible kind. Cruelty practised here by black slave owners, is heart-rending to witness. Some chiefs (black) own thousands–they sell, torture, or kill them at pleasure."

The above is an extract from a letter written by an officer of the United States Navy to a friend of his in Boston. The writer is a son of a late distinguished Senator from one of the New England States. There is no doubt but that the statement made by this gentleman, is the true condition of the negros in Africa. Coming, as it does, from an officer of the United States Navy, a man in whom the rulers of our Government have placed confidence and promoted to distinction–and, moreover, from an individual, no doubt, whose early teachings were antagonistic to slavery, no man can indulge for a moment the belief that the report is fabulous. . . . There is no mistake about the condition of the negros of the barren soil of Africa. They are certainly the most degraded and worthless beings in their present state imaginable. As is stated in a paragraph of the letter quoted, "a few of the chiefs act as directors and tyrants to the lower portion of them, treating them in the most cruel manner known to humanity." In another part of the letter mentioned, the writer uses the following language: "Having seen our negros at home in our Southern States, and having seen them here, I regard the 'institution' as it exists there as a benign, nay heavenly institution, and our Southern brethren deserve the thanks of the whole christian world for having ameliorated, in such striking contrast with their brethren here, three and a half million of negros."

It will scarcely be controverted, we presume, that the slaves of the Southern States of this Union are to-day in a better state of physical and enlightened existence than the host of poor, indolent negros now in Africa. After seeing that such is the true state of things, we have not the least scruple in believing that those negros that are brought from the coast of Africa to the United States, receive a great human blessing by the change; and although the people of this continent bring them here for the purpose of making them slaves, yet, we say, they perform the part of benefactors, and ought to be so considered by all enlightened people. . . .

Questions

1. The arguments against slavery contained both logical and emotional aspects. Which works best? Use Garrison's "A Short Catechism Adapted to All Parts of the United States" and Greeley's "A Great Slave Auction" for the comparison.
2. Why do you think people believed the arguments supporting slavery as made by James De Bow and Clayton Banner? Explain with examples from their writings.
3. How do you think it was possible for Americans to call on the words of the Declaration of Independence, "All men are created equal," and not apply them to *all* people?

Notes

1. See Samuel Sewall, *Selling of Joseph* (Philadelphia, 1700).
2. Thomas C. Parramore, *Carolina Quest* (Englewood Cliffs, N.J.: Prentice-Hall, 1969), 61.
3. Quoted in Lorenzo J. Greene, *The Negro in Colonial America, 1620–1776* (New York: Columbia University Press, 1942), 60.
4. Mark A. Noll et al., eds. *Christianity in America* (Grand Rapids, Mich.: William B. Eerdman, 1983), 188–89.
5. *United States Gazette* (Philadelphia), 28 October 1835.
6. William E. Huntzicker, *The Popular Press, 1833–1865* (Westport, Conn.: Greenwood Press, 1999), 64.
7. *New-York Times,* 7 December 1859.

CHAPTER 9

Nat Turner and Slave Insurrections, 1831

On August 13, 1831, Nat Turner—a slave born in Southampton County, Virginia—received the sign for which he had long searched. The sun changed colors. It was now time to act on the visions he had experienced in 1825. In one Turner saw black and white spirits fighting in the clouds with blood flowing like streams down from them. Turner knew exactly what God wanted him to do. He had revealed to no one what he had seen or what was to be done, but now it was time to act. Turner told his closest friends, and they met on the night of August 20, to have a meal and make final plans. Turner and the other slaves agreed to begin their revolt by murdering Turner's owner and his family as they slept on Sunday, August 21. All five members of Joseph Travis's family died in their beds, including an infant. From there, the slaves continued on what Turner called "the work of death," killing whites, including children, with axes and swords. They continued into Monday morning before running into whites who were now alerted to what Turner and the others were doing. Turner and his band escaped into the Dismal Swamp of Virginia and North Carolina, where Turner eluded capture for nearly six weeks. His revolt left fifty-five whites dead.[1]

Nat Turner, born in 1800, had been taught to read by his first owner, who believed that it was imperative to the salvation of slaves to be able to read the Bible. Turner learned and became a preacher. For him, religion became a way to salvation both spiritually and physically. Though he was still required to toil in fields, Turner knew something greater lay in store for him. His visions confirmed this, especially those in which Jesus spoke to him. Ultimately, his revolt was, Turner believed, what God had planned for him. Turner, therefore, had no choice but to obey. Many slaves believed Turner was God's messenger and that he, endowed with special gifts and prophecy, was one they needed to follow.

Slave revolts were not new in America. As early as 1712, the *Boston News-Letter* reported on a slave rebellion in New York.[2] Colonial American newspapers repeated news of slave revolts anywhere in the Americas as much as any available news in the eighteenth century. In 1739, South Carolina slaves revolted in what became known as the Stono Rebellion. The slaves killed twenty whites, and forty slaves died as they tried to make their way to freedom in Florida. Fear of slave rebellions became a real part of everyday life wherever large numbers of slaves were held.[3] In 1755, for example, New York passed a law that allowed the killing of slaves who were more than one mile from their masters' residences if there was a general alarm or any kind of disturbance.[4] As the number of slaves in the United States grew, as slavery became an area of contention politically and between sections, and as the abolition movement grew, the fear of slave revolts grew, too.

The fear of insurrection was not unfounded in nineteenth-century Virginia or other parts of America. In 1800, an African American blacksmith named Gabriel Prosser organized hundreds of slaves, who planned to march on Virginia's capital, burn the city, and capture the governor. Slaves fearful of repercussions revealed the revolt, and Prosser and other leaders of the planned revolt were arrested and executed. In 1822, Denmark Vesey, a free-black carpenter in Charleston, South Carolina, planned a revolt to take control there. Again, slaves concerned about what might happen exposed the plot. Vesey and his compatriots were arrested to thwart the plot, which—just as with the proposed Prosser rebellion—included hundreds of slaves. Vesey was hanged.

Countless other rebellions, either real or imagined, were revealed from 1822 on in the South. None, however, could have spurred the fear of Turner's revolt. Within days, slaves in the regions surrounding Southampton, Virginia, were suspected of conspiring to revolt. Many slaves in the Tidewater regions of Virginia and North Carolina had been given increased freedom to attend religious revivals, just as Turner had from the early part of the century on. It was, as Turner's original owner Benjamin Turner had believed, the duty of the master to save the souls of the slave, a common belief during the early days of the Second Great Awakening, a religious revival that spread to Virginia and North Carolina from Kentucky around 1800.[5] But, increasingly, the white population came to believe religion was just another means for abolitionists to spread insurrection fever among slaves. Slaves, on the other hand, found liberation in the scriptures that justified their being free. As a result, North Carolina Governor John Owen said that religion and revival were abolitionist tools used to "sow sedition among our slaves . . . to prepare the minds of that portion of our population for any measure however desperate."[6] Teaching slaves to read or write soon became illegal in many Southern states, and allowing slaves to mingle freely at revival or church meetings decreased greatly.

This chapter looks at the reaction to Nat Turner's rebellion and slave insurrections in general. The first section deals with opposition to slave rebellions. It begins with a piece by William Lloyd Garrison, the owner and editor of the *Liberator,* America's most well-known abolitionist newspaper. In the *Liberator*'s second issue, Garrison wrote about a book titled *Walker's Appeal,* a narrative written by a free black that advocated insurrection and violence as a means to end slavery. Garrison at this time said revolt was wrong, but he did predict that a major slave uprising would take place soon. Garrison's editorial is followed by two of the initial reports out of Virginia concerning Turner's rebellion. The first plays down what happened, while the second uses terminology that no doubt created fear among the whites of the region who read it. The next reading deals with Turner's capture. The final reading in the section comes from South Carolina. It is an official request by the state for the North to help in limiting abolitionist activities in the South to stir slaves to revolt.

The section that supports insurrections begins, as does the opposition section, with an editorial by William Lloyd Garrison. Eight months after the initial editorial of the first section, Garrison writes in support of Turner's actions, calling for immediate emancipation for slaves. The next editorial, by George Goodwin of the *Connecticut Courant,* used Turner's rebellion to advocate the back-to-Africa movement, which proposed returning Africans to the newly formed country of Liberia. The next entry, also by Garrison, uses the Turner revolt as the basis for demanding that slavery be eradicated from the Constitution. The final selection was written by an Ohio minister, A.J. Glover. Though written in 1857, it still deals with the repercussions of the Turner revolt, arguing that slaves should use any amount of force necessary to achieve freedom.

Opposition to Insurrections

William Lloyd Garrison: "Walker's Appeal"

William Lloyd Garrison was adamant in his writings that slavery was evil and should be eradicated. He did not, however, advocate slave rebellions as a means for Africans to obtain their independence. In 1829, a pamphlet written by David Walker, who was a North Carolina free-born black, circulated through Boston first and then through other parts of America including the South. It advocated violence and rebellion as a means to correct the evils of slavery. While it is doubtful that many slaves saw or read Walker's writings, what he proposed would come to fruition with Nat Turner's rebellion eight months later. In this editorial, Garrison decries violent rebellion but acknowledges such could well happen.

Liberator (Boston), 8 January 1831

Believing, as we do, that men should never do evil that good may come; that a good end does not justify wicked means in the accomplishment of it; and that we ought to suffer, as did our Lord and his apostles, unresistingly—knowing that vengeance belongs to God, and he will certainly repay it where it is due;—believing all this, and that the Almighty will deliver the oppressed in a way which they know not, we deprecate the spirit and tendency of this Appeal. Nevertheless, it is not for the American people, as a nation, to denounce it as bloody or monstrous. Mr. Walker but pays them in their own coin, but follows their own creed, but adopts their own language. We do not preach rebellion—no, but submission and peace. Our enemies may accuse us of striving to stir up the slaves to revenge but their accusations are false, and made only to excite the prejudices of the whites, and to destroy our influence. We say, that the possibility of a bloody insurrection at the south fills us with dismay; and we avow, too, as plainly, that if any people were ever justified in throwing off the yoke of their tyrants, the slaves are that people. It is not we, but our guilty countrymen, who put arguments into the mouths, and swords into the hands of the slaves. Every sentence that they write—every word that they speak—every resistance that they make, against foreign oppression, is a call upon their slaves to destroy them. Every Fourth of July celebration must embitter and inflame the minds of the slaves. And the late dinners, and illuminations, and orations, and shoutings, at the south, over the downfall of the French tyrant, Charles the Tenth, furnish so many reasons to the slaves why they should obtain their own rights by violence.

Some editors have affected to doubt where the deceased Walker wrote this pamphlet.—On this point, skepticism need not stumble: the Appeal bears the strongest internal evidence of having emanated from his own mind. No white man could have written in language so natural and enthusiastic.

T. Trezevant: "Disagreeable Rumors"

The news of the slave revolt in Southampton County, Virginia, came out of Virginia and North Carolina following Nat Turner's uprising with varying degrees of alarm. This news story in the Richmond Whig, *written by the postmaster in Jerusalem, Virginia, downplays the revolt, does not give specific numbers of casualties, and is certain that the slaves will not succeed.*

Whig (Richmond), 23 August 1831

Disagreeable rumors having reached this city of an insurrection of the slaves in Southampton county, with loss of life; in order to correct exaggeration, and at the same time to induce all salutary caution, we state the following particulars:

An express from the hon. James Trezvant to the executive, states that an insurrection had broken out, that several families had been murdered, and that the negroes were embodied, requiring a considerable military force to reduce them. The names and precise numbers of families are not mentioned. A letter to the postmaster corroborates the intelligence. Prompt and efficient measures are being taken by the governor, to call out a sufficient force to put down the insurrection, and place lower Virginia on its guard.

Serious danger of course, there is none. The deluded wretches have rushed on assured destruction.

An Anonymous Report: "Insurrection of the Blacks"

Hezekiah Niles printed a number of reports on the Southampton County slave revolt in this issue of the Register. *This one, from the August 24 Norfolk, Virginia,* Herald, *was one of the first printed on the revolt and contains language sure to instill fear in those living in slaveholding regions who read it. The letter also listed the names and numbers of those killed, but they are omitted here.*

Niles' Weekly Register (Baltimore), 27 August, 1831

I have a horrible and heart-rending tale to relate, and lest even its worst features might be distorted by rumor and exaggeration, I have thought it proper to give you all and the worst information, that has as yet reached us through the best sources of intelligence which the nature of the case will admit.

A gentleman arrived here yesterday express from Suffolk, with intelligence from the upper part of Southampton county, stating a band of insurgent slaves (some of them believed to be runaways from the neighboring swamps), had turned out on Sunday night last and murdered several whole families, amounting to 40 or 50 individuals. Some of the families were named, and among them was that of Mrs. Catherine Whitehead, who, with her son and five daughters, fell a sacrifice to the savage ferocity of these demons in human shape.

The insurrection was represented as one of the most alarming character, though it is believed to have originated only in a design to plunder, and not with a view to a more important object—as Mrs. Whitehead, being a wealthy lady, was supposed to have a large sum of money in the house. Unfortunately, a large number of the effective male population was absent at camp meeting in Gates county some miles off, a circumstance, which gave a temporary security to the brigands in the perpetration of their butcheries; and the panic which they struck at the moment prevented the assembling of a force sufficient to check their career. . . .

To-day another express arrived from Suffolk; confirming the disastrous news of the preceding one and adding still more to the number of the slain. The insurgents are believed to have from 100 to 150 mounted men, and about the same number on foot. They are armed with fowling pieces, clubs, &c. and have had a recontre with a small number of the militia, who killed six and took eight of them prisoners. They are said to be on their way to South Quay, probably making their way for the Dismal Swamp, in which they will be able to remain for a short time in security. For my part, I have no fears of their doing much further mischief. There is very little disaffection in the slaves generally, and they cannot muster a force sufficient to effect any object of importance. The few, who have rushed headlong into the arena, will be shot down like crows or captured and made examples of. The militia are collecting in all the neighboring counties, and the utmost vigilance prevails. . . .

In haste, yours.

T. Trezevant: "Nat Turner Apprehended"

News of Nat Turner's arrest appeared immediately in Norfolk, the closest major city to the insurrection. In this account, Turner is said to be contrite for his actions. It was written by the postmaster of Jerusalem.

American Beacon **(Norfolk), 31 October 1831**

Messrs. Shields and Ashburn, Editors of the Beacon, Norfolk, Va.

Gentlemen—Last night the 30th inst. about 9 o'clock, news reached our little village that Gen. Nat was taken alive: today at a quarter after one o'clock, he reached this place, (well guarded) and was delivered into the hands of James W. Parker and James Trezevant, gentlemen, Justices, and after 1 1/2 or 2 hours close examination was committed to Prison.—During all the examination, he evinced great intelligence and such shrewdness of intellect, answering every question clearly and distinctly, and without confusion or prevarication. He acknowledges himself a coward and says he was actuated to do what he did, from the influence of fanaticism, he says the attempt originated entirely with himself, and was not known by any other Negroes, but those to whom he revealed it a few days before, and then only 5 or 6 in number!—he acknowledges now that the revelation was misinterpreted by him, and says it was revealed to him not to follow the inclination of his spirit—he is now convinced that he has done wrong, and advises all other Negroes not to follow his example. He was taken about 12 o'clock on Sunday, in a Cave that he had just finished and gotten into; and while in the very act of fixing the bushes and bows to cover him, a gentleman by the name of Benjamin Phipps, walked up near the spot, and was only led to examine it by accidentally seeing the brush shake; after removing the covering he discovered Nat., and immediately pointed to kill him with his gun, but he exclaimed "don't shoot and I will give up," he then threw his sword from the Cave, that being his only weapon, and came out and went with Mr. Phipps, until they reached some other gentlemen, when after staying at the Keys all night they proceeded here today.

Respectfully, T. Trezevant, P.M.

Joint Committee on Federal Relations: "Preamble"

In South Carolina, the African slave population had been larger than that of whites from the colonial period. Slave rebellions, therefore, were feared and a threat. In 1739, the Stono Revolt left more than sixty people dead, and South Carolina increased its control and surveillance over slaves. In 1822, Denmark Vesey—who purchased his freedom years earlier—instigated another revolt. Though it was crushed as the Stono Revolt nearly a century earlier, it reminded South Carolinians of their precarious relationship between whites and slaves. Many in South Carolina felt that abolitionist literature was instigating slave revolts like that of Nat Turner. As a result, Governor George McDuffie organized a committee on federal relations that requested Northern states limit the activities of abolition societies whose purposes were to "excite the slaves of the Southern States to insurrection and revolt."[7] The preamble to what the committee produced charged that abolitionists' acts left the South in a state of "perpetual panic."

Journal and Southern Whig (Camden, South Carolina), 28 November 1835

Let it be admitted, that the three millions of free white inhabitants in the slave-holding States are amply competent to hold in secure and pacific subjection the two million of slaves. . . . Let it be admitted, that, by reason of an efficient police and judicious internal legislation, we may render abortive the designs of the fanatic and incendiary within our own limits, and that the torrent of pamphlets and tracts which the Abolition presses of the North are pouring forth with an inexhaustible completeness, is arrested the moment it reaches our frontier. Are we to wait until our enemies have built up, by the greatest misrepresentation and falsehoods, a body of public opinion against us, which it would be almost impossible to resist, without separating ourselves? . . . Or are we to sit down content, because from our own vigilance and courage the torch of the incendiary and the dagger of the assassin may never be applied? This is impossible. No people can live in a state of perpetual excitement and apprehension, although real danger can be long deferred. Such a condition of the public mind is destructive of all social happiness, and consequently must prove essentially injurious to the prosperity of a community that has the weakness to suffer under a perpetual panic.

Support for Insurrections

William Lloyd Garrison: "The Insurrection"

In the first issue of the Liberator, *William Lloyd Garrison predicted that slave rebellions would soon begin in the South. In this editorial, Garrison tells readers that the nation can expect more unless there is "IMMEDIATE EMANCIPATION" for all slaves.*

Liberator **(Boston), 3 September 1831**

What we have long predicted—at the peril of being stigmatized as an alarmist and declaimer,—has commenced its fulfilment. The first step of the earthquake, which is ultimately to shake down the fabric of oppression, leaving not one stone upon the other, has been made. The first drops of blood, which are but the prelude to a deluge from the gathering clouds, have fallen. The first flash of lightning, which is to ignite and consume, has been felt. The first wailings of a bereavement, which is to clothe the earth in sackcloth, have broken upon our ears.

In the first number of the Liberator, we alluded to the hour of vengeance in the following lines:

Wo if it come with storm, and blood, and fire,
When midnight darkness veils the earth and sky!
Wo to the innocent babe-the guilty sire—
Mother and daughter-friends of kindred tie!

Stranger and citizen alike shall die!
Red-handed Slaughter his revenge shall feed,
And Havoc yell his ominous death-cry,
And wild Despair in vain for mercy plead—
While hell itself shall shrink and sicken at the deed!

Read the account of the insurrection in Virginia, and say whether our prophecy be not fulfilled. What was poetry—imagination—in January, is now a bloody reality. 'Wo to the innocent babe-to mother and daughter!' Is it not true? Turn again to the record of slaughter! Whole families have been cut off-not a mother, not a daughter, not a babe left. Dreadful retaliation! 'The dead bodies of white and black lying just as they were slain, unburied'—the oppressor and the oppressed equal at last in death-what a spectacle!

True, the rebellion is quelled. Those of the slaves who were not killed in combat, have been secured, and the prison is crowded with victims destined for the gallows!

'Yet laugh not in your carnival of crime Too proudly, ye oppressors!'

You have seen, it is to be feared, but the beginning of sorrows. All the blood which has been shed will be required at your hands. At your hands alone? No—but at the hands of the people of New-England and of all the free states. The crime of oppression is national. The south is only the agent in this guilty traffic. But, remember! the same causes are at work which must inevitably produce the same effects; and when the contest shall have again begun, it must be again a war of extermination. In the present instance, no quarters have been asked or given.

But we have killed and routed them now—we can do it again and again—we are invincible! A dastardly triumph, well becoming a nation of oppressors. Detestable complacency, that can think, without emotion, of the extermination of the blacks! We have the power to kill all—let us, therefore, continue to apply the whip and forge new fetters!

In his fury against the revolters, who will remember their wrongs? What will it avail them, though the catalogue of their sufferings, dripping with warm blood fresh from their lacerated bodies, be held UP to extenuate their conduct? It is enough that the victims were black—that circumstance makes them less precious than the dogs which have been slain in our streets! They were black-brutes, pretending to be men—legions of curses on their memories! They were black—God made them to serve us!

Ye patriotic hypocrites! ye panegyrists of Frenchmen, Greeks, and Poles! ye fustian declaimers for liberty! ye valiant sticklers for equal rights among yourselves! ye haters of aristocracy! ye assailants of monarchies! ye republican nullifiers! ye treasonable disunionists! be dumb! Cast no reproach upon the conduct of the slaves, but let your lips and cheeks wear the blisters of condemnation!

Ye accuse the pacific friends of emancipation of instigating the slaves to revolt. Take back the charge as a foul slander. The slaves need no incentives at our hands. They will find them in their stripes—in their emaciated bodies—in their ceaseless toil—in their ignorant minds—in every field, in every valley, on every hill-top and mountain, wherever you and your fathers have fought for liberty—in your speeches, your conversations, your celebrations, your pamphlets, your newspapers—voices in the air, sounds from across the ocean, invitations to resistance above, below, around them! What more do they need? Surrounded by such influences, and smarting under their newly made wounds, is it wonderful that they should rise to contend—as other 'heroes' have contended—for their lost rights? It is not wonderful.

In all that we have written, is there aught to justify the excesses of the slaves? No. Nevertheless, they deserve no more censure than the Greeks in destroying the Turks, or the Poles in exterminating the Russians, or our fathers in slaughtering the British. Dreadful, indeed, is the standard erected by worldly patriotism!

For ourselves, we are horror-struck at the late tidings. We have exerted our utmost efforts to avert the calamity. We have warned our countrymen of the danger of persisting in their unrighteous conduct. We have preached to the slaves the pacific precepts of Jesus Christ. We have appealed to Christians, philanthropists and patriots, for their assistance to accomplish the great work of national redemption through the agency of moral power–of public opinion–of individual duty. How have we been received? We have been threatened, proscribed, vilified and imprisoned–a laughing-stock and a reproach. Do we falter, in view of these things? Let time answer. If we have been hitherto urgent, and bold, and denunciatory in our efforts, –hereafter we shall grow vehement and active with the increase of danger. We shall cry, in trumpet tones, night and day,–Wo to this guilty land, unless she speedily repents of her evil doings! The blood of millions of her sons cries aloud for redress! IMMEDIATE EMANCIPATION can alone save her from the vengeance of Heaven, and cancel the debt of ages!

George Goodwin: "To Be Secure and Free"

Nat Turner's revolt stirred many emotions and sentiments in all parts of America. In this untitled editorial from the Connecticut Courant, *editor George Goodwin uses the revolt as an opportunity to denounce slavery and to push efforts to re-colonize slaves in Liberia through the American Colonization Society. Goodwin notes in the editorial that his paper is filled with Southern accounts of the revolt. Indeed, this paper and those in the following weeks were filled with reports of the hysteria that followed in the South as suspected insurrections were uncovered and slaves punished and killed.*

Connecticut Courant **(Hartford), 13 September 1831**

In another column will be found an interesting sketch of the late insurrection among the blacks in Virginia. . . . The account is calculated to awaken painful reflections in the mind of every considerate reader. The fact that we have in the bosom of our country so large a population, held in slavery, possessing no interests in common with our citizens with feelings alienated by a sense of wrong and injustice, ignorant, and easily excited by injudicious or mischievous men, and their numbers, already formidable, increasing with a fearful rapidity, is enough to fill the firmest mind with alarming apprehensions—and these apprehensions are not a little increased, by the serious difficulties which lie in the way of any effectual remedy for the evil. That the evil however exists, and that it is a curse and a reproach to a nation professing to hold sacred the great principle that "all men are born free and equal," will not be denied, and it is not the part of wisdom to avert our eyes from it, because the evil is fraught with danger, and the remedy beset with difficulties.

We feel no disposition to cast reproaches upon that portion of our countrymen who are more immediately interested in this subject, as if they were the only offenders. We choose rather to regard slavery as a national sin in which all are involved—a national sin in which all are implicated. We doubt not that multitudes of slave holders lament the evil of slavery as much as others who are so fortunate as not to stand in the same relation to their fellow men—the difficulties and dangers connected with it, they can better apprehend than we can, and it ought not to be a matter of surprise, or complaint, that they should view with jealousy any measures having a bearing on this subject.... We have neither the slightest doubt that many slaves are treated by their owners with the greatest kindness, so that in truth they fare better than many of their free colored brethren at the North. But still the fact remains that they are slaves, held in bondage by their fellow men, regarded as property, and bought and sold as merchandize. At the same time they are human beings like ourselves, possessing the same feelings, and endowed by their Creator with the same capacity for moral and intellectual improvement.... We do not believe it possible at the present day, entirely to exclude from their minds the light of knowledge which shines so brightly around them—some rays will penetrate the darkness and break in upon their minds; enough at least will reach them to make them sensible of their situation and their wrongs, and to stimulate them to a struggle for deliverance. The issue of such a struggle, like the Southampton tragedy, may prove fatal to them, but it would be attended with scenes from the contemplation of which the mind shrinks with horror.

With such a population in the midst of them, how can any people be secure and free from constant danger and alarm. And how important that every effort designed to mitigate such an evil should be sustained and encouraged by national patronage. Such efforts are making by the American Colonization Society. . . . The most favorable prospects of independence and happiness are held out to all such as are disposed to emigrate to Liberia. Many are waiting for an opportunity to go; many slave holders are ready to manumit their slaves, as soon as means are provided for their transportation; and nothing is wanting but resources, to render this institution a blessing to Africa, and the means of mitigating, if not ultimately removing, the evil which now presses with such dreadful weight upon our country. We rejoice that this institution is fast gaining ground in the affections of the people—that prejudices and opposition are giving place to more correct views and more generous support. And we cannot but hope the day is not far distant, when an enlightened public sentiment will encourage and sustain the Government in taking this society under its fostering care and promoting its benevolent designs by a liberal and adequate patronage.

William Lloyd Garrison: "The Great Crisis"

Nat Turner's rebellion helped reopen discussion in America about the Constitution's "allowance" of slavery in the United States. In this editorial, William Lloyd Garrison reminds people in New England that unless slavery is purged from America and made illegal it will end the Union.

Liberator (Boston), 29 December 1832

There is much declamation about the sacredness of the compact which was formed between the free and slave states, on the adoption of the Constitution. A sacred compact, forsooth! We pronounce it the most bloody and heaven-daring arrangement ever made by men for the continuance and protection of a system of the most atrocious villany ever exhibited on earth. Yes—we recognize the compact, but with feelings of shame and indignation; and it will be held in everlasting infamy by the friends of justice and humanity throughout the world. . . .

People of New-England, and of the free States! is it true that slavery is no concern of yours? Have you no right even to protest against it, or to seek its removal? Are you not the main pillars of its support? How long do you mean to be answerable to God and the world, for spilling the blood of the poor innocents? Be not afraid to look the monster SLAVERY boldly in the face. He is your implacable foe—the vampyre who is sucking your life-blood—the ravager of a large portion of your country, and the enemy of God and man. Never hope to be a united, or happy, or prosperous people while he exists. He has an appetite like the grave—a spirit as malignant as that of the bottomless pit—and an influence as dreadful as the corruption of death. Awake to your danger! the struggle is a mighty one—it cannot be avoided—it should not be, if it could.

It is said if you agitate this question, you will divide the Union. Believe it not; but should disunion follow, the fault will not be yours. You must perform your duty, faithfully, fearlessly and promptly, and leave the consequences to God: that duty clearly is, to cease from giving countenance and protection to southern kidnappers. Let them separate, if they can muster courage enough—and the liberation of their slaves is certain. Be assured that slavery will very speedily destroy this Union *if it be let alone*; but even if the Union can be preserved by treading upon the necks, spilling the blood, and destroying the souls of millions of your race, we say it is not worth a price like this, and that it is in the highest degree criminal for you to continue the present compact. Let the pillars thereof fall—let the superstructure crumble into dust—if it must be upheld by robbery and oppression.

A.J. Grover: "Slave Insurrections"

By 1857, the controversy over slavery had reached a boiling point in America. Two weeks after A.J. Grover of Earlville, Illinois, wrote this February 24 letter to the Liberator, *the Supreme Court handed down its decision in the Dred Scott case (see Chapter 27). That decision said slaves were property solely and could not be citizens of the United States. This letter speaks of revolution, of enemies (Southern slave holders), and of violence if needed.*

Liberator (Boston), 13 March 1857

DEAR MR. GARRISON:

I am glad to see many of the leading Abolitionists coming fully up to the sticking-point of endorsing, by speech and resolution, the efforts of the slave to gain his liberty by the same means that his oppressors use to keep him in bondage.

Admitting the Non-Resistant idea to be true . . .I see not why the non-resistant Abolitionist cannot sympathize with and even encourage slave insurrections. The existing relation of slave and slaveholder is one of intrinsic war, which results in the greatest injustice to the slave, and an appalling sacrifice of human life, all on one side! Let the case be partially reversed. The slave, by a successful rebellion, regains his liberty, justice is restored, and human life is sacrificed on the *other* side. . . . Clearly, the conclusion is, that if there is a reasonable prospect that the slaves of the South can gain their liberty by insurrection, non-resistants could aid them in doing so, for the reason that it is better to *save life,* and *do justice, than to destroy life that injustice may be done* . . . .

Twenty-five years of anti-slavery debate ought to have resulted at least in a programme of action—to have prepared the way for some practical steps toward bringing about the desired object. Certainly, we are not going to continue the discussion twenty-five years longer without testing our theory by some practical experiments! I would suggest that the time has come to hit the Slave Power whenever and wherever it seems to hurt the most, provided the blows do not recoil upon ourselves. The only questions necessary to ask are, Is it wrong? and, Do the slaveholders like it? If the answer is No, then pay on; the more they dislike it, the more they should take. Nothing scares the slaveholders like insurrection. The mere report of the secret intention of half-a-dozen slaves to rise turns every slaveholder south of Mason and Dixon's line pale as death—no matter what his natural complexion may be. The bloody ghost of insurrection haunts the Slave Power perpetually with visions of a terrible retribution at the hands of those it has so long crushed and degraded. While it yet trembles with the fright caused by the late rumors let Abolitionists not fail to seize the moment to encourage the slave by a timely expression of sympathy in his behalf, and to remind the slaveholder that this sympathy is fast hardening into something more substantial—that peradventure it may take the form of lead and steel. Would this be equivalent to revolution? The justification is, that revolution is the only hope of the slave; consequently, the quicker it comes, the better. . . .

While we have not strength to meet this issue in the ordinary way, owing to the advantageous entrenchment of our enemies, we have strength to *revolutionize.* We can count on the assistance of at least three million slaves in the enemy's country, who would join the standard of revolution, three-fifths of whose strength would be against us in a political contest. Change the *interests* of the Northern allies of slavery, and you would change *their Principles,* and thereafter they would trouble us no more than weathercocks trouble the wind; so that, if we did not gain their strength, the party of slavery would at least lose it.

But it is said we should have the United States Government to contend against. The United States Government is the people, and if the people are with us, the Government is with us. There is no power above the people, except a superstitious regard for the Constitution, and the moment the people will it, this great American juggernaut will be broken in pieces, and an emancipated nation will be prepared to worship the true God. Revolution, peaceably if we can, but—*Revolution!*

Yours, for the slave, A.J. GROVER

QUESTIONS

1. Increasingly, religion seems to be a justification for violence to achieve certain goals. In the case of American slaves in the antebellum period, was violence their only recourse, or do you think other means of manumission could have been found? Explain.
2. What can you tell about white attitudes toward blacks from the chapter selections?
3. The Constitution allowed slavery in America. How might each side in this argument use this fact to support their cause?

Notes

1. Nat Turner, *The Confessions of Nat Turner, the Leader of the Late Insurrection in Southampton, Va.* (Baltimore: T.R. Gray, 1831).

2. *Boston News-Letter,* 12 April 1712.

3. David A. Copeland, *Debating the Issues in Colonial Newspapers* (Westport, Conn.: Greenwood Press, 2000), 81–82.

4. David A. Copeland, *Colonial American Newspapers: Character and Content* (Newark: University of Delaware Press, 1997), 121.

5. Lemuel Burkitt and Jessee Read, *A Concise History of the Kehukee Baptist Association from Its Original Rise Down to 1803,* rev. Henry L. Burkitt (Philadelphia: Lippincott, Grambo and Co., 1850), 147.

6. *Register* (Raleigh, North Carolina), 18 November 1830.

7. William W. Freehling, *Prelude to Civil War: The Nullification Controversy in South Carolina 1816–1836* (New York: Harper & Row, 1966), 343–44.

CHAPTER 10

The Nullification Act, 1832

In the 1830s, many South Carolinians felt that the federal government no longer cared about their welfare. Congress had just passed another tariff bill on imported and exported products. Led by the Palmetto state, many Southerners believed that the taxes were too high and unjustified—and unconstitutional. South Carolina, through the *South Carolina Exposition and Protest,* had said so in 1828 when Congress passed the initial tariff in this conflict (see Chapter 6). Even though the new tariff reduced taxes on some goods, it kept those on cotton—South Carolina's and the South's chief export—at about 50 percent. South Carolina, as a result, passed the South Carolina Ordinance, which nullified the tariffs of 1828 and 1832 and made it a crime to attempt collection of the taxes within the state. A confrontation years in the making and that would ultimately be decided by civil war was at a crisis point.[1]

The initial concept of nullification had been raised in the unsigned *Exposition and Protest.* Its author, however, was John C. Calhoun, vice president and citizen of South Carolina who continued along with others to promote and refine the concept of nullification during the next four years. Calhoun's concept of nullification said that states ultimately had the right to annul a federal law if in passing the law the state believed Congress exceeded the powers delegated to it by the Constitution. Calhoun said the tariffs in question overstepped the bounds of federal power by limiting the rights of the states. The states, he said, had entered into a compact with other states by ratifying the Constitution. Ratification of the Constitution, he reckoned, did not take away states' rights. Calhoun said that each state—if it deemed a federal law overstepped constitutional limits—could meet in a state convention and rule null and void the law in question. After that, Congress could repeal the law or retool it into a constitutional amendment. If the amendment was added to the Constitution, the objecting state or states could accept the edict as the law of the land or leave the Union.

The debate on nullification reached a new level in 1830 when it became the center of a heated debate in the Senate between Robert Hayne of South Carolina and Daniel Webster of Massachusetts. Hayne outlined South Carolina's position as conceived by Calhoun. Webster countered with the concept of nationalism, saying that to be able to nullify federal law at the whim of a state made the "Union a rope of sand." He said that all states live under a government of uniform laws that are equal among the states. If, Webster reasoned, under such a system, one state can dispense of a law while another accepts it, "Does not this approach absurdity?" Such a system, Webster said, would prove the end of the Union. "When my eyes shall be turned to behold for the last time the sun in heaven," Webster emphasized in flowing rhetoric, "may I not see him shining on the broken and dishonored fragments of a once glorious Union; on States dissevered, discordant, belligerent. Liberty *and* Union, now and for ever, one and inseparable!"[2]

Following the Webster–Hayne debate, the lines on nullification were clearly drawn, and the differences were nowhere more obvious than between President Andrew Jackson and his vice president, Calhoun. Calhoun, who had withdrawn from the 1824 presidential election to run unopposed for the vice presidency, wanted to succeed Jackson in the White House. Having served as second in command under two presidents, Calhoun no doubt felt he was in position to move upward. His position on states' rights, however, and the fact that Jackson severed all ties with him during the nullification controversy, ended his hopes. Knowing he would not receive any support from Jackson, Calhoun resigned the vice presidency at the 1832 South Carolina Ordinance convention and assumed the senatorial seat of Hayne, who was elected governor. Calhoun continued the nullification fight in the Senate, reiterating South Carolina's position that tariff acts—if rejected by the states—were "utterly null and void."

The president's reaction to the South Carolina Ordinance and Calhoun's nullification was a threat to send troops into South Carolina. Working with Henry Clay of Kentucky, Calhoun reached a compromise on tariffs that gradually reduced them by 30 percent during the next decade. The president signed the compromise bill in March 1833, the same day he signed another bill that said the federal government had the right to use military force to stop insurrections, which South Carolina quickly nullified but the president chose to ignore. The crisis of nullification and of the possible separation of states from the Union was over for now.

The first chapter reading deals with toasts given by President Jackson and Vice President Calhoun. The toasts set the stage for the battle between South Carolina and the president over nullification. It is followed by an article that says tariffs are unconstitutional and can be ignored. The next discusses the anti-tariff convention. The last is a challenge to states that subscribed to South Carolina's nullification position. They are asked to stand with the state or go down fighting with it.

The opposition section begins with an article on "submission men," those in South Carolina opposed to nullification. The next attacks the nullifiers and the Charleston *Mercury* for spreading propaganda. The third entry discusses a pro-tariff convention, and the last says that South Carolina's actions will not wreck the Union.

SUPPORT FOR NULLIFICATION

Henry L. Pinckney: "Our Union"

In April 1830, the nation's top politicians came together for the "Jefferson Day Dinner," an annual event to honor Thomas Jefferson's birthday. President Andrew Jackson and Vice President John C. Calhoun were to give toasts. Calhoun planned to use the affair to promote nullification. Jackson, ever wily, bested his vice president when—just before Calhoun was to speak—he toasted, "Our Union—It must be preserved." Calhoun, caught totally off guard, could only respond by saying, "The Union, next to our liberty most dear!" Henry Pinckney of the Charleston Mercury *used the toasts as a chance to make it sound as if Jackson supported the actions threatened by South Carolina, and he also makes it sound as if Jefferson would have approved. He also notes that Jackson said "federal union," not simply union.*

Mercury **(Charleston), 24 April 1830**

The president's toast at the late Jeffersonian celebration was "the federal union—it must be preserved."—To this we respond, amen. But how preserved? There is but one mode, and that is by inducing the majority to respect the rights and feelings of the minority—or, in other words, by inducing the north and east to repeal or modify the iniquitous measures by which the south is impoverished and enslaved. And that the president alludes to this mode, is too evident, we think, to admit the shadow of doubt. His message to congress distinctly recognizes the rights of the states; and solemnly cautions congress to beware of encroachments on them. He is a disciple of Jefferson, whose whole life was devoted to the establishment of state right doctrines, and who first pointed out the mode by which a lone federal usurpation can be resisted and repressed. When the president, therefore, under such circumstances, says that the union "must be preserved," it follows necessarily that he refers to the mode of preservation pointed out by Mr. Jefferson. And that is, by the exercise of the sovereignty of the states. . . .

The president's toast we think, taken in connexion with his well known principles, and the peculiar circumstances under which it was pronounced, completely puts an end to whatever little doubt may have heretofore existed as to his feelings or opinions in relation to the momentous question, now at issue between the federal government and the whole southern section of the union. Indeed it is a distinct recognition of Jeffersonian principles. . . . Those are the principles for which the south is contending. . . . They are the true principles of the constitution, and the more they are discussed, the more surely will they triumph. Let the south be but true to itself, and abundant aid will be given it by the followers of Jefferson in every other quarter.

An Anonymous Report: "Union–Disunion"

Niles' Weekly Register, *which followed the events of the nation as closely as any publication of the period, generally presented both sides of the issues of the day, even though its editor, Hezekiah Niles, held strong opinions on subjects. Though he opposed South Carolina's rationale for nullification, Niles still printed the state's side in his publication. In this issue, Niles ran numerous articles from South Carolina. These come from the Columbia* Telescope.

Niles' Weekly Register (Baltimore), 22 May 1830

Sir. . . . I presume no friend to the state will venture to say, that for the sake of preserving the union, we are bound to perpetual submission to the injuries we complain of. A man that will hold that doctrine, is not a man to be reasoned with, but to be opposed; it is the language of our oppressors, and he who uses it, joins them. . . .

A law enacted by incompetent authority, is not binding. Power exerted without, and beyond the jurisdiction actually conferred, may, in all cases, be rightfully opposed. A law enacted by congress, not authorized by the constitution of the United States, is no more obligatory upon us, than if it were enacted by the king of France.

The tariff of protection is not sanctioned by the powers given to congress in the constitution of the United States. If we mean, therefore, to support that constitution, and by so doing to support the American union, we must declare the law imposing taxes on imports by the benefit of domestic manufactures, *unconstitutional, null and inoperative in the State of South Carolina* . . . .

The course by nullification is practicable and right, it is not disunion, and even if it were, in the language of Mr. Jefferson, disunion is preferable to a government of unlimited powers. If this course should be adopted, the legislature of each suffering state would know, what and who to depend upon, in the time of trial; all would be united as to the course to be pursued.

. . . In doing justice to herself, Carolina would do no more than her duty to the constitution, to the union; and would act on the same principle as an individual citizen does who refuses to pay an unjust demand. . . . *They* will then be forced to calculate the value of the union, and we doubt not they will appreciate its value. We repeat our solemn conviction that resistance by nullification will not lead to war.

Thomas Ritchie: "Anti-Tariff Convention"

The concept of nullification spread to other states. In this editorial from the Enquirer, *Thomas Ritchie suggests that Virginia should follow South Carolina's lead and hold an anti-tariff convention.*

Enquirer **(Richmond), 12 July 1831**

We have published the proposition for holding an *anti-tariff convention* on the 30th of September–and also a paper explaining the advantages of such a meeting–it appears from the following resolutions, that *both parties* in Charleston have adopted the measure.–May we not respectfully recommend it to the citizens of Virginia? It is a peaceful and constitutional measure for uniting the friends of free trade against this "bill of abominations." It will bring together the *facts*–It will concentrate the *arguments* in one point of view. It will produce a co-operation, "a pull, and a strong pull, and a pull all together," among the enemies of the tariff–not confined to one section of the country but extending from Maine to Georgia. . . . It will organize a plan of opposition, which is best calculated to effect the object without mischief. It will bring all the lights on this great subject to one focus; and pour the full force of them upon the next congress of the U.S.–This too is the very moment for such an united effort. . . .

Now, then, is the time to act–now is the time to throw upon the subject all the lights which can be collected from every quarter, and rally together the friends of free trade–not to passionate exertions, but to a peaceful, constitutional, and united effort. What! shall the manufacturers combine, and shall we not associate? Shall *they* hold their conventions; and not we? Shall they appeal to interests, and we not to principles?–They employ sophistry and delusion–and shall we not resort to argument? Shall we not oppose fact to fact–and appeal to appeal?

We would recommend it, therefore, to the citizens of Virginia, at their respective courthouses, in the month of July or August–perhaps on the great election day, in the latter month–to assemble in their primary capacities, and appoint delegates to represent them in the anti-tariff convention. The moment one meeting is held in Virginia, the spirit will move over the land–and the example will be followed elsewhere. *So mote it be!*

Robert Hayne: "Stand or Fall with Carolina"

Robert Hayne had been one of South Carolina's Senators, but in 1832 he resigned to become the state's governor. His senatorial spot was filled by then Vice President John C. Calhoun. Calhoun's and Hayne's rationale for nullification was wrapped in states' rights, and this address firmly calls on South Carolinians to stand or fall with South Carolina.

Messenger **(Pendleton, South Carolina), 26 December 1832**

Fellow citizens, THIS IS OUR OWN—OUR NATIVE LAND, It is the soil of CAROLINA, which has been enriched by the precious blood of our ancestors, shed in defense of those rights and liberties, which we are bound, by every tie divine and human, to transmit unimpaired to our posterity. It is *here* that we have been cherished in youth and sustained in manhood . . . *here* repose the honored bones of our Fathers . . . *here,* when our earthly pilgrimage is over, we hope to sink to rest, on the bosom of our common mother. Bound to our country by such sacred, and endearing ties—let others desert her, if they can, let them revile her, if they will—let them give aid and countenance to her enemies, if they may—but for us, we will STAND OR FALL WITH CAROLINA.

Opposition to Nullification

C.F. Daniels: "Submission Men"

Many in South Carolina who favored nullification referred to those who supported strong Union ties as "submission men." At times, the bickering went beyond the printed page, and in 1831, Daniels and nullification editor James H. Hammond got into a fist fight over the issue.[3] *In this editorial, Daniels proudly states that he is a "submission man," which, he says, means that he believes in the Constitution.*

Journal **(Camden, South Carolina), 9 April 1831**

For a year or two past it has appeared to afford great comfort to the advocates of nullification, war, bloodshed, and brimstone to call people who have little relish for a tournament with windmills submission men, and they keep it up with undiminished zeal and good sense. . . . We *are* submission men. . . . We profess to submit to the Constitution of our country. We submit to the laws framed under the forms of that Constitution. We submit to the voice of a majority of the nation. We submit to government in preference to submission to anarchy, and we finally submit to the oaths we have taken to support all these things in their integrity. This is what we submit to; and now tell us whether these are any of the items to which you do not submit. It is but a subterfuge to say one submits to the Constitution, but since it has been violated one is absolved from allegiance. We do ourselves believe the spirit of the Constitution to have been violated; but a violation of the Constitution must be constitutionally remedied. Because A has cheated B out of his lawful rights, is B at liberty to knock A's brains out for the offense? The national legislature has enacted an unconstitutional law. Who says so? A state, a town, an individual. Does the state, the town, or the individual set itself up for judge upon the question, or does it submit to the expounders provided by the Constitution? The Nullifiers tell us that it is a base and cowardly 'submission' to obey the government when its requirements militate with their own notions of individual 'sovereignty.' Is there anything but Jacobinism, sheer, rank, unadulterated anarchy and opposition to every well-settled notion of government in this? Nothing under Heaven! And in this sense we glory in the name of submission men. . . .

Furioso: "A Well Organized Party"

The issue of nullification led to the organization of political parties in South Carolina in anticipation of elections. The Nullifiers were centered in Charleston but had supporters throughout the state. In this letter, the anonymous Furioso, a Unionist, attacks the Nullifiers' strategy and their principal newspaper, the Mercury. *He says both exaggerate the extent to which South Carolinians support nullification.*

Courier **(Charleston), 10 August 1831**

What a fine thing is a well organized party. How beautifully its different parts play into each other. The big Nullifiers in Charleston have a meeting; organize a club; pass resolutions and huzzah; they then send circulars to the little Nullifiers in the interior and beg them to make haste and kick up a dust at the country Court Houses. The circular arrives; the lawyers at the Court House dash off and bring together the constables, the hangers-on at the taverns, and a dozen others; they meet in the court room and flourish a resolution or two; denounce General Jackson; organize a political club; get some old fellow to come out; call him a Revolutionary worthy; vote thanks to one another; and send their proceedings to the *Mercury,* countersigned by Tom, the Pres;. and Jack Copias, the Sec. And now behold the columns of the *Mercury* the day after the receipt of the proceedings. Oh, what congratulations! What rejoicings it pretends to make! Pieces appear, headed with the words 'Glorious News,' and 'Interesting Proceedings,' and all that kind of thing, and the people are gravely told that these are evidences of public opinion. O tempora! O mores! how this world is given to gulling; what authentic evidences of public opinion!!

George Goodwin: "The Tariff Convention"

Nullification was, naturally, tied closely with the issue of protective tariffs. In this untitled editorial from the Connecticut Courant, *George Goodwin discusses a national pro-tariff convention, the importance of the tariff to manufacturing, and the hope that the convention exposes the fallacies of nullification.*

Connecticut Courant **(Hartford), 8 November 1831**

We have devoted considerable space this week to the proceedings of the Tariff Convention, believing that a great portion of our readers cannot fail to be deeply interested in what has so important a bearing on the industry and prosperity of the country. The Convention was composed of a large body of men, from remote sections of the Union, embracing in their number, statesmen, agriculturists, manufacturers, mechanics and merchants. . . . The results of their labors, embodied in the address to the people, and in the reports of the various committees, will shortly be laid before the public, and, so far as our limits will admit transferred to our columns. . . . The information which it will be the means of spreading before the public, must exert a salutary influence. It will place in a conspicuous light the extent and importance of our manufacturing interests–It will lay open the great source of our national prosperity and independence–direct public attention to the rapid improvements which have taken place in our manufacturers, under the protective system, and point out the disastrous consequences which must ensue to all claims of the community from the overthrow of this system. We would hope also the Convention will not be without a good effect in exposing the fallacy of the theories and reasonings which are urged against the system by the nullifying and free trade party. . . . At any rate we trust the effect will be to concentrate the strength of the advocates of protection, and cause them to maintain with firmness the principles which they consider intimately connected with the highest welfare of the nation.

William Cullen Bryant: "Wreck of the Republic Not at Hand"

When South Carolina threatened nullification following the tariff duties in 1828, Bryant and his newspaper supported their efforts because of the effects the tariff had on South Carolina as well as on other states. In 1832, however, after a South Carolina convention declared both the 1828 and 1832 tariffs null and void, the Evening Post *sided against anyone who would attempt to "wreck our republic."*

Evening Post (New York), 29 August 1832

It is the destiny of all republics to be agitated occasionally by the desperate plans of disappointed and ambitious men, resolved to rule or ruin. Such might succeed with a corrupt people, but not in our intelligent and free land. Public opinion has indignantly rejected every proposition to dismember our confederacy, and has pronounced a just judgment on those who prefer themselves to their country—we have already among us more than one blasted monument of selfish ambition. The wreck of our republic is not yet at hand—the people's devotion to the Union is invincible, and the same verdict awaits every man, whether of the North, the South, the East, or the West, who would dare to violate its integrity.

Questions

1. Do you think Calhoun's theory of nullification has any validity? Explain.
2. Newspaper editors such as Thomas Ritchie of the Richmond *Enquirer* hoped that if states united against the tariff they could force its repeal. Is this the way democratic government should work?
3. A number of people involved in the debate over the tariff and nullification could remember the Revolutionary War. What was their argument against nullification?

Notes

1. For a full explanation of the nullification controversy, see Merrill D. Peterson, *Olive Branch and Sword: The Compromise of 1833* (Baton Rouge: Louisiana State University Press, 1982); William W. Freehling, *Prelude to Civil War: The Nullification Controversy in South Carolina 1816–1836* (New York: Harper & Row, 1966); Charles S. Sydnor, *The Development of Southern Sectionalism, 1819–1848* (Baton Rouge: Louisiana State University Press, 1948); Chauncey Samuel Boucher, *The Nullification Controversy in South Carolina* (Chicago: University of Chicago Press, 1916).

2. "Webster's Second Reply to Hayne–January 26th and 27th, 1830," *Daniel Webster, Defender of the Constitution,* http://www.danorr.com/webster/webster_second.html.

3. Boucher, *The Nullification Controversy,* 132. This work also contains numerous newspaper clippings.

CHAPTER 11

The Bank of the United States, 1832

Andrew Jackson was president; Henry Clay wanted to be. The two most powerful politicians in America from west of the Appalachians had run for president against each other in 1824 (see Chapter 4). In that election, Clay's decision to throw his support to John Quincy Adams ensured the election of the son of the second president, despite the fact that Jackson had won the popular vote but not enough electoral votes to win in the general election. Clay's alliance with Adams had become one of the nation's foci following that election. Now another difference between Jackson, the hero of the Battle of New Orleans, and Clay, Kentucky's favorite son, was taking center stage–their positions on the Bank of the United States. Jackson wanted it abolished; Clay supported it. In fact, he urged Nicholas Biddle, president of the bank, to push for renewal of the bank's charter in 1832 instead of 1836. This would make the Bank of the United States a campaign issue, something that infuriated Jackson.[1]

Congress chartered the Bank of the United States for twenty years in 1816, but it was not the nation's first national bank. Alexander Hamilton, America's first secretary of the treasury, proposed and created the first Bank of the United States in 1791. Congress chartered that bank for twenty years, making it responsible for control of the nation's money and for issuing currency. The bank helped the young nation establish a sound economy, but its charter was not renewed in 1811. Following the War of 1812 and a period of uncertain economics, Congress created the Second Bank of the United States along similar lines to those of the first bank. Initially, the bank did nothing to help the nation's economy, and America slipped into depression in 1819. The Panic of 1819 hurt many Americans, especially those who had borrowed heavily from the bank because it called in its notes. One of its eight branches–the one in Baltimore–was involved in embezzlement. Though the bank pulled through and the nation returned to stronger economic times, many Americans, especially those in the South and West, distrusted and disliked the bank because, in setting the nation's economy on more solid footing, it had seriously hurt many individuals from those regions.[2]

Jackson was one of those Westerners who distrusted the bank, and he promised that, once elected, he would not recharter it when its charter came up for renewal in 1836. But the president was forced to play his hand four years before he had intended. Clay was certain that Congress would approve the early renewal, so he urged Biddle on. Both houses approved the renewal with ease. The votes, however, were not a two-thirds majority. Jackson knew that the early rechartering was a political ploy, and he said, "The Bank is trying to kill me, *but I will kill it*."[3] He vetoed the bill. In vetoing the bank's renewal, Jackson delivered a lengthy address. He used social class and the distinction of rich versus poor to gain popular support from the people. "It is to be regretted that the rich and powerful too often bend the acts of government to their selfish purposes," Jackson said. "Many of our rich men have not been content with equal protection and equal benefits, but have besought us to make them richer by act of Congress. . . . If we can not at once, in justice to interests vested under improvident legislation, make our Government what it ought to be, we can at least take a stand against all new grants of monopolies and exclusive privileges, against any prostitution of our Government to the advancement of the few at the expense of the many, and in favor of compromise and gradual reform in our code of laws and system of political economy."[4]

Clay responded to Jackson's message in the Senate, hoping to override the veto. "General distress, certain, widespread, inevitable ruin, must be the consequences of an attempt to enforce the payment," he said in describing what the veto would do to hardworking Americans. "Depression in the value of all property, sheriff's sales and sacrifices, bankruptcy, must necessarily ensue, and, with them, relief laws, paper money, a prostration of the courts of justice, evils from which we have just emerged, must again, with all their train of afflictions, revisit our country."[5] Despite Clay's best efforts, the veto could not be overridden. Jackson had won; the bank was dead and was not revived when its charter expired in 1836.

The chapter readings begin with those supporting the bank. The first comes from *Niles' Weekly Register*. Hezekiah Niles and Thomas Ritchie of the Richmond *Enquirer* rarely saw eye to eye on anything. The bank was no different. In this article, Niles chastises Ritchie for criticizing the Baltimore editor for his pro-bank position. The next entry is from the *National Intelligencer*. Editors Joseph Gales and W.W. Seaton reprinted articles from various papers supporting the bank, their position in the controversy. The next new article is a speech delivered in the Senate during an unsuccessful attempt to resurrect the bank in 1841.

The section opposing the bank begins with an article from Alabama. Strongly opposed to the bank, the paper complains about a flier sent to Americans who opposed the bank as a form of propaganda to gain bank support. The next entry is Thomas Ritchie's attack on Niles and on the bank. It is followed by the resolves of the people of Hartford, Connecticut, who opposed the bank's recharter. The final selection comes from the New York *Daily Advertiser.* Using misspelled words and what is supposed to be backwoods grammar, the article insinuates that President Jackson cannot run the government without the help of his close aide, Major J. Downing.

Support for the Bank

Hezekiah Niles: "Remarks by the Editor of the *Register*"

Editors in antebellum America were not subtle in their support of their political views or attacks against those who opposed them. In this editorial, Hezekiah Niles, editor of Niles' Weekly Register *of Baltimore, lashes out against Thomas Ritchie, editor of the Richmond* Enquirer. *Niles's editorial is more of an attack on Ritchie than a defense of the Bank of the United States, but belittling Ritchie also disparaged his cause. Ritchie's editorial is included in the section below. Both discuss a letter written by James Madison to Jared Ingersoll concerning the bank.*

Niles' Weekly Register (Baltimore), 30 July 1831

I thank Mr. Ritchie for the extraordinary magnanimity that he has shewn, in *permitting* me to *speak for myself!* It is so unusual for him to allow any one, whose misfortune it is to incur his "sovereign" displeasure, to be at all seen by the readers of the "Enquirer" except "as through a glass dimly," in the editor's *own* sublime presentations, that I have "stuck a pin" here to his everlasting praise! . . .

Mr. Ritchie is sorry—very sorry, indeed—melancholy, very melancholy, indeed, that Mr. Madison should have written his letter of June 25, 1831, to Mr. Ingersoll. Poor old man! Does not the infallible never-wavering guide in *all* things, whether of "faith hope or charity, or in whacking at the pope"—the incorruptible editor of the Richmond Enquirer, "*pity*" "the father of the constitution" in his dotage—though that letter has more beauty and power than *all* the Ritchies since the creation have displayed? But let that pass. Mr. Ritchie *pities* Mr. Madison and has *pitied* "Mr. Niles." How shall WE survive it?

For the information of my readers, though the editor of the Enquirer cannot any more *comprehend* what I say than a Highlander ascertain the use of a kneebuckle, I shall explain the *reason* of the offensive paragraph that he has quoted.

It is well known that, for years past, (when the present president of the United States thought on such subjects as I did), I oftentimes endeavored to shew the *constitutionality* of laws to protect the NATIONAL INDUSTRY, or appropriate money for INTERNAL IMPROVEMENTS; and that, having established such constitutionality, at least to my own satisfaction, I frequently exhorted others, who honestly differed in opinion with me, to yield up their opposition to the repeatedly established interpretations of the constitution in favor of the principles which I contended for. It is now several years since—I recollect it well—when privately reflecting upon the contents of one of my own essays in which the point alluded to was involved, that I stood self-accused of *sheer impudence* or *palpable dishonesty,* in offering a rule to others that I would not abide by myself, as to the bank of the United States; and, though I could not yet fully give up the prejudices or opinions that I had formed in by-gone days, I consented to waive them; holding myself "*corrupt*" if I should not "*practice upon the maxims recommended to others*"—however high the authority may be for earnestly advising many things and recklessly doing their opposites. In this frame of mind, I read Mr. Madison's letter—and I thought that it became me, as an honest man, to acknowledge the invincible power of his argument, so far as the *constitutionality* of the bank was concerned. To accept the monster proposed in place of that institution, was more difficult than to accept a president for life, with liberty to name his successor!—about which *strict-construction* Mr. Ritchie has been as mute as a "bull-frog frozen up in a pond." What a croaking would he have made, had the *late* president of the United States recommended a thing so preposterous? . . .

An Anonymous Report: "The Bank Veto"

As the number of newspapers in America grew and the nation faced a variety of issues in the antebellum period, editors often pulled opinions from other newspapers that supported their own political views. That is exactly what the editors of the National Intelligencer—*Joseph Gales and W.W. Seaton—did following Jackson's veto of the renewal of the Bank of the United States' charter. The editorials here come from the Boston* Daily Atlas *and the Portland, Maine,* Daily Advertiser. *The* National Intelligencer *had received the bulk of the federal government's printing patronage until Jackson's election, so Gales and Seaton had reasons more than political principle to oppose Jackson's veto. The first editorial refers to Jackson's "kitchen cabinet," the name given to Jackson's unofficial advisors. He relied on this group, not those who comprised the actual executive cabinet, for most of his decisions. The second attacks Jackson's attempts to portray the national bank as a tool of the wealthy to be used to keep the poor impoverished.*

National Intelligencer (Washington, D.C.), 9 August 1832

The Bank Veto.—This is the most wholly *radical* and basely *Jesuitical* document that ever emanated from any Administration, in any county. It violates all our established notions and feelings. It arraigns Congress for not asking permission of the Executive before daring to legislate on the matter, and fairly imitates a design to save the two houses in future from all such trouble. It imprudently asserts that Congress have acted prematurely, blindly, and without sufficient examination. It falsely and wickedly alleges that the rich and powerful throughout the country are waging a war of *oppression* against the poor and the weak; and attempts to justify the President on the ground of its being his duty thus to protect the humble when so assailed. Finally, and unblushingly it denies that the Supreme Court is the proper tribunal to decide upon the constitutionality of the laws!!

The whole paper is a most thoroughgoing *electioneering* missile, intended to secure the mad-caps of the South, and as such, deserves the execration of all who love their country or its welfare. *This veto* seems to be the production of the whole *kitchen* cabinet—of hypocrisy and arrogance; of imbecility and talent; of cunning, falsehood, and corruption—a very firebrand, intended to destroy their opponents, but which now, thanks to Him who can bring good out of evil, bids fair to light up a flame that shall consume its vile authors.

If the doctrine avowed in this document do not arouse the Nation, we shall despair that any thing will, until the iron hand of despotism has swept our fair land, and this glorious Republic, if not wholly annihilated, shall have been fiercely shaken to its very foundations.

There is no part of the Veto Message more deservedly reprobated, and more reprehensible, than that part which attempts to array the poor against the rich, and thus to set in opposition the prejudices which one class may have against another. The object of all banks, it is more than insinuated, is to make the rich richer and the poor poorer. We will not dwell upon the refutation of so unworthy an insinuation. But we ask the property-holders, if they are willing to lend a hand for some new Agrarian project, which shall upset all the rights of estates and chattels. A more deranging, radical, law upsetting document was never promulgated by the wildest Roman fanatic. The revolutionists of France went but little further. But how undignified, how disreputable is it, in the President of a constitutional republic to lay his blows not only upon the laws and upon the Judiciary, but even to degrade his station with insinuations, which would do discredit to Cromwell or the *people-loving* Robespierre. Is the President preparing for a crown by cajoling us with the prospect of an equal division of goods—by offering his aid to overturn the rights of property, to humble the wealthy, and to put down the exalted? If so, we ask, which is worth the most, monarchy, despotism the tyranny of one man—or, honorable poverty, and the present enjoyment of a constitution and laws which throw the field of exertion wide open to industry, energy, and economy? Let it be remembered that every military chieftain, Sylla, Caesar, Cromwell, all have obtained unlimited and despotic power by pretending to be the sole friends of the People and often by denouncing the rich, and by cajoling the poor with prospects, which they never intended to be realized, or only realized with chains and slavery, and dungeons, or enrollment in the legions assembled to add to the power of the tyrant.

Isaac Bates: "Speech of Mr. Bates"

In 1841, the Senate was debating again whether to establish another national bank. This speech by Isaac Bates of Massachusetts notes the constitutionality of the bank and the need for it.

Massachusetts Spy **(Worcester), 21 July 1841**

. . .I have no doubt as to the power of Congress to establish a Bank of the United States within the District of Columbia, or without it, nor of the power of Congress to establish branches within the States, either with their consent or without it, any more than I have of the right of Congress, under the commercial power, in order to prevent the wreck of property and the loss of human life, to establish a lighthouse at the land's end of Cape Charles or Cape Henry. And further, I hold that if, upon a fair construction of the Constitution, and a just survey of the great purpose for which the Constitution was designed—not the government of a petty corporation, beginning and ending in the matter of dollars and cents, but the Government of a great and growing nation, whose destiny, in the vicissitude of human affairs, it was impossible to foresee, and yet was to be provided for, and whose duration, it is to be hoped, will be limited only by that of time—a doubt should arise upon any of its provisions, as doubts must arise, the Constitution itself has provided its own appointed expositor of its own meaning—the judicial power—of resolving such doubt, and definitively settling such questions. . . . And until reversed, the official oath to support the Constitution embraces it as much as if there was no other provision in it. It is an obligation to support it in the provision for its construction as much as it is any other part of it. How can a man who respects and reveres the Decalogue set at naught the development and exposition of the amplitude of its meaning by Him who commanded it. I mean no irreverence, but it seems to me the principle which governs in one case must govern the other.

The question is not, what Mr. Jefferson, or Mr. Madison, or Mr. Monroe, or Gen. Jackson, or Mr. Adams, Hamilton, or Washington has said or thought—great names, I admit, and for some of which I have the most profound respect and the highest admiration. But circumstances change, influences change, men change, and opinions change, admonishing us not to be too confident of that of which we are not certain, and to be a little more indulgent than we are. There are comparatively but very few things of which a man can be certain he sees the whole. But the question is, what saith the judicial power—the scripture—the only power authorized and commissioned to speak on this subject, and to speak authoritively[*sic*] as well as definitely, and to all who acknowledge the supremacy of the Constitution? . . .

It follows that I think a National Bank *necessary*, in the administration of the finances, as a fiscal agent of the Government. In my judgment, it will be useful in expediting the return of specie payments by the banks. In my judgment, it will be useful in equalizing the exchanges. And in my opinion, a Bank of the United States is indispensable to give a uniform currency to the People. How can twenty-six independent States, organized as the banks now are, furnish a uniform currency? It is idle to talk of it. And how can Congress do it without the intervention and instrumentality of a National Bank, the sphere of whose influence shall be co-extensive with the limits of the Union? . . .

This, then, is our relative position. What is to be done? A bank we must have. The People look to it for redemption from the thraldem in which their business is involved, They wait for it as for the dawn of a bright and glorious morning after a disturbed, dark night of distress and suffering. They demand it; they have a right to it, and they shall have it if any agency of mine can help to give it to them. I will stay here not only to August, but to December, and from December to March, and from March to March again, but they shall have it. I will sacrifice every opinion that will leave me a conscience undefiled to provide it for them. I will overleap every barrier that is not absolutely impassable. Sir, the spirit that prevailed upon a memorable occasion elsewhere must predominate and prevail here. We must have a union for the sake of union, and union for the sake of cause, and for the sake of the People, for whom this Government was formed, worthy to have a feather's weight of influence upon our deliberation or our action. . . .

Again: I shall vote for the amendment because I can do it without a surrender of principle. Non-user is not abandonment. I do not, as seems to be supposed, erase my judicial decision. I blot out no provision of the Constitution. Congress itself can do neither. The People only, in the way provided by the Constitution, can do either or both. . . .

Finally, I shall vote for the amendment because if the bill, thus amended, becomes a law, it will have the effect I confidently believe, either to answer the purpose for which it is designed, or will remove the doubts and scruples that stand in the way of one that will. These are the reasons, summarily, that will govern me in the vote I shall give. . . .

Opposition to the Bank

An Anonymous Report: "United States Bank"

In the summer of 1831, the pro-bank forces sent a "supplement" of the National Gazette *to regions of the country that supported President Jackson and his efforts to kill the* National Bank. *This report from Huntsville, Alabama, attacks the report and those who want the bank to continue at the beginning and end of the news item. In the middle are excerpts of the* Gazette*'s flier. Part of the* Democrat*'s argument centers on monied aristocracy versus hardworking Westerners, the same rationale Jackson would use in his veto of the recharter. The Richmond* Enquirer *reprinted this report along with numerous others about the bank on July 1, 1831.*

***Huntsville (Ala.) Democrat,* 16 June 1831**

The veil that has so long covered and concealed the motives and conduct of the ruling spirits of this iniquitous institution, is, at length removed; and they stand forth in all their native deformity. It must now be acknowledged, even by bank partizans, that the question of re-charter will depend upon the firmness and incorruptible patriotism of the several states, on the one hand, and upon the unremitted exertions, and the seducing influence of a monied aristocracy, on the other.—Our last northern mail came literally loaded with "Supplements to the National Gazette," containing the argument of *hireling writers* in favor of the re-charter of the Bank. . . . Our limits will not permit us to present to our readers anything like a review of this document; so we must be content with one single extract. . . . Here it is.

TO THE MEMBERS OF THE STATE LEGISLATURES OF THE UNITED STATES

"*Gentlemen:*—The President of the United States has offered to you a great temptation. He has invited you to break down an Institution established by Congress to regulate the currency, and thus to possess yourselves of the uncontrolled privilege of issuing paper money. If, therefore, you immediately instruct the Representatives in Congress from your State to destroy the Bank of the United States, you will in all probability influence so large a portion of that body, as to succeed in the design of prostrating the General Government, by placing the revenues and the currency of the country at your mercy."

Here, the following questions naturally present themselves.—Who are addressed?—Who are those addressing:—What is the motive of the address? and—What are, "*The Members of the State Legislatures.*" Those to whom the people may delegate the power of passing laws for their security and happiness—those, whom the people will hold responsible if they fail to further the views of the man, namely, Andrew Jackson, whom they have appointed to rule over them—those whom, it is presumed, money cannot corrupt—those who are inaccessible to bribery—those, who, in addition to their responsibility to their constituents, will be bound by a solemn oath to support the Constitution of the United States. Those who make the address, belong to a rich, *banking fraternity—A lordly band of money dealers;* for whom the sound of liberty has no charms, unless recommended by the more "spirit-stirring" sound of gold and silver—who have attempted to take the discussion of the question, whether the Bank shall be re-chartered or not, out of the regular channel of inquiry; and who are striving to suppress opposition by the magic influence of money. The motive of this bold, and we may add, insolent, address, is too evident to need comment.

The people of the west will not bear this.—They know too well the price of liberty; and we hope we shall hear their sentiments, through their Legislatures next winter, in stronger terms than they have yet been expressed. . . .

Thomas Ritchie: "Mr. Niles—and the Bank of the U.S."

The Bank of the United States became the principal issue of the presidential campaign of 1832, and Andrew Jackson knew that his opposition to the bank could win him many votes in the South where states' rights and less national interference in local affairs was growing in popularity. He also knew that many business people believed the national bank restricted their financial dealings. This editorial, written by the Enquirer*'s outspoken editor, Thomas Ritchie, attacks editor Hezekiah Niles, who supported the bank. The editorial banter between the two was common during the antebellum period as publications chose political sides and supported fervently the positions of their respective political parties. Niles's response may be found in the first section of readings in this chapter. Ritchie refers to James Madison and Jared Ingersoll in his editorial. Madison pushed for the Second Bank during his tenure as president. Ingersoll, a representative of Pennsylvania, did the same.*

***Enquirer* (Richmond), 22 July 1831**

We to-day lay before our readers Mr. Madison's letter to Mr. Ingersoll. We confess we have seen it with regret. The doctrine does not appear to us as sound and satisfactory. What is it but to say, that an encroachment on the constitution, if recognised by all the departments of the government, consecrates itself? That the sedition act, for instance, was at one time constitutional? . . .

We are not surprised to see Mr. Niles swerving from his moorings on this occasion—He *now* has no doubt as to the constitutionality of the bank. But hear him! in his last paper:

"Mr. Madison's letter concerning the bank of the U. States, must go far, indeed, to correct the judgment of those who have sincerely believed in the unconstitutionality of that institution. It was after his manner, but with much less power, that we have often reasoned with ourselves for several years past—and by so doing, had nearly retired from those opinions which we formerly entertained on that subject. But thus guided by the FATHER OF THE CONSTITUTION—one of the ablest and best men, too, that ever lived, we have no hesitation in saying, frankly and openly, that we now have no doubt as to the *constitutionality* of the bank of the United States, and that the question of re-chartering it should be decided according to the *expediency* of the proceeding—as presented, when the time to act upon the matter shall arrive."

An Anonymous Report: "No Need for a National Bank"

The United States Bank became an election issue in 1832, just as Andrew Jackson's opponents wanted. Sides would align on the bank based upon their devotion to Jackson or to his opponents. In the case of the petition listed below, George Goodwin, editor of the Courant, *tells his readers in this untitled article that most of those who attended this meeting did not support Jackson's re-election, but they also did not support rechartering the bank. The initial comments in this report are from Goodwin; the remainder comes from the petition of the citizens of Hartford.*

***Connecticut Courant* (Hartford), 31 January 1832**

We give below the proceedings of a public meeting, held in this city, last Friday evening, on the subject of the United States Bank. The notice calling this meeting was artfully framed, so as to embrace not only all political parties without distinction, and not only all opposed to an unqualified renewal of the present charter of the Bank, but all opposed to a renewal without essential modifications. . . .

In regard to the general question of re-chartering the Bank, we believe there can be little doubt as to the sentiments of this community. . . .

At a meeting held by the citizens of Hartford on the evening of the 27th day of January, to consider the subject of the renewal of the charter of the Bank of the United States, Ward Woodbridge, was appointed Chairman, and Albert Day, Secretary. . . .

Resolved, That we view with deep interest, the application of the President, directors and company of the Bank of the United States for a renewal of their present charter.

Resolved, That we object to the renewal of the Bank charter as at present organized for the following reasons. . . .

The powers of the Bank over the circulating medium are dangerous, from its enormous capital, subject to the will of a single Board, and enabling them, for purpose of speculation in stocks and exchange, suddenly to check their own issues and those of the State Banks. . . .

It has unlimited power to locate branches in all the States without the consent or approbation of the same; having already located no less than three branches in one State. . . .

The Branches refuse to receive the notes of other Branches and of the Parent Bank in payment of debts due themselves. . . .

The Bank receives the deposits of the nation, without making any adequate compensation for the many millions constantly standing to the credit of the Government. . . .

Resolved, That there exists no necessity for a bank with such powers at the present, for a bank with less capital and essential modifications would it is believed be acceptable to American stockholders and afford sufficient bank facilities. . . .

J. Downing: "I'm Stump'd"

In 1833, a series of letters appeared in the Daily Advertiser *of New York. The letters were said to be written by Major J. Downing, a close personal friend of Andrew Jackson. The grammar and humor in the letters, however, lead one to believe that instead they use Jackson's "backwoods" roots to poke fun at his decision to veto the Bank of the United States, since the controversy over it did not die in 1832.*

Daily Advertiser **(New York), 23 September 1833**

To Mr. Dwight of the New York Daily Advertiser.

My Good Old Friend—I'm stump'd. I jist got a letter from the Gineral, and until got that letter I thought all the stories about the Bank was jist got up by the opposition folks, to hurt the Gineral and Mr. Van Buren, and Zekel Bigelow thought so too. But the Gineral's letter tells me pretty much all about it, and a leetle more too. As soon as I read it to Zekel, "well," says he,

"Major, my notion is there is some plagy foul birds in Washington, and if some on em haint siled their own nests I'm mistaken."

The Gineral says he wants me to come right on, for tho the folks about him say all works well, he's afraid they'll git him in a tangle—consarn em, I don't know what on earth has got in em and the Gineral too, jist so sure as I quit him he gits in trouble. I must go right back to Washington and try and put things strait if I can but I'm afraid they'll git the Government in a plagy snarl afore I git there. I was a leetle afraid on't when I left, and I telled the Gineral as much, be he said he'd do nothin till I got back. . . .

Zekel Bigelow says "its an ill wind that blows nowhere." and seein that the Government is goin to try to break the Bank, he's goin to turn broker in Wall street, he says there will be no better business stirrin, for then folks will have to pay a trifle for eny most every draft thats drawn. . . .

If I had'nt promised the Gineral to stick to him threw thick and thin, I'd go right home to Downingville and have nothin more to do with the Government; but if I quit him now, the Government will go all to smash, jist as sure as I am in haste and wrath.

Your friend,

J. DOWNING, Major.

Questions

1. What were the arguments for the National Bank?
2. What were the arguments against the bank? Were these valid? Explain.
3. Read the articles by Hezekiah Niles and Thomas Ritchie. What was the basis for the disagreement between these two powerful editors?

Notes

1. For discussions of the Second Bank of America, see John M. McFaul, *The Politics of Jacksonian Finance* (Ithaca: Cornell University Press, 1972); Robert V. Remini, *Andrew Jackson and the Bank War: A Study in the Growth of Presidential Power* (New York: W.W. Norton, 1967); T.P. Govan, *Nicholas Biddle: Nationalist and Public Banker* (Chicago: University of Chicago Press, 1959); Bray Hammond, *Banks and Politics in America from the Revolution to the Civil War* (Princeton: Princeton University Press, 1957); W.B. Smith, *Economic Aspects of the Second Bank of the United States* (Cambridge: Harvard University Press, 1953).

2. George Brown Tindall, *America: A Narrative History*, 2 vols. (New York: W.W. Norton, 1984), 1:370–71.

3. Quoted in Robert V. Remini, *Andrew Jackson and the Course of American Freedom, 1822–1832* (New York: Harper & Row, 1981), 366.

4. "Veto Message, Washington, July 10, 1832," in James D. Richardson, *Compilation of the Messages and Papers of the Presidents,* 20 vols. (Washington, D.C., 1908), 2:1152–54.

5. Calvin Colton, ed., *The Works of Henry Clay,* 10 vols. (New York: G.P. Putnam's Sons, 1904), 7:523–35. This version of Clay's speech may be found at the "Nineteenth Century Documents Project," http://www.furman.edu/~benson/docs/clay.htm.

CHAPTER 12

The Penny Press and the Moral War, 1833

On August 21, 1835, an innocent blurb appeared in the *Sun*, the first of New York's newspapers to sell for a penny an issue. The paragraph stated that "some wonderful discoveries of the most wonderful description" had been detected with a new and powerful telescope. On August 25, the *Sun* printed a longer article, claiming that it came from the *Edinburgh Journal of Science*. More revelations came the next day, including the fact that the discoveries were on the moon and a discussion of vegetation. This meant that the moon could support life. On August 28, the *Sun* disclosed the most amazing information. The scientist, Sir John Herschel, saw winged people flying and then landing on the moon's surface: "They averaged four feet in height, were covered, except on their face, with short and glossy copper-colored hair, and had wings composed of a thin membrane." Some newspapers picked up the *Sun*'s stories and ran them. Others blasted editor Benjamin Day for pulling an elaborate hoax on thousands, with one New York competitor asking, "how any man of common sense should read it without at once perceiving deception."[1] And, they were right. The *Sun*'s fabulous series that revealed life on the moon was the product of the imagination of one of the *Sun*'s writers, Richard Adams Locke.[2]

The *Sun*'s "moon hoax," as the stories have come to be known, is one of the more famous aspects of the newspaper era known as the Penny Press. Benjamin Day's *Sun* was the first of America's penny papers. It appeared September 3, 1833, and it differed greatly from the other New York newspapers. First, it was small in comparison to the staid papers that served the city. Bigger seemed to be better to editors in the late 1820s and early 1830s. The *Journal of Commerce* and the *Courier*, two of New York's best, had pages about two feet by three feet in size. The *Sun*, in contrast, had four pages, each one about eight by ten inches.[3] There was one other striking contrast—cost. The *Sun* cost readers a penny an issue. Newspapers up to that time were rarely sold individually. Usually, one had to have a yearly subscription, but if a paper was sold by individual copy, it cost at least six cents. The penny paper caught on quickly. In fact, in the next five years, at least thirty-four

THE  SUN.

NUMBER 1.] NEW YORK, TUESDAY, SEPTEMBER 3, 1833. [PRICE ONE PENNY

PUBLISHED DAILY,

AT 222 WILLIAM ST .... BENJ. H. DAY, PRINTER.

The object of this paper is to lay before the public, at a price within the means of every one, ALL THE NEWS OF THE DAY, and at the same time afford an advantageous medium for advertising. The sheet will be enlarged as soon as the increase of advertisements requires it—the price remaining the same.

Yearly advertisers, (without the paper,) Thirty Dollars per annum—Casual advertising, at the usual prices charged by the city papers.

☞ Subscriptions will be received, if paid in advance, at the rate of three dollars per annum.

FOR ALBANY—PASSAGE ONLY $1.

The large and commodious steamboat COMMERCE, Capt R. H. Fitch, will leave the foot of Courtlandt street on Friday, at five o'clock, P. M. for Albany stopping at the usual landing places to land and receive passengers. Passage $1. For particulars apply to the Captain on board.

REGULAR DAYS.

From New York, Mondays, Wednesdays, Fridays.
From Albany, Tuesdays, Thursdays, Saturdays. a29

FOR NEWPORT AND PROVIDENCE.

The splendid steamboat BENJAMIN FRANKLIN, Capt. E. S. Bunker, and the PRESIDENT, Capt. R. S. Bunker, will leave New York at 5 o'clock, P. M. and Providence at 12 o'clock, M. every Monday, Wednesday and Friday. For further information apply to the Captain on board foot of Courtlandt-st. or at the office, 11 Broad st. s2

FOR HARTFORD—PASSAGE 1 DOLLAR.

THROUGH BY DAYLIGHT.

The splendid low-pressure steamboat WATER WITCH, Capt. Vanderbilt, leaves the foot of Catherine street every Tuesday, Thursday, and Saturday mornings, at 6 o'clock, and arrives in Hartford at 7 o'clock the same evening. Passage One Dollar—meals extra.

The above boat leaves Hartford on Mondays, Wednesdays, and Fridays, at the same hours. s2 tf

FOR LONDON—To sail 10th of Sept.—The new packet ship Montreal, Champlin, Master, will sail on the 10th inst. For freight or passage, having elegant accommodations, apply to the Captain, on board, Pine-st. wharf, or to
s2 JOHN GRISWOLD, Agent, 68 South st.

FOR LIVERPOOL.—The fast-sailing ship Tallahasse, S. Glover, Master, will be ready to receive cargo in a few days, and have despatch. She has excellent accommodations for both cabin and steerage passengers. For freight or passage, apply to
s2 WOOD & TRIMBLE, 157 Maiden-lane.

FOR HAVRE.—The Packet ship Formosa, Orne, master, will sail on the 8th Sept. For freight or passage apply to the captain on board, or to
WM. WHITLOCK, Jr. 46 South st. s2

FOR LIVERPOOL.—Packet of the 8 Sept.—The packet ship Roscoe, J. C. Delano, master, is now in readiness to receive cargo. For freight or passage apply to the captain on board, foot of Maiden lane, or to
s2t10 FISH, GRINNELL & CO. 134 Front st.

FOR KINGSTON, JAM.—Packet 10th Sept. The elegant coppered ship Orbit will sail as above. For freight or passage, having splendid accommodations, with state rooms, apply to
s2 D. AYMAR & Co. 34 South st.

FOR NEW ORLEANS.—Packet of the 8th September, the very fast-sailing coppered ship, Nashville, Capt. Rathbone, will sail as above.—For freight or passage, having handsome accommodations, apply to E. K. COLLINS, 68 South st.

N. B. A lighter is in readiness to receive cargo at Pine street wharf. s2

FOR NEW ORLEANS—Packet of Sept. 15. The ship Tennessee, Capt. Sears, will sail as above. For freight or passage, having handsome accommodations, apply to
SILAS HOLMES & CO. 62 South st.
A lighter is in readiness to receive cargo. s2

AN IRISH CAPTAIN.

"There are as sweet a pair of pistols as any in the three kingdoms," said an officer, showing a pair to a young student of his acquaintance, "and have done execution before now; at the slightest touch, off they go, as sweet as honey, without either recoiling or dipping. I never travel without them."

"I never heard of highwaymen in this part of the country."

"Nor I," replied the officer, "and if I had I should not trouble myself to carry the pistols on their account—Highwaymen are a species of sharks who are not fond of attacking us lobsters; they know we are a little too hard to crack. No, my dear sir, highwaymen know that soldiers have not much money, and what they have they fight for."

"Since that is the case, how come you to travel always with pistols?"

"Because," answered the officer, "I find them very useful in accommodating any little difference I may accidentally have with a friend, or which one friend may chance to have with another."

"Do you often settle differences in that way?"

"Why, I was twice out before I arrived at your age.—The first time was with a relation of my own, who said he would see my courage tried before he would contribute with the others towards the purchase of my first commission; so I sent him word that I would be happy to give him one proof the very next morning, and when we met, I touched him so smartly in the leg, that he has halted ever since. But all his doubts being now removed, he cheerfully contributed his quota with the rest of my relations, and we have been very good friends ever since."

"Pray what gave you occasion for the second?" said the young student.

"How it began originally is more than I can tell," answered the captain; all I know is, that a large company of us dined together, we sat long, and drank deep, and I went to bed rather in a state of forgetfulness, and was awaked in the morning from a profound sleep, by a gentleman who began a long story, how I had said something that required explanation; and also, that I had accidentally given him a blow, but he supposed I had no intention to affront him, and so he continued talking in a roundabout kind of way, without coming to any point. So I was under the necessity of interrupting him, "upon my conscience, Sir, (said I,) I am unable to declare, with certainty, whether I had any intention of affronting you or not, because my head is still a little confused, and I have no clear recollection of what passed, nor do I fully comprehend your drift at present, but I conjecture that you wish to have satisfaction; if so, I must beg you will be kind enough to say so at once, and I shall be at your service." Finding himself thus cut short, he named the place and the hour. I met him precisely at the time. His first pistol missed fire, but I hit him in the shoulder. At his second shot, the bullet passed pretty near me, but mine lodged in his hip, and then he declared he was quite satisfied. So as I had given a blow the preceding night, and two wounds that morning, upon declaring himself satisfied, I said I was contented."

"You would have been thought very hard to please, if you had made any difficulty."

"I thought so myself," rejoined the captain, "and so the affair ended, he being carried home in a coach, and I marching from the field of battle on foot."

"Pray, may I ask if you ever was in a battle?"

"No," replied the captain with a sigh, "I never was; I never had that good fortune, though I would give all the money I have in the world, and all the money I am owing, which is at least treble the sum, to be in one to-morrow."

"Provided you had a good cause," replied the young student.

"I should not be squeamish respecting the cause, provided I had a good battle: that, my dear, is what is the most essential to a conscientious officer, who wishes to improve himself in his profession. I have much reason, therefore, to wish for a war; and at the present juncture, it would be much to the advantage of the nation in general, as it is dwindling into a country of ploughmen, manufacturers, and merchants. And you must know, too, that I am pretty fortunate, having already stood thirteen shots, and I never was hit but once."

"Thirteen! what, have you fought thirteen duels?"

"No, no!" replied the captain, "the last shot fired at me completed only my sixth duel."

Wonders of Littleness.—Pliny and Elian relate that Myrmecides wrought out of ivory a chariot, with four wheels and four horses, and a ship with all her tackling, both in so small a compass, that a bee could hide either with its wings. Nor should we doubt this, when we find it recorded in English history, on less questionable authority, that in the twentieth year of Queen Elizabeth's reign a blacksmith of London, of the name of Mark Scaliot, made a lock of iron, steel, and brass, of eleven pieces, and a pipe key, all of which only weighed one grain. Scaliot also made a chain of gold, of forty-three links, which he fastened to the lock and key, and put it round the neck of a flea, which drew the whole with perfect ease. The chain, key, lock, and flea, altogether weighed but one grain and a half!

Hadrianus Junis saw at Mechlin in Brabant, a cherry-stone cut into the form of a basket; in it were fourteen pair of dice distinct, the spots and numbers of which were easily to be discerned with a good eye.

But still more extraordinary than this basket of dice, or any thing we have yet mentioned, must have been a set of turnery shown at Rome, in the time of Pope Paul the Fifth, by one Shad of Mitelbrach, who had purchased it from the artist Oswaldus Norhingerus. It consisted of sixteen hundred dishes, which were all perfect and complete in every part, yet so small and slender that the whole could be easily enclosed in a case fabricated in a peppercorn of the ordinary size! The Pope is said to have himself counted them, but with the help of a pair of spectacles, for they were so very small as to be almost invisible to the naked eye. Although his holiness thus satisfied his own eyes of the fact, he did not, we are assured, require of those about him to subscribe to it on the credit of his infallibility; for he gave every one an opportunity of examining and judging for himself, and among the persons thus highly favored, particular reference is made to Gasper Schioppius, Johannes Faber, a physician of Rome.

Turrianus, of whose skill so many wonderful things are related, is said to have fabricated iron mills, which moved of themselves, so minute in size, that a monk could carry one in his sleeve; and yet it was powerful enough to grind in a single day, grain enough for the consumption of eight men.

A Whistler.—A boy in Vermont, accustomed to working alone, was so prone to whistling, that, as soon as he was by himself, he unconsciously commenced. When asleep, the muscles of his mouth, chest, and lungs were so completely concatenated in the association, he whistled with astonishing shrillness. A pale countenance, loss of appetite, and almost total prostration of strength, convinced his mother it would end in death, if not speedily overcome; which was accomplished by placing him in the society of another boy, who had orders to give him a blow as soon as he began to whistle.

The Penny Press. *On September 3, 1833, Benjamin Day released the first issue of the* Sun, *price: one cent. Day and his newspaper started a newspaper revolution in New York and other large cities. The established press, which charged six cents per issue and only sold its papers by subscription, now had to compete with papers that all could afford and that were hawked on street corners. The penny papers were more sensational in their content. The extensive coverage of the murder of a prostitute named Ellen Jewett is a good example.*

Moon Hoax. *In 1835, the* Sun*—New York's first penny paper—ran a series of stories on an amazing discovery—life on the moon. The* Sun *described "man-bat" families. This is the image that many Americans saw, depicting what a scientist with a new and powerful telescope had seen. The "Moon Hoax," as the series came to be known, was the work of the imagination of Richard Adams Locke. One of Locke's contemporaries, Edgar Allan Poe, claimed that he had given Adams the inspiration for the hoax series in a story Poe had published in the* Southern Literary Messenger *titled "The Unparalleled Adventures of One Hans Pfall." Few believed Poe's claim, however, and many "claimed" they were not fooled by the* Sun*'s series.*

daily newspapers were started in New York City alone, capitalizing on the success of Day's newspaper.[4]

The idea for inexpensive newspapers did not originate with Day. Some British printers published one-cent papers within the first decade of the eighteenth century, and they continued producing them until tax laws made it impossible in the 1740s.[5] In America, Philadelphia printer William Cobbett published a paper costing two cents in 1816 in an effort to get around a tax placed on folded newspaper, and Christopher Conwell printed a paper called the *Cent* in Philadelphia in 1830, naming his paper after its cost.[6] The first American effort at producing a cheap newspaper, however, may have been the effort of Benjamin Mecom, nephew of Benjamin Franklin, who printed, irregularly, a paper called the *Penny Post* in Philadelphia in 1769.[7] Dr. H.D. Sheppard tried it, too, with the *New York Morning Post.* The *Post,* which went on sale on January 1, 1833, attempted to break with traditional newspaper sales practices. Most papers were sold only by subscription. Sales of individual issues rarely occurred, but Sheppard—who published medical tracts—thought papers hawked on the streets by newsboys at a cheap price could reach an eager public. Sheppard's paper initially sold for two cents, and he then dropped the price to a penny. A massive snow storm on the first day of publication coupled with poor editing by Sheppard killed the *Post* and opened the way for the *Sun*.[8]

Though the *Sun* was America's first successful penny paper, it was not the one that made the Penny Press notorious to many. James Gordon Bennett and the New York *Herald* did that. Bennett began his paper in 1835, and the next year set the nation on its ear with his reporting of the murder of Ellen Jewett, a prostitute. Bennett's description of her murder contained fact mingled with conjecture. "He then drew from beneath his cloak the hatchet," Bennett explained, "and inflicted upon her head three blows, either of which must have proved fatal, as the bone was cleft to the extent of three inches in each place." Two days later, after his story of April 11 drew criticism, Bennett claimed, "The courts of law have not alone a right to investigate this crime—this red-blooded atrocity. The whole community have an interest." Not only did he describe the murder, but he told readers about Jewett's body, covered with a sheet. "The perfect figure—the exquisite limbs—the fine face—the full arms—the beautiful bust," were a part of Bennett's article.[9] Many newspapers ran Bennett's stories of Jewett's murder and the subsequent trial, and the other penny papers covered the events, too. Richard Robinson, a dry-goods clerk, was acquitted of the murder.[10]

The financial success of the *Herald* spurred Bennett on. He continued with his exaggerated stories and pompous comments, and he explained his story style this way: "There is a moral—a principle—a little salt in every event of life—why not extract it and present it to the public in a new and elegant dress?"[11] Even the penny editors began to hate Bennett. In 1840, Park Benjamin and James Watson Webb, two Wall-Street editors, spearheaded an attack on Bennett and the *Herald*. Known as the moral war, the six-penny editors and some penny editors claimed Bennett's "immoral" stories were hurting society. In many ways, Bennett provoked what happened. "My great purpose is to upset—reform—knock up—and revolutionize the impudent, blustering, corrupt, immoral Wall street press," he said.[12] Bennett's attackers argued that decent people should not read the *Herald*. They asked that advertisers stop advertising in the paper and that subscribers stop their subscriptions. The moral war, or "the War of the Holy Alliance" as Bennett called it, cost him more than 9,000 subscriptions to his daily and weekly papers from 1840 to 1842.[13] The war ended before the end of 1840, but bad feelings about Bennett by many editors and Americans continued well after his death in 1872. Others, it should be pointed out, greatly admired the *Her-*

ald's editor, and following the moral war he initiated changes in the paper that made it more respectable.

This chapter looks at the reaction to the rise of the Penny Press. Its first section includes articles that support it. The first, appropriately, comes from James Gordon Bennett and his proposal for a penny paper—the *Globe*—that failed in 1832. It is followed by Benjamin Day's prospectus for the *Sun* and Bennett's for the *Herald.* Praise for the penny papers from a Wall- Street editor, Gerald Hallock, is next. Hallock's paper was one of those that attacked Bennett in 1840, however. The last two readings in this section come from Bennett.

The second section of the chapter presents attacks on the Penny Press's morals and ethics. As a result, most of the entries are aimed at James Gordon Bennett or the controversies he caused, particularly reporting in the Ellen Jewett case. The first two entries discuss the morals of papers. The second is particularly interesting because it comes from a penny paper targeted to a female audience. The next selection praises a public beating of Bennett and is followed by the first attack on Bennett during the moral war. The last two entries come from later papers. The first is Henry Raymond's prospectus for the *New-York Daily Times.* It offers a paper, according to the announcement, that varies from Bennett's version of the press. The last is an 1860 article that shows how long the dislike of Bennett lasted.

Support for the Penny Press

James Gordon Bennett: "To the Public"

Although James Gordon Bennett would later become the epitome of the Penny Press publisher with the New York Herald, *he proposed a paper with the characteristics of a penny paper in 1832, specifically a small, easy-to-manage size that was in direct contrast to the large, unhandy blanket sheets. The* Globe *failed, but the prospectus may well have set the stage for Benjamin Day's* Sun, *even though its cost—$8 per year—was much more than the annual cost of penny sheets.*

Globe (New York), 29 October 1832

I publish this evening, at No. 20 William Street, the first number of a new daily journal called the *New York Globe,* price eight dollars a year. Early arrangements will be made to issue a weekly and a semi-weekly paper from the same office. . . .

A word on the size of my paper. *For years past the public has been cloyed with immense sheets—bunglingly made up—without concert of action or individu-*

ality of character—the reservoirs of crude thoughts from different persons who were continually knocking their heads against each other, without knocking any thing remarkably good out of them. I have avoided this inconvenience. . . .

I am now embarking on my own account—on my own responsibility. . . . With these remarks I commit my bark to the breeze.

JAMES GORDON BENNETT

Benjamin Day: "Published Daily"

Benjamin Day came to the conclusion after the failed attempts by Dr. H.D. Sheppard with his penny paper, the Morning Post, *that New York City was ready for a penny paper. The penny paper would be possible, Day thought, because new printing practices meant thousands of papers could be printed quickly and cheaply. He also felt that a small-sized paper—not one of the blanket sheets that might measure three-feet wide or more—would be more acceptable to the general public and also more profitable. Day's* Sun *measured about the size of a book, 71/2 inches by 10 inches, and contained Day's rationale at the top of the left-hand column of its first issue.*

***Sun* (New York), 3 September 1833**

The object of this paper is to lay before the public, at a price within the means of every one, all the news of the day, and at the same time afford an advantageous medium for advertising. The sheet will be enlarged as soon as the increase of advertisements requires it, the price remaining the same.

Yearly advertisers (without the paper), Thirty Dollars per annum. Casual advertising at the usual prices charged by the city papers.

Subscriptions will be received, if paid in advance, at the rate of three dollars per annum.

James Gordon Bennett: "The Herald and the Great Role of a Newspaper"

James Gordon Bennett never thought small. He expected great things from his newspaper and became a millionaire in the process. The following is the prospectus for the Herald, *which lays out what Bennett expected to do with his newspaper.*

***Herald* (New York), 6 May 1835**

James Gordon Bennett & Co. commence this morning the publication of the MORNING HERALD, a new daily paper, price $3 per year, or six cents per week. . . .

We have had an experience of nearly fifteen years in conducting newspapers. On that score we can not surely fail in knowing at least how to build up a reputation and establishment of our own. In *débuts* of this kind many talk of principles—political principle—party principle, as a sort of steel-trap to catch the public. We want to be perfectly understood on this point, and therefore opening disclaim all steel-traps, all principle, as it is called—all party—all politics. Our only guide shall be good, sound, practical common sense, applicable to the business and bosoms of men engaged in every-day life. We shall support no party—be the organ of no faction or *coterie*, and care nothing for any election or any candidate from President down to a Constable.

We shall endeavor to record facts on every public and proper subject, stripped of verbiage and coloring, with comments when suitable, just, independent, fearless, and good-tempered. If the *Herald* wants the mere expansion which many journals possess, we shall try to make it up in industry, good taste, brevity, variety, point, piquancy, and cheapness. . . .

I mean to make the *Herald* the great organ of social life, the prime element of civilization, the channel through which native talent, native genius, and native power may bubble up daily, as the pure sparkling liquid of the Congress fountain at Saratoga bubbles up from the centre of the earth, till it meets the rosy lips of the fair. I shall mix together commerce and business, pure religion and morals, literature and poetry, the drama and dramatic purity, till the *Herald* shall outstrip everything in the conception of man. The age of trashy novels, of more trashy poems, of most trashy quarterly and weekly literature, is rapidly drawing to a close.

This is the age of the Daily Press, inspired with the accumulated wisdom of past ages, enriched with the spoils of history, and looking forward to a millennium of a thousand years, the happiest and most splendid ever yet known in the measured span of eternity!

Gerald Hallock: "Penny Papers"

Gerald Hallock was not a Penny Press editor. His newspaper, the Journal of Commerce, *served the economic interests of New York City. While many editors of the blanket newspapers attacked penny papers, Hallock defended them and challenged blanket editors to be more like penny editors by showing less political partisanship. By 1840, however, the* Journal of Commerce *and many other "Wall Street papers" would attack James Gordon Bennett's brand of penny reporting in the moral war.*

***Journal of Commerce* (New York), 29 June 1835**

It is but three or four years since the first Penny Paper was established. Now there are half a dozen or more of them in this city, with an aggregate circulation of twenty or thirty thousand, and perhaps more. These issues exceed those of the large papers, and, for aught we see, they are conducted with as much talent and *in point of moral character we think candidly they are superior to their six-penny contemporaries.* By observing the course of these papers, we have been led to regard them as quite an accession to the moral and intellectual machinery among us. The number of newspaper readers is probably doubled by their influence, and they circulate as pioneers among those classes who have suffered greatly from want of general intelligence. Let all classes of the community but read, and they will thin, and almost, of course, will become less entirely the dupes of designing individuals. There is hardly any thing which his Holiness of Rome has more reason to be afraid of than the Penny Papers. Those who have read them will, as a natural consequence, come more or less to the commission of the execrable offense of forming opinions for themselves. But for the subserviency which, from the nature of their circulation, they are compelled to exercise towards Trade Unions and such like humbug affairs, we see not why the effect of the little papers should not be almost wholly good. They are less partisan in politics than the large papers, and more decidedly American, with one or two exceptions. The manner in which their pecuniary affairs are conducted shows how much may come of small details. They are circulated on the London plan, the editors, and publishers doing no more than to complete the manufacture of the papers, when they are sold to the newsmen or carriers for 67 cents per 100. The carriers distribute the papers, and on Saturday collect form each subscriber six cents, so that for each call their net income to the carriers is but one third of a cent. We wish our penny associates all success, hoping that they will grow wise, good, and great, until they make every six penny paper ashamed that tells a lie, or betrays its country for the sake of party, or does any other base thing.

James Gordon Bennett: "The *Herald*"

Bennett's brash reporting style quickly made the Herald *the most widely read New York newspaper. Though many complained about his sensational news coverage, most papers ran his coverage of the Ellen Jewett murder. In this editorial, Bennett brags that his paper covers the news better than any other.*

Herald **(New York), 16 August 1836**

The Herald alone knows how to dish up the foreign news—or indeed domestic events, in a readable style. Every reader—*numbering between thirty and forty thousand daily*—acknowledge this merit in the management of our paper. We do not, as the Wall-street lazy editors do, come down to our office about ten or twelve o'clock–pull out a Spanish segar–take up a scissors–puff and cut–cut and puff for a couple of hours–and then adjourn to Delmonico's to eat, drink, gormandize and blow up our cotemporaries. We rise in the morning at five o'clock–write our leading editorials, squibs, sketches &c., before breakfast. From nine till one we read all our papers, and the original communications, the latter being more numerous than those of any other office in New York. From these we pick out facts, thoughts, hints and incidents, sufficient to make up a column of original spicy articles. We also give audience to visitors–gentlemen on business–and some of the loveliest ladies in New York, who call to subscribe–God bless them. At one, we sally out among the gentlemen and loafers of Wall-street–find out the state of the money market–return, finish the next day's paper–close every piece of business requiring thought, sentiment, feeling or philosophy, before four o'clock. We dine moderately and temperately–thank God for his mercies–read our proofs–take in cash and advertisements, which are increasing like smoke–and close the day by going to bed always at ten o'clock, seldom later.

That's the way to conduct a paper with spirit and success.

James Gordon Bennett: "Price Increase"

The success of the Herald *following the Jewett stories led Bennett to increase the price of his paper. This made a number of competitors mad, but the announcement was typical of Bennett, who equated himself to Napoleon in this notice and, no doubt, angered many when he said his paper could send more to heaven than the church.*

Herald **(New York), 19 August 1836**

After the usual quantity of reflection which I give any thing, I have come to the determination to advance the price of the Herald to TWO CENTS PER COPY to every subscriber and purchaser in the city or country. With my usual rapidity of thought and action, the new arrangement goes into effect TO DAY. There are Napoleons of the press, as well as of the camp. . . . I want to be rich–I shall be rich. . . .

I am determined to make the Herald the greatest paper that ever appeared in the world. The highest order of mind has never yet been found operating through the daily press. Let it be tried. What is to prevent a daily newspaper from being made the greatest organ of social life? Books have had their day–the theatres have had their day–the temple of religion has had its day. A newspaper can be made to take the lead of all these in great movements of human thought, and of human civilization. A newspaper can send more souls to Heaven, and save more from Hell, than all the churches or chapels in New York—besides making money at the same time. Let it be tried.

Opposition to Penny Press Tactics

William M. Swain: "Venal and Corrupt"

William M. Swain edited a penny paper in Philadelphia, but that does not mean he approved of all that the penny sheets printed, even his own. Shortly after James Gordon Bennett began running stories of the murder of prostitute Ellen Jewett, Swain penned the following lines. His own paper would publish the controversial accounts of Jewett's murder in June.

Public Ledger (Philadelphia), 20 April 1836

The press in our country is venal and corrupt beyond that of any other free country. It is immeasurably behind that of France in dignity, candor, truth, knowledge, deep investigation and bold averment; indeed inferior in every thing which a free press ought to be. It is far behind that of England in bold and fearless exposition of error, defence of right and denunciation of wrong. Why is this? Because in neither country does the press condescend to flatter prejudices; because in each, the editor dares to teach and scorns to follow. But in our own country, most editors are seekers of patronage, and governed by the corrupt, and corrupting principle that *they must cater for the public taste*, and too large a portion of the public, unwilling to endure disagreeable truth, address corrupting appeals to the pecuniary interests of the editors.

William Newell: "Subverse to Any Valuable Moral Purpose"

In 1836, William Newell attempted to found a new penny paper, one aimed specifically at a female audience. Increasingly, women were playing a larger role in society, as witnessed by the number of benevolent societies they operated or participated in—temperance and abolition being but two examples. Newell hoped that he could target women with a cheap paper and, at the same time, clean up the content of the pennies. Newell's editorial is a reaction to the Jewett murder series.

Ladies' Morning Star (New York), 23 April 1836

The *manner* in which many of the daily occurrences of the police department have been communicated to the public, is not in keeping with our opinions of propriety, or calculated to subserve any valuable moral purpose. That some portions of the police reports, as given in the penny journals, are useful to citizens, we do not pretend to deny, as they contribute to guard the unsuspecting against the arts of the vicious, to promote vigilance in the unwary, and to expose to deserved opprobrium the incorrigibly wicked. Thus far we commend them. But to chronicle every story of the vices, associated with the names of those miserable and degraded beings, who are lost to all senses of femenine [*sic*]modesty and virtue, is apparently a work of supererogation, and ought better be witheld [*sic*]; as the disgusting details of infamy can never convert the wretched victims of vice into virtuous women, and is calculated to shock the delicacy of the virtuous, to plant the burning blush of shame on the cheek of the "pure in heart," and to prostrate the honourable feelings of the chaste of *one sex*, by an exposure of the frailties of its unworthy members, by means of the corrupt devices and unworthy arts of *the other*.

Benjamin Day: "Beat"

James Watson Webb of the New York Courier *and* Enquirer *threatened Bennett in January 1836. In May, he assaulted him. Day greatly appreciated the attack.*

Sun **(New York), 10 May 1836**

Upon calculating the number of public floggings which that miserable scribbler, Bennett, has received, we have pretty accurately ascertained that there is not a square inch of his body which has not been lacerated somewhere about fifteen times. In fact, he has become a common flogging property; and Webb announced his intention to cowskin him every Monday morning until the Fourth of July, when he will offer him a holiday. We understand that Webb has offered to remit the flogging upon the condition that he will allow him to shoot him; but Bennett says:

"No; skin for skin, behold, all that a man hath will he give for his life!"

Park Benjamin: "Utter Scoundrelism"

Park Benjamin may be better known as a poet, but he edited the Evening Signal *and the* New World, *the latter carrying extensive literary works. Benjamin, however, detested James Gordon Bennett, and the comments below were the first shots fired in the moral war. The Phillips mentioned at the beginning of this article was James P. Phillips, and he and Bennett were carrying on a public discussion concerning the authorship of a play.*[14] *Benjamin used the argument as an opportunity to attack "the conductor of the* Herald."

Evening Signal (New York), 27 May 1840

The case mentioned by Mr. Phillips is but one of the innumberable instances of the utter scoundrelism of the fellow known as the conductor of the Herald. We hope, for the character of our population, that it is indeed true that the daily lies and libels coined by this venal wretch neither "affect" nor "injure" those against whom they are directed.

His daily habits of blasphemy, obscenity and falsehood–his shocking displays of contempt for the most sacred mysteries of religion–the levity and profane familiarity of all his allusions to the Deity, of whom he never speaks save with an assumed air of patronage, more repulsive to the feelings of the devout than the ravings of the most daring infidel–his personal lampoons upon private and public men–and his libels upon the country and its institutions–all these, exhibited, day after day and year after year in a widely circulated newspaper cannot but exercise a most deleterious influence upon the community and imperceptibly blunt its moral sense.

His paper is held up as false to honor and to principle. He is "an habitual liar" and an "active utterer of obscenities." He is a "notorious scoffer, liar and poltroon, scourged, kicked, cuffed, tweaked by the nose, trodden on and spit upon in the open street, times without number."

Henry Raymond: "The *Times* Will Speak for Itself"

Although Henry Raymond started the New-York Daily Times *nearly two decades after the first penny paper appeared, the principal penny editors–James Gordon Bennett and Horace Greeley–were still the most powerful American editors. Raymond promised a newspaper that covered "all the news fit to print," and the final line of his prospectus is directed toward Bennett, Greeley, and other penny editors.*

New-York Daily Times, 18 September 1851

We publish to-day the first number of the NEW-YORK DAILY TIMES, and we intend to issue it every morning, (Sundays excepted) for an indefinite number of years to come.

We have not entered upon the task of establishing a new daily paper in this city, without due consideration of its difficulties as well as its encouragements. We understand perfectly, that great capital, great industry, great patience are indispensable to its success, and that even with all these, failure is not impossible. But we know also, that within the last five years the reading population of this city has nearly doubled, while the number of daily newspapers is no greater now than it was then;–that many of those now published are really *class* journals, made up for particular classes of readers;—that others are objectionable upon grounds of morality;—and that no newspaper, which was really *fit* to live, ever yet expired for lack of readers.

As a *Newspaper*, presenting all the news of the day from all parts of the world, we intend to make THE TIMES as good as the best of those now issued in the City of New-York;—and in all the higher utilities of the Press—as a public instructor in all departments of action and of thought, we hope to make it decidedly superior to existing journals of the same class. . . .

Upon all topics,—Political, Social, Moral and Religious,—we intend that the paper shall speak for itself;—and we only ask that it may be judged accordingly. We shall be *Conservative*, in all cases where we think Conservatism essential to the public good;—and we shall be *Radical*, in everything which may seem to us to require radical treatment and radical reform. We do not believe that *everything* in Society is either exactly right, or exactly wrong;—what is good we desire to preserve and improve;—what is evil, to exterminate, or reform. . . .

We do not mean to write as if we were in a passion,—unless that shall really be the case; and we shall make it a point to get into a passion as rarely as possible.

An Anonymous Report: "A Curse from Providence"

In December 1860, the United States was on the verge of civil war. South Carolina would secede from the Union in one week, but many still considered James Gordon Bennett the bane of America. From the stories about the murder of the prostitute Ellen Jewett, to the gaudy announcement of his engagement, through the moral war, the dislike for Bennett continued for decades, as witnessed by this story in the Morning Herald and Daily Gazette.

Utica (N. Y.) Morning Herald and Daily Gazette, 14 December 1860

We suppose that even the greatest apparent curses have their latent uses in the great plan of Providence. It may puzzle human wisdom to understand how partial evil results in universal good; but we must accept the axiom or impeach the Great Architect himself. We must assume that in some mysterious manner or other, plagues and pestilences, earthquakes and volcanic upheavings, venomous reptiles and devastating tempests, fleas and the diphtheria, ophthalmia and the toothache, droughts and fever-breeding miasma, hydrophobia and Upas trees, wars and famine, floods and railroad slaughters;—are but so many cogs and wheels—so many springs and shafts—in the mechanism of creation. On this theory, we charitably suppose that in the great economy of Nature, even the New York *Herald* has its "hidden uses." JAMES GORDON BENNETT was doubtless created for some wise purpose. Whether it was to *illustrate* the doctrine of total depravity, to show what Nature could do in the line of getting up a mean man, or by way of reminder to his fellow-beings of how near the human could approach the diabolic without entirely losing physical similitude to the former, will naturally remain a moot point. Perhaps, indeed, he was intended to serve as a terrible warning to those deluded mortals who cultivate the brain at the expense of the heart, and believe that wealth and position can confer respect upon a ruffian and blackguard. An editorial ISHMAEL, his hand raised against every man, and every man's hand raised against him; a social and intellectual pariah, whom society has cast from its bosom with loathing: a creature without heart and apparently without human affections; an outlaw, from whom honest men instinctively recoil; a craven, cowardly ruffian, whom the discipline of a dozen horsewhippings has failed to chasten into decency;—his name has long been a synonym for all that was venal, cowardly and abject. Grown rich by iniquitous labor, and aping respectability in his outward demeanor, he carries into old age all the vileness and venom of youth. . . .

Questions

1. What were James Gordon Bennett's claims about himself and his paper? What reasons might be given to explain why so many disliked him?
2. According to Gerald Hallock, what positive things did the Penny Press do for newspapers in general?
3. What were the problems associated with the blanket or Wall-Street papers, according to the penny-paper editors?

Notes

1. *Commercial Advertiser* (New York), 29 August 1835.

2. The story of the "moon hoax" may be found in Frank M. O'Brien, *The Story of The Sun* (New York: D. Appleton, 1928). It is explained as a form of literature, circulation booster, and business tactic in Ulf Jonas Bjork, "'Sweet is the Tale': A Context for the *New York Sun*'s Moon Hoax," *American Journalism* 18 (2001):13–27.

3. Frederic Hudson, *Journalism in the United States, from 1690 to 1872* (1873; reprint, New York: Harper & Row, 1969), 408.

4. Frank Luther Mott, *American Journalism, A History: 1690–1960,* 3rd ed. (New York: Macmillan, 1962), 219–20, 228.

5. For information on British penny papers, see Michael Harris, *London Newspapers in the Age of Walpole, A Study of the Origins of the Modern English Press* (London: Associated University Presses, 1987).

6. Michael Buchholz, "The Penny Press, 1833–1861," in *The Media in America,* ed. Wm. David Sloan, 5th ed. (Northport, Ala.: Vision Press, 2002), 126; Mott, *American Journalism,* 239.

7. Isaiah Thomas, *The History of Printing in America* (1810; reprint, New York: Weathervane Books, 1970), 449.

8. Mott, *American Journalism,* 219–20.

9. *Herald* (New York), 11 and 13 April 1836.

10. For more details on Ellen Jewett's murder and Richard Robinson's trial, see Andie Tucher, *Froth & Scum: Truth, Beauty, Goodness, and the Ax Murder in America's First Mass Medium* (Chapel Hill: University of North Carolina Press, 1994).

11. *Herald* (New York), 31 August 1835.

12. *Herald* (New York), 12 August 1836.

13. Circulation figures in the *Herald* (New York), 30 May 1840, 16 December 1851; cited in Willard Grosvenor Bleyer, *Main Currents in the History of American Journalism* (Boston: Houghton Mifflin, 1927), 194.

14. Merle M. Hoover, *Park Benjamin: Poet & Editor* (New York: Columbia University Press, 1948), 105. This selection, "Utter Scoundrelism," is taken from this book.

CHAPTER 13

The Alamo and Texas Annexation, 1836

In 1830, Mexico had a problem. Part of its territory–Texas–had more Americans living in it than Mexicans, and nothing appeared to be slowing the tide of American emigration. Mexico's National Colonization Law of 1825, which offered land to emigrants had attracted thousands of Americans from Southern states. Nearly 20,000 had settled there by 1830, with at least another 10,000 arriving in the next five years. The rich soil of East Texas was perfect for growing cotton, which also meant that the Americans brought slaves with them to work this highly labor-intensive crop. Mexico wanted to slow American emigration and passed laws to inhibit immigration, but Mexico never seriously enforced those laws. In addition, Mexico outlawed slavery. Nothing seemed to stop the flood of Americans, however, who outnumbered Mexicans 10 to 1 in Texas by 1835.[1]

Texas was part of the Mexican state Coahuila, and in 1833 the Americans living in the Texas portion of the state asked the Mexican government to make Texas a state independent from Coahuila. Stephen F. Austin, whose father Moses initiated American emigration to Texas shortly after Mexico gained independence from Spain in 1821, traveled to Mexico City with the request. That petition was denied, and the next year General Antonio Lopez de Santa Anna declared himself dictator of Mexico, abolishing its Congress and all state legislatures. Because most of the inhabitants of the Coahuila–Texas region were Americans, they called upon the example of their old home and revolted. Delegates on March 2, 1836, declared for Texans "*that our political connexion with the Mexican nation has forever ended, and that the people of Texas, do now constitute a* FREE SOVREIGN [*sic*], *and Independent Republic.*"[2] Appropriately, the delegates titled their document the Declaration of Independence. The move incensed Santa Anna, and the general himself led troops to punish the Texans.

More than 4,000 Mexican troops marched into Texas, and on March 6, they surrounded the mission in San Antonio–called the Alamo. Promising no quarter to those inside, the Mexicans attacked the mission all night.

NILES' WEEKLY REGISTER.

BALTIMORE, MARCH 19, 1836.

Niles' Weekly Register. *Hezekiah Niles started the* Weekly Register *in 1811. Part newspaper, part magazine, Niles's publication offered Americans a comprehensive understanding of the issues the nation faced. Though Niles wrote editorials supporting certain policies and politicians, he still ran opposing viewpoints in his periodical. This one, from 1836, contained extensive coverage of the Texas war of independence and the Battle of the Alamo.*

When the fighting ended, 187 people inside the Alamo were dead, including former Tennessee Congressman David Crockett and other notable Americans who had left the United States to help Texas when troubles began in 1835. Only one woman and a slave survived the attack on the Alamo. News of the massacre spread quickly after it appeared in the *Telegraph and Texas Register* on March 17, and Texans prepared to strike back. Led by Sam Houston, Texans, joined by large numbers of volunteers from America, regrouped and attacked Santa Anna's army on April 21, shouting, "Remember the Alamo" as they charged. The unsuspecting Mexican soldiers were quickly defeated, and Santa Anna was taken prisoner.

Most Texans expected that their new republic would not remain an independent nation for long. Even though they made Houston the nation's president, they expected Texas would soon be a state, especially since Houston and President Andrew Jackson were close friends. Friendship, however, could not convince many Americans that Texas needed to be part of the Union. Many feared a war between Mexico and the United States. Others looked at the massive amount of territory in Texas, the fact that 90 percent of Texans were from Southern states, and that its constitution made it illegal for the government to interfere in any way with slavery, and they concluded the worst thing that could happen to the United States was the addition of Texas. Indignant at the United States' response, Texas began life as the Republic of Texas, opening trade and diplomatic relations with European countries. All the while, Mexico refused to accept Texas as an independent nation, but it did not move to force Texas to rejoin Mexico.

Even though Texas journeyed on an independent course, the ties of its citizens to the United States were strong, and in 1843, the United States secretly began to discuss annexation with representatives of Texas. Many Americans, ever since the nation acquired the Louisiana Territory in 1803, had envisioned the United States as a land stretching from Atlantic to Pacific, and some even argued that Texas was a part of the original purchase from France that somehow ended up in Spain's possession. Sensing the time was right, President John Tyler pushed a resolution through Congress in February 1845 that offered Texas statehood. Texas accepted in July, and Texas officially joined the Union on December 29. Before, during, and after these dates, the nation argued over Texas annexation, with slavery being the principal issue. The concept of Manifest Destiny (see Chapter 18) played a part, too. Texas became the twenty-eighth state, but its admission into the Union led to war with Mexico (see Chapter 19), something that many Americans believed the new president, James K. Polk, wanted in order to obtain even more territory.

The readings in this chapter begin with those that favor Texas annexation and the Texas cause in the 1836 war for Texas independence. The first comes from a Texas newspaper and refers to ten friends of Texas—the Southern states from Virginia southward. The next is the report of the massacre at the Alamo, news of which inflamed passions in many Americans. The third entry directly ties Texans to the United States, by declaring there is no doubt that they—the Texans—are really Americans who deserve American assistance. The next entry predicts Northern resistance to Texas annexation. Following it is a letter from Thomas Gilmer of Virginia, a reply to one by John Quincy Adams, which is included below, and one by Andrew Jackson. The last entry in this section is by John O'Sullivan. O'Sullivan, who was the press's strongest proponent of Manifest Destiny, believes Texas annexation is right and cannot be stopped.

The readings that oppose Texas annexation begin with two that bring up the specter of the division of the nation because of slavery in Texas. The first is written by a Northern editor; the second comes from John Quincy Adams, who believed annexing Texas was unconstitutional and a way to spread slavery. The next entry comes from a Whig perspective. Whigs as a whole in the 1840s opposed territorial expansion.

Support for Annexation and/or Texas Independence

Jefferson: "Shall We Declare Independence?"

The ties of many Texans to America was evident in numerous ways. The pseudonym used here is one example. The newspapers that began in Texas in the 1820s with their decidedly United States' view is another. Here, the anonymous writer in this Austin paper wants Texas to free itself from Mexico and expects the United States to provide an army for protection. The writer talks about one enemy—Mexico—and ten friends—referring no doubt to the southernmost American slave states.

Telegraph and Texas Register (Austin), 27 February 1836

Shall we declare for independence is a question now upon every tongue; the idle and the thinking, the patriot and the speculator. The subject is near every heart that is capable of feeling, and involves in its decision the future destiny of Texas. Our representatives are about to assemble; we have invested them with power to determine this important query, and should now, by free discussion, if possible, enlighten their path.

We may rejoice that, at this crisis, we are not entirely on untrodden ground. We have a bright example before us, in the United States; and by observing the similarity of our situation, we may more correctly judge the propriety of our course. . . .

In the first place, have the causes which led to the separating, been as aggravated with the people of Texas as with the patriots of the revolution. *They* complained of imposing an unjust tax, of stationing armed troops amongst them, in time of peace, of carrying citizens out of the country for trial, &c. *We* complain of their imposing heavy duties upon us, and expending none of the revenue within our borders; of not only harboring armed troops amongst us, in time of peace, but of sending them with *hobbles* to literally confine our people in disgraceful fetters, or destroy their lives. . . .

It is said our declaring for independence would unite all Mexico against us. It will give us ten strong friends, where it makes us one imbecile enemy. . . .

There is one consideration, that alone ought to be final, in influencing the mind of every patriot in favor of independence. It is that our friends from the United States who now almost compose our army, and have assisted in gaining our proudest laurels, have, in anticipation of that event alone, offered their services and lives in our defence. Our friends in the United States are looking upon us with fraternal affection: their arm is already extended, clothed with power terrible to tyrants. Let us not deceive them, or their countenance will be withdrawn, and we will be left, our wives and children, to the mercy of Mexicans. If we put the contest on a footing worthy of their assistance, by declaring for independence, "a thousand friends will leap from their scabords," and ten thousand voices answer our appeal for assistance. The blood and treasures of citizens of the United States will flow freely out, when offered in the cause of liberty and independence. . . .

JEFFERSON.

An Anonymous Report: "Highly Important from Texas"

The New Orleans newspapers kept America apprised of what was happening in Texas. This report contained numerous details about the fighting there, but in the middle, there was a paragraph about the Alamo. The slaughter there struck a chord with many Americans because many of those killed were Americans who had volunteered to protect Texas.

True American (New Orleans), 28 March 1836

On the 6th of March about midnight the Alamo was assaulted by the whole force of the Mexican army commanded by Santa Anna in person; the battle was desperate until daylight, when only 7 men belonging to the Texan garrison were found alive, who cried for quarter, but they were told that there was no mercy for them—they then continued fighting until they were all butchered. One woman, Mrs. Dickinson, and a negro of Col. Travis were the only persons whose lives were spared. We regret to say that Col. David Crockett, and companion, Mr. Benton, and Col. Bonhan of S.C. were among the number slain—Col. Bowie was murdered in his bed, sick and helpless. The bodies of the slain were thrown into a mass in the centre of the Alamo and burned. The loss of the Mexicans in storming the place was not less than 1000 killed and mortally wounded, and as many wounded, making with their loss in the first assault between 2 and 3,000 men. . . .

An Anonymous Report: "Distresses of the Colonists"

In this anonymous report from New Orleans, the writer leaves no doubt that the attacks in Texas are attacks by the Mexican government on American citizens. He says that "they are Americans—their blood is ours." Though the article does not say it, it seems implied that Texas should be considered a part of the United States.

Courier **(New Orleans), 13 May 1836**

The Schr. Coralla arrived this morning from Matagorda, (Texas) loaded with the unfortunate wives and children of the colonists—grief and despair is depicted on all their countenances—many who were in easy, if not affluent circumstances, are now reduced to abject poverty. A scene so distressing we feel assured has never before been witnessed in the United States—even the miseries of the unfortunate inhabitants of St. Domingo, with all their sufferings, can bear no parallel to this. Many of them being unable to escape with money, whereby they could supply their wants until such time as employment could be procured; but the people of Texas are pastoral, their riches were their flocks and lands, which they have been compelled to abandon, and are now flung on our shores destitute in every thing, and broken in spirit. It should be recollected they are Americans—their blood is ours; and it behoves [*sic*] us to alleviate their afflictions and sufferings. Many of them have lost their fathers, husbands, sons, and brothers—let therefore some of our worthy fellow citizens call a meeting for their relief—the call will not, cannot be made in vain—every man will throw in his mite, and even our ladies, who are proverbial for their benevolence, will not let such an occasion pass unnoticed. An thing more from us, we deem unnecessary—the feelings of pity and charity in our inhabitants are such, that it is sufficient for them to know, that any of their fellow creatures are in need of a helping hand from them to extend it.

An Anonymous Report: "The Storm Is Gathering"

Most Southerners expected Texas annexation to happen immediately after the Texas republic formed in 1836. This comment from Richmond rightly predicts the rising sectional dispute that annexation will cause.

***Whig* (Richmond), 11 January 1837**

Some of the Northern papers are beginning to take ground against the admission of Texas into the American Union, on the ground that it will strengthen the interests of the slave holding states. We shall soon hear the whole Northern phalanx in the cry, and the alarm will be sounded in every plausible form calculated to awake cupidity and fanaticism. . . . The coming sessions of Congress will develop signs which cannot be mistaken. The storm is gathering.

Thomas Walker Gilmer: "To the Editor"

Thomas Walker Gilmer was a congressional representative from Virginia and the commonwealth's former governor. In this letter to Niles' National Register, *he responds to an open letter by John Quincy Adams that appears in the second section of readings in this chapter. Gilmer asks what slavery has to do with annexation.*

***Niles' National Register* (Baltimore), 1 July 1843**

Having recently published a letter signed by Messrs. ADAMS, GATES, SLADE, WM.B. CALHOUN, GIDDINGS, SHERLOCK J. ANDREWS, BORDEN, CHITTENDEN, MATTOCKS, MORGAN, HOWARD, BIRDSEYE, and HALL, members of the 27th congress, addressed "To the people of the free states of the union," . . .I am sure you will not withhold from me the privilege of being heard by *the people of all the states* through the medium of your columns. . . .

What has slavery to do with this question? Will the number of slaves in the United States be increased by the annexation of Texas? Will the number of slaveholding states be increased? It is true that the climate and soil of Texas are peculiarly adapted to the culture of cotton, sugar, &c—crops which render slave-labor more profitable than it can be in grain-growing regions, and this may induce the slave population now in the United States to advance southward in the event of annexation. But as this population advances to the South, will it not recede from the North? Is it the object of your correspondents to confine the slave population of the United States within a compass so narrow as to multiply the hardships of the slave, and to compel the master to turn him loose upon the North and the West, nominally free, but really a burden to himself, an scourge to "*the people of the free States!*" . . .

I will not believe that your correspondents have spoken advisedly, or by any authority, when *they* claim to reflect the feelings of the people of the free states. . . . I am persuaded that they will find a more practical as well as a more liberal spirit pervading the population of the nonslaveholding States. The union is as necessary now as it always was for the protection of all. It can be preserved only by preserving the Constitution which formed it. . . . Our Union has no danger to apprehend from those who believe that its genius is expansive and progressive, but from those who think that the limits of the United States are already too large and the principles of 1776 too old-fashioned for this fastidious age.

THOMAS W. GILMER

Andrew Jackson: "Texas Annexation"

Andrew Jackson hesitated to push for Texas annexation in 1836 because he feared it might cost Martin Van Buren the 1836 election. Jackson, however, favored annexing Texas. In this letter, he says if America does not do it soon, the chance will be lost forever. In addition to the issue of slavery, many Americans worried that Great Britain might work to obtain Texas, and that would put the U.S. in the untenable position of being surrounded by British territory, Canada to the north and Texas to the south and west, and unable to expand territorially. That greatly worried America's hero of the War of 1812.

***Madisonian* (Washington, D.C.), 3 April 1844**

The present golden moment to obtain Texas must not be lost, or Texas must, from necessity, be thrown into the arms of England, and be forever lost to the United States–England in possession of Texas, or in strict alliance, offensive and defensive, and contending for California. How easy would it be for Great Britain to interpose a force sufficient to prevent emigration to California from the United States, and supply her garrison from Texas! Every *real American,* when they view this, with the danger to New Orleans from British arms from Texas, must unite, heart and hand, in the annexation of Texas to the United States. It will be a strong iron hoop around our Union, and a bulwark against all foreign invasion or aggression. I say, again, let not this opportunity slip to regain Texas, or it may elude our grasp forever, or cost us oceans of blood and millions of money to free us from the evils that may be brought upon us. I hope and trust there will be as many *patriots* in the Senate as will ratify the treaty, which I have no doubt will be promptly entered into.

John L. O'Sullivan: "Annexation"

Many Americans wanted the United States to control all the territory it possibly could. Texas was but one piece of property. It was, however, one ripe to become part of America since many of its inhabitants were United States citizens. And, the United States offered statehood to the Republic of Texas in March 1845. Texas accepted in July, something O'Sullivan rightly anticipated.

United States Magazine and Democratic Review (New York), July/August 1845

It is time now for opposition to the Annexation of Texas to cease, all further agitation of the waters of bitterness and strife, at least in connexion with this question. . . . It is time for the common duty of Patriotism to the Country to succeed;. . .it is at least time for common sense to acquiesce with decent grace in the inevitable and the irrevocable.

Texas is now ours. Already, before these words are written her Convention has undoubtedly ratified the acceptance, by her Congress, of our proffered invitation into the Union; and made the requisite changes in her already republican form of constitution to adopt it to its future federal relations. Her star and her stripe may already be said to have taken their place in the glorious blazon of our common nationality; and the sweep of our eagle's wing already includes within its circuit the wide extent of her fair and fertile land. She is no longer to us a mere geographical space. . . . The next session of Congress will see the representatives of the new young State in their places in both our halls of national legislation, side by side with those of the old Thirteen. . . .

Why, were other reasoning wanting, in favor of now elevating this question of the reception of Texas into the Union, out of the lower region of our past party dissensions, up to its proper level of a high and broad nationality, it surely is to be found, found abundantly, in the manner in which other nations have undertaken to intrude themselves into it, between us and the proper parties to the case, in a spirit of hostile interference against us, for the avowed object of thwarting our policy and hampering our power, limiting our greatness and checking the fulfilment [*sic*]of our manifest destiny to overspread the continent allotted by Providence for the free development of our yearly multiplying millions. . . .

It is wholly untrue, and unjust to ourselves, the pretence that the Annexation has been a measure of spoliation, unrightful and unrighteous—of military conquest under forms of peace and law—of territorial aggrandizement at the expense of justice, and justice due by a double sanctity to the weak. . . . The independence of Texas was complete and absolute. It was an independence, not only in fact but of right. No obligation of duty towards Mexico tended in the least degree to restrain our right to effect the desired recovery of the fair province once our own—whatever motives of policy might have prompted a more deferential consideration of her feelings and her pride, as involved in the question. If Texas became people with an American population, it was by no contrivance of our government, but on the express invitation of that of Mexico herself; accompanied with such guaranties of State independence, and the maintenance of a federal system analogous to our own, and constituted a compact fully justifying the strongest measures of redress on the part of those afterwards deceived in this guaranty, and sought to be enslaved under the yoke imposed by its violation. She was released, rightfully and absolutely released, from all Mexican allegiance, or duty of cohesion to the Mexican political body, by the acts and fault of Mexico herself, and Mexico alone. . . .

With no friendship for slavery, though unprepared to excommunicate to eternal damnation, with bell, book, and candle, those who are, we see nothing in the bearing of the Annexation of Texas on that institution to awaken a doubt of the wisdom of that measure, or a compunction for the humble part contributed by us towards its consummation. . . .

Opposition to Annexation

Theodore Dwight: "The Purchase of Texas"

Theodore Dwight was the editor of the Daily Advertiser *in New York. His paper opposed slavery, and the editor believed—as did many Northerners—that if Texas were added to the United States it would be purely to expand slave territory. Discussions of Texas annexation began early, this editorial coming from 1828. Dwight's multiweek commentary was published by other newspapers, and it is taken from the* Connecticut Courant *here, another newspaper that strongly opposed slavery and its spread.*

***Connecticut Courant* (Hartford), 13 October 1828**

The view of this question presented by the papers in favour of it, is obviously introduced for stage effect. Its object is, by prejudice, to make it a party affair, in the hope doubtless of having it decided by party feelings and passions. The project of procuring a sufficient amount of territory, south of the line below which, by the adjustment of the Missouri controversy, slavery may be admitted, is one of vast importance to the future concerns and existence of the Union. There are now twenty-four States. Of these there are twelve slave holding States, if Delaware and Maryland are fairly to be considered as such. How many States may eventually be made out of the territory now owned by the United States south of the 36th degree of latitude, we have no means of conjecturing. But if in addition to them we are to purchase enough for eight or ten more, for the mere purpose of strengthening the power, increasing the influence, and securing to them the absolute control of the political concerns of this republic, it is a matter of the deepest possible concern to those States that are free from this great national curse. If Texas should be added to the United States, it is not an extravagant supposition that there may in process of time be twelve or fifteen additional slave States incorporated into the Union. This would give them, even if Delaware and Maryland are ranked among the free States, no less than from *forty to fifty senators,* with a proportionate number of members in the other branch of the national legislature. The slave States, even when in a minority, have always been able, by their address and management, to govern the country. What may not then be expected from them when they can command such an overwhelming majority?

If, then, the free States do not intend to surrender themselves at discretion, if, they do not feel inclined to yield up their weight and influence in the national affairs, if they are not disposed to become tributary to the slave States, and to see all the wealth and energy of the republic placed under the sovereign controul and disposal of these States, it is incumbent on them to watch this project with the deepest solicitude and care, and to check at the outset every effort at the accomplishment of such a wild and pernicious undertaking. . . .

It is not at all improbable, that when the new States become the majority; when the Arkansas Territory, and Texas, and all the other vacant regions, become States, measures will be adopted to sequester fro the use of those States, all the domains of the nation;—and among others, that this immeasurable, invaluable province, now about to be bought for the purpose of multiplying the slave States, and increasing General Jackson's glory, will be declared to be the property of the four or five slave States made therefrom, though purchased by the nation.

John Quincy Adams: "Address to the People of the Free States of the Union"

John Quincy Adams, the sixth president and now a representative from Massachusetts, opposed slavery, but he found another reason to oppose Texas annexation. He believed that it was unconstitutional, that the United States had no right to annex an independent nation. In this letter, signed by Adams and others, he outlines the seriousness of the annexation issue for the North. This open letter appeared shortly after secret negotiations between the Tyler administration and the government of Texas were uncovered.

National Intelligencer (Washington, D.C.), 4 May 1843

We, the undersigned, in closing our duties to our constituents and our country as members of the 27th congress, feel bound to call your attention very briefly to the project, long entertained by a portion of the people of these United States, still pertinaciously adhered to, and intended soon to be consummated—THE ANNEXATION OF TEXAS TO THIS UNION. . . .

The last election of President of the Republic of Texas is understood to have turned *mainly* upon the question of *annexation* or *no annexation,* and the candidate favorable to that measure was successful by an overwhelming majority. The sovereign States of Alabama, Tennessee, and Mississippi have *recently* adopted resolutions, some if not all of them *unanimously,* in favor of annexation, and forwarded them to Congress.

The honorable HENRY A. WISE, a member of Congress . . .said, in a speech delivered January 26, 1842:

"True, if Iowa be added on the one side, Florida will be added on the other. But there the equilibrium is gone—gone forever. The *balance of interests* is gone—the *safeguard* of American property—of the American Constitution—of the American Union vanished into thin air. *This must be the inevitable result, unless, by a treaty with Mexico,* THE SOUTH CAN ADD MORE WEIGHT TO HER END OF THE LEVER! *Let the South stop at the Sabine,* (the eastern boundary of Texas), while the North may spread unchecked beyond the Rocky Mountains, AND THE SOUTHERN SCALE MUST KICK THE BEAM!" . . .

At the present session the resolutions of the State of Alabama in favor of annexation, and sundry petitions and remonstrances against it, were referred to the Committee on Foreign Relations. . . . At the same time Mr. Adams asked, as an individual member of the committee, for leave to present the following resolutions: . . .

"*Resolved,* That any attempt of the Government of the United States, by an act of Congress or by treaty, to annex to this Union the Republic of Texas or the people thereof, would be a violation of the Constitution of the United States, null and void, and to which the free States of this Union and their people ought not to submit."

Objections being made, the resolutions were not received, the Southern members showing a disinclination to have the subject agitated in the house *at present* . . . . [W]e submit to you whether the project of annexation seems to be abandoned, and whether there be not *the most imminent danger* of its speedy accomplishment, unless *the entire mass of the people in the free States become aroused to a conviction of this danger,* AND SPEAK OUT AND ACT IN REFERENCE TO IT IN A MANNER AND WITH A VOICE NOT TO BE MISUNDERSTOOD EITHER BY THE PEOPLE OF THE SLAVE STATES, OR THEIR OWN PUBLIC SERVANTS AND REPRESENTATIVES. . . .

We know their present temper and spirit on this subject too well to believe for a moment that they would become *particeps criminis* in any such subtle contrivance for the *irremediable perpetuation* of AN INSTITUTION which the wisest and best men who formed our Federal Constitution, as well from the slave as the free States, *regarded as an evil and a curse,* soon to become extinct under the operation of laws to be passed prohibiting the slave trade, and the progressive influence of the principles of the Revolution.

To prevent the success of this nefarious project—to preserve from such gross violation the Constitution of our country, adopted expressly, "*to secure the blessings of liberty*" and not the perpetuation of slavery—and to prevent the speedy and violent dissolution of the Union, we invite you to unite, without distinction of party, in an immediate expression of your views on this subject, in such manner as you may deem best calculated to answer the end proposed. . . .

William G. Brownlow: "Texas Against Annexation"

The question of Texas annexation was an issue in the 1844 presidential election. The Democratic candidate, James K. Polk, advocated adding Texas and other lands. The Whig party supported Henry Clay and strongly opposed annexation. In this article, Brownlow quotes from a Texas newspaper to support his position against annexation.

Jonesborough (Tenn.) Whig, and Independent Journal, 24 July 1844

What will the Texas party in this country do, now that the intelligent and influential portion of the citizens of that country, have come out against the scheme? When it is understood here, that Texas herself is opposed to annexation, and it is only advocated *here* by men who wish to make a little capital for a sinking cause, and avoid the real issues before the country, upon which they were whipped out in 1840, their own partizans will turn from the humbug in disgust.

The following is a part of an editorial from the *Civilian,* the leading organ of the Texas Government, published at Galveston.

"The annexation fever, is, we are happy to state, now confined principally to the other side of the Sabine. Like the *grippe* it has been of a much milder type and passed off much sooner here than in the United States. Solitary and alone we have until recently held the only pen, a feeble one it is true, which has been directed against this measure, but succor has at length come forward, and the large intelligent and respectable class of citizens who have stood opposed to the measure are likely to find other and abler advocates of their opinions. At the outset of the negotiations it was assumed with more confidence than circumstances warranted, that nine tenths of the people of Texas were in favor of the measure. This was a mere guess, like the one which gave rest to it, viz: that two thirds of the United States Senate would vote for the treaty. And a better knowledge of facts has proved that were erroneous. Its friends here are astonished to find the opposition to it so strong and successful. The fact is not to be concealed that from all quarters the evidences are strong and palpable of a growing aversion to the scheme."

There does indeed seem to be a powerful demon employed counteracting and undoing all that we have done or can do against slavery and the slave trade. Nowhere has it more completely baffled our efforts than on this very land of Texas. But the struggle was from the first a vain one. Had we, indeed, on first recognizing the independence of Texas, procured a recognition of it from Mexico, and poured European capital and population into it, we might have reared an independent state; but capital refused to repair thither, the American alone migrated to Texas. In such circumstances to hope that Texas would not declare itself politically Anglo-American, as it was left to become in population and commercial connexion, was idle. How strong the national current ran in that direction we see from the unanimity of the Texas assemblies. They are all American to a man. . . .

President Polk has . . .cajoled the Texans into a vote of annexation, and acted thereon promptly by the despatch of ships and regiments to the Rio Grande. . . .

Questions

1. Why do you think the writings supporting Texas annexation talk so little about slavery, while those that oppose it make it the central issue of their argument?
2. How do you think most Americans felt about Texas during its war of independence from Mexico? Explain through the articles, especially those from the New Orleans papers.
3. From the readings, which region—North or South—seems to make annexation more of a sectional issue? Give examples.

Notes

1. For information on the Texas war of independence and Texas annexation, see Stephen L. Hardin, *Texian Iliad: A Military History of the Texas Revolution, 1835–1836* (Austin: University of Texas Press, 1996); Frederick Merk, *Slavery and the An-*

nexation of Texas (New York: Alfred A. Knopf, 1972); Stanley Siegel, *A Political History of the Texas Republic 1836–1845* (Austin: University of Texas Press, 1956); Justin Harvey Smith, *The Annexation of Texas* (SS: AMS Press, 1971); Lon Tinkle, *Thirteen Days to Glory: The Siege of the Alamo* (New York: McGraw Hill, 1958). For the events from a Mexican perspective, see Jeff Long, *Duel of Eagles: The Mexican and U.S. Fight for the Alamo* (New York: Morrow, 1990).

2. *Telegraph and Texas Register* (San Felipe de Austin), 5 March 1836.

CHAPTER 14

The Trail of Tears, 1838

In the summer of 1838, a writer to the *Savannah Georgian* commented, "Georgia is, at length, rid of her red population, and this beautiful country will now be prosperous and happy."[1] For nearly forty years, the state of Georgia had waged a political war with the Native Americans who lived there–principally Cherokee–to nullify any political treaties the nation had with the state or federal government and to assume control of Cherokee lands.

In 1802, the federal government agreed to annul all Indian claims within Georgia if the state would cede its western lands to the United States. In 1804, Congress passed a law that allowed the president to exchange lands owned by Indians east of the Mississippi River for land west of it. In 1825, President James Monroe announced to Congress plans to repeal Indian claims to land in Georgia and elsewhere. Georgia followed with a series of acts that took away the rights of the Cherokees. The laws made it illegal for the Cherokees to assemble in council except to relinquish lands to the state, and they took away any legal recourse for the Cherokees by making it illegal for them to bring suit in a court or to testify against any white person for any reason.[2] Finally, in 1830, at the insistence of President Andrew Jackson, Congress passed the Indian Removal Act, which called for the forced removal of the "Five Civilized Tribes"–the Cherokee, Choctaw, Creek, Chickasaw, and Seminole–to the Oklahoma territory (see Chapter 7).

Of the five Southern tribes, the Cherokee were by far the most powerful, and they fought against removal through federal courts since the Georgia courts were closed to them. The first case, *Cherokee Nation v. Georgia,* sought negation of Georgia's recently passed laws. That effort failed. In another case, *Worcester v. Georgia,* the Cherokees won. Chief Justice John Marshall noted that federal treaties took precedence over those of the states. This gave the Cherokees some hope that they might hold onto their lands in Georgia, North Carolina, Tennessee, and Alabama. The Cherokees, however, had not reckoned on the response of the president. Jackson, an Indian fighter and a chief architect of Indian removal, refused to enforce the Court's ruling[3] and reportedly said, "Marshall has made his decision, now let him enforce it!"[4]

Most of the "Civilized Tribes," so-called because they assimilated white customs of dress, housing, religion, and the like more than most Native Americans, had neither the populations nor resources of the Cherokees and were forced to move west sooner. One group of Seminoles, led by Osceola, rebelled in 1835 and lived in the Everglades before being defeated in the 1840s. By 1836, nearly all of the Indians, except the Cherokees and those fighting in Florida, had either been removed to Oklahoma or were on their way there. The Cherokees were split over whether to capitulate and move or to hold on to their lands. Some Cherokees agreed to leave voluntarily. Over the next two years, they followed one of the three routes established to move Indians from the South into the territory west of the Mississippi. One route went overland through Alabama to Mobile, where Indians traveled by boat to New Orleans then up the Mississippi and Arkansas rivers. A second route went through Alabama, Mississippi, and Arkansas. The third and longest overland route sent Indians through Tennessee and Kentucky, across the Ohio River, and either across Southern Missouri or south through Northern Arkansas. The final route, with the last part passing through Missouri, is the one the Cherokees named "the trail where they cried"–the Trail of Tears–even though all routes collectively are deemed the Trail of Tears today.

Before the first Cherokees voluntarily left for Oklahoma, the nation issued its Memorial and Protest of the Cherokee Nation. It stated:

> The Cherokees were happy and prosperous under a scrupulous observance of treaty stipulations by the government of the United States. . . . Little did they anticipate, that when taught to think and feel as the American citizen, and to have with him a common interest, they were to be despoiled by their guardian, to become strangers and wanderers in the land of their fathers . . . and to seek a new home in the wilds of the far west, and that without their consent.[5]

Tired of waiting for all Cherokees to voluntarily leave their homeland, Georgia officials first arrested Chief John Ross, the tribe's spokesman. They only agreed to free him if the Cherokees agreed to leave the state. President Martin Van Buren then sent in federal troops to force the Cherokees to leave Georgia in May 1838, driving them, according to one report, "like cattle through rivers, allowing them no time even to take off their shoes and stockings."[6]

The trip west for all Native Americans was difficult. Nearly one in four of the 15,000 Cherokees who traveled west died on the forced march. Once in Oklahoma, the Cherokees and other members of the "Civilized Tribes" discovered smaller amounts of land on which to live than they had had in the East. The land was also inferior to that in the East.[7] Despite this last fact, the Cherokees and other Indians would not be able to hold this land forever, either, something another Trail of Tears observer, Alexis de Tocqueville, noted. "In a few years the same white population that now flocks around them will doubtless track them anew," Tocqueville said of the Indians removed to the West. He realized all too well what would eventually happen to the Indians. Their lands in the West would be wanted, too, and concluded for the Indians, "their only refuge is the grave."[8]

This chapter looks at America's reaction to and comments about the removal of Native Americans as a result of the 1830 Indian Removal Act. The first section looks at Indian removal positively and begins with a story from *Niles' Register* about the deplorable conditions of some of the Indians as they were force-marched west. The second is President Andrew Jackson's 1836 letter on the rationale behind the move. It is followed by a graphic story that describes atrocities committed by the Creek in Georgia in 1836. The next comes from the Columbus, Georgia, *Enquirer*. This extended editorial bemoans when the Indians will ever be removed, makes disparaging remarks about the Cherokees, and threatens physical action by Georgia against the Cherokees if the federal government does not act for removal.

The articles that react negatively to Indian removal begin with a speech by David Crockett, frontier hero and political adversary of Andrew Jackson. The next entry, an anonymous letter written by a New York visitor to Georgia, discusses the conditions of the Cherokees as they wait to be removed. An anonymous story titled "The Last Indian" follows. It speaks of the last Native American left after the actions of white Americans. The last selection is written by a missionary to the Cherokees. It talks about the last days of the Cherokees in Georgia.

Support for Indian Removal

An Anonymous Report from Georgia: "The Incessant Cry of Bread!"

The United States government began preparations for the removal of some Native Americans from the South almost immediately after the passage of the Indian Removal Act. As a means to show that Native Americans would be better off moving west, stories appeared that described the current destitute conditions of Native Americans. In this story, which first appeared in Georgia, the plight of the Creek is described. What might be considered a negative report becomes part of the validation for removing the Indians so that they might be saved from horrible conditions.

***Niles' Weekly Register* (Baltimore), 16 July 1831**

To see a whole people destitute of food—the incessant cry of the emaciated creatures being *bread! bread! bread!* is beyond description distressing. The existence of many of the Indians is prolonged by eating roots and the bark of trees. The berries of the Indian or China tree of last year's growth were ate by them as long as they lasted—nothing that can afford nourishment is rejected however offensive it may be.

Andrew Jackson: "President Jackson's Message"

Even though Texas was not a part of the United States in 1836, many of its inhabitants were American immigrants. Just as other Americans who migrated west, those in Texas started newspapers. The Texas newspapers followed closely events in America. In this report, the Telegraph and Texas Register *provides President Jackson's message on removal of the Cherokees from Georgia. Note the promises in the message, especially that the territory given to the Cherokees and the other "Civilized Tribes" would never be inhabited by whites or turned into American states.*

***Telegraph and Texas Register* (Austin), 23 January 1836**

The plan of removing the aboriginal people who yet remain within the settled portions of the United States, to the country west of the Mississippi river, approaches to its consummation. It was adopted on the most mature consideration of the condition of this race, and ought to be persisted in till the object is accomplished, and prosecuted with as much vigor as a just regard to their circumstances will permit, and as fast as their consent can be obtained.

All preceding experiments for the improvement of the Indians have failed. It seems now to be an established fact, that they cannot live in contact with a civilized community, and prosper. Ages of fruitless endeavors have, at length, brought us to a knowledge of this principle of intercommunication with them. The past we cannot recall, but the future we can provide for. . . .

The plan for their removal and re-establishment is founded upon the knowledge we have gained of their character and habits, and has been dictated by a spirit of enlarged liberality. A territory exceeding in extent that relinquished, has been granted to each tribe. Of its climate, fertility, and capacity to support an Indian population, the representations are highly favorable. To these districts the Indians are removed at the expense of the United States, and with certain supplies of clothing, arms, ammunition, and other indispensible article; they are also furnished gratuitously with provisions for the period of a year after their arrival at their new homes. In that time, from the nature of the country, and of the productions raised by them, they can subsist themselves by agricultural labor, if they choose to resort to that mode of life. If they do not, they are upon the skirts of the great prairies, where countless herds of buffalo roam, and a short time suffices to adapt their own habits to the changes which a change of the animals destined for their food may require. . . . Funds have been set apart for the maintenance of the poor. The most necessary mechanical arts have been introduced, and blacksmiths, gunsmiths, wheelwrights, millwrights, &c., are supported among them. . . .

Such are the arrangements for the physical comfort, and for the moral improvement of the Indians. The necessary measures for their political advancement, and for their separation from our citizens have not been neglected. The pledge of the United States has been given by Congress, that the country destined for the residence of this people, shall be for ever "secured and guaranteed to them." A country west of Missouri and Arkansas has been assigned to them, into which the white settlements are not to be pushed. No political communities can be formed in that extensive region, except those which are established by the Indians themselves, or by the United States for them, and with their concurrence. A barrier has thus been raised for their protection against the encroachments of our citizens, and guarding the Indians, as far as possible, from those evils which have brought them to their present condition. Summary authority has been given by law to destroy all ardent spirits in their country, without waiting the doubtful result, and slow process of a legal seizure. . . .

After the further details of this arrangement are completed, with a very general supervision over them, they ought to be left to the progress of events. These, I indulge the hope, will secure their prosperity and improvement, and a large portion of the moral debt we owe them, will then be paid.

An Anonymous Report: "Creek War Incidents"

All members of the Five Civilized Tribes did not meekly surrender to the Indian Removal Act of 1830. In some cases, war resulted. War reports were often designed to inflame fears toward Native Americans. In this report, which appeared in the Connecticut Courant, *the gruesome aspects provide realism for readers but also help Americans who do not live in the Carolinas, Georgia, and Florida understand why it is imperative that "the wild savage" be removed from these states. References to Florida are to the Seminole uprising led by Osceola that began in 1835. Such reports originating from the South were further proof that the government needed to step up Indian removal, which was to be completed by the end of 1838. Similar reports of Indian uprisings appeared throughout the nation.*

***Connecticut Courant* (Hartford), 30 May 1836**

In the Creek nation, at this moment, the scenes of Florida are being acted over. The wild savage, frenzied by the smell of blood in his nostrils, is prowling the wilderness, skulking around plantations, levelling the deadly rifle at the breast of the white man, scalping the unoffending wife and mother, and beheading the innocent and unsuspecting babe! We have heard of some cases which make the blood chill in our veins. A house in which lived a man, his wife, and six children, was suddenly surrounded by a savage band, who entered the peaceful domicil, inhumanly massacred every soul, securing the scalps of all, and severing each child's head from its body! The house of a Mr. Colton was attacked, and himself butchered, without a moment's warning, or the least opportunity for resistance. We believe in all, from 40 to 50 murders have been committed, besides numbers of negroes on plantations. Fires have been kindled in every direction–farm houses, cotton gins, out houses, corn cribs, and all of the value swept away from the honest and industrious planter, who was laudably striving to locate himself comfortably for life, and provide for his children. . . .

Mark S. Flournoy: "Cherokee Affairs"

Most Georgia newspapers supported the removal of the Cherokees. This editorial, by Enquirer *editor Mark Flournoy, wonders why the federal government has not yet removed the remaining Cherokees from Georgia, referring to the Cherokees as disturbers of the peace and people who inflict savage cruelties. Flournoy suggests that if the government does not act, Georgia, under direction of its governor, has the right to take matters with the Cherokees into its own hands.*

***Enquirer* (Columbus, Georgia), 31 May 1838**

We had hoped until now that the treaty with the Cherokees would be executed, and the tribe removed without the scenes of blood and desolation that had marked the conduct of the other Indians in our vicinity. We knew that some of them were dissatisfied, and manifested a desire to remain–we knew that there were evil disposed white men in different sections of the country, who, under the influence of a mawkish sensibility, were encouraging a spirit of resistance to the policy and pledged faith of the Government, but we were unprepared to believe that, after the treaty was made, and armed men by thousands collected to enforce it, the President would interpose the influence and authority of his administration to procrastinate the justice due to Georgians, and delay the emigration of the Indians. But so it is. A message has been sent to both branches of Congress, containing a proposition allowing the Cherokees *two years* longer to disturb the peace, and become better prepared to murder, burn and destroy the persons and property of our fellow citizens. Such a proposition, from such a source, must arouse in the bosom of every true Georgian feelings of mingled indignation, contempt, and disgust.

What can the President and his advisers mean? Do they allow that this trifling with long delayed justice due a sovereign State, this indirect encouragement to the commission of savage cruelties, will be submitted to by those who have wanted for more than thirty years, in the vain expectation that the government would remove the Indians and fulfill her solemn engagement? Or did they deem that the arm of federal power is strong enough to crush or curb the wronged and insulted spirit of a people who have waited the tardy footsteps of that faltering justice? The President and his Secretary of War have surely forgotten the true condition of things, or they have strangely mistaken the determination with which their proposition will be met by every man that has a drop of Georgia blood in his veins. What are the facts? Georgia had extended her laws over the territory and disposed of it to her citizens, thousands of whom had removed to and settled on their lands; the government was bound by compact to extinguish the Indian title, and in compliance with its obligation made a treaty with the tribe by which the right of soil, occupancy and jurisdiction was ceded in this State, and the Indians bound to emigrate in this month; fearing that difficulties might arise from the known unwillingness of a portion of the tribe to emigrate, thousands of soldiers were called from their homes and ordered to the scene in anticipated danger. Every thing gave promise that the Indians would shortly leave for their home in the West. . . .

This business can take what course the President and his advisers see cause to give it, so far as they are concerned. . . . If Congress refuses, on the suggestion of Mr. Van Buren, to execute the treaty, Mr. Gilmer has only to go ahead in the path before him, cheered by the voice and backed by the right arm of this whole people.

Opposition to Indian Removal

David Crockett: "Speech of Colonial David Crockett"

Davy Crockett was a political opponent of President Andrew Jackson, and the differences between the two Tennesseans was easy to see in their views on the treatment of Native Americans. As part of his bid for a congressional seat, Crockett stumped across Tennessee, taking on Jackson at all stops.

These comments come from his speech delivered in Trenton, Tennessee, in which he directed a quick jab at Jackson for his treatment of Indians and for violating the Constitution in the process.

Augusta (Ga.) State-Rights' Sentinel, 7 August 1835

I could not, would not believe that Andrew Jackson understood the Constitution better than the makers of it.

I believe he violated the Constitution again upon the Indian Bill. By this bill a handful of Indians were smashed up. Are we justified in this because we are a great and mighty people? In the name of God, if we are great, let us be gracious.

A Gentleman of New York: "Cherokee Treatment"

Visitors to different regions of the country would often comment on what they saw on their journeys. This letter, signed "A Gentleman of New York, Now Travelling in the Upcountry of Georgia," is an example. The New York visitor attacked both slavery and the treatment of the Cherokees by Georgia. In the section on the Cherokees, the writer talks about the deplorable conditions the Cherokees face as their land is being taken away.

Augusta (Ga.) State-Rights' Sentinel, 1 September 1835

Nothing has been spared to dislodge them from their country, and the miserable pittance of land left them for a temporary abiding place has from time to time been taken from them by the most arbitrary an[d] unjust means. I do not believe that the good people of Georgia are acquainted with the proceedings that are carrying on among these poor injured and destitute people. . . .

It is a well known fact that the wives and children of these defenceless creatures, have been turned out of their homes, expelled from their cabins and set adrift upon a friendless community to exist as they can. It is enough to draw tears from stones to listen to the wrongs of this once brave and now persecuted people. . . .

Would you believe it, that in one of the old thirteen States, known for its orderly, moral, intelligent bearing, in which the religion of the meek and lowly Saviour is preached, where the principles of republican government are so well known . . . should, *at this very moment*, permit a suspension of civil laws of the country . . . for the arbitrary purpose . . . of enforcing obedience to the authority of the State?

An Anonymous Report: "The Last Indian"

News reports of the removal of the Cherokees and other Southern tribes were often terse statements about the groups of Native Americans who were passing through an area. Those sympathetic to the Indian cause often spoke of the tragic conditions faced by those being moved West. In this article from Franklin, Tennessee, an unknown writer tells of the genocide of Native Americans. Franklin was the site of President Andrew Jackson's meeting with several Native American groups in 1830, during which the leaders of those groups agreed to move to lands west of the Mississippi. Although the destruction of Indians is not described, the blame is placed squarely on white Americans. Although Indians will disappear from America, the writer says, the nobleness that they obtained will never be forgotten.

Western Weekly Review (Franklin), 29 June 1838

I looked, and lo, I beheld a great Continent. Its length extended from Cape Horn to the North Pole; its eastern side was dashed by the wrathful surge of the Atlantic, and the waters of the Pacific dashed in angry billows against its western shore. . . .

While I was yet gazing, my eye caught the glimpse of a tall and stately figure as it glided across a distant plain. It was an Indian. . . .

From the elevated station he looked down upon the sun-lit valley below, where the smoke ascended in mystics [*sic*] wreaths from the rude wig-wams of his kindred. A dark and pretentous [*sic*] cloud began to gather in the far-off west–the heavens were shrouded in darkness, and the troubled elements began their frightful ragings. . . .

Years wore apace. I looked again, and saw an Indian standing on a rugged cliff that over-hung the great Pacific.–He was the last of his race!–the remaining memento of a once powerful and magnanimous nation! . . . As he continues to gaze the fire of youthful vigor begins again to kindle on his bosom; his eyes too, begin to sparkle as the scene of other days recurs to his mind; and he almost conceives that the fate of his countrymen and the story of their wrongs are only the horrid airy visions of fancy. With stature erect, and eyes turned homeward, he continued to gaze, and with a strong voice of hope he exclaims, "Where are they?" He listens–the tones of his voice sound through the surrounding mountains–presently he hears the voice of echo answer–"Where are they!"

Now he begins to realize all the horrors of his situation. He turns around to look at the setting sun and then begins to weep. "Oh my country!" he ejaculates, "my prostrated and degraded country! The white man has robbed me of my country, and exterminated my countrymen." . . .

But will this blot out forever the Indian's name!–will this be the last that we shall ever hear of this sad and mournful history.–will the recollections of this daring people be forever erased from the enlivening pages of memory? No! When the bones of their cruel persecutors shall have dissolved in their native dust–when their names shall have been forgotten and swallowed up in the dark waters of oblivion, the history of the Indian will still live in the recollections of poetry—will still be subject of praise and panegyric, and from the theme of discussion for both orator and historian . . . What? forget the Indian? no, never! . . .

Evan Jones: "With the Cherokees"

Evan Jones was a Baptist missionary to the Cherokees and one of only three whites to accompany the nation on its move west. Jones wrote letters about the trip to the Baptist Missionary Magazine. *Religious periodicals were one of the principal ways many Americans received their information in the middle of the nineteenth century. The magazine published portions of Jones's letters in its September magazine and more in April 1839. In this letter, Jones describes the deplorable conditions the Cherokees faced on their evacuation.*[9]

Baptist Missionary Magazine (Boston), September 1838

The Cherokees are nearly all prisoners. They have been dragged from their houses, and encamped at the forts and military posts, all over the nation. In Georgia, especially, multitudes were allowed no time to take any thing with them, except the clothes they had on. Well-furnished houses were left a prey to plunderers, who, like hungry wolves, follow in the train of the captors. These wretches rifle the houses, and strip the helpless, unoffending owners of all they have on earth. Females, who have been habituated to comforts and comparative affluence, are driven on foot before the bayonets of brutal men. Their feelings are mortified by vulgar and profane vociferations. It is a painful sight. The property of many has been taken, and sold before their eyes for almost nothing—the sellers and buyers, in many cases, being combined to cheat the poor Indians. These things are done at the instant of arrest and consternation; the soldiers standing by, with their arms in hand, impatient to go on with their work, could give little time to transact business. The poor captive, in a state of distressing agitation, his weeping wife almost frantic with terror, surrounded by a group of crying, terrified children, without a friend to speak a consoling word, is in a poor condition to make a good disposition of his property and is in most cases stripped of the whole, at one blow. Many of the Cherokees, who, a few days ago, were in comfortable circumstances, are now victims of abject poverty. Some, who have been allowed to return home, under passport, to inquire after their property, have found their cattle, horses, swine, farming-tools, and house-furniture all gone. And this is not a description of extreme cases. It is altogether a faint representation of the work which has been perpetrated on the unoffending, unarmed and unresisting Cherokees. . . .

The principal Cherokees have sent a petition to Gen. Scott, begging most earnestly that they may not be sent off to the west till the sickly season is over. They have not received any answer yet. The agent is shipping them by multitudes from Ross's Landing. Nine hundred in one detachment, and seven hundred in another, were driven into boats, and it will be a miracle of mercy if one-fourth escape the exposure to that sickly climate. They were exceedingly depressed, and almost in despair.

Questions

1. Read carefully the promises made to Native Americans by President Jackson in his 1836 letter. Which of these promises to the Indians did the United States keep? Do you think Jackson truly believed these conditions were possible? Explain.
2. Two basic perceptions of Native Americans exist in these readings. Describe each of them.
3. What do you think stimulated the hostile reaction toward the Cherokees as found in the Columbus *Enquirer*?

Notes

1. *Savannah Georgian,* quoted in *Niles' Weekly Register,* 21 July 1838.

2. Barbara F. Luebke, "Elias Boudinot and 'Indian Removal,'" in *Outsiders in 19th-Century Press History: Multicultural Perspectives,* ed. Frankie Hutton and Barbara Straus Reed (Bowling Green: Bowling Green University Popular Press, 1995), 121.

3. John M. Coward, *The Newspaper Indian: Native American Identity in the Press, 1820–1860* (Urbana: University of Illinois Press, 1999), 67–68. The Supreme Court cases are *Cherokee Nation v. Georgia,* 1831, U.S. Supreme Court *Reports,* 5 Peters, 15–18; and *Worcester v. Georgia,* 1832, U.S. Supreme Court *Reports,* 6 Peters, 559–61.

4. George Brown Tindall, *America: A Narrative History,* 2 vols. (New York: W.W. Norton, 1984), 1:407.

5. Memorial and Protest of the Cherokee Nation, 22 June 1836, quoted in John M. Blum, et al., *The National Experience,* 2 vols. (San Diego: Harcourt Brace Jovanovich, 1985), 1:233.

6. *Niles' National Register,* 18 August 1838.

7. James West Davidson, et al., *Nation of Nations,* 2 vols. (New York: McGraw-Hill, 1990), 1:391.

8. Alexis de Tocqueville, *Democracy in America,* 2 vols. (New York: Alfred A. Knopf, 1980), 1:352.

9. Theda Perdue and Michael D. Green, eds., *The Cherokee Removal: A Brief History with Documents* (Boston: Bedford Books, 1995), 163.

CHAPTER 15

The *Amistad* and Cinque, 1839

In January 1841, John Quincy Adams received a letter. One of the sentences in the simply written note summed up the reason it had been sent to the seventy-four-year-old former president: "All we want," the writer pleaded, "is make us free."[1] The author of the note and other Africans had been taken illegally by Spanish slave traders from Africa's west coast in 1839. Now, they were about to have their case heard by the United States Supreme Court. The case would determine whether the Africans were free or whether they were the property of Spanish slave traders.

How did a group of Africans—never intended to be brought to the United States—end up in front of America's highest tribunal? Early in 1839, a Portuguese slave boat left Africa with perhaps six hundred Africans on board, all slated to be sold into slavery in the Western Hemisphere.[2] The slave trade had been outlawed by most countries in Europe and in America in the early nineteenth century. That, however, did not stop the slave trade because it was enormously profitable to slave traders and to African chiefs.[3] The boat sailed to Cuba, where the captives were divided out and sold. Fifty-three[4] boarded the *Amistad*, a schooner owned by Raymon Ferrer. Bad weather kept the *Amistad* from reaching its destination as it should have in three days. On the night that the ship should have been in port, one slave—who has been called Cinque in the writings about the event—broke out of his shackles and led the others in a revolt. The slaves killed Captain Ferrer and the cook, and two other sailors escaped by jumping overboard. Two Africans were also killed, but those remaining captured the other two ship hands and demanded the Spaniards take the Africans home since the Africans knew nothing about navigating the schooner.

Cinque knew enough about his location to know that the *Amistad* needed to sail east so that he and his fellow captives could return home. He made sure that the Spaniards sailed east during the day. But at night, the sailors reversed course and headed west. As a result, the *Amistad* wandered the Atlantic, running out of food and water, and making it necessary for the

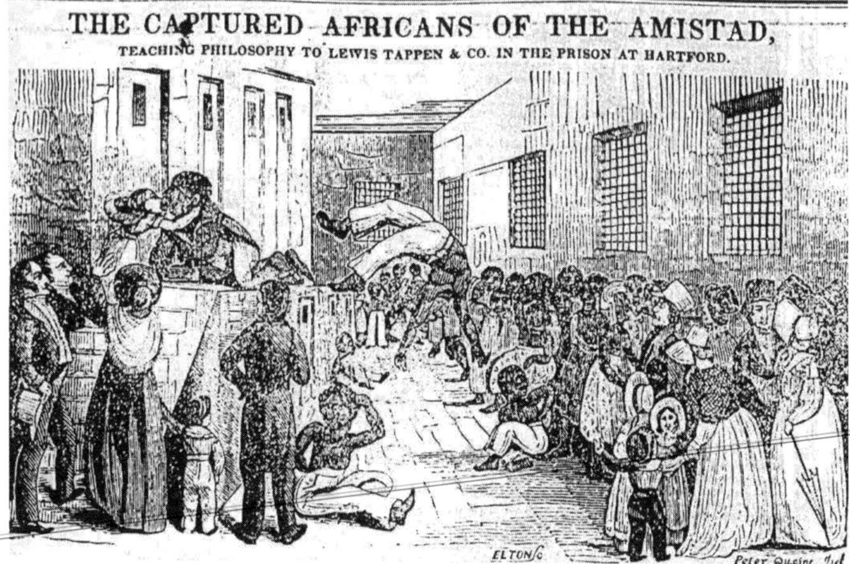

The Captured Africans of the *Amistad*. *On October 4, 1839, the New York* Herald *ran a lengthy article on the Africans who had been on board the* Amistad *and destined for slavery. James Gordon Bennett supported slavery, and his paper's articles on Cinque and the other* Amistad *captives depicted them in derogatory ways. The* Herald *did the same with abolitionists, in this case Lewis Tappan. The information that accompanied this image, in part, said, "On the left hand is Lewis Tappan, with his white hat, attended by another abolitionist, looking at Cinque kissing a pretty young girl, who was handed up to him by her sympathetic mother. . . . Away to the right is the fashionable, pious, learned, and gay people of Connecticut, precisely as they appeared during these amusing scenes in Hartford prison, receiving lectures and instructions in African philosophy and civilization."*

ship to hail down other ships to purchase supplies. Finally, the ship ended up off the coast of New York. The boat landed on Long Island to buy supplies, but that encounter ultimately led to the Africans' capture. When American sailors reached the *Amistad,* one of the Spaniards explained what had happened, and Cinque and company were taken into custody. The *Amistad* was towed to New London, Connecticut.

Even though the *Amistad* landed in a free state and had been towed to a port in another nonslave state, questions arose as to whether the Africans were free or the property of the Spaniards. Many in America, including President Martin Van Buren, paid special attention to the case because they felt the outcome could have implications for the 1840 elections. Van Buren, especially, thought he could use the case to win proslavery votes. The Spanish said the United States had no jurisdiction over the event and needed to return the *Amistad*, its surviving crew, and the Africans to Cuba for a trial. That did not happen. Instead, the trial judge ruled that the Africans were free since Spain had signed a treaty in 1817 with England that made African slave trading illegal. The United States government, however, appealed the case, setting up Cinque's and the other Africans' Supreme Court appearance and the entry of John Quincy Adams into the fray. Spain and Portugal also joined the case as claimants against the ruling to set the Africans free.

Adams's arguments in front of the Court included more than the rights of those taken from Africa. He claimed that what the government proposed violated the freedoms of the Constitution and might ultimately be used to remove the freedoms of white Americans. In the end, Justice Joseph Story, for the Court, "ordered the said negroes to be delivered to the president of the United States, to be transported to Africa."[5] In November 1841, the Africans who were still living sailed for Africa with a group of missionaries.

America's newspapers followed the story of the *Amistad* and its "cargo" closely. Daily reports of the trial appeared in newspapers, and many abolitionists used the event and the trial to argue against slavery. The correspondence found in two New York papers, however, the *Journal of Commerce* and the *Morning Herald*, typify the nation's dialogue surrounding the event. Some newspapers sympathized with the plight of the Africans, while others, with proslave leanings, tended to belittle what was being done to free Cinque and his compatriots. Most of the readings in the chapter come from the two papers, the *Journal* printing the abolitionist message surrounding the *Amistad*, and the *Morning Herald* belittling the abolitionist effort and the Africans. The *Journal* portrayed the Africans as noble; the *Morning Herald* poked fun at their appearance, intelligence, language, and—most importantly—the abolitionists. The last article in the section of articles and editorials that supported the *Amistad* victims comes from the *Colored American*, a New York newspaper published by and for African Americans. It offers a view of Cinque radically different from that found in the *Morning Herald*.

Support for the Africans

George Day: "Narrative of the Africans"

The account of the Amistad *was replayed in numerous newspaper accounts from numerous perspectives. In this one, recorded by abolitionist George Day, readers received an interpretation of the events from one of the Africans.*

Journal of Commerce (New York), 10 Oct. 1839

To the Editors of the Journal of Commerce:

Gentlemen.–The following short and plain narrative of one or two of the African captives, in whose history and prospects such anxious interest is felt, has been taken at the earliest opportunity possible, consistently with more important examinations. It may be stated in general terms, as the result of the investigations thus far made, that the Africans all testify that they left Africa about six months since; were landed under cover of the night at a small village or hamlet near Havana, and after 10 or 12 days were taken through Havana by night by the man who had bought them named *Pipi*, who has since been satisfactorily proved to be Ruiz; were cruelly treated on the passage, being beaten and flogged, and in some instances having vinegar and gunpowder rubbed into their wounds; and that they suffered intensely from hunger and thirst. The perfect coincidence in the testimony of the prisoners, examined as they have been separately, is felt by all who are acquainted with the minutiae of the examination, to carry with it overwhelming evidence of the truth of their story. Yours respect'ly,

GEORGE E. DAY.

This afternoon, almost the first time in which the two interpreters Covey and Pratt have not been engaged with special reference to the trial to take place in November, one of the captives named Grabaung was requested to give a narrative of himself since leaving Africa, for publication in the papers.... Grabaung first gave an account of the passage from Africa to Havana. On board the vessel there was a large number of men, but the women and children were far the most numerous. They were fastened together in couples by the wrists and legs, and kept in that situation day and night. Here Grabaung and another of the Africans named Kimbo, lay down upon the floor to show the painful position in which they were obliged to sleep. By day it was no better. The space between decks was so small,–according to their account not exceeding four feet,–that they were obliged, if they attempted to stand, to keep a crouching posture. The decks, fore and aft, were crowded to overflowing. They suffered (Grabaung said) terribly. They had rice enough to eat, but had very little to drink. If they left any of the rice that was given to them uneaten, either from sickness or any other cause, they were whipped. It was a common thing for them to be forced to eat so much as to vomit. Many of the men, women, and children, died on the passage.

They were landed by night at a small village near Havana. Soon several white men came to buy them, and among them was the one claiming to be their master, whom they call *Pip*, said to be a Spanish nick name for *Jose*. Pip, or Ruiz, selected such as he liked, and made them stand in a row. He then felt each of them in every part of the body; made them open their mouths to see if their teeth were sound, and carried the examination to a degree of minuteness of which only a slave dealer would be guilty. . . .

The men bought by Ruiz were taken on foot through Havana in the night, and put on board a vessel. During the night they were kept in irons, placed about the hands, feet, and neck. They were treated during the day in a somewhat milder manner, though all the irons were never taken off at once. . . . In addition to this there was much whipping, and the cook told them that when they reached land they would all be eaten. This "made their hearts burn." To avoid being eaten, and to escape the bad treatment they experienced, they rose upon the crew with the design of returning to Africa.

Such is the substance of Grabaung's story, confirmed by Kimbo, who was present most of the time. He says he likes the people of this country, because, to use his own expression, "they are good people—they believe in God, and there is no slavery here." . . .

John Quincy Adams: "Victims of the Slave Trade"

The Journal of Commerce *under the editorial guidance of Gerald Hallock and David Hale was decidedly antislavery. In this letter from Adams, who was the nation's sixth president and the lawyer for Cinque and the other slaves, the former chief executive explains what has happened to those Africans aboard the* Amistad, *and the illegality of it all.*

***Journal of Commerce* (New York), 19 November 1839**

The Africans of the Amistad were cast upon our coast in a condition perhaps as calamitous as could befall human beings, not by their own will—not with any intention hostile or predatory on their part, not even by the act of God as in the case of shipwreck, but by their own ignorance of navigation and the deception of one of their oppressors whom they had overpowered, and whose life they had spared to enable them by his knowledge of navigation to reach their native land.

They were victims of the African slave trade, recently imported into the island of Cuba, in gross violation of the laws of the Island and of Spain; and by acts which our own laws have made piracy—punishable with death. They had indicated their natural right to liberty, by conspiracy, insurrection, homicide and capture and they were accused by the two Cuban Spaniards embarked with them in the ship, of murder and piracy—and they were claimed by the same two Cuban Spaniards, accessories after the fact to the slave-trade piracy, by which they had been brought from Africa to Cuba, as their property, because they had bought them from slave-trade pirates.

They knew nothing of the Constitution, laws or language of the country upon which they were thus thrown, and accused as pirates and murderers, claimed as slaves of the very men who were their captives, they were deprived even of the faculty of speech in their own defense. This condition was sorely calamitous; it claimed from the humanity of a civilized nation compassion;—it claimed from brotherly love of a Christian land sympathy;—it claimed from a Republic professing reverence for the rights of man justice—and what have we done?

A naval officer of the United States seizes them, their ship and cargo, with themselves; tramples on the territorial jurisdiction of the state of New York, by seizing, disarming and sending on board their ship, without warrant of arrest, several of them whom he found on shore; releases their captives; admits the claim of the two captives to fifty masters as their slaves; and claims salvage for restoring them to servitude. They are then brought before a court of the United States, at once upon the charge of piracy and murder, upon a claim to them as slaves, and upon a claim against their pretended masters for salvage, by kidnapping them again into slavery. The Circuit Judge decides that the United States do not exercise the right of all other civilized nations to try piracies committed in foreign vessels; that he thereupon cannot try them for piracy or murder, but that the District Court may try whether they are slaves or not; as it is doubtful whether this trial will be held in Connecticut or New York, and it must take time to ascertain in which, they shall in the mean time be held as slaves to abide the issue.

Is this compassion? Is it sympathy? Is it justice? But here the case now stands.

Quere: "More Amistad Questions"

As the court date for Africans who were on board the Amistad *approached, many wondered whether a fair trial would be possible. The anonymous Quere poses questions on the situation in a series of letters, of which this is the third. The most interesting is the fourth question. Here, the writer foreshadows the Dred Scott Supreme Court decision of 1857 (see Chapter 27) by asking if the* Amistad *Africans are lawful property and by answering that they are men.*

Journal of Commerce **(New York), 25 December 1839.**

THE AFRICANS OF THE AMISTAD.

Question l. By what authority or *process*, are the Africans now held, seeing that the Circuit Court of the United States for the State of Connecticut, has dismissed the complaint charging piracy and murder upon the high seas, and declared itself to have no jurisdiction in the premises, or that no offence has been committed?

Answer. A *libel* upon the schooner Amistad and its cargo for *salvage* having been filed by an officer of the U.S. Navy, a *warrant* was issued out of the District Court of the U. States for the State of Connecticut, directed to the Marshal of that District, commanding him to take into his custody and detain the said schooner and cargo till the claim for salvage should be investigated and decided. Upon *this warrant,* the schooner and cargo not only, but *all the Africans,* who came in her, were taken into custody. Subsequently other and various claims were interposed, but that warrant, it is believed, is the only process by which they are now held.

Question 2. Has the District Court of the U. States for the State of Connecticut, *jurisdiction* in the matter, *to the extent* its process has been used or exercised?

Answer. So far as the schooner *and cargo* are the subject of inquiry, it may be doubtful; for as much as the locality in which she was taken, may be such as to oust that Court of jurisdiction and give it to the U. States District Court for the Southern District of New York: and if the Africans are lawful *slaves,* the same Court which exercises jurisdiction over the schooner and cargo, must exercise jurisdiction over them. But if they are not lawful slaves, then process against them, no matter from which court issued, would be exercised to *an extent* unwarranted by law.

Question 3. But how does it appear that such exercise of jurisdiction would be to *an extent* unwarranted by law?

Answer. The District Court is one of limited jurisdiction—and its *admiralty powers only,* are invoked in the case of this libel: it is to ascertain, under this claim for salvage, whether "meritorious services" have been rendered in saving *property* from the perils and dangers of the sea, and if so found to be the case, to decree payment of a reasonable sum of money by the owners, or out of the *sale of the property*: Its powers are limited to the adjustment of the rights *of salvor and owner,* touching the *property saved,* that which is *conceded to be property of somebody*: it cannot entertain the question, whether that which is saved, *be property*; its province is, to determine *how* that which is *conceded to be property,* and has been saved, shall be disposed of as between owner and *salvor.* . . .

Question 4. Does it not then follow, that the question, whether the Africans are *lawful slaves* or *property,* ought to be settled in some other way, than that which is now pursued?

Answer. Yes—and it belongs to some COURT OF COMMON LAW, to determine whether the Africans are *men* or things: and if such Court, on full evidence that they are *slaves, lawfully held as such* , under and by virtue of some constitutional provision, act of Congress or treaty stipulation, shall pronounce them *things* or *property,* it will then be in time for an Admiralty Court to dispose of *such things,* to remunerate an officer of the U. States

Navy for towing a schooner and her cargo from Montauk Point into New London!...

QUERE.

An Anonymous Report: "A High-Minded People"

President Martin Van Buren was openly supportive of returning the Africans to Spain and retaining them as slaves. In this anonymous report in the Hartford Courant, *the writer reports on the president's position, one Van Buren took as much as a political ploy for re-election as one in which he believed.*

Courant (Hartford), 10 February 1840

We are informed by a gentleman from New Haven that a short time previous to the trial of the Africans of the Amistad, before the U.S. District Court at New Haven, Judge Judson presiding, Martin Van Buren addressed a letter to the Judge recommending and urging him to order the Africans to be taken back to Havana in a government vessel, to be sold there as slaves—and that about the same time the U.S. schooner Grampus was ordered to New Haven for the purpose of receiving them. The schooner, we learned from several sources, arrived at New Haven about the time of the trial under "sealed orders" and, after learning the decision of the court again, "made off." The letter of the President, recommending that these poor unfortunate Africans be sent into perpetual bondage, is said to contain statements disgraceful to the high station of its author, and which, were they published, would excite the indignation of every Republican freeman in the land. What will the friends of liberty say to this? Surely Martin Van Buren is playing the part of a tyrant with a high hand—else why this tampering with our courts of justice, this Executive usurpation, and this heartless violation of the inalienable rights of man? Of the truth of the above there is no doubt, and we leave the unprincipled author of such a proceeding in the hands of a just and high-minded People.

Charles Bennett Ray: "Cinque and Heroes of the American Revolution"

The Colored American *was originally called the* Weekly Advocate *under the guidance of Samuel Cornish and Philip A. Bell. The name was changed in an effort to prove that blacks, indeed, were Americans. In 1839, Ray assumed the paper's editorship. Most of the newspaper's financial support came from abolitionists, and when this piece was printed, the* Colored

American was the only paper in America with an African American editor. Here, Cinque is elevated to a status comparable with America's most notable founding fathers.

Colored American **(New York), 27 March 1841**

CINQUE.—This noble hero, by his defence of liberty, has placed himself side by side with Patrick Henry, John Hancock, Thomas Jefferson, and Samuel and John Adams fathers of the Revolution. The justice of the nation has stood up in vindication of his deeds, in defence of his course, and decreed them right. How could they have done otherwise, with an example so illustrious as the American Revolution before them. Were he not an African, a black man, his fame would be emblazoned forever on the tide of time, and written in high eulogium by the historian's pen. Robert Purvis has done himself great honor, in causing to have so correct a likeness taken of him on steel, to be handed down to posterity. His character and his acts certainly deserve to be written in song. Either would form a subject for those who muse in poetry. Now that the victory is won, will it not inspire the poet of the Merrimac. May it not be a subject for C.L.R. or H.H.G., or D.A.P. or Philomath. These, our own brethren, sometimes appear in song.

Opposition to the Africans

James Gordon Bennett: "Abolition and the *Amistad* Case"

The Morning Herald *and* Journal of Commerce *were New York rivals in the newspaper business. They, like many newspapers in America at the time, reflected a political point of view. In this letter, James Gordon Bennett, who was sympathetic to Southerners and slavery, attacks the* Journal *and abolitionist leaders. One of those leaders, Lewis Tappan, led the public pleas for the* Amistad *victims. The fact that his brother, Arthur, began the* Journal *should not be overlooked by readers. Bennett charges that the* Journal *and its correspondents are fabricating stories and stretching the truth to evoke sympathy.*

Morning Herald **(New York), 13 September 1839**

The "Journal of Commerce" and several other abolition papers, are very busy trying to create excitement out of the Amistad case and captured Africans. The Rev. David Hale, with a hypocritical, squinting, cast of the eye—not an honest, downright squint like mine—is publishing the correspondence of Lewis Tappan & Co., who intend, out of this case, to revive the dying embers of abolition in the north.

It seems there is a treaty in existence between Spain and the United States, by a clause of which the former claims the restoration of the Amistad and her cargo, and the latter government is bound in good faith, to deliver it, with all its appurtenances. The Rev. David Hale, and his correspondents, however, close their eyes to the faith and obligations of this treaty, and are busy, day and night, in stirring up the elements of popular resistance to the laws, under the form of studied, elaborate, and ridiculous appeals to their passions and feelings.

We are credibly informed, from authentic sources, that the stories told by Lewis Tappan in the Journal, like those first published in a penny paper, are one half fabulous, and the other half exaggerated.—In order to correct fables and exaggerations, we have again despatched a correspondent to New Haven, to track the footsteps of the abolitionists, and to tell the whole country the truth of this singular and extraordinary affair. We have already corrected many of the outrageous fabrications of the "Journal of Commerce," and its exciting adjuncts, and we presume we shall have a good month's work on hand to correct the fabrications they intend to make for the next four weeks, for when men with long black coats, under the name of religion, begin to lie, they don't stick at trifles—they beat the Father of Lies all to pieces. . . .

Already this strange affair bids fair to excite a stronger feeling throughout the Union, than any event that has happened in a long time. Whatever disposition be made of these Africans, the laws and treaties between nations ought to govern its course, in exclusion of those mischievous appeals to the passions of the mob of pious or profane loafers. We should not be surprised even, if the Amistad case entered deeply into the next election. Every thing about it looks black enough for a squall. Get out your great coats and umbrellas—we know not the moment the clouds will pour down, or the wind may blow.

An Anonymous Report: "The Captured Africans"

James Gordon Bennett sent a number of correspondents to cover the Amistad *situation. This report exposes the attitudes that many Americans had about Africans as witnessed in the descriptions of Cinque and others.*

Morning Herald **(New York), 18 September 1839**

Mr. Bennett: The Abolitionists are of course greatly annoyed by your exposure of their hypocrisy; and are endeavoring to attract the sympathy and extract the money of the humane by accusing those who have desired to divest the main question of the perplexing difficulties thrown around it by Tappan & Co. of subserviency to the views of the slave holders. But such charges are too preposterous to receive a moment's consideration, and the effect of the indiscreet and foolish movements of the Abolitionists has been highly prejudicial to the Africans. I heard one of our most distinguished citizens remark yesterday, that his sympathies had at first been warmly enlisted in favor of the blacks—that he had been induced to believe, by the representations of the pseudo-philanthropists, that they were a set of hapless beings who had been torn from the enjoyments of social and domestic life and sold to hopeless misery, to feed the insatiate avarice of a blackhearted planter; and he should have rejoiced at their escape, even if they had reached our shores dyed to the elbows in the blood of their oppressors. He thought of Cinguez as he had been represented by Leavitt and his coadjutors, the heroic liberator of his enslaved brethren, who nobly preferred death to the degrading bondage of the white man; and was almost ready to wink at an infraction of our treaty with Spain, if necessary, to protect him from the consequences of his daring gallantry. But a look at the *hero* and his *compatriots* had wrought an instantaneous change in his sentiments. Instead of a chivalrous leader with the dignified and graceful bearing of Othello, imparting energy and confidence to his intelligent and devoted followers, he saw a sullen, dumpish looking negro, with a flat nose, thick lips, and all the other characteristics of his debased countrymen, without a single redeeming or striking trait, except the mere brute qualities of strength and activity, who had inspired terror among his companions by the indiscriminate and unsparing use of the lash. And instead of intelligent and comparatively civilized *men,* languishing in captivity and suffering under the restraints of the prison, he found them the veriest animals in existence, perfectly contented in confinement, without a ray of intelligence, and sensible only to the wants of the brute. No man, he said, more thoroughly appreciated the hideous horrors of the slave trade, or had conceived a more decided aversion to slavery in all its phases; but he was certain that the natives of Africa would be improved and elevated by transferring them to the genial climate of Carolina, and the mild restraints of an intelligent and humane planter. Still although the abstract idea of liberty was utterly incomprehensible to an African, and ridiculous as applied to him; and his physical condition was made better by the change, he has natural rights which it is enormous wickedness to invade. The previous impressions, as well as present views of this gentleman, are precisely coincident to my own, and the effect of my examination of the condition and character of the captured blacks was identically the same.

The conclusion that I arrive at, therefore, is, that the monstrous perversions of the fact of which the Abolitionists have been guilty, and their hypocritical and insidious appeals to the sympathies of the public, have operated to the serious disadvantage of the blacks, and will have a greater influence in precluding a fair trial, than all other causes combined. . . .

An Anonymous Report: "The Captured Africans of the *Amistad*"

The Morning Herald*'s correspondents enjoyed making both the Africans and the abolitionists appear foolish. This news story was accompanied by a woodcut that showed the Africans turning somersaults. It also portrayed Cinque on top of a white girl kissing her while an inquisitive crowd looks on. Within the news account, the author continually pokes fun at the Africans and their language.*

Morning Herald (New York), 4 October 1839

A change has passed over the entire spirit of the existence of the negroes since their confinement at Hartford. Their animal spirits are greater than ever; they eat more, drink more, chatter more, gambol more, and turn more somersets than ever. In short, they are as merry as crickets, and as satisfied as pigs in clover. . . .

These blacks have created a greater excitement in Connecticut than any event that has occurred there since the close of the last century. Every kind of engine is set in motion to create a feeling of sympathy and an excitement in their favor. . . . A few weeks since Lewis Tappan arrived in Hartford, accompanied by his black tail; consisting of a great number of negroes of all ages and sizes, and colors, and speaking all languages from the Monshee down to the Mandingo. The appearance of this patron of pious negroes was exceedingly singular, as he paraded the streets of Hartford with a dozen negroes forming a black tail. . . .

The black fellows in confinement are astonished at all these singular movements, and begin to think, from the number of negroes brought to talk and jabber with them, that the blacks are the principle men in this country. They laugh heartily at all the movements of the whites, and consider them poor loafers, with ungraceful movements, and very much to be pitied because they are totally unable to turn a somerset. This is the *ne plus ultra* of accomplishments and refinements with them. If a man cannot turn a somerset they think very little of him in the way of civilization. They listen to what Lewis Tappan and the others have to say; and although Cinguez understands scarce a word that is said, and is conversed with often by signs; he replies merely by taking Lewis Tappan and his friends into the middle of the floor, and by signs asking them to turn a somerset. When he finds they are unable to oblige him in this particular, he throws a somerset himself by way of a lesson to them, laughs heartily, tries to turn up his flat nose, and walks off to his comrades, evincing the greatest contempt for the white chiefs who can't throw a somerset. . . .

At New Haven ladies were not allowed to visit the negroes generally; but at Hartford all who wish to enter are admitted. . . . They have invested in this affair, with all the romance of an eastern fairy tale, and they consider the black fellows as worthy of as much honor as the colored Moorish Knights of old; and if they get clear, it is probable some Yankees will pick them up in detail, and take them around the country to show them by way of a speculation. . . . And the negroes show their astonishment by eating an additional quantity of rice and throwing a few extra somersets to assist digestion. . . .

On Thursday Cinguez underwent an examination at the hands of a phrenological professor, who has paid great attention to the Africans, and is understood to have made himself exceedingly popular with them all . . . fumbling over his head with an air of solemn wisdom that would have done credit to a conventicle of jackasses or abolitionists, comparing his organs with a printed scale, and announcing the result of his examination to the admiring audience with unspeakable satisfaction. . . .

"That will do. Ladies and Gentlemen, this very happy experiment illustrates the truth of what I have stated to you. Those unfortunate men, whom a kind Providence has thrown upon our shores, are capable of the highest intellectual achievements. . . . But, Ladies and Gentlemen, I am detaining you from eloquence far more impressive than my own. Shinquah will make an address to his faithful followers, which the interpreters will render into English as accurately as possible. It is necessary to observe, however, that the idiom of the Mandingoes is somewhat peculiar, and that it is so much more significant than our language, as to be capable of conveying in a few sentences, ideas that cannot be expressed in English without using more than quadruple the number of words."

Cinguez, after this flourish of the phrenologist, delivered himself of a most eloquent oration in this wise:—Yah ullah hoo yumbu hek goo èèeh geroo wung boo wullah nah looh heèè dloa nahen wah tomah poo jumba Ke Tapan ke lah kos wooh tee pouh jee hee yah kon waun ka woo ne fee leh etap nee yal manding bum se moo tah as um su ti ye hah whoo sha nah ah e so ya do oh po oh yoh so poo oh yahu de wahah. Wooh pee lah.

This speech of Cinguez produced a great sensation amongst the white ladies, who could not understand a word of it; and amongst the black fellows, who chuckled and laughed at it. The interpreter gave the following as a rough translation:

"Hear, brothers. The white men fools. We are better. They not swim, not jump, not tumble, not turn somersets. We do all this. White chief feel my head. It is hard. I feel his head. It is soft. White women handsome. Our women better. White women turn no somersets; not swim, not jump, not tumble. They talk too much. Our women swim, tumble over, roll, turn somersets. White man's rice good, sun good; water bad. Tappan talk much, fool, do nothing; cannot turn a somerset: want to teach us, but very much fool to know nothing. We go home to Mandingo and eat and drink, and swim and jump again. Yes." . . .

An Anonymous Report: "Abolitionists Going to the Devil"

James Gordon Bennett truly detested the abolitionist movement and used every opportunity during the early stages of the Amistad *event to ridicule and belittle them. Here, an anonymous letter writer uses biblical scripture to portray abolitionists as the Devil in their work with Cinque and company. In addition, the paper delivered a jab at Lewis Tappan whenever it could, something that occurs here.*

Morning Herald **(New York), 23 October 1839**

MR. BENNETT:—We have the authority of Holy Writ for the fact that the devil, on a certain occasion therein described, inserted himself in the bodies of a parcel of swine, which swine ran down a hill into the sea, and so perished; and from this we come to the conclusion that Mr. Devil carried his pigs to a bad market. And now you have the authority, not of the scriptures, but of your humble servant, and many other persons of equal credibility, for the fact, that the same devil has lately entered the abolitionists, and is now rapidly driving them where they must, as a party, meet the fate of the swine. The parallel between the two cases, runs well until you come to the catastrophe, and there it fails—for the pigs were really valuable, and the devil erred in not endeavoring to *save his bacon*; while the abolitionists are good for nothing except mischief, and the devil will compensate for much of the evil he has wrought, if he makes an end of them in this way.

The excitement that had prevailed here on the subject of the Africans has nearly subsided. The presumptuous folly of Tappan and his coadjutors was only matter for ridicule. . . .

How long the abolitionists are to be permitted to practice their impositions on the public remains to be seen. The impression here is, however, that they have overreached themselves by this last act of fraud and rascality. They may rest assured, at any rate, that any further attempts to abuse the indulgence granted them by the Marshal and Col. Pendleton, by pampering the negroes, and thus rendering them insolent and troublesome, will meet with a suitable rebuke. It was but two or three days since, that the keeper discovered a large knife in possession of one of the blacks, and on instituting a scrutiny among them he found eight knives. They all denied having any most positively, and when the keeper found where they were hid, he was obliged to take them by force. Cinguez had two hid in his bunk. They were the largest kind of pruning knife, with the blades between three and four inches long, and very sharp at the point. These knives were furnished them by the abolitionists, or their agents, with what intent is not known; probably for the purpose of regaining their liberty, of which they are said to be unjustly restrained.

Questions

1. In what ways, do you think, the dialog concerning the *Amistad* reflected opinions on slavery and its validity in America?
2. From the readings that opposed the *Amistad* Africans, do you think the Africans or abolitionists were disliked more by those favoring the return of the Africans to Spanish control? Explain.
3. From the readings, what opinions do the abolitionists hold concerning the Africans in reference to their abilities to be free, independent people?

Notes

1. Kali to John Quincy Adams, 4 January 1841, quoted in Iyunolu Folayan Osagie, *The* Amistad *Revolt* (Athens: University of Georgia Press, 2000), 14.

2. A number of sources contain the *Amistad* account. The report may be found in the Supreme Court case, *United States v. Amistad*, 40 U.S. 518 (1841), 522–30; Osagie, *The* Amistad *Revolt;* Howard Jones, *Mutiny on the* Amistad (New York: Oxford University Press, 1987); Arthur Abraham, *The* Amistad *Revolt* (Freetown: USIS, 1987); Eugene D. Genovese, *From Rebellion to Revolution: Afro-American Slave Revolts in the Making of the Modern World* (Baton Rouge: Louisiana State University Press, 1979). The sources on which most scholars depend, however, are *The African Captives: Trial of the Prisoners of the "Amistad" on the Writ of Habeas Corpus before the Circuit Court of the United States for the District of Connecticut, at Hartford, Judges Thompson and Judson, September Term, 1839* (New York: American Antislavery Society, 1839); and John W. Barber, *A History of the* Amistad *Captives* (New Haven, Conn.: E.L. & J.W. Barber, 1840). Newspaper accounts also provide good coverage of the *Amistad* captives and trial.

3. Osagie, *The* Amistad *Revolt*, 3–4.

4. Most scholarly works list the number of slaves on the *Amistad* at fifty-three. The Supreme Court synpopsis of the event, however, lists fifty-four.

5. *United States v. Amistad*, 597.

CHAPTER 16

The Dorr Rebellion, 1842

In 1842, civil war loomed in the United States. Slavery had nothing to do with this civil war. States' rights being overrun by federal law had not drawn the ire of those who were ready to rebel. This civil war, in fact, was confined to the nation's smallest state, Rhode Island, but the cause of this rebellion was, those who instituted it believed, a bedrock of what America was all about—the right to vote. Those who rebelled in Rhode Island in 1842 were not fighting for the right of all Rhode Island citizens to vote, however. They were fighting solely for the rights of white males.

When James Madison inked the Constitution and delegates to the constitutional convention approved it in 1787, not one of the thirteen original colonies unconditionally allowed all white males to vote. Pennsylvania came the closest by permitting all white males who paid taxes to vote, but in most colonies and, subsequently, in most states, only white males who owned property could vote. When Vermont—which had been part of New Hampshire and New York originally—ratified the Constitution in 1791 to become the fourteenth state, it was the nation's first to accept universal suffrage for its white male citizens. Most of the states that joined the Union after Vermont did the same. Increasingly, states allowed white manhood suffrage. They also turned to the popular vote for elections rather than having delegates to state conventions elect officeholders from governor to judges.[1]

This did not happen in Rhode Island, though. The last of the original thirteen colonies to ratify the Constitution, the state that began as Providence Plantation elected to keep its charter, granted by Charles II in 1663, as its governing document. Owning property was a requirement of suffrage. By 1842, however, many of Rhode Island's residents were artisans and mechanics who were already or who would soon be workers in a growing industrial community, especially in the Providence area. They were not property owners, and as a result, the more rural parts of the state had more representation than the highly populated areas. By 1841, suffrage groups seeking voting rights for all white males developed throughout the state,

Laws of Rhode Island.

STATE OF RHODE ISLAND AND PROVIDENCE PLANTATIONS.

In General Assembly,—April Session, A. D. 1842.

—

AN ACT in amendment of an act entitled "An act to prevent Routs, Riots and Tumultuous Assemblies, and the evil consequences thereof."

Be it enacted by the General Assembly as follows:

—

The act to which this is in amendment, is hereby so far amended, as that if in the making or attempting to make Proclamation as mentioned in said act, the persons assembled as therein specified do not forthwith disperse themselves, they are to be dealt with as is in said act provided: And that so much of said act as requires the delay of an hour after making or attempting to make Proclamation as aforesaid, is hereby repealed.

True copy—witness,

HENRY BOWEN, Sec'ry.

Dorr Rebellion. *In May 1842, two governments existed in Rhode Island. One was the official government of the state. The other was known as the People's Government, with Governor Thomas Dorr at its head. Worrying that civil war loomed on the horizon, the General Assembly passed this act. This announcement appeared in the* Newport Mercury *on May 7. The* Mercury *served as the official newspaper of the government organized under Rhode Island's Charter, which was granted by Charles II in 1663 and still remained the official governing document of the state. The lack of a constitution that allowed all white males to vote was the root cause of the Dorr Rebellion. Under the charter, only male landowners could vote.*

and most of them accepted a Declaration of Principles, drawn up by one group. The declaration's propositions stated that all men were created free and equal and that property ownership should not create political advantages. In addition, every state needed a written constitution and a bill of rights. Rhode Island, the declaration said, had neither because the 1663 charter was not a constitution. It functioned, therefore, without a republican form of government, and that kept the majority of citizens from participating in state affairs. Consequently, Rhode Island citizens had a right to draft a new constitution that accurately represented all of the state's citizens.[2]

In response, suffragists and the state legislature called for constitutional conventions. Each drew up new constitutions; that of the suffragists was called the People's Constitution, and that of the legislature, the Freemen's Constitution. A prominent Providence lawyer, Thomas Dorr, had joined the cause of manhood suffrage and was instrumental in the design of the People's Constitution, but the Freemen's Constitution was the only one legally authorized. It was, however, narrowly voted down in a March election. Rhode Island's 1663 charter remained the law of the land, but the state was in limbo. With Dorr guiding the suffragists, the state held elections, and two separate governments were elected. The suffragists chose Dorr as governor, but the state's official ballots re-elected Samuel Ward King. Now two governments existed in the state. Both sides jockeyed for power. Dorr traveled to New York to seek support from its political machinery. King sought aid from the federal government and from President John Tyler. King began to arrest some of the leaders of the People's Party. Other members of the People's government resigned. The only solution appeared to be a military confrontation. Dorrites, led by their governor, attacked the arsenal in Providence, but the attempt fell apart. Dorr fled the state, the People's government collapsed, and King established martial law in the state. Dorr was captured, returned to the state, and tried for high treason. He was sentenced to prison "for the term of his natural life, and there kept at hard labor in separate confinement."[3]

Although Dorr's Rebellion was defeated, Rhode Island began to rethink its position on property ownership as a requirement to vote. In May 1843, a new constitution liberalized voting requirements, but the state continued to require white males either to pay taxes or own property—depending upon whether they were native- or foreign-born—until 1860. Dorr, after one year in prison, was pardoned, and in 1854—just before his death—the state legislature annulled his court conviction. The concept of universal male suffrage, just as the concept of a nation run not by an aristocracy but by the everyday people, became reality for white males in antebellum America. For many, no better example existed than Andrew Jackson, considered one of the common people, who was able to ascend to the presidency (see Chapter 4). "The great constitutional corrective in the hands of the people against usurpation of power," Jackson said, "is the right of suffrage."[4] Jackson no doubt meant white males, though in some states free blacks could also vote. The right of women to vote would have to wait (see Chapter 21).

This chapter looks at writings that center on the Dorr Rebellion and on male suffrage. The first readings support the rebellion, male suffrage, and the revolt. It begins with two articles from the *New Age,* the official Rhode Island suffrage newspaper. They are followed by a letter from President John Tyler that was sent to Governor Samuel King. King asked for federal intervention in Rhode Island, but Tyler refused to do so unless more proof of actual danger to the state could be provided. The next entry is a report of the activities of the People's Party government. What is interesting is that it is reported just as papers would report actions in Congress or in the state legislature. Here, a body usurping the traditional state power is treated as an official body. The last article in this section, by Horace Greeley, is part of a longer editorial that looks at the entire Rhode Island situation. Both parts of the editorial are included, one in each set of chapter readings. This part acknowledges the right of all males to vote.

The section of opposition to the rebellion and suffrage begins with the other part of Greeley's editorial. Though few would come out and deny any white males the right to vote, Greeley said more than gender was needed to determine voting credentials, and any effort to usurp a government needed to be closely scrutinized. This editorial is followed by articles that deal with events of the revolt. The last entry is an extended poem by the editor of the *Providence Journal* that explains the events of the Dorr Rebellion.

SUPPORT FOR THE REBELLION AND MALE SUFFRAGE

Rhode Island Suffrage Association: "Petition"

The New Age *was a newspaper begun expressly to support the manhood suffrage movement in Rhode Island. It was run by a committee appointed by the Rhode Island Suffrage Association.*[5] *This petition was written in polite language so as not to irritate the state's assemblymen, but it is obvious that the association wanted universal male suffrage for the state.*

New Age (Providence), 18 December 1840

To the Honorable the General Assembly of the State of Rhode Island: The undersigned, inhabitants and citizens of the State of Rhode Island, would respectfully represent to your honorable body, that they conceive, that the dignity of the State would be advanced, and that the liberties of the citizens better secured, by the abrogation of the Charter granted unto this State by King Charles the Second of England, and by the establishment of a constitution which should more efficiently define the authority of the Executive and Legislative branches, and more strongly recognize the rights of the citizens.

Your petitioners would not take the liberty of suggesting to your honorable body, any course which should be pursued, but would leave the whole affair in your hands, trusting to the good sense and discretion of the General Assembly.

Your petitioners would further represent to the General Assembly, that they conceive that an extension of the suffrage to a greater portion of the white male residents of the State, would be more in accordance with the spirit of our institutions, than the present system of the State and for such an extension they ask. Your petitioners would not suggest any system of suffrage, but would leave the matter to the wisdom of the General Assembly.

Upon both the prayers of your petitioners, they would ask the immediate and efficient action of the General Assembly, and as in duty bound will ever pray. . . .

An Anonymous Report: "No Confidence"

When the state assembly called for a constitutional convention, the New Age *issued this article. It doubted anything would happen to help those disenfranchised and said that the people had a right to hold a convention of their own, something the suffrage associations did.*

New Age, and Constitutional Advocate (Providence), 18 February 1841

Though we have but little confidence in the results of the deliberations of the Convention ordered by the General Assembly, yet the very fact that such a Convention has been ordered proves conclusively that there is a growing disposition on the part of the freeholders of the State to consider and remedy the abuses of its government. There has been a time when a petition like the one of Smithfield would have been quietly laid upon the table. But the General Assembly know that it would not do at this lat day to pass over in contempt a document of such character. As for this *Convention for the framing of a Constitution,* which they have called, we do not suppose it will do anything for the advancement of freedom in our State. It will be seen that the representation in the Convention will be nothing more than a representation of freemen, and taking this into view, it will be only the General

Assembly elected over again, and therefore we have no more to hope from such a body than we have from the General Assembly. Of course the over-represented towns will send their quota of representatives, and the under-represented towns will be voted down in precisely the same manner as if the General Assembly had themselves taken up the question of a Constitution. We are of the opinion that the whole affair will result precisely as did the last attempt of the kind. These contradictions only show the necessity of the people's taking the matter into their own hands. They are the persons most interested in the result. If then the General Assembly will not meet the wants of the people, nor in all probability will a Convention acting under them, it is high time *they* took the matter into their own hands, resolved if they cannot obtain redress of their grievances in the ordinary way, they will take extraordinary measures to obtain it.

John Tyler: "Letter from the President"

Rhode Island Governor Samuel Ward King appealed to the president for help in quelling what he feared would be an uprising in Rhode Island. The president's answer was no doubt not exactly what Governor King wanted. The president essentially said he would not send in federal troops unless an insurrection took place. Even then, he would be hesitant because he did not want to make the president the "armed arbitrator between the people."

***Newport (R.I.) Mercury,* 16 April 1842**

To His Excellency.

The Governor of Rhode Island:

SIR.—Your letter dated the 4th inst. was handed me on Friday . . .I shall not adventure the expression of an opinion upon those questions of domestic policy, which seem to have given rise to the unfortunate controversies between a portion of the citizens and the existing Government of the State. They are questions of Municipal regulation, the adjustment of which belongs exclusively to the people of Rhode Island, and with which this government can have nothing to do. For the regulation of my conduct in any interposition which I may be called upon to make, between the Government of a State and any portion of its citizens who may assail it with domestic violence, or may be in actual insurrection against it, I can only look to the Constitution and Laws of the United States, which plainly declare the obligations of the Executive Department, and leave it no alternative as to the course it shall pursue. . . .

By a careful consideration of the . . .acts of Congress, your Excelency [*sic*] will not fail to see, that no power is vested in the Executive of the United States to anticipate insurrectionary movements against the Government of Rhode Island, so as to sanction the interposition of the military authority, but that there must be an actual insurrection manifested by lawless assemblages of the people or otherwise, to whom a proclamation may be addressed, and who may be required to betake themselves to their respective abodes. . . . I have also to say . . . the Executive could not look into real or supposed defects of the existing government in order to ascertain whether some other plan of government proposed for adoption was better suited to the wants and more in accordance with the wishes of any portion of her citizens. To throw the Executive power of this Government into any such controversy would be to make the President the armed arbitrator between the people of the different States and their constituted authorities, and might lead to an usurped power, dangerous alike to the stability of the State Government and the liberties of the people. . . .

I render to your Excellency assurances of my high respect and consideration.

JOHN TYLER.

Washington, April 11, 1842.

An Anonymous Report: "Meeting of the Legislature Under the 'People's Constitution'"

The inability of Rhode Island's voters to approve a new constitution opened the door for the People's Party. After its own elections and approval of its own constitution, the new government began operation in Providence. This report, which is identical to those that newspapers ran of "official" governments, gave some credence to Dorr's activities.

***Newport (R.I.) Mercury*, 7 May 1842**

On Tuesday last, the Government under the "People's Constitution" was organized at Providence. The procession was formed at the Hoyle Tavern and consisted of about 2,000 persons of whom about 700 were armed, and proceeded through some of the principal streets to Eddy street, to a building intended for a Foundry, (an in an unfinished state,) where arrangements had been made for the organization of the Government. . . .

The House convened at 3 o'clock and a committee was appointed to wait on Gov. Dorr and inform him the Legislature was ready to receive any communication he may have to lay before them.

The Committee reported that the Governor would address the two Houses forthwith.

The Governor then delivered his message which was of great length, and ordered to be printed.

An act passed repealing the act passed by the General Assembly at their April session.

Resolutions were passed to the effect that the Governor be requested to inform the President of the United States, that the Constitutional Government had gone into operation. . . .

Horace Greeley: "The Rhode Island Question"

Horace Greeley disagreed with the methods of the Dorr Rebellion, but he agreed with the principle for which they were founded–the right to vote. The end of this editorial supports this point. The first part of the editorial, that which condemns Dorr and the rebellion, is included in the readings below.

Daily Tribune **(New York), 13 May 1842**

We appeal to both parties in Rhode Island for moderate counsels and conciliatory measures.–Having at last agreed with regard to essentials, why should they shed each other's blood on a punctilio? The non-Freeholders have long and justly demanded an extension of the Right of Suffrage; the Landholders have at length wisely conceded it. Why fight now? Why should not the Suffrage men take what is offered them as an instalment, since it secures to seven-eights of them the fullest Political Rights, and thereby the power to make such further modifications as they choose in a legal manner? Long will the day be rued by every lover of Freedom and of a Government of Laws wherein the first drop of blood is shed in this most deplorable quarrel.

Opposition to the Rebellion and Male Suffrage

Horace Greeley: "The Rhode Island Question"

The issue of manhood suffrage was not a simple one to Horace Greeley. People cannot simply take government into their own hands, he said. But, people have a right to vote, and Greeley believed that suffrage should not be based on gender but on other criteria. This editorial provides fuel for both sides of the manhood suffrage issue, and the section that supports the Rhode Island suffrage issue is included in the section above.

Daily Tribune **(New York), 13 May 1842**

Gov. Dorr and his supporters base the lawfulness of their proceedings on the assumption that *a majority of the People* have an inalienable right to change their form of Government, or establish an entirely new one, at such time and in whatever manner they may choose. Suppose we admit this, the question instantly presents itself—*Who are the People* possessing this right? If all persons are intended, then their Constitution has not been adopted.... 'Ah, but,' says the governor, 'we mean by the People all adult male citizens.' Yea, sir; so we understand; but by *what right do you draw this line?* Who authorized you to say who are and who are not entitled to a voice in the primordial organization of a commonwealth? How are you empowered to decide that a citizen may vote and an alien may not?—that an intelligent native, 20 years old, shall not vote, while an ignorant immigrant of 21, being naturalized, may do so?—that a drunken and vicious husband may vote while his exemplary and well informed wife may not? . . . All must see that the Suffrage party are condemned by their own principles.... If Mr. Dorr's government is recognized at Washington, a government *de facto* of revolted Africans in South Carolina or Mississippi must be by the same rule....

The right of a majority to form and alter Governments, the right of individuals to vote, must have *some* limitations. If a President or a majority in Congress should be chosen, and the beaten party by adding up their popular votes, were able to show a majority, would they thence be authorized peaceably to oust the President and Congress so chosen? A Government in which Law and Prescription are nothing but aggregate physical majorities of to-day every thing, has certainly no existence in any State but Rhode Island....

Samuel Ward King: "1,000 Dollars Reward"

Following the failed assault on the arsenal, the People's government fell into disarray, and Thomas Dorr fled. Below is Governor King's announcement of a $1,000 reward for Dorr's capture.

Newport (R.I.) Mercury, 11 June 1842

WHEREAS, THOMAS W. DORR, of Providence charged with treason against the said State of Rhode-Island and Providence Plantations is a fugitive from justice, and supposed to be now within the limits of our sister State of Connecticut; and from credible information, is still pursuing his nefarious enterprise against the peace and dignity of said State of Rhode Island and Providence Plantations . . . I made a requisition on the 25th of May last, addressed to his Excellency Chauncey F. Cleveland, Governor of said State of Connecticut, for the apprehension and delivery of the said Thomas Wilson Dorr, according to the constitution of the United States....

I do, therefore pursuant to authority in me vested, and by advice of the Council, hereby offer a reward of One Thousand Dollars for the delivery of the said Thos. Wilson Dorr to the proper civil authority of this State, within one year from the date hereof, that he may be dealt with as to law and justice shall appertain. . . .

SAMUEL W. KING

An Anonymous Report: "Dorr Fled and His Fort Taken"

Though the cause was lost, Dorr and a few faithful continued their efforts. Dorr, who had been in New York, returned, and he and his company set up camp in Chepachet, a small town on the Connecticut border. The government learned of the encampment and Dorr's attempts to fortify it, interceded, and caused Dorr to flee for his life, as this "extra" from the Providence Journal *explains.*

***Providence (R.I.) Journal,* 28 June 1842**

. . . Dorr fled last evening, at 7 o'clock, with fifty men, in the direction of Connecticut. His own men were ignorant of his flight, and many of them declared that they would shoot him, could they find him. A large body of them went through Burrillville, in the direction of Massachusetts. The fugitives were in considerable parties and well armed.—They will therefore be dangerous to the peaceful inhabitants, unless they are taken. . . .

Henry B. Anthony: "The Dorriad"

The Providence Journal *captured the failed Dorr Rebellion in an extended poem that was published over a two-week period in January 1843. The opening stanza refers to Dorrites' failed attempt at firing cannons on the arms house in Providence. Later, Dorr brandished a sword he said belonged to a Revolutionary soldier, but that was probably not true. Algerine refers to a law passed by the legislature that made it treason for anyone to hold a state office if elected under the People's Constitution—that drawn up by the suffragists and so named by those who opposed it. Though the poem, written by the paper's editor Henry Bowen Anthony, tends to poke fun at the suffragists, the last stanza seems to imply that they were correct.*

***Providence Journal,* 7 and 13 January 1843**

TH' impatient chief looked on with ire,
Blanched was his cheek, but tenfold fire
    Was flashing in his eye.
And, *waddling* up—he meant to *stride*—
"Give me the torch," with fury cried,
    "And d—it, let me try!"

He seized the match with eager hand,
While backward his brave soldiers stand;
Three times he wave it in the air,
The cursed Algerines to scare,
And bid them all for death prepare;
Then down the glowing match-rope thrust,
As though he'd have the cannon burst.
Had they not *put the ball in first,*
It very likely would.
But, hark! what sounds astound the ear?
Why turns each hero pale with fear?
What blanches every lip with fright?
What makes each "General" look so white?
And e'en the Governor looks not quite
As easy as a Governor might. . . .
"The ALGERINES have come at last!
They're turning out in every street,
Their tyrant swords we soon shall meet.
Already in the torches' glare,
Their bayonets gleam in MARKET SQUARE. . . .
Enough was said, enough was heard,
They needed not another word.
Away, like frightened sheep, they ran,
And save himself, they cried, who can. . . .
For now the martial Governor Dorr
Hath buckled on *that sword* for war,
And swears he is determined for
        The Algerines to rout. . . .
The Governor saw with conscious pride,
The men who gathered at his side;
That bloody sword aloft he drew,
        And "list my trusty men," he cried–
"Here do I swear to stand by you,
        As long as flows life's crimson tide;–
Nor will I ever yield, until
I leave my bones upon this hill." . . .
Tremble, ye Algerines: the hour
Is hastening, when, with sovereign power,
The people shall their rights demand,
And rise in vengeance through the land.
        Morton, with twice ten thousand men
For Governor Dorr, shall cross the line; . . .
The exiles shall their footsteps turn
Where freedom's hopes forever burn.
On Acote's height, o'er Dexter's Plain,
Freedom's wild shout shall burst again,

And franchised freemen join the cry,
For beauty, banks and liberty. . . .
The cause is safe, the State is won!

Questions

1. How could the Dorr Rebellion have been avoided? Could it have been avoided? Explain.
2. What were Horace Greeley's beliefs on the rights of people to vote?
3. The Dorr Rebellion raises questions about government of and for the people. Are there situations of which you can think in which Dorr's actions would be justifiable? Were his actions warranted? Explain.

Notes

1. George Brown Tindall, *America: A Narrative History,* 2 vols. (New York: W.W. Norton, 1984), 1:388–89.

2. Details on Dorr's Rebellion come from Arthur May Mowry, *The Dorr War, or the Constitutional Struggle in Rhode Island* (Providence, R.I.: Preston & Rounds, 1901; reprint, New York: Johnson Reprint Corp., 1968); and Marvin E. Gettleman, *The Dorr Rebellion: A Study in American Radicalism, 1833–1849* (New York: Random House, 1973).

3. *Republican Herald* (Providence), 29 June 1844.

4. Andrew Jackson to James Buchanan, June 25, 1825, Buchanan Papers, Historical Society of Pennsylvania, Philadelphia, quoted in Robert V. Remini, *Andrew Jackson and the Course of American Freedom, 1822–1832* (New York: Harper & Row, 1981), 30–31.

5. Mowry, *The Dorr War,* 55.

CHAPTER 17

Joseph Smith and the Mormons, 1844

In 1844, Joseph Smith sat in a jail cell in Carthage, Illinois. It was not the first time the thirty-eight-year-old founder of the Church of Jesus Christ of Latter-day Saints had been arrested. Trouble seemed to travel with Smith and the Latter-day Saints. This time, however, Smith and his brother, Hyrum, would not leave their cell alive. On the afternoon of June 27, a mob opened fire, killing the Smiths.

The death of Joseph Smith ended a religious journey that began when the Vermont-born prophet uncovered a set of golden tablets near Palmyra, New York, around 1827.[1] That Smith might find religious artifacts or even begin a religious movement in Palmyra was not inconsistent with what had been happening in the area for years. Western New York had been the site of numerous religious revivals in the 1820s and was referred to as the burned-over district by many because of the continuous fires that dotted the countryside providing light for revival meetings. Smith's tablets, however, were something new. Written in a hieroglyphic-type text that Smith could read, the tablets told how Hebrews had traveled to North America after the fall of the Tower of Babel and of how evil subsequently triumphed over good in the New World. Then evil finally succumbed to God's prophet—Mormon—and his son Moroni. Smith published the golden tablets as *The Book of Mormon* in 1830 and based his new religion, the Church of Jesus Christ of Latter-day Saints, on the new book and the Bible.

Smith and his new church, which had many traditions compatible with established Christian beliefs, appealed to some people who had grown disillusioned with mainline Christian denominations. Revivalism had already sparked several new denominations, and, increasingly, many in America believed the second coming of Jesus was imminent. Therefore, Mormonism was not initially seen as a radical step. Being a member of the LDS required total devotion, a tenet to which most who believed the second coming was nearly at hand freely subscribed. Smith advocated living in closed communities, another facet of Mormonism that was not out of line with the com-

WHIG—Extra.

Friday Morning July 12, 1844.

Arouse!—Arouse!—The Standard flies,
High sounds our *Bugle* call,
The voice of battle's on the breeze,
Arouse Whigs!—one and all!

Buffalo meeting-house near Willliams' Mill, Carter co	"	21,
Stoney Creek Campground, Carter co	"	22,
Scotts' Saw-Mill, Carter co	"	23,
Carter's Furnace, Johnson co	"	24,
Howard's Forge, "	"	26,
Wills' meeting house, "	"	27,
Paperville, Sullivan co	"	28,
Reedy Creek, Sullivan co	"	29,
Gammon's School-house, Sullivan co	"	30,
Rogersville Circuit Court,	Sept.	23,
Greeneville "	Oct.	14,
Jonesboro' "	Oct.	28.

Life and health permitting, I will address the people at the above times and places, unless the appointments should come in conflict with religious meetings. As I do not consider my health perfectly restored, if I should be unable to attend any of the above appointments, I will procure the attendance of some Whig speaker, so that the people will not, in any case, be disappointed. My engagements are such that I do not at present expect to make or attend, any other appointments during the canvass, and my Whig friends are respectfully requested to give the above notice as general a circulation as possible. Col Haynes has been invited to attend, and has promised to do so.

TH·MAS A. R. NELSON.

June 8th 1844

McMULLEN'S TRINITY!

Death of Joe Smith.

JOE SMITH, the infamous Mormon Prophet, his brother Hiram, and another leading Mormon have all been killed. Another Presidential candidate out of the way, which makes Polk the stronger, as the Mormons are all Locos! This rascal ought to have been shot ten years ago. The subjoined article from the Quincy Illinois Herald, gives the particulars:

"DEATH OF THE PROPHET!!

Joe and Hiram Smith are Dead!

The steamboat Boreas just in from Warsaw, brings shocking intelligence from the marching order. Maj Flood has ordered out the militia of this regiment, and the steamer Boreas is waiting to convey them to the scene of action.

There is no knowing where this dreadful affair will end. Many have expressed fears that our city is in danger, because most of the Warsaw families have taken refuge here—but we believe there is no danger, we are too far from the scene of action.

Messengers have just left for Hannible and the other town below, for the purpose of arousing the Missourians. The excitement in our city is intense and the anxiety to hear the fate of Gov Ford and his men very great.

LOCOFOCOISM EXEMPLIFIED.

Read it Boatsmen!

At the late Session of our Legislature, Mr Williams of Knox, submitted a memorial No. 117, having for its object the removal of obstructions in the Tennessee and Holston Rivers.

By a reference to the House Journal, page

Extra! Extra! *When news that was considered too important to wait for a regular issue of a newspaper was received at the printing office, editors sometimes published supplements of "extras" to get out the news. This is a special edition of the* Jonesborough (Tenn.) Whig. *William Brownlow, the paper's editor, used the extra to call attention to the candidate his paper supported for president–Henry Clay. He also used the special issue to announce the death of Joseph Smith, founder of the Latter-day Saints. In the next regular issue of the paper, Brownloe praised those who murdered Smith in Carthage, Illinois.*

BRIGHAM YOUNG MUSTERING HIS FORCES TO FIGHT THE UNITED STATES TROOPS.

The Mormon War. *The Church of Jesus Christ of Latter-day Saints—known to most as the Mormon church—had stirred controversy wherever its founder, Joseph Smith, and his followers went from 1830 until their migration to Utah. The Mormon War of 1857 and 1858 began after Brigham Young was replaced as territorial governor by a non-Mormon. The LDS officially introduced their practice of polygamy in 1852, and it stirred the ire of most non-LDS Americans. The Republicans even attacked polygamy in their party platform, saying they opposed the "twin pillars of barbarisms," slavery and polygamy. The government sent 3,000 troops to Utah to force Young to relinquish the governorship, which he did. Only one battle was fought in the war, and the government outlawed polygamy in 1862. This image appeared in* Harper's Weekly *on November 28, 1857.*

munal movements taking place in Oneida, New York, and elsewhere. Where Smith's new religion differed was in its strong mission call. Proselytizing members of other religious groups was advocated. Good works by a person were an essential part of the teachings of Smith's LDS, so becoming a missionary took on nearly mandatory requirements. But, as the Mormons increased in numbers and moved westward to gain new members and to find a new Promised Land in which to settle, hostility toward them grew. In 1837, one Missouri writer called the LDS "a mass of human corruption, a tribe of locusts, that still threatens to scorch and wither the herbage of a fair and goodly portion of Missouri by the warm of emigrants from their pestilent hive in Ohio and New York."[2]

Because the LDS believed a new Jerusalem existed somewhere in North America, Smith sent people westward to look for it. Some believed they had found it in the Northeast corner of Ohio, in the town of Kirtland. Numbers of the town's residents joined the church, and Smith and other Mormons moved there in 1831. Initially accepted, the Mormons soon angered many, and Smith was tarred and feathered. Smith moved again in 1837, this time to the area near Independence, Missouri, where some LDS members had been living for years. The large influx of Mormons was met with resistance and forced a move north in the state. Hostilities intensified, especially after Smith announced on July 4, 1838, "I will be the Second Mohamed."[3] The Mormon War, as it was called by many, had begun, with Governor L.W. Boggs proclaiming war on the LDS. Boggs decreed, "The Mormons must be treated as enemies, and must be exterminated or driven from the State, if necessary for the public peace. Their outrages are beyond all description."[4] As a result of the war, Smith was arrested, but he and other incarcerated Mormons escaped and fled to Illinois in 1839.[5] There, the LDS established their new home in Commerce, a name changed to Nauvoo, the Hebrew word for beautiful.

Nauvoo quickly turned into a prosperous and thriving community and Illinois' second-largest city behind Chicago. The LDS also prospered. There were at least 35,000 proselytized members by 1844, principally in the United States but also in England.[6] While in Nauvoo, Smith disclosed that he had received a number of revelations. The most offensive of these was polygamy. Although it did not become church doctrine until 1852, Smith revealed the practice to some church leaders, and news of it leaked to the press. Increasingly, Smith claimed greater power for himself, declaring himself King of the Kingdom of God and establishing the Nauvoo Legion, a militia. He also announced his intentions to run for president in 1844.

Smith began to make many enemies, both among Mormons and among the gentiles–the term the LDS used to refer to non-Mormons–in Illinois. One group found a way to attack Smith; it began a newspaper in Nauvoo. The *Nauvoo Expositor* published its only issue June 7, 1844. The *Expositor* called the LDS, as originally taught, verily true. But editor Sylvester Emmons went on to attack Smith, saying he had pretensions to righteousness and that the effort being made by Joseph Smith for political power and influences was not commendable in the sight of God. Smith ordered the Nauvoo Legion to close down the *Expositor,* which it did by destroying the press, the type, and any newspapers it could find. Those who opposed Smith had charges brought against him and other LDS leaders for inciting riots, and he, his brother, and two other LDS leaders were jailed in nearby Carthage. "Can you stand by and suffer such infernal devils!" one letter writer in nearby Warsaw railed. "We have no time for comments; every man will make his own. Let it be made with powder and balls!!!"[7] The letter's suggestions were followed two weeks later when Illinois troops stopped guarding the jail, and a mob of up to 250 surrounded the jail and opened fire on the second-story jail cell. Though many predicted the demise of the LDS following Smith's death, the Mormons continued to thrive. Under Brigham Young's guidance, they moved the base of their operations to Utah.

This chapter looks at how the press reacted to Smith and the Mormons. The chapter's first section focuses on attacks on Mormons and begins with a report from Geauga County, Ohio, where Smith and other Mormons moved when they left New York. It is followed by reports that describe Mormonism and Smith. These are followed by an expose written by John C. Bennett, once a Mormon himself, who wrote actively against Smith and the LDS from 1842 on. The next readings revolve around the murder of Joseph Smith. These are followed by a report from Hawaii on the evils of polygamy. The section opposing Mormons ends with Horace Greeley's interview of Brigham Young.

In the second section, writings that dealt favorably with Mormons are included. They begin with a review of *The Book of Mormon* by the newspaper in Palmyra, New York, near where Smith found the golden tablets. It is followed by a letter written to the *Messenger and Advocate*, a Mormon newspaper. The chapter ends with two accounts that discuss the unfair treatment Mormons received in Missouri during the Mormon War of 1837–1839.

Opposition to Mormons

An Anonymous Report: "The Golden Bible, or Book of Mormon"

When Joseph Smith and his followers left New York, they moved to Ohio. Although this report is not overtly critical of Mormons and is more informative in its presentation, the author obviously believes Smith and the Latter-day Saints are inaccurate in their beliefs and professions.

Geauga Gazette **(Painesville, Ohio) 31 January 1831**

The Golden Bible, or Book of Mormon.

The believers in the sacred authenticity of this miserable production, are known by the name of "Mormonites," and their book is commonly called "the book of Mormon." It is asserted by them that their number in this vicinity is four hundred. . . .

They have recently received an additional revelation from the prolific prophet, Smith, which is generally understood to say that Kirtland is within the precincts of the holy land; but by others is said to mean only that in that town will be a great gathering of mighty multitudes, preparatory to their westward general migration. . . .

They profess to receive sensible demonstrations of the presence of the Deity. A few days since, a young man gave information to some of his brethren that he was about to receive a message from heaven. They repaired to the spot designated, and there, as they solemnly assert, a letter descended from the skies and fell into the hands of the young man.—The purport was to strengthen his faith and inform him that he would soon be called to the ministry. They declare their solemn belief that this letter was written by the finger of God. The style of writing was the round Italian, and the letters of gold. The favored youth immediately attempted to copy the communication, but as fast as he wrote, the letters of the original disappeared until it entirely vanished. It is alledged that some of them have received white stones promised in the 2d chapter of the Revelations. Such of them as have "the spirit" will declare that they see a white stone moving about the upper part of the room, and will jump and spring for it, until one more fortunate than the others catches it, but he alone can see it. Others however profess to hear it roll across the floor. These two stories, and others of a similar character, are told by them with solemn assertations of their truth. . . .

An Anonymous Report: "Mormonism—Religious Fanaticism—Church and State Party"

The Courier and Enquirer *was one of America's best-known and respected newspapers at the beginning of the 1830s. By printing this anonymous letter, editor J. W. Webb joined most American editors in denouncing Smith and Mormonism. This letter attempts to show that Smith and his son were simply gullible dupes in the get-rich-scheme of an Ohio man.*

Morning Courier and New-York Enquirer, 1 September 1831

You have heard of MORMONISM—who has not? Paragraph has followed paragraph in the newspapers, recounting the movements, detailing their opinions and surprising distant readers with the traits of a singularly new religious sect which had its origin in this state. Mormonism is the latest device of roguery, ingenuity, ignorance and religious excitement combined, and acting on materials prepared by those who ought to know better. It is one of the mental exhalations of Western New York.

The individuals who gave birth to this species of fanaticism are very simple personages, and not known until this thrust them into notice. . . . Old Joe

Smith had been a country pedlar in his younger days, and possessed all the shrewdness, cunning, and small intrigue which are generally and justly attributed to that description of persons. He was a great story teller, full of anecdotes picked up in his peregrinations—and possessed a tongue as smooth as oil and as quick as lightning. . . . Young Joe, who . . .figured so largely in the Mormon religion, was at that period a careless, indolent, idle, and shiftless fellow. He hung round the villages and strolled round the taverns without any end or aim—without any positive defect or as little merit in his character. . . .

A few years ago the Smith's [*sic*] and others who were influenced by their notions, caught an idea that money was hid in several of the hills. . . . They dug these holes by day, and at night talked and dreamed over the counties' riches they should enjoy, if they could only hit upon an iron chest full of dollars. . . . At last some person who joined them spoke of a person in Ohio near Painesville, who had a particular felicity in finding out the spots of ground where money is hid and riches obtained. He related long stories how this person had been along shore in the east—how he had much experience in money digging—how he dreamt of the very spots where it could be found. "Can we get that man here?" asked the enthusiastic Smiths. "Why," said the other, "I guess as how we could by going for him." . . .

After the lapse of some weeks the expedition was completed, and the famous Ohio man made his appearance among them. This recruit was the most cunning, intelligent, and odd of the whole. He had been a preacher of almost every religion—a teacher of all sorts of morals. . . . He knew every turn of the human mind in relation to these matters. He had a superior knowledge of human nature, considerable talent, great plausibility, and knew how to work the passions as exactly as a Cape Cod sailor knows how to work a whale ship. His name I believe is Henry Rangdon or Ringdon, or some such word. About the time that this person appeared among them, a splendid excavation was begun in a long narrow hill, between Manchester and Palmyra. This hill has since been called by some, the Golden Bible Hill. . . . In the face of this hill, the money diggers renewed their work with fresh ardour, Ringdon partly uniting with them in their operations.

Jesse Townsend: "Mormonism"

As Smith and his followers moved westward, people who had any knowledge of the man and movement would often write letters that appeared in newspapers. This letter from Palmyra, New York, found its way into a number of publications. The author, Jesse Townsend, hoped to reveal Smith's questionable past and that of his followers.

Christian Register (Boston), 30 December 1834

A lazy fellow who was formerly a county pauper, has lately attempted to raise recruits for "Joe Smith," on Pillar Point, near this place. He pretended that he had a withered arm miraculously cured. From a knowledge of this bold attempt at imposition, and with a view of getting correct information on this subject of Mormonism, a person in this village addressed a letter to a gentleman of the first respectability in Palmyra and received the following answer:

PALMYRA, County of Wayne.
State of N.Y., August 16th, 1834.

Dear Sir,—Your letter of the 5th ult. requesting information concerning the people called Mormonites, and concerning their origin and leaders, has been received.

This imposition was begun by Joseph Smith, in the vicinity of this village.

However incredible it may appear, the following statement is correct, and shows the great folly and weakness of the people who have credited the impositions with falsehoods which Joseph Smith and his associates in iniquity have propagated.

I begin with the leader "Joe" as he is and has been called here for 20 years past. For ten years he has been a man of questionable character, of intemperate habits, and a noted money-digger. . . . Joe pretended that he had at length found, by digging, a wonderful curiosity, which he kept closely concealed.

After Joe had told different stories, and had called the pretended curiosity by different names, he at length called it, The Golden Plates of the Book of Mormon. . . .

In the meantime, Joe visited a visionary fanatic, by the name of Harris and told him he had received some golden plates from the Lord with directions to call on Martin Harris for fifty dollars, to enable him to go to Pennsylvania and there translate the contents of those plates. . . .

At the same time, Smith affirmed that it would be immediate death for any one to see those plates besides himself and the writers of the book of Mormon.—Poor Martin, through his lack of faith and his having, at a certain time refused to hand over to Joe more money, was excluded from a view of the plates. . . .

Thus dear sir, you have a general, but true delineation of the Mormonites in their origin and the character of their prominent characters. Smith and Harris. Make what use of this communication you please. Such use as you may judge the cause of true religion requires; such as may prevent the propagation of error and delusion. Yours respectfully,

JESSE TOWNSEND.

John C. Bennett: "Objections to the Gathering of Saints"

John C. Bennett waged a campaign against Smith and the Latter-day Saints that culminated in History of the Saints, *a book written in 1842 attacking their practices. In this article, which appeared before the book, Bennett outlines the evils of Smith and the LDS church.*

Daily Journal (Louisville, Kentucky), 27 July 1842

To the Editors of the Louisville Journal:—

As I promised to lay before you some of the strong points of objection to "*the gathering of the Saints,*" or the congregating of THE MORMONS at *one point, or general head-quarters,* I now proceed to redeem the pledge.

1st. Nine hundred and ninety-nine thousandths of all the *faithful* of the Mormon Church regard Joe Smith as God's vice-regent on earth, and obey him accordingly . . .If, therefore, any State officer, in the administration of public justice, happens to give offence to His Holiness the Prophet, it becomes the will of God, *as spoken by the mouth of his Prophet,* that that functionary should DIE; and his followers, *the faithful Saints,* immediately set about the work of assassination, in obedience, as they suppose, to their Divine Master; and for which NOBLE DEED, they expect to receive an excellent and superior glory in the celestial kingdom!!! . . .

2d. Where a large community, like the Mormons, are under the absolute dictation of a vacillating and capricious tyrant, like Joe Smith, who acts under the influence of reason, but is wholly governed by impulses and selfish motives, political demagogues will become fawning sycophants, and the best interests of the country will be sacrificed in the ambitious views of an ancient or modern Prophet—a Mahomet or a Smith! This state of things is fraught with the most fearful consequences—the subversion of governments; the fall of kingdoms and empires; the destruction of nations by the shedding of rivers of human blood; and, where consequences of a less serious nature accrue, it destroys natural affection, hardens the heart against the better feelings of our nature, and produces a state of savage barbarity, which causes a civilized man to shudder, and from which he turns with loathing and disgust.

3d. The standard of morality and Christian excellence with them is quite unstable. Joe Smith has but to speak the *word,* and it becomes the LAW which they delight to obey—BECAUSE IT COMES FROM GOD!! Acts, therefore, which but yesterday were considered the most immoral, wicked, and devilish, to-day are the most moral, righteous, and God-like, because God, who makes right, has so declared it *by the mouth of his anointed Prophet!*

4th. Joe Smith designs to abolish all human laws, and establish a *Theocracy,* in which the word of God, *as spoken by his (Joe's) mouth,* shall be the only law; and he now orders that his followers shall only obey such human laws as they are *compelled* to do, and declares that the time is at hand when all human institutions shall be abrogated! Joe's *will* is to become the *law of right,* and *his power is to execute it.*

5th. Under the new order of things, *all* the property of *the Saints,* with their wives and little ones, is to be *consecrated* to Joe, to subserve his purposes and gratify his passions! . . .

With high consideration of respect and esteem, suffer me to subscribe myself—Yours, respectfully,

JOHN C. BENNETT.

Charles A. Foster: "Unparalleled Outrage at Nauvoo"

The animosity between Joseph Smith and those who opposed him came to a head in June 1844. A newspaper in Nauvoo—the center of the LDS—attacked Smith. Smith ordered the paper shut down. The report of these actions appeared in the Warsaw Signal. *Thomas C. Sharp, editor of the* Signal, *added the introductory and closing paragraphs of this report of the events in Nauvoo that resulted in the arrest of Joseph and Hyrum Smith. Charles Foster, who was connected with the* Expositor, *provided the* Signal *with the basic report of what occurred in Nauvoo in relation to the closing of the* Nauvoo Expositor. *It is Sharp, though, who advocated violence toward Smith.*

Warsaw (Ill.) Signal, 12 June 1844

Below we give the particulars of the diabolical outrage that has ever been perpetrated in this free country. Had it been the act of an excited multitude, it would have appeared much more excusable; but it was the deliberate work of men who acted not from the impulse of a sudden emotion, nor amid the tumult of an intoxicated multitude. It was done in cold blood! and is there any thing further needed to exhibit the fiendish and tyrannical disposition of Joe and his sattelites. To comment on this most wanton act would be an insult to our readers. . . .

Mr. Sharp:—I hasten to inform you of the unparalleled outrage, perpetrated upon our rights & interests, by the ruthless, lawless, ruffian band of Mormon mobocrats, at the dictum of that unprincipled wretch Jo Smith . . . declared the Nauvoo Expositor, a nuisance, and directed the police of the city to proceed immediately to the office of the Expositor and DESTROY THE PRESS AND ALSO THE MATERIALS, BY THROWING them into the STREET!!!!

If any resistance were made, the officers were directed to demolish the building and property, of all who were concerned in publishing said paper;

and also take all into custody, who might refuse to obey the authorities of the City.

Accordingly, a company consisting of some 200 men, armed and equipped, with muskets, swords, pistols, bowie knives, sledge hammers, &c, assisted by a crowd of several hundred minions, who volunteered their services on the occasion, marching to the building, and breaking open the doors with a sledge hammer, commenced the work of destruction and desperation.

They tumbled the press and materials into the street, and set *fire to them, and demolished the machinery with sledge hammer, and injured the building very materially.* We made no resistance; but looked on and felt revenge, but leave it for the public to avenge this climax of insult and injury.

C.A. Foster.

We received the above communication by the hands of Charles A. Foster, about 1/2 past 11 o'clock to-day. We have only to state, that this is sufficient! War and extermination is inevitable! Citizens ARISE, ONE AND ALL!!!– Can you stand by, and suffer such INFERNAL DEVILS!! to ROB men of their property and RIGHTS, without avenging them. We have no time for comment, every man will make his own. Let it be made with POWDER AND BALL!!!

William G. Brownlow: "Death of Joe Smith"

The Jonesborough Whig*'s editor was a Methodist minister named William Brownlow. He printed a "extra" on July 12 to announce the death of Joseph and Hyrum Smith. In this article, Brownlow praises those who killed Smith, saying he should have been killed ten years earlier.*

Jonesborough (Tenn.) Whig, and Independent Journal, 24 July 1844

Some of the public Journals of the country, we are sorry to see, regret the death of that blasphemous wretch *Joe Smith,* the Mormon Prophet. Our deliberate judgement is, that he ought to have been dead ten years ago, and that those who at length have deprived him of his life, have done the cause of God, and of the country, good service.

What lead [*sic*] to his death? This question answered properly and no one will be found to regret his death. By order of Smith and his villainous Council, a newspaper press was destroyed on the 10th ultima [i.e., this month, July], for the reason too, that it did not advocate Mormonism! This was followed by a declaration of *Martial Law,* and the adoption of other *arbitrary measures,* to the injury and annoyance of other peaceable citizens.

These things led to a war, and Smith was killed, as he should have been. Three cheers to the brave company who shot him to pieces!

Jon Hyde, Jr.: "Utah as It Is "

Jon Hyde was a Mormon missionary sent to the Sandwich Islands (Hawaii) in early 1856. Although the islands were an independent nation, their inhabitants had a great deal of contact with the United States, especially with California. A large number of Hawaiians came to California during the 1849 gold rush, as did Mormons. As part of the LDS's proselytizing efforts, missionaries traveled to the islands. Hyde was a convert to Mormonism, but he rethought his conversion on the ocean voyage. In this letter, Hyde discusses the errors of Mormonism, particularly polygamy, referred to as the abominable doctrine.

Polynesian (Honolulu, Hawaiian Islands), 18 October 1856

To the Editor of the Polynesian:

It is ignoble to attack the weak and foolish to meddle with the ridiculous. Mormonism, however, is not weak. Between 2,000 and 3,000 professors of this cruel delusion will have arrived before this date at Salt Lake, as this year's emigration; it is not therefore decreasing. A system that has sufficient pretence of truth to obtain the acquiescence of a hundred thousand men and women of different countries, persuasions, abilities and prejudices, to combine them into one active co-operating body, and from 40,000 to 50,000 persons, who are gathered in one location, knocking at the gate of the Union, demanding admission as a state, is certainly not ridiculous. Its religious pretensions are too arrogant and presumptuous to deserve any thing but contempt; but the attention it has attracted, the abominations it practices, the moral depravity and religious ruin it is consummating in its many devotedly deluded followers, demands more serious consideration.

The Mormons arouse the rest of mankind with adultery, prostitution and corruption–point to disease and misery as their consequences–offer a better plan, polygamy, for the salvation of the world, the purification of our morals, the increase of our happiness, and to prepare, say they, for the coming of Jesus Christ. If their plan be effectual, surely it must result in good at *home*. . . . But if we find them more corrupt, men and children less happy, more degraded, and the children more depraved we must reject the system as false and their claims to divine inspiration as infamous blasphemy. . . .

On the 7th April, 1852, polygamy was publicly avowed, and a pretended revelation of J. Smith's commanding its practice was read and commented upon: since then this principle has formed a part of their public preachings. The whole of the apostles abroad had lied in denying it; positively, deliberately, willfully lied,—wrote lies,—published and circulated lies,—the heads of the church sanctioned and commanded them and claimed for it the approval of that Being who cannot lie! What confidence can we place in the statements of such men, or the pretensions of such a system? . . .

That polygamy owes its rise to the lusts of Joseph Smith; that it is subversive of man's happiness; that it is degrading to the women, who feel bitterly their degradation; that it is not productive of peace, but heart-wringings, anguish and despair; that it produces an unruly, swearing, lying, precocious and profligate race of children; that it is not beneficial to the increase of the population nor improving to the physical or mental development of their offspring, and that instead of purifying and elevating man, it is a most depraving curse.

I who have been an eye and ear witness to its practical operation at Salt Lake City. . . .

Last Spring I left Salt Lake for these Islands, dissatisfied and unhappy. On recalling to my memory all I had witnessed; what I had seen of tyranny and wrong, corruption and sorrow, vice and crime—what I had heard of contradictions and inconsistencies in doctrine, ridiculous pretensions miserably supported, outrageous imposture and intolerant bigotry, I determined to forsake this system. My reasons have been repeatedly asked, and by many persons. I have selected, Mr. Editor, your columns as my means of communicating the above brief sketch of some of them, and am sir.

Yours respectfully, JON HYDE, Jr.

Horace Greeley: "Brigham Young Interview"

From the time that the Latter-day Saints came into existence, they were of interest to Americans because of their views. Interviews became a way for newspapers to gain information during the early part of the Penny Press era. Horace Greeley, one of America's most outspoken and popular editors—he would run for president as the Democratic candidate in 1872 against U.S. Grant—traveled to Utah for this interview with Brigham Young. The interview, despite the sectional conflict that raged in 1859, caused considerable discussion. Greeley's interview is reasonably unbiased, but Young's answers no doubt angered many, as he supported slavery and polygamy and called any church other than that of the LDS apostate.

Tribune **(New York), 20 August 1859**

H.G.: Am I to regard Mormonism (so-called) as a new religion, or as simply a new development of Christianity?

B.Y.: We hold that there can be no true Christian Church without a priesthood directly commissioned by and in immediate communication with the Son of God and Savior of Mankind. Such a church is that of the Latter-Day Saints, called by their enemies Mormons; we know no other that even pretends to have present and direct revelations of God's will.

H.G.: Then I am to understand that you regard all other churches professing to be Christian as the Church of Rome regards all churches not in communion with itself—as schismatic, heretical, and out of the way of salvation?

B.Y.: Yes, substantially.

H.G.: What is the position of your church with respect to slavery?

B.Y.: We consider it of divine institution and not to be abolished until the curse pronounced on Ham shall have been removed from his descendants. . . .

H.G.: How general is polygamy among you?

B.Y.: I could not say. Some . . .have each but one wife; others have more; each determines what is his individual duty.

H.G.: What is the largest number of wives belonging to any one man?

B.Y.: I have fifteen; I know no one who has more; but some of those sealed to me are old ladies whom I regard rather as mothers than wives, but whom I have taken home to cherish and support.

H.G.: Does not Christ say that he who puts away his wife, or marries one whom another has put away, commits adultery?

B.Y.: Yes; and I hold that no man should ever put away a wife except for adultery—not always even for that. Such is my individual view of the matter. I do not say that wives have never been put away in our church, but that I do not approve of that practice. . . .

Support for Mormons

O. Dogberry: "Gold Bible"

The region surrounding Palmyra was the home of Joseph Smith and where he uncovered the golden tablets that revealed new scripture. In this issue of The Reflector, *its publisher, O. Dogberry, reprinted Chapter One of "The First Book of Nephi" from the* Book of Mormon, *about which there were rumors, though it had not yet been released. After the chapter, Dogberry made the following comments, which proposed that the golden tablets might be genuine since most people knew too little of scripture to make any other evaluation.*

The Reflector **(Palmyra), 2 January 1830**

We do not intend at this time to discuss the merits or demerits of this work, and feel astonished that some of our neighbors, who profess liberal principles, and are probably quite as ignorant on the subject as we are, should give themselves quite so much uneasiness about matters that so little concern them. The Book, when it shall come forth before the public, it must stand or fall, according to the whims and fancies of its readers. How it will stand the test of criticism, we are not prepared to say, not having as yet examined many of its pages.—We are, however, prepared to state, that from a part of the first chapter, now before us, and which we this day publish, we cannot discover anything treasonable, or which will have a tendency to subvert our liberties. As to its religious character, we have as yet no means of determining, and if we had, we should be quite loth to meddle with the tender consciences of our neighbors.

Orson Hyde: "To the Editor of the *Messenger and Advocate*"

The Latter-day Saints realized the power of the press and began the Messenger and Advocate *in 1834. The author of this letter to the editor, Orson Hyde, along with Hebert Kimball, traveled to England in 1837 as part of the first LDS mission to Europe. Kirtland, Ohio, was the center of LDS activity in the early to mid-1830s, with about 2,000 Mormons living there by 1835.*[8] *Hyde and others used Kirtland as a base of missionary activity in the Ohio Valley and Missouri. This letter discusses one of those mission trips.*

Messenger and Advocate (Kirtland), April 1836

DEAR BROTHER:—Having just returned from a short mission, say about three weeks, in the county of Portage Ohio, I feel disposed to drop you a few lines that you may know something how the cause of truth has prospered in my hands during this short period.

I commenced preaching in the township of Hiram, the place where our beloved brethren, Joseph Smith jr. and Sidney Rigdon were most shamefully beaten, tarred and feathered some three or four years since by the inhabitants of that place and vicinity. . . .

There is an opportunity of doing much good in those regions, if some faithful laborer would go into that part of the vineyard.

I expect to leave town to-morrow for the purpose of sounding the ram's horn again around Jericho, that her walls may be broken down, but may God bless and spare those who entertain the spies, (or the servants of the Most High.)

The cause of God will roll on in the face of an opposing world, and I cannot but make the expression of the Prophet, saying, "no weapon formed against thee shall prosper." . . .

The servants of God are declaring boldly the counsel of the Most High, as contained in the book of Mormon, the Scriptures and the book of Covenants–Many are repenting and coming to baptism that they may obtain the remission of their sins through faith in the name of Christ.

May the Lord pour out his Spirit upon the Elders abroad, and may the angel of thy presence go before them,–may they be endowed with wisdom and power from on high, to stop the mouths of gainsayers, and to heal the sick, and cast out devils in the name of the Lord.

I am, Sir, Yours in the Bonds of the new Covenant,

ORSON HYDE

S.M. Bartlett: "Gross Outrage"

Mormons led by Brigham Young moved to the Quincy, Illinois, area following the troubles and expulsion the LDS experienced in Missouri in 1839. They soon migrated north of Quincy to Commerce, renaming it Nauvoo. Most residents of Quincy welcomed the LDS to their community. In this report by S.M. Bartlett, editor of the Quincy Whig, *readers of the paper are given an account of Mormon persecution in Missouri. Bartlett's account describes the torture of several Mormons. Readers should know that the paper's positive portrayal of the LDS soon gave way to attacks.*

***Quincy (Ill.) Whig*, 18 July 1840**

We readily give place below to the proceedings of a public meeting held at Nauvoo, Hancock county. They but briefly allude to the inhuman outrage lately perpetrated by certain persons of Missouri, upon four citizens of the Mormon persuasion, living in Hancock county, in this State. . . . Here, with their victims in their power, the Missourians proceeded to inflict a severe punishment upon them.–One was immediately stripped, a halter placed around his neck, and attached to a limb above his head, and so tightly drawn that to prevent choking to death, he was obliged to stand on the tip of his toes; in this situation, with his arms fastened around the tree, so that his bare back was fully exposed, the tormentors swore they would take his life unless he would confess. In vain he urged his innocence, that he had nothing to confess, that he had never committed any theft, &c., they still plied their whips until his back was so dreadfully lacerated, that to save his life, he agreed to confess any thing they would desire. He was taken down from the tree, with scarcely any life in him, and actually confessed whatever his tormentors wished! . . .The old gentleman . . .one of the four abducted, behaved with such resolution, and pointed out to them so clearly their injustice and inhumanity, that after stripping, and fastening him to the tree, and taunting him with epithets of the foulest character, they took him down and finally set him at liberty. One of the victims by some means, succeeded, all cut in pieces as he was to make his escape . . . to the river closely pursued by his persecutors, where, finding a canoe, he made all haste for this shore; upon arriving at which, he staggered out of the boat and fell exhausted on the beach, seemingly resolved to die, if die he must, upon a soil where the laws were respected. Two other of the victims, by our latest intelligence, were still in the hands of the people of Tully, if death, of which there is some probability, has not put an end to their sufferings. . . .

The Governor, with commendable spirit, we learn, has taken hold of the matter, and avows his intention of investigating all the circumstances connected with these outrages—and to protect the Mormons from future outrage and aggression, to the utmost of his authority. . . .

An Anonymous Report: "A Glance at the Mormons"

This description of the Latter-day Saints came at a time when the LDS were still enjoying a "honeymoon" period with many in western Illinois. It includes a favorable description of what the LDS had done with the area surrounding Nauvoo and a positive view of LDS beliefs. It was written by an unnamed visitor to Nauvoo.

Quincy (Ill.) Whig, 17 October 1840

Since the Mormons were expelled from the State of Missouri, they have purchased the town of Commerce, a situation of surpassing beauty, at the head of the lower rapids, on the Illinois shore of the upper Mississippi river. The name of the place they recently changed to Nauvoo, the Hebrew term for Fair or Beautiful. Around this place, as their centre, they are daily gathering from almost every quarter: and several hundred new houses, created within the last few months; attest to the passing traveller the energy, industry, and self-denial with which the community is imbued. . . .

The signal success which every where attends their exertions, proves how well their religious system is adapted to give expression to the various forms of enthusiasm that pervade the religious sentiment of the day. Retaining many truths which are held in common by different denominations of Christians and covering their own absurdities with imposing forms and lofty pretensions, their system opens a winning asylum for all the disaffected or dissatisfied of other persuasions, and much that is congenial to almost every shade of erratic or radical religious character. . . .

They teach that all who are baptized by immersion and under proper authority, are legally entitled to the remission of their sins, and the gift of the Holy Ghost. Among other religious exercises, they meet together to testify, to prophecy, to speak with tongues to interpret, and to relate their visions and revelations, and, in short, to exercise all the gifts of God, as set in order among the ancient churches. They believe that the restoration of Israel to Palestine, the rebuilding of Jerusalem, and the second advent of the Messiah are near at hand. . . .

As to the Book of Mormon, while they place implicit confidence in its truth, they deny that it is a new Bible, to exclude the old but a historical and religious record, written in ancient times, by a branch of the house of Israel that peopled America, from whom the Indians descended. . . .

Questions

1. Why might people react so negatively to Joseph Smith and Mormonism?
2. After reading the writings in this chapter, do you think Americans of the nineteenth century were a religious people? Explain your reasoning.
3. From the readings, can you determine what the Mormons may have done that caused such disdain?

Notes

1. A number of sources tell the story of the development of Mormonism, Mormon conflicts in the 1830s and 1840s, and the arrest and murder of Joseph Smith and his brother Hyrum. See Jan Shipps, *Mormonism: The Story of a New Religious Tradition* (Urbana: University of Illinois Press, 1985); Richard L. Bushman, *Joseph Smith and the Beginnings of Mormonism* (Urbana: University of Illinois Press, 1984); Leonard J. Arrington and Davis Bitton, *The Mormon Experience: A History of the Latter-day Saints* (New York: Vantage Books, 1980); Donna Hill, *Joseph Smith, the First Mormon* (Garden City, N.J.: Doubleday, 1977); Sydney Ahlstrom, *A Religious History of the American People* (New Haven, Conn.: Yale University Press, 1972); Loy Otis Banks, "The Role of Mormon Journalism in the Death of Joseph Smith," *Journalism Quarterly* 27 (1951): 268–81. A contemporary account of the development of the Latter-day Saints and the Mormon troubles from 1838–1844 is E.D., "The Rise and Progress of the Mormon Faith and People," *Southern Literary Messenger* 10 (September 1844): 526–38. The story of Joseph Smith and Mormonism was also a popular newspaper topic from 1829 forward.

2. *Gazetteer of the State of Missouri* (St. Louis) 1837, quoted in Arrington and Bitton, *The Mormon Experience*, 47.

3. Quoted in Ahlstrom, *A Religious History*, 506.

4. Quoted in E.D. "Rise and Progress of the Mormon Faith," *Southern Literary Messenger*, 534.

5. *Daily Evening Gazette* (St. Louis, Missouri), 1 May 1839.

6. *Deseret Church News Almanac* (Salt Lake City, Utah, 1974), 205.

7. *Warsaw (Ill.) Signal,* 12 June 1844. See Banks, "Role of Mormon Journalism," *Journalism Quarterly,* for a complete discussion of the beginning and the destruction of the *Nauvoo Expositor.*

8. Arrington and Bitton, *The Mormon Experience,* 21.

CHAPTER 18

Manifest Destiny, 1845

In 1663, eight Britons who supported the return of Charles II to the British throne received a charter for land in the New World. That charter was for a land to be called Carolina after the king, and it stretched from the Atlantic Ocean "to the west as far as the south seas."[1] Though no one at the time knew exactly how far west the lands may have stretched, there was a belief that America was a vast land spanning thousands of miles. Colonial Americans did not initially focus their attention to the west. They looked eastward back across the Atlantic to England for laws, trade, and the necessities of life.

But by the middle of the 1750s, American colonists were moving into what they called the backcountry. Within a generation, they would be an independent nation and living beyond the Appalachian Mountains, turning Kentucky and Tennessee into states before the end of the eighteenth century. When President Thomas Jefferson purchased Louisiana from Napoleon Bonaparte in 1803, the young United States suddenly owned twice the amount of land it had before the purchase. Reports from explorers Lewis and Clark and from Zebulon Pike of this region created a fascination with a land that held great promise for Americans. Jefferson remarked:

> However our present interests may restrain us within our own limits, it is impossible not to look forward to distant times when our rapid multiplication will expand itself beyond those limits, and cover the whole northern, if not the southern continent, with a people speaking the same language, governed in similar forms, and by similar laws; nor can we contemplate with satisfaction either blot or mixture on that surface.[2]

Another forty years would pass before the term Manifest Destiny would be coined when the *United States Magazine and Democratic Review* stated, "Our manifest destiny is to overspread the continent allotted by Providence for the free development of our yearly multiplying millions."[3] Jefferson, however, captured the essence of American expansionism in his comment to Monroe.

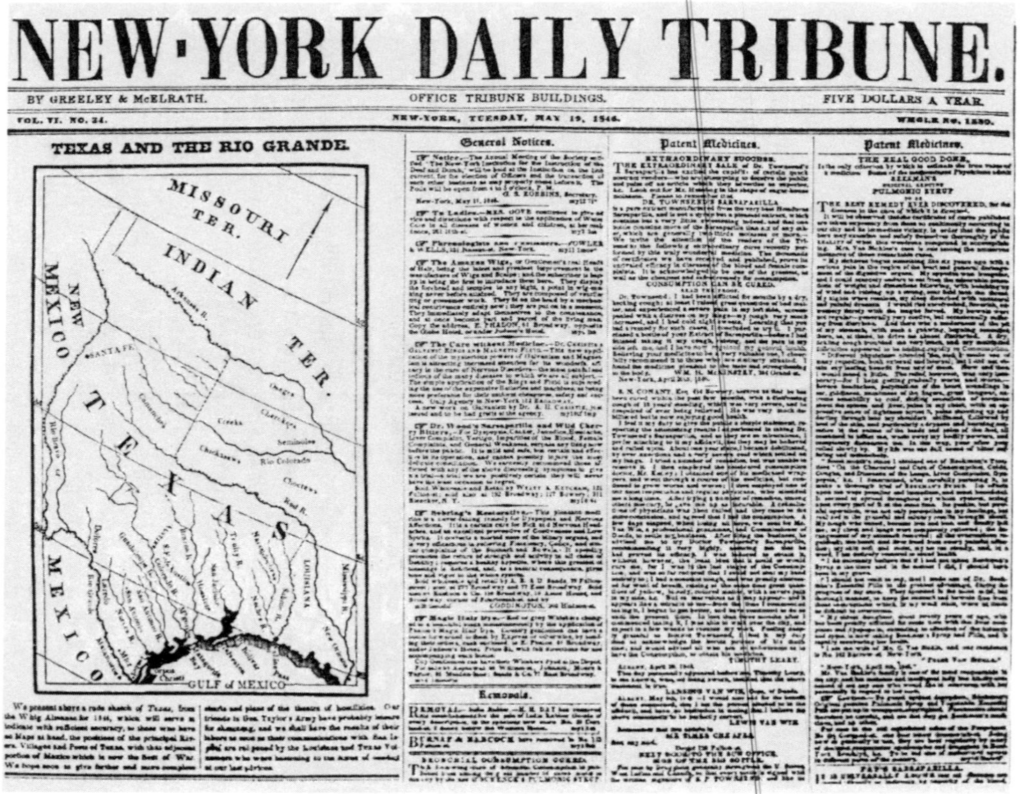

NEW-YORK DAILY TRIBUNE.

BY GREELEY & McELRATH. OFFICE TRIBUNE BUILDINGS. FIVE DOLLARS A YEAR.

VOL. VI. NO. 34. NEW-YORK, TUESDAY, MAY 19, 1846. WHOLE NO. 1530.

TEXAS AND THE RIO GRANDE.

MISSOURI TER.

INDIAN TER.

NEW MEXICO

TEXAS

MEXICO

LOUISIANA

GULF of MEXICO

General Notices.

Patent Medicines.

Patent Medicines.

Removals.

Texas annexation. *In 1845, Texas became America's twenty-eighth state. As the nation discussed adding the Republic of Texas to the nation, Horace Greeley ran this map of Texas to give readers a better idea of its location and features.*

The concept of Manifest Destiny combined religious, nationalistic, and ethnocentric beliefs. From the first New England settlements, those living in America thought of it as a new "Promised Land" and of themselves as God's chosen. Religion was an integral part of Americans' lives, and they viewed much of what they saw through a religious lens heavily tinted with Protestantism. Jefferson's notion that the continent would one day be governed with the same type of government everywhere would not have discounted Protestantism. Government would, of course, be republican in nature. Through the American lens, the world also contained a white pigment. White Americans were racially superior to Indians, Africans, and any other indigenous peoples who could be imagined, in their world-view concept. White American superiority also applied to any group, even others with European origins. American Manifest Destiny was never stronger than during the Mexican War. "To *liberate* and *ennoble*–not *enslave* and *debase*–is our mission," Moses Y. Beach wrote in the New York *Sun* on November 20, 1847. "Well may the Mexican nation, whose great masses have never yet tasted liberty . . . accept the ranks and rights of freeman at our hands." Americans thought the same way of Russian or British occupation on the Pacific Northwest coast. Many Americans also assumed that Canada would one day join the United States.

By 1848, the United States controlled the lands between the Atlantic and Pacific oceans. America obtained those lands through treaty and war, thanks in no small part to the policies of President James K. Polk, an expansionist advocate. Other Americans believed that even more territory should belong to the United States, especially Cuba and Mexico. The latter surrendered territory to the United States in the Treaty of Guadalupe-Hidalgo in 1848. The United States never gained either, but did eventually obtain the Sandwich Islands–Hawaii–and Alaska along with other smaller island territories in the Caribbean and the Pacific.

American editors may have been the strongest advocates of Manifest Destiny, coining the term and continually pushing American superiority. The ideas behind Manifest Destiny could appear in any form in newspapers. The *New World*, a New York City paper, for example, carried a woodcut of Christopher Columbus and his men first landing in the Western Hemisphere in its nameplate of the1830s. Under that image, the paper declared, "No pent-up Utica contracts our powers: The whole unbounded Continent is ours!"

This chapter looks at American thought on Manifest Destiny, beginning with readings that advocated the concept. The first reading comes from the *United States Journal* and advocacy for the election of Polk, who believed in Manifest Destiny. The next editorial, by John O'Sullivan, discusses all that comprised American Manifest Destiny–religion, nationalism, and ethnocentrism. It is followed by the editorial that introduced the term Manifest Destiny. The next editorial, by H. W. Bellows in the *American Review*, glorifies American greatness and superiority. The last entry in the first section promotes American control of territories from Cuba through Mexico.

The readings opposing Manifest Destiny begin with an editorial that combines expansionism with the annexation of Texas. It promotes the idea that America cannot control all territory and must stop its borders somewhere. The next reading opposing expansionism is a political platform from Ohio that demands that the United States cease with its expansionist mentality. In this statement, the Mexican War is the impetus, and those who provided the statement believed the only reason for the war was to acquire the lands of Mexico.

Support for Manifest Destiny

Theophilus Fisk: "Young America"

America's Manifest Destiny could not be denied, even if it meant fighting for land, which is what Theophilus Fisk suggested in this editorial. He refers to "Young America," the concept of democracy, and the United States' right to the continent.[4] *Because of his views on Manifest Destiny, Fisk pushed the policies of James K. Polk in his newspaper.*

United States Journal **(Washington, D.C.), 3 May 1845**

There is a new spirit abroad in the land, young, restless, vigorous and omnipotent. It manifested itself in infancy at the Baltimore Convention. It was felt in boyhood in the triumphant election of James K. Polk; and in manhood it will be still more strongly felt in the future administration of public affairs in this country. . . . It sprang from the warm sympathies and high hopes of youthful life . . .it is Young America, awakened to a sense of her own intellectual greatness by her soaring spirit. It stands in strength, the voice of the majority. . . . It demands the immediate annexation of Texas at any and every hazard. It will plant its right foot upon the northern verge of Oregon, and its left upon the Atlantic crag, and waving the stars and the stripes in the face of the once proud Mistress of the Ocean, bid her, if she dare, "Cry havoc, and let slip the dogs of war."

John L. O'Sullivan: "The Popular Movement"

John L. O'Sullivan edited two publications, the Democratic Review *and the* Morning News, *both in New York. He used them to promote Manifest Destiny. This editorial glorifies all aspects of Manifest Destiny and plainly states that all would be better off under the American scheme of government, religion, and point of view.*

Morning News (New York), 24 May 1845

From the time that the Pilgrim Fathers landed on these shores to the present moment, the older settlements have been constantly throwing off a hardy, restless and lawless pioneer population, which has kept in advance, subduing the wilderness and preparing the way for more orderly settlers who tread rapidly upon their footsteps. It is but a short time since Western Massachusetts, Connecticut and Rhode Island, although now proverbially the land of "steady habits" and good morals, presented a population no ways superior socially to that of Texas at the present day. As their numbers increased, law and order obtained control, and those unable to bear constraint sought new homes. Those latter have rolled forward in advance of civilization, like the surf on an advancing wave, indicative of its resistless approach. This is the natural, unchangeable effect of our position upon this continent, and it must continue until the waves of the Pacific have hemmed in and restrained the onward movement.

To say that the settlement of a fertile and unappropriated soil by right of individual purchase is the aggression of a government is absurd. Equally ridiculous is it to suppose that when a band of hardy settlers have reclaimed the wilderness, multiplied in numbers, built up a community and organized a government, that they have not the right to claim the confederation of that society of States from the bosom of which they emanated. An inalienable right of man is to institute for themselves that form of government which suits them best, and to change it when they please. On this continent communities grow up mostly by immigration from the United States. Such communities therefore inevitably establish the same form of government which they left behind and *demand* of them that they *come* into the Union. Mexico, in whole or in part, becomes so settled by the Anglo-Saxon race that they have a majority and decide to alter the system to that of the United States model, and ask for admittance into the Union, the same inalienable right will exist and who will deny it?

John L. O'Sullivan: "Annexation"

The annexation of Texas provided the event at which the term Manifest Destiny was inserted into the rhetoric of American expansion across North America. O'Sullivan's authorship of this editorial has long been assumed, but it may have been written by one of his reporters, Jane Storm.[5]

United States Magazine and Democratic Review (New York), July/August 1845

It is time now for opposition to the Annexation of Texas to cease, all further agitation of the waters of bitterness and strife, at least in connexion with this question.... But, in regard to Texas, enough has now been given to Party. It is time for the common duty of Patriotism to the Country to succeed;—or if this claim will not be recognized, it is at least time for common sense to acquiesce with decent grace in the inevitable and the irrevocable.

Texas is now ours. Already, before these words are written her Convention has undoubtedly ratified the acceptance, by her Congress, of our proffered invitation into the Union; and made the requisite changes in her already republican form of constitution to adopt it to its future federal relations. Her star and her stripe may already be said to have taken their place in the glorious blazon of our common nationality; and the sweep of our eagle's wing already includes within its circuit the wide extent of her fair and fertile land. She is no longer to us a mere geographical space.... She comes within the dear and sacred designation of Our Country; no longer a "*pays,*" she is a part of "*la patrie;*" and that which is at once a sentiment and a virtue, Patriotism, already begins to thrill for her too within the national heart. The next session of Congress will see the representatives of the new young State in their places in both our halls of national legislation, side by side with those of the old Thirteen....

Why, were other reasoning wanting, in favor of now elevating this question of the reception of Texas into the Union, out of the lower region of our past party dissensions, up to its proper level of a high and broad nationality, it surely is to be found, found abundantly, in the manner in which other nations have undertaken to intrude themselves into it, between us and the proper parties to the case, in a spirit of hostile interference against us, for the avowed object of thwarting our policy and hampering our power, limiting our greatness and checking the fulfillment of our manifest destiny to overspread the continent allotted by Providence for the free development of our yearly multiplying millions....

H.W. Bellows: "The Destiny of the Country"

The American Review *was a publication of the Whig party and promised "to stand by the Constitution," with this slogan under its name. In this article by H.W. Bellows, the greatness and superiority with which many Americans viewed their nation in the 1840s is easily evident. The splendor of "national destiny," the granting of "providential advantage," and America as God's "ultimate triumph" are all part of the rhetoric.*

American Review (New York), March 1847

Notwithstanding the proverbial pride of Americans, few have yet attained any due sense of the magnificence of their country and the splendor of their national destiny. . . . There is more to sober than to intoxicate, to awe than to addle, in a true estimate of ourselves and our country. Our vanity springs from the contemplation of what we have done, or what we are, and is often based upon comparisons which nothing but our own ignorance renders possible or flattering. . . . Every providential advantage in our possession we appropriate as the result of our own intentions and labors. We attribute our institutions wholly to the sagacity of our Fathers, and the maintenance of them to the wisdom of their Sons. Our national importance seems to us to have been wrought out by our own right arms. And there is a very amusing feeling throughout the nation, that Americans are a different order of beings from others; that one American soldier is at least equal to four Mexicans, three French or two Englishmen. . . . If we understood better our real claims to the respect and confidence of the world; if we appreciated the greatness, not which we have achieved, but which has been thrust upon us by Destiny; if we valued ourselves upon our real advantage and upon a greatness not dependent upon contrast or admitting comparison, but of a totally different kind from any the world has yet seen, we should cease to be vain and become self-respectful. . . .

There is no nation on the face of the earth or in the records of history, if we except the Jews, whose origin, circumstances and progress have been so purely providential as ours; none which owes so little to itself and so much to the Ruler of its destiny. . . .

And this broad continent, this new world, with lakes like oceans and rivers like seas, penetrated to the heart with bays and gulfs; this region comprising every clime and furnishing the products of all—the furs of the north and the fruits of the tropics—the bread stuffs of temperate zones—the woolens of cold, and the cottons of warm climates—stretching from one great ocean of the globe to the other, and from the frozen serpent almost to the equator—this vast area with natural divisions to indicate it as the home of many nations, is, by the Providence of God, one country, speaking one language, rejoicing in one common Constitution, honoring the same great national names, celebrating the same great national events. It is one nation. And it is a free nation. It possesses an ideal form of government, the dream of ancient heroes no longer a vision of the night; the prophetic visionary song of poets become the prosaic language of matter-of-fact men. It is without hereditary rulers, without a legalized aristocracy. It is self-governed. It is a land of equal rights. It is a stable republic.

And what a marvelous and providential history has it had! . . .

Have we often considered the wonderful and providential aptitude of our country for deriving the greatest and most indispensable advantages from the most brilliant discoveries of modern times in science and art? . . . Was not the railroad expressly invented to hold together in its vast iron cleets our broad and otherwise unbound country, threatening to fall to pieces by its own weight? . . . Let its fiery horse, with a continent for his pasture, speed as swiftly as he can; where there is land to sustain his hoof, he cannot take us off our own soil, or away from the sound of our native tongue! Is not the lightning-winged telegraph, that puts a girdle of intelligence round the earth in the eighth of a second, a providential angel whose mission is peculiar to our own land an all but omnipotent spirit whose business it is to facilitate the intercourse of a nation whose territories stretch into different climates, and are divided by chains of mountains, and which yet depends for its united existence upon agreement of sentiment, frequency of intercourse, concurrence of sympathies and central unity of operations? If the providence of God, choosing out a theatre for the ultimate triumph of his earthly purposes toward our race, had selected this land after having long, and until the fullness of time, kept it back from civilized possession, would not the whole world have recognized the justice and expediency of the choice? . . .

Moses Y. Beach: "Cuba Under the Flag of the United States"

Westward expansion was not the only manifestation of Manifest Destiny. Moses Y. Beach, editor and owner of the New York Sun, *was not alone in considering it America's right to control other territories, specifically Cuba. In this editorial, Beach calls for the annexation of the Caribbean island. Beach wrote the editorial as the United States and Mexico were at war. He believed America should own territory from Florida to Yucatan, which included Cuba.*

Sun (New York), 23 July 1847

When in Havanna last winter, we had a consultation with a meeting of the most influential and wealthy men of that city upon the union of Cuba to the United States, and promised to lay the matter before the people of this country as soon as the Mexican question had been disposed of. Mexico, to all intents and purposes, is now in our possession. All parties in the United States, and even foreign nations look upon that question as settled so far as conquest and occupation are concerned, and we now hasten to fulfil our promise, and that promise must be our apology for this article. Cuba by Geographical position, necessity and rights belongs to the United States, it may be and must be ours. The moment has arrived to place it in our hands and under our flag. Cuba is in the market for sale, and we are authorized by parties eminently able to fulfil what they propose, to say that if the United States will offer the Spanish government one hundred millions of dollars, Cuba is ours, and that, with one week's notice, the whole amount will be raised and paid over by the inhabitants of the Island. One week is all they ask, if our Government will only make the offer for them to act upon, and which Spain is ready to accept. This is no vision, but a fixed fact, of which we have seen, and now hold the most undoubted proofs. The possession of Cuba will complete our chain of territory, and give us the North American Continent. It is the garden of the world, the key to the Gulf, and the richest spot of its size on the face of the earth. From Florida Point to its northeastern coast is only fifty miles, bringing the Island almost within cannon shot and sight of the United States. Cuba yields to Spain an annual revenue of seven millions . . . which will double the amount the moment it comes under the United States. . . . Cuba must be ours! Stretching from Florida to Yucatan it commands the Gulf and coast of Mexico. . . . To us it is indispensable. We want its harbors for our ships to touch at, to and from Mexico. . . . Give us Cuba, and our possessions are complete.

Opposition to Manifest Destiny

Weston Gales: "The Texas Fever"

Manifest Destiny encompassed many issues. One of them was the annexation of Texas. In this editorial, Weston Gales of the Register *seems to be uncertain as to what should happen with Texas and other land in North America. He believes that adding more land will be detrimental to the South because it is unlikely that any of it will be slaveholding. For that reason, the nation needs to add no more land. Gales ultimately concludes that the United States should set an example for all with republican liberty, acting perhaps as the "mother of republics" in America—the one to whom they look for guidance. They may, if they choose, join the United States, but should never be forced.*

***Weekly Raleigh Register, and North Carolina Gazette,* 21 May 1844**

Should not those impatient spirits who raise the banner-cry of "Texas, now or never," look at least the length of their noses before them! Should they be so awfully patriotic as madly to shut their eyes and rush on, "uncaring of consequences?" Do they suppose that our Government can embrace all North America, from the North Pole to Panama, from Cape Cod to California? . . . As Southern men—as identified with the Slaveholding interest—should they not look ahead? Is it not prudent to look boldly to the future?

Let them face it like men. Let them look at the map and say whether the acquisition of Texas would add even temporary strength to our peculiar interests? Texas has territory sufficient for about five States. Two of them would be Slave States, and in them would Slave labor be profitable. The other three must, out of necessity, be *free* States, inasmuch as Slave labor in grazing countries is never profitable—and, at least, three-fifths of Texas is only a grazing country. Would three against us, and two in our favor, add greatly to our relative strength? Not according to our Arithmetic.

Again: Let our greedy annexationists look on the map, and tell us, what other country, besides Texas, in all North America, can be hereafter added to our Union by which the Slave interest can gain any strength? Let them remember that Slavery is not tolerated in Mexico. Let them also remember, that by the Missouri compromise, Slavery cannot, for all time to come, exist north of 36 degrees. . . . Every argument used now for the Annexation of Texas, may be used hereafter for other accretions, from this large extent of Territory, with this difference indeed in their favor, that they are already ours and will not cost us Ten Millions in purchase—and the further difference, that we should not entangle ourselves in a War with foreign nations in making the acquisition. . . .

And we ask those who are so passionately devoted to the acquisition of Texas, that their war-cry is "Texas of Disunion"—whether they can lay the flattering unction to their souls, that *when* Texas is safely housed, that immediately after that, the door will be closed? Can they be so short sighted? Let them go to their horn books and study Geography. It may reduce their temperature to the proper point.

It may be asked what is to be our destiny then? What should be our true policy? We answer that we are obliged to *stop somewhere.* We must have a limit to our acquisition of Territory. If we annex Texas—there is Mexico and beyond—we are obliged to have an outer boundary. Our true policy, we believe to be this: Let the United States be for this continent, the *mother of Republics.* They have already been reared on our principles in South America, in Mexico, in Texas; some of these Republics have adopted almost precisely our Constitution. Let the Canadas constitute one or two Republics—when their time shall arrive. Let our Territories over the Mississippi, as they get old enough, be set up as Republican daughters around us. Let them extend to the Pacific. Let Texas continue as she undoubtedly will a Republic. Let Mexico, with her government in form, whatever it is in practice, similar to ours, be admitted into our family of Republics, and treated kindly. Let there be treaties of amity and commerce between this Union of Republics and let us show that we are the true advocates of Republican liberty throughout the continent, and that we are willing others should enjoy the blessing in its purity, whether under our control or not.

An Anonymous Report: "No More Territory—Nine Reasons Against the New Platform"

The National Era *opposed the spread of slavery into any new American territory. It also opposed the Mexican War, but the paper's editor, Gamaliel Bailey, did not oppose ethical national expansion. These excerpts, taken from an editorial that disagreed with them, presents Whig-party sentiment on annexing more territory. Though it is not included here, Bailey believed this platform, which staunchly opposes Manifest Destiny, was really a ploy to protect slaveholding interests.*

National Era (Washington, D.C.), 16 September 1847

The Whigs of Cuyahoga county, Ohio, in Convention assembled, lately passed the following resolutions:

"*Resolved,* That while we regard the 'Wilmot Proviso' as the 'freeman's platform,' we at the same time declare the WHIG DOCTRINE TO BE STILL BROADER; namely, *Unqualified opposition to any further annexation of territory to this Union; that upon* THIS GROUND *the Whigs of the North and South, East and West,* SHOULD UNITE AND DO BATTLE AGAINST ALL ATTEMPTS TO BRING IN ANY MORE TERRITORY, either by purchase or by conquest, or under the cunning pretext of payment of the expenses of the war.

"*Resolved,* That, in carrying out our principles, we can support no man for the Presidency unless he be a staunch, tried Whig, approved by a Whig National Convention, and who is openly pledged against any further annexation of territory or extension of slavery."

These resolutions present distinctly the issue, "No More Territory," without qualification. . . .

"Provided, always, and it is hereby declared to be the true intent and meaning of Congress in making this appropriation, that the war with Mexico ought not to be prosecuted by this Government with any view to the dismemberment of that Republic, or to the acquisition, by conquest, of any portion of her territory; that this Government, ever desirous to maintain and preserve peaceful and friendly relations with all nations, and particularly with the neighboring Republic of Mexico, will always be ready to enter upon negotiations with a view to terminate the present unhappy conflict, on terms which shall secure the just rights and preserve inviolate the national honor of the United States and of Mexico; that it is especially desirable, in order to maintain and preserve those amicable relations which ought always to exist between neighboring Republics, that the boundary of the State of Texas should be definitively settled, and that provision be made by the Republic of Mexico for the prompt and equitable adjustment of the just claims of our citizens on that Republic."

Questions

1. After reading the selections, why might Americans consider it their "divine right" to own as much land as possible, especially that which turned into the continental United States?
2. Why did Moses Beach want the United States to own all territory from Cuba through the Yucatan?
3. Why did the Ohio Whigs and Weston Gales–also a Whig–want no more expansion of territory?

Notes

1. Oscar Theodore Barck, Jr. and Hugh Talmage Lefler, *Colonial America* (New York: Macmillan Company, 1958), 158.

2. Thomas Jefferson to James Monroe, 24 November 1801, in Paul L. Ford, ed., *Works of Thomas Jefferson,* 10 vols. (New York, 1892–1899), 9:315–19; quoted in Frederick Merk, *Manifest Destiny and Mission in American History* (New York: Alfred A. Knopf, 1963), 9.

3. "Annexation," *United States Magazine and Democratic Review* 17:85 (July and August 1845).

4. Frederick Merk, *Manifest Destiny,* 54.

5. Linda S. Hudson, *Mistress of Manifest Destiny: A Biography of Jane McManus Storm Cazneau, 1807–1878* (Austin: Texas State Historical Association, 2001).

CHAPTER 19

The War with Mexico, 1846

In 1844, the United States elected James K. Polk as the eleventh president. A year earlier, no American would have even conceived that the representative from Tennessee would be the nation's chief. But the nation's top presidential candidate–Henry Clay–opposed annexation of Texas, and much of America was in favor of expansion, believing it to be the nation's "manifest destiny" to control the continent. Specifically, expansionists looked to Oregon and Texas as natural extensions of the United States. Texas had declared its independence from Mexico in 1836, though the Mexican government did not recognize it. Since that time, the large number of Americans who emigrated there had sought to become a part of the United States. Clay said annexation of Texas was "dangerous to the integrity of the Union."[1] Polk favored immediate Texas annexation. In November, Polk defeated Clay for the presidency by less than 40,000 votes. In March 1845, Congress offered statehood to Texas, Polk took office, and Mexico broke diplomatic ties with the United States–all within a week. On December 29, 1845, Texas officially joined the Union; in April 1846, Mexican forces attacked American troops in Texas; and in May, the United States declared war on Mexico.[2]

Texas was not the only territory with Mexican ties that American expansionists wanted to add to the United States. They had their eyes on California and New Mexico, too. Polk was willing to fight for this new territory, to buy it, or both. Americans who opposed slavery, generally, thought the war was wrong. Polk was aligned too closely to the Southern states for them, and many feared that the war with Mexico was an effort to expand Southern slavery and power. Some Southerners believed Mexico was not worth taking, thinking the region unsuited to slavery, and feeling that Mexicans were inferior beings. Most Americans, though, had no doubt that Mexico would be defeated. As a result, camps developed in the nation. One called for control of all of Mexico. The "All Mexico" faction was comprised of those who believed strongly in Manifest Destiny (see Chapter 18). Others did not op-

THE TEXAS GAZETTE.

PRINTED AND PUBLISHED, WEEKLY, BY **GODWIN BROWN COTTEN**, AT SIX DOLLARS, PER ANNUM, IN ADVANCE.

VOL. I. AUSTIN, TEXAS, SATURDAY, OCTOBER 3, 1829. NO. 2.

MILITIA LAW.

(CONCLUDED.)

Passed 23d June, 1828.

The Governor of the State of Coahuila and Texas to all its Inhabitants—KNOW YE, that the Congress [illegible] as follows:

No. 58.—The Constitutional Congress of the free, independent and sovereign state of Coahuila and Texas have enacted the following

REGULATIONS,

ART. 43. Such retired officers shall not be entitled to any other distinction in the militia, than what their grade in it gives them, nor shall they have any rank other, than that given by their commissions in the militia.

ART. 44. Whenever, in national festivals, or other service, a force of regular troops, or active militia is united to the local militia, the provisions of articles 27, 28 and 29, of the national militia law shall be observed. (*Note*—the militia called out and actually in the national service, as troops of the army, are called active militia.)

CHAPTER. IV.

INSTRUCTION.

ART. 45. The officers, sergeants and corporals shall receive their first instruction from the retired officers of the army, who may belong to the militia, or other officers of the army who may be present—and should there be none neither, the ayuntamientos will report that fact through the chief of department, or of *partido* to the governor, who will make application to the commandant general of the district, to send the number of officers necessary for the above purposes.

ART. 46. After the officers and sergeants are instructed, they will proceed to drill their respective commands, on such festival days as may be designated by the commandants of corps for that purpose, during the six months next following the first organization of the militia.

ART. 47. The inspector general, the commandants of battalions, squadrons and companies, shall all be responsible for the discipline, and for the establishment of the most efficient subordination in the service, and whatever may be conducive to good order, within their respective commands, and they can apply to the local civil authority of the jurisdiction to which they appertain, for the purpose of promoting whatever may be necessary to effect these important objects.

ART. 48. After the militia is organized, there shall be four mustering months in each year, to be designated by the governor, after receiving the report and advice of the ayuntamientos as to the principal occupations of the inhabitants, and the situation and peculiar circumstances of each municipality, or place, in order that the mustering months may be selected, so as to cause the least injury or inconvenience to the militiamen.

ART. 49. During the four months, mentioned in the last article, the commandants will cause the militia to muster on every solemn festival day, (*dias festivos solemnes*,) and drill them three hours in the forenoon, and the same in the afternoon, for the purpose of instructing them in all the evolutions and tactics used in the regular army.

CHAPTER V.

SUBORDINATION AND CORRECTIONAL PENALTIES.

ART. 50. The chiefs of the militia in the interior service of the state, shall conduct themselves as citizens who command citizens.

ART. 51. Every militiaman, who has fulfilled the service for which he was called out, shall return to the station of a citizen; he will therefore, only be subject to the rules of military subordination while in such service.

ART. 52. When this militia is in the service of the nation, it shall be subject to the rules and regulations of the army, and when in the service of the state, this law will govern it.

ART. 53. No officer shall call a muster of the whole or any part of this militia, without the approbation (*anuencia*) of the superior local civil authority, of the jurisdiction to which it appertains; the militiamen, shall however, always obey the calls and orders of their officers without any hesitation—whatever may be the responsibility which the officer takes upon himself, and for which he will be responsible to his superiors. The musters appointed by this law for instruction and drill, are exceptions to the provisions of this article.

ART. 54. The penalties for disobedience, disrespect to superior officers, or neglect of duty, shall be the same for officers, sergeants, corporals and privates.

ART. 55. Simple disobedience shall be punished by arrest, not to exceed three days.

ART. 56. Should the disobedience be accompanied with disrespect, or slight insult to any officer, sergeant or corporal, the penalty shall be four days arrest, or close confinement for two days.

ART. 57. Should the insult be an aggravated one, the arrest shall be for ten days, or close confinement for five days.

ART. 58. Whoever neglects or fails in his duty to the service, or in complying with an order, shall be tried and sentenced, militarily, and fined not less than ten, nor more than two hundred dollars, according to the capacity of the individual to pay, and the nature of the offence, which fine shall be applied in all cases, to the militia fund. Should it appear after proper investigation, that the person fined was unable to pay it, he shall be imprisoned in close confinement, not less than fifteen days, nor more than [illegible].

ART. 59. Should the penalty imposed by virtue of the last article, exceed fifty dollars fine, or two months and a half imprisonment, the sentence shall not be executed, until it shall have been approved of by the court martial, hereinafter mentioned.

ART. 60. Any soldier, placed on sentry, who shall desert his post, shall suffer imprisonment for eight days.

ART. 61. He who is found asleep on his post shall be punished with six days close imprisonment: should he suffer himself to be relieved by any other than the proper corporal, he shall be subject to four days close imprisonment, and he will also incur the same penalty, for not giving due notice of any alarm, or other event in the line of his duty which may occur.

ART. 62. If any militiaman on guard, shall leave it without permission from the commander of the same, he shall be punished by arrest, for four days, or close confinement for two.

ART. 63. If the whole guard shall abandon their post, they shall suffer eight days close confinement, and if the commander be implicated, he shall be dismissed from office.

ART. 64. If any one in a quarrel, shall take up arms to defend another employed in the same service, to whom he is not subordinate, he shall suffer imprisonment for eight days.

ART. 65. He who in the same case shall take up arms to offend a superior, of whatever rank, shall be arrested immediately and prosecuted by an officer of the corps, whom the commandant shall nominate for that purpose, and the offender shall be delivered over to the civil authority, together with a summary of the facts and circumstances of the case, in order that he be tried and the penalty inflicted, which the laws designate for disrespect or resistance to the judicial authority, proportioning it to the circumstances of the case.

ART. 66. He who unsuccessfully excites insubordination, shall be imprisoned eight days, but should he occasion disorder, he shall be imprisoned ten days, and also suffer the fine designated in article 58, or in case of not being able to pay the fine, the imprisonment prescribed in said article, in lieu thereof.

ART. 67. A repetition of any of the above expressed offences shall be punished with double the penalty designated for the first offence; those who transgress a third time, shall suffer double the penalty designated for those who transgress a second time, and those who transgress a fourth time shall be dismissed from the militia and deprived of all the rights of citizenship, for four years, and it will then require a special decree of the legislature to re-instate them.

ART. 68. He who at the same time shall commit an offence against the civil law, and also against this regulation, shall be punished for the latter, agreeably to the provisions of this regulation, and for the former, he shall be punished agreeably to the laws, for which purpose he shall be delivered over to the competent judicial authority, together with a summary of the facts and circumstances of the case.

ART. 69. The provisions of the preceding article are to be understood, as applicable; only to offenders in a faction, or quarrel; for except in this case and other acts of the service, they are subject to the civil authority.

ART. 70. The authority of imposing the penalties belongs to the commandant of the force engaged in the act of service, in which the fault may be committed.

ART. 71. The militiaman is obliged to suffer the penalty imposed upon him, but after having complied with it, he can appeal for redress, except in cases under the 59th article, which come within the 59th article, and have been examined by the court martial before mentioned, for after this procedure, there can be no farther appeal.

ART. 72. The appeals in cases of correctional penalties will be decided by a court martial, to be called the court of subordination and discipline.

ART. 73. This court martial shall be convened by the commandant, in cases of appeals which are not excepted in article 71, or examine and revise sentences in the cases mentioned in article 59. It shall be composed of the commandant, as president, of the two captains, the two first lieutenants, two sub-lieutenants, and the two sergeants, oldest in age, (*mayores de edad*) of the whole battalion or squadron, and the two corporals, likewise the oldest in age, of the company whose turn it may be to furnish them, for which purpose the companies in their regular numerical order, will designate two corporals every six months, and when it shall come to the turn of a company to supply two corporals as members of the court, those who have previously served, cannot be re-selected until all the corporals of the companies shall have served their turns. The secretary of the court shall be one of its members, appointed by a plurality of votes.

ART. 74. In districts where the militia do not amount to a battalion or squadron, or where those corps are formed from two or more municipalities, the court martial shall be composed of all the militia officers of the municipality where it is convened, and of the two sergeants, two corporals, and four militiamen of the greatest age. The person who acts as commandant shall be president; and should the militia not compose a company, the court shall be formed of the alcalde and two militiamen of each grade, or one of each, should there be no more.—Sergeants, corporals and soldiers, to be eligible for members of the court must know how to read and write.

ART. 75. The court cannot impose upon such as appeal without just cause, any higher penalties than those designated; but should it appear that the penalties imposed by the commandant in the act of service are unjust, the court can impose the same punishment upon the person in fault, and also cause him to remunerate the injured person, for the damages he may have sustained at the rate of from four bits to two dollars, per day, according to the judgment of the court.

Texas Gazette. *As Americans migrated west, they carried printing presses with them. That did not change when they emigrated to Texas—a part of Mexico—in the 1820s. The* Texas Gazette *and other newspapers had a decidedly American flavor and carried large amounts of news from the United States.*

pose obtaining new territory, but they opposed the spread of slavery into lands obtained from Mexico, which gave rise to the Wilmot Proviso (see Chapter 20). Still others wanted no new territory.

Following America's declaration of war, United States troops under General Zachary Taylor crossed the Rio Grande. They captured Monterrey and defeated Santa Anna at Buena Vista. The United States then controlled the northern portion of Mexico. General Winfield Scott led an assault on Mexico City, taking Mexico's capital in September 1847. At the same time, John C. Frémont, Robert Stockton, and other Americans living in California entered the fray. Another American force led by Stephen Kearney captured Santa Fe and marched on to San Diego. In slightly more than a year, the United States defeated Mexico, and in January 1848, the two nations entered peace talks in Guadalupe-Hidalgo. Mexico relinquished any claims to Texas, ceded California and New Mexico to the United States, and established a border with the United States that ran along the Rio Grande and Gila rivers. America gave Mexico $15 million in compensation and agreed to pay claims that American citizens might have against Mexico. The nation spent nearly $100 million to fight the war, with nearly 13,000 dying either in action or from disease, but the land additions from the Mexican War—plus gaining Oregon in the Buchanan–Pakenham Treaty of 1846—created the continental United States of today with only one small land exception, which the nation obtained from Mexico in 1853.

This chapter looks at the press's response to the Mexican War. The nature of the nation's response to the war makes the pairings of the readings a bit complicated. The first set of readings include those that opposed the war and opposed annexation of Mexico into the United States. What complicates the issue is that all who opposed annexation did not necessarily oppose the war. Also, the issue of slavery in territories was a part of the discussion. Should slavery be allowed in territory obtained from Mexico or in all of Mexico if the nation claimed the entire area as spoils of war. The idea of Manifest Destiny played a role, too, that is, the concept that it was America's destiny to control all the land from the Atlantic to the Pacific, and perhaps all of North America. The second set of readings include those in favor of war and supported incorporating all of Mexico into the nation as a result of the war. Generally, those who supported war would have been advocates of "all Mexico," but some supporters of the war did not think America should take in all of Mexico.

The readings against annexation and war begin with two that protest the war, one from the North and the other from the South. The next, by editor Gamaliel Bailey, discusses the immorality of the war. It is followed by two editorials that oppose Mexican annexation primarily because the writers consider Mexicans inferior to white Americans. The readings supporting the war and annexation begin with a news account from the *New Orleans Bee.* The papers of New Orleans became the principal source of news of the war for Americans, and the telegraph helped get news to the people faster than ever. The next entries advocate the annexation of all of Mexico, the last being a "trial balloon" floated by the Polk administration through a letter written by James Buchanan, secretary of state, to ascertain public sentiment toward claiming all of Mexico at the end of the war.

Opposition to Annexation and War

Horace Greeley: "Who Can Make Wrong Right?"

Horace Greeley strongly opposed the Mexican War just as he strongly opposed slavery and would support the Wilmot Proviso. In this editorial that accompanied the president's proclamation of war, Greeley questions America's motives and places the blame directly on those who wanted to annex Texas.

Daily Tribune **(New York), 15 May 1846**

Can the President and Congress? This is a grave question, and concerns us nearly. Its correct solution determines whether a load of guilt shall rest on a few souls or on many. Three months ago, if a party of our people had gone down to the Rio Grande, halted opposite Matamoros, threatened that city with cannon, and blockaded the River, they would have been marauders and land-pirates, and every body would have admitted that Mexico was justified in so treating them. The peremptory orders of Polk & Co. relieve Gen. Taylor and our army of the direct responsibility of the invasion which has taken place, and places that responsibility—where? Who meets it? Who? Depend on it, the blood which must be shed, the misery which is inevitable, rests somewhere. Swindlers of '44! with your 'peaceable Annexation,' do not skulk! Here is the fruit of *your* doings! Look it in the face!

Ten days ago, if a Baltimore clipper had overtaken a Mexican trading ship at sea, captured and plundered her, it would have been piracy by all law, and the perpetrators must have swung for it. Now that same act would be pronounced laudable by our Courts, and the Mexican vessel and cargo a lawful prize to the captors. But can any man imagine that the distinction made by our Courts be respected in the Chancery of Heaven? No! never! Abhorred be this War, its authors and abettors! 'O my soul, come not thou into their secrets—unto their assembly, mine honor, be not *thou* united!'

Weston Gales: "The War with Mexico"

Weston Gales's opposition to the Mexican War was tied up in his belief that any more land acquisition would be detrimental to the South (see Chapter 18 readings). Here, he states that most Americans did not want the war, but he still thinks the nation needs to support the cause.

Weekly Raleigh Register, and North Carolina Gazette, 22 May 1846

When one's country becomes involved in war with a foreign nation, however strong the sense of the indignation against those who may have unnecessarily and wickedly brought about such a calamity, there is a feeling of reluctance to the utterance of the condemnation which a crime so great against humanity and the common weal justly incurs. Such has been our feeling, and, as far as possible, our course, in regard to the war with MEXICO and its contrivers. . . .

There is a solemn task devolved upon us by the circumstances under which the country has been placed; and it shall be faithfully discharged—but not at this moment, when anxiety on the fate of our arms on the Rio Grande occupies not ours only, but almost exclusively every mind.

In the act of Congress, which we publish officially to-day, the two Houses of Congress have, we conceive, given the seal and sanction of their authority to a false principle and to a false fact in the form of the highest act of legislation which they can ever be called upon to perform; an act such as has never before been approached but with the greatest reluctance and caution, and after months of deliberation. No man who will suffer his reason to pass upon the facts in the case, and will obey the dictates of his conscience but must admit that this War was deliberately begun by the Executive of the United States; and that it was begun by an usurpation of power which the Constitution has denied to the President. The unsustained pretence for this war, that it is the act of Mexico, has been approved, and the usurpation of the war power by the President recognised as constitutional, by the act of Congress. . . .

Our political friends in Congress have suffered themselves, in giving apparent sanction to that which they themselves in many instances severally declared to be false and unsubstantial, to be led into error by a dread of the reeling of the People, who, they seem to have thought, had the bill passed without their votes, would not be able to appreciate the motives by which they would have been influenced. We trust, that in acting thus, they undervalue the intelligence of the People.

The *People,* moreover, do not want this war, *not any* war, set on foot by the Executive, solely in pursuance of plans of his own. *They* want no war, moreover, which like this, could have been not only honorably but profitably avoided, had the wise and safe and humane course of his predecessors been followed by the President of the United States. They want no war for conquest merely. Still less do they want a war which is to exhaust the public treasury, to harass the citizens with the most fatiguing military service—in which the climate will be far more fatal than the bullets of the enemy—and which is, according to the President's avowed intention, to end, after all, in *negotiation,* which, upon every principle of common sense as well as of public law, ought to have preceded instead of following the bloody fray. . . .

Gamaliel Bailey: "Policy—Principle—What Might Be"

Gamaliel Bailey started the National Era, *in part, to fight slavery. Later in 1847, he wrote a series of three extremely long editorials on the war, in which he talked about not taking any territory from Mexico, or, if we did, making Mexico into states on a par with the United States and without slavery. In this editorial, which was written much closer to the beginning of the conflict, Bailey attacked those who promoted and voted for the war as immoral people. Principle, he said, should get America out of Mexico immediately with no new territory.*

National Era (Washington, D.C.), 25 February 1847

When the President first announced that Americans and Mexicans had met in hostile encounter, on the banks of the Rio Grande, and his friends introduced in Congress a bill declaring, in its preamble, that war existed between Mexico and the United States, by the act of the former, two modes of action presented themselves to the opponents of the war—one of party policy, the other of principle. It was a critical moment—a grand opportunity for the exhibition of noble daring. A favorite General of the American people, with this soldiers, was reported to be surrounded by enemies. His peril was exaggerated. The honor of the national flag was in jeopardy. The public press gave voice to a fiery, headlong, uninquiring patriotism.

On the other hand, it was affirmed by the Whigs that the President had usurped power in occupying by the army of the United States the line of disputed territory between Mexico and Texas—that the immediate cause of the war was his own act, directing General Taylor to march from Corpus Christi to the Rio Grande; that the bill, therefore, embodied in its preamble a positive falsehood.

There were many honorable men, Christian men, in Congress. What should they do? IF they voted against the bill, they must encounter the press and the people, the fierce anathemas of a misguided but burning patriotism;

they might seal their own political doom, and the fate of the party with which they acted. If they voted for the bill, they would affirm what they believed to be a falsehood—they would stand self-condemned at the bar of posterity, for having done what in them lay to impose a falsehood upon history—they would become supporters of an act of Executive despotism of fearful precedent, and assume with him the responsibility of a war, which they held to be aggressive, and therefore violative of every principle of justice.

It was a time to try men's souls—a crisis in which single-eyed, courageous devotion to the Right, might have commanded instant peace, rebuked Executive usurpation with such power as to have forever prevented its repetition, established the virtue and honor of the Government on a perpetual basis. What a triumph might here have been achieved by principle—ay, would have been! For, as we now know, General Taylor was abundantly able to extricate himself from the perilous position, in which obedience to the instructions of the President had placed him. A resolution then passed by Congress, directing the President to desist from the attempt to occupy the disputed territory, and withdraw the army, would have re-settled things upon their original basis. But, in an evil hour, party policy triumphed, principle was disregarded, a falsehood was voted, a wicked war endorsed, the assumption of unconstitutional power by the Executive enforced; and now the country is involved in a struggle which is debauching the youth of the nation, wasting our energies, accumulating debt, concentrating power in the central Government, especially the Executive department—a struggle with a weak, distracted sister republic, in which no victory won by us can bring glory to our arms, while it postpones the hour of reconciliation—a struggle over which hang clouds and darkness, and fearful apprehension of coming calamities.

Evil begets evil, and "Things bad begun, make strong themselves by ill." That one wrong step has plunged the opponents of the war into irretrievable difficulties. . . .

Would to God that our politicians dared to act out their convictions of duty? Why cannot men rely upon the Right, live for the Truth, die for the Truth? Who shall harm you, if ye be followers of that which is good? The Government is not our country; party is not our country; nor is our country our God. Duty to our Maker—in other words, justice—may demand that we stand up in the face of our country, and resist her wrong doing; and Principle may command the abandonment of even party. It is in scenes of peril, in exigencies of great moment, that the Man is called upon to appeal to his own convictions; to rely upon his own decisions. Then, when his conscience and his God are his only counsellors, he can look down upon party spirit and popular indignation, and feel tranquil in the consciousness that knows no guilt.

How easy it were to act like honest men! However it may have been in the beginning of the war, now, evidently, it would cost nothing to be honest.

The American army has triumphed, with far inferior numbers, in the open field, in the deadly defile, against the almost impregnable city. Mexico has been humbled, stricken to the dust. Two-thirds of her territory is in our occupation. We are in the plentitude of our power, united, inexhaustible in resources. She is sunk so low that none do her reverence. Her commerce destroyed; her ports in our possession; with no force in the field to make head against our armies; she stands tottering on the brink of destruction.

How easy to be magnanimous! Withdraw our armies to American territory; call home the squadron. Let us say to her that conquest is not our aim; her territory shall not be dismembered; let strife cease between us; let perpetual peace and concord reign. It would be such a spectacle as earth has never witnessed—a sublime example of justice and moderation, to be emulated in all future ages—such a demonstration of the ennobling influences of Democratic institutions as would command the admiration of the nations of the old world, and more than realize the brightest dreams of the authors and supporters of the principle of self-government: while Mexico herself would be regenerated, restored, secured as our fast friend forever.

As it is, this great nation is acting precisely like a bully, who has got his adversary under and is beating him for no other than the glorious purpose of making him cry, *enough!* It is a vulgar feeling of insolent triumph—a mean disposition to extort an acknowledgment of our superior brute force, that can take any pleasure in the continuance of the war with Mexico.

Waddy Thompson: "Mexico"

Waddy Thompson of South Carolina served as America's ambassador to Mexico from 1842–1844. After returning, he wrote a book titled Reflections *about his experiences there. Thompson did not necessarily oppose the war; he opposed taking Mexico. Some editors used parts of his book to support the same view. Here, Thompson says that taking Mexico is morally wrong, but, more importantly, it offers the United States nothing, reflecting America's view of superiority over other groups.*

National Intelligencer **(Washington, D.C.), 21 October 1847**

I would take no more Mexican territory—first, because we have no right to it; none is pretended but the ruffian—the robber right of conquest. . . .

Secondly, I would not take more territory, because it will be worse than valueless. It will be a heavy charge upon our Government instead of an indemnity to our citizens who have claims upon Mexico. A friend said to me today that we will not take the people, but the land. Precisely the reverse will be the case; we shall take the people, but no land. It is not the country of a savage people whose lands are held in common, but a country in which grants have been made for three hundred and twenty-five years, many of them two and three hundred miles square; nothing paid for these grants when they are [*sic*] made, and no taxes upon the lands afterwards; it is all private property, and we shall get no public domain which will pay the cost of surveying it. I speak of the country beyond the Rio Grande. We shall get no land, but will add a large population, aliens to us in feeling, education, race, and religion—a people unaccustomed to work, and accustomed to insubordination and resistance to law, the expense of governing whom will be ten times as great as the revenues derived from them.

William Cullen Bryant: "The Mexicans Are Indians"

The title of this editorial no doubt said much to antebellum Americans. Native Americans were inferior to white Americans, and Bryant's reference to America's "Civilization" and "Christianity" in opposition to Mexico's "barbarism and anarchy" played well to the Manifest Destiny concept that drove much of the rationale for the Mexican War. Here, it says it would be immoral of America to leave Mexico to its own inferior devices when the United States could provide enlightened guidance to these Indians. Still, Bryant intimates, we would never want to make these people Americans because of their inferiority.

Evening Post **(New York), 24 December 1847**

The Mexicans are *Indians*—Aboriginal Indians. Such Indians as Cortez conquered three thousand years ago, only rendered a little more mischievous by a bastard civilization. . . . They do not possess the elements of an *independent* national existence. The Aborigines of this country have not attempted, and cannot attempt to exist *independently* along side of us. Providence has so ordained it, and it is folly not to recognize the fact. The Mexicans are *Aboriginal Indians*, and they must share the destiny of their race.

Now we ask whether any man can coolly contemplate the idea of recalling our troops from the territory we at present occupy, from Mexico. . . . Why, humanity cries out against it. Civilization, Christianity, protest against this reflux of the tide of barbarism and anarchy. . . .

No party in this country contemplates the dismemberment of Mexico proper, or the annexation of any portion of her population to our own. It would be a disastrous event for the whole confederacy. But we owe it as a duty to ourselves and the general cause of freedom to keep our flag flying . . . till the progress of time, and the silent effect of our presence, our customs, our busy commerce, our active intelligence, our press, shall have breathed a new life into this unfortunate country, and we have some security that she will not be a curse to herself and to her neighbors.

Support for Annexation and War

An Anonymous Report: "Important Movement of Troops"

New Orleans newspapers and the newly invented telegraph played vital roles in coverage of the Mexican War. In this article, the Bee *provides information about American troop deployment in preparation for Texas joining the United States in December, and for possible military strikes either against Mexican advances or directly against Mexico.*

New Orleans (La.) Bee, 16 August 1845

We hasten to lay before our readers the important intelligence we have just received relative to the movements of troops for the purpose of protecting the newly acquired territory of Texas, from the dangers of a projected Mexican invasion. Gen. Gaines, now in our city, having received authentic Information to the effect that TEN THOUSAND Mexican troops, were within eight days march of Gen. Taylor, who is posted at St. Joseph's Island, immediately despatched a messenger to Gov. Mouton, at Pass Christian, claiming a requisition of TWO REGIMENTS OF VOLUNTEERS. . . .

The two Volunteer Regiments are to be stationed at the Forts and Barracks on the Gulf, subject to the orders of the Government; and the United States troops at present in garrison at those stations are to be immediately transferred to Texas. The two Companies of Volunteer Artillery will leave on Wednesday on board the steamship Alabama, together with four companies of United States troops. . . .

The above information may be relied upon as authentic.

In addition to this news we see it stated that a Steamer has been hired for 30 days, by the government officers, to send troops to Texas, at the modern rate of $3.00 per day, amounting only to 9 THOUSAND DOLLARS!!! . . .

Arunah S. Abel: "Conquest"

The Sun *was a penny paper of Baltimore. Part of the rationale behind the "All Mexico" movement was the principle that the Mexicans would be better off under the moral guidance of the United States. This is Arunah Abel's argument here, especially if the Mexicans continued fighting America.*

Sun (Baltimore), 15 October 1847

. . . [W]e are disposed to regard . . . as auspices for good, the harbingers of a new and glorious era to the benighted and oppressed people of Mexico.

In the contemplation of such a conquest as that which ours must be, if accomplished at all, even those who cannot approve the project, must be sensible to the moral grandeur of the achievement. Considered in its simplest aspect, it is really nothing more than the overthrow and systematic suppression of a gross and heartless military despotism on one hand, and the elevation of the people on the other. It is the rescue of the constitutional energies of republicanism from the degradation, selfishness, and prostitution of factious ambition, and the restoration of the same in all the renovated beauty and efficiency with which our experience can invest them, to the enraptured apprehension of the popular mind.... Would it not be an act of benevolence, clothed too with an inexpressible moral sublimity, to revolutionize such a state of things, and restore the powers of government to the sovereignty of the people?

William M. Swain: "A Directing Providence"

As has been said, Manifest Destiny and the Mexican War were entwined. In this editorial, William Swain speaks of America's war with Mexico as divine Providence because it will mean that all the land from the Atlantic to the Pacific will repose "in peace and prosperity" with "the same religious, civil, and political rights." His ideals are reminiscent of those used by Thomas Jefferson after the Louisiana Purchase.

Public Ledger **(Philadelphia), 25 October 1847**

We are believers in the superintendence of a directing Providence, and when we contemplate the rise and amazing progress of the United States, the nature of our government, the character of our people, and the occurrence of unforseen events, all tending to one great accomplishment, we are impressed with a conviction that the decree is made and in the process of execution, that this continent is to be but one nation, under one system of free institutions. This is said in no spirit of prophecy, but in the conclusion of reason.... On this hemisphere principles have been developed calculated to revolutionize the old habits of thinking among men, to disprove the divine right of kings, to explode the reverenced maxims of tyranny, and to establish a rational political liberty for the human race.... When the spectacle of a whole continent, reposing in peace and prosperity, where every one enjoys the same religious, civil and political rights, is beheld from beyond the Atlantic and Pacific, the principles of despotism, no matter how mild their form, must give way, and men will resume their rights and prerogatives. The progress of events points to a time when men will be astonished.

James Buchanan: "Mexico"

Secretary of State James Buchanan was one of the politicians who favored making Mexico a part of the United States. This letter, which appeared in Washington on Christmas Eve, was originally read in Philadelphia and was a way for the Polk administration to decipher public sentiment on annexation.[3] Note, the United States would never make Mexico part of its territory unless there were no other choice, according to Buchanan.

Union (Washington, D.C.), 24 December 1847

Heaven has smiled upon the just cause; and the character of our country has been illustrated by a rapid succession of brilliant and astonishing victories. The exploits of our army have elevated our National character, and shed a lustre upon our name throughout the civilized world. . . .

The war has not been prosecuted for conquest. At every stage in its progress, we have been willing to conclude a just and honorable peace. Indeed, we can never wage a war for conquest in the popular sense of that term. Our free institutions forbid that we should subject nations to our arbitrary sway. If they come within our power, we must bestow upon them the same blessings of liberty and law, which we ourselves enjoy. Should they be annexed to the Union . . .they must participate in the freest and best Government upon earth—on equal terms with ourselves.

The Capital of Mexico is now the Head-Quarters of our conquering Army, and yet such is the genius of our free institutions, that, for the first time, its peaceful and well-disposed citizens enjoy security in their private rights, and the advantage of a just and firm Government. From all that can be learned, they appreciate our protection at its proper value; and dread nothing so much as the withdrawal of our army. They know this would be the signal for renewed and fierce dissensions among their military leaders, in which the Mexican people would become the victims. In this wretched condition of affairs, justice to them and to ourselves may require that we should protect them in establishing, upon a permanent basis, a Republican Government, able and willing to conclude and maintain an equitable Treaty of Peace with the United States. After every effort to obtain such a treaty, should we finally fail in accomplishing the object, and should the military factions in Mexico still persist in waging upon us a fruitless war, then we must fulfill the destiny which Providence may have in store for both countries.

Questions

1. What are the principal reasons those who oppose the war cite for that opposition?

2. What is William Swain's rationale for our participation in the war, and what should America obtain from it?
3. What religious implications are used by both sides to justify either opposing or supporting the war, and for or opposing the annexation of Mexican territory?

Notes

1. *National Intelligencer* (Washington, D.C.), 27 April 1844.

2. Specific details of the Mexican War are taken from George B. Tindall, *America: A Narrative History*, 2 vols. (New York: W. W. Norton, 1984), 1:520–35.

3. Frederick Merk, *Manifest Destiny and Mission in American History* (New York: Alfred A. Knopf, 1963), 119.

CHAPTER 20

The Wilmot Proviso, 1846

In August 1846, three months after war with Mexico had begun, President James K. Polk requested $2 million. He wanted money to use to negotiate with the Mexican government for territory that the nation might obtain from Mexico. Americans knew that Polk favored expansion, and they knew he had his eye on the Mexican territories of New Mexico and California to go with the recently annexed Texas. Texas joined the Union as a slave state, and many Northern members of Congress reckoned that any new territory acquired from Mexico and entering the Union would likely be the same. Enter a first-year Pennsylvania representative named David Wilmot. Wilmot, like many other Americans, favored expansion. He favored admitting Texas to the Union as a slave state, but no Mexican cessations, he said in a speech on the House floor, should become a part of the United States as slave-holding territory.[1]

Wilmot proposed that if the president were to be given the $2 million, slavery should be barred from any territories acquired. He based his reasoning on two points. First, Mexico had already abolished slavery, and reintroduction of the practice into a free-soil region was morally wrong. Second, Wilmot harkened back to the Northwest Ordinance of 1787 for the wording of his amendment to the $2 million bill. In the 1787 legislation, Americans agreed that slavery would be barred from the Northwest Territory.[2] Wilmot's amendment to the $2 million bill stated:

> Provided, That as an express and fundamental condition to the acquisition of any territory from the Republic of Mexico by the United States by virtue of any treaty which may be negotiated between them, and to the use by the Executive of the money herein appropriated, neither slavery nor involuntary servitude shall ever exist in any part of said territory except from crime, whereof the party shall first be duly convicted.[3]

The House of Representatives passed the amendment the same day Wilmot introduced it, but the Senate did not discuss the bill until the last day of the congressional session. The Polk administration wanted the amendment stricken from the Senate version, but a filibuster by Senator John Davis of Massachusetts not only kept the Senate from removing Wilmot's attachment, it kept the Senate from voting on the bill altogether. By the time Davis finished speaking, the Senate learned that the House had adjourned, and so, too, did the Senate without taking any action on the $2 million bill or its rider.[4]

The vote on legislation that would become known as the Wilmot Proviso did not develop along traditional party lines; it followed sectional lines. Few Southerners supported the amendment in the House. Few Northerners voted against it. Most Americans initially missed the significance of the vote, but one newspaper, as if it had a crystal ball with which to peer into the future, remarked, "As if by magic, it [the Proviso] brought to a head the great question which is about to divide the American people."[5] Sectionalism was about to become the basis for American politics, and leading Southern politicians such as John C. Calhoun initiated a new level to the conflict by introducing Southern rights and block-Southern voting to the mix.

Even though Congress did not approve the $2 million bill to purchase land from Mexico or the Wilmot rider in 1846, neither went away. In the next Congress, the request for money reappeared and so did the Proviso. The Proviso never passed into law, even though the House voted on it dozens of times before 1850. In 1850, Congress approved the Compromise of 1850 (see Chapter 23). It approved the possibility for slavery to exist in the ceded Mexican territory, but part of that region—California—applied for admission as a free state and was admitted. The Wilmot Proviso appeared to be dead, but as the battle raged over the Proviso, a new ingredient was added to the debate—popular sovereignty. Popular sovereignty, which said that "all questions pertaining to slavery in the Territories, and in the new states to be formed therefrom are to be left to the people residing therein, through their appropriate representatives,"[6] became law in 1854 (see Chapter 25). David Wilmot's Proviso was now officially dead, but its essence remained the foundation of American political action until the Union dissolved.

This chapter looks at the heated debate that grew in the wake of the Wilmot Proviso. The first section looks at support of the Proviso and begins with an editorial from the *Jefferson Democrat* of Adams, New York, that says support or opposition to the Proviso will be the central issue of the elections of 1848. It calls for no more concessions to the South. The next entry comes from the *Daily Atlas* of Boston. As was customary, the paper reprinted editorials from other newspapers supporting its own political position. It suggests that those who favor the Proviso should work through the House of Representatives, not the presidency, to end slavery in the territories. The next article in the section attacks the Southern premise that the Wilmot Proviso usurped the rights of those living in territories. The last selection, from a Southern newspaper, says Congress has the right to limit slavery in the territories since it has been doing so since the passage of the Northwest Ordinance.

The readings that attack the Wilmot Proviso start with one from a series of anti-Proviso editorials that appeared in the Charleston *Mercury*, one of the South's most vocal newspapers for Southern rights. It is followed by two articles by two other champions of the South. The first was written by James De Bow of New Orleans, an editor who fought as hard as those of the *Mercury* to promote the South. John C. Calhoun's resolutions, which were introduced in the Senate to counteract those of David Wilmot, follow. An article from New York that says the Wilmot Proviso attacks the foundations of the Constitution concludes the readings.

Support for the Proviso

An Anonymous Report: "Democracy–North and South"

The Wilmot Proviso became a central issue of the 1848 elections. Here, the National Era *republishes an article from a democratic paper, the* Jefferson Democrat *of Adams, New York, calling for Democrats North and South to rally behind the Proviso.*

National Era (Washington, D.C.), 29 July 1847

"The deep has been stirred," and the great principle round which the *true* Democracy of the *whole* country will rally in '48, as one man, will be, "NO more concessions to the South–no further extension of Human Chattelship." There is an enflexible [*sic*] determination–not the less efficient because it is quiet, seeking no relief in present ebullitions–on the part of a large majority of the North, to give their suffrages to no man for President who would interfere by the exercise of his prerogative, with their wishes in this respect, or to delegate any one as their Representative who will further succumb to Southern Overseerism, or consent "to bedabble with the blood of brethren their skirts," by implanting in territory yet to be acquired, and where now it has no legal existence, this–according to South Carolina philosophy–"basis and support of our *free* institutions."

We interfere not with this institution where it already exists; we leave each State to manage its own domestic affairs as seems proper to its own sovereign will; but we never can permit, in the noble country soon to be unlocked to the Saxon advance, that a worse than Saxon serfdom should again settle like a nightmare, forcing Freemen of New York to compete, side by side, on degrading and destructive terms, with the Chattel of Georgia; no, never! never! Southern Holy Alliances and Northern Doughfaceism will we oppose with Northern Combination and Southern Sense of Right; and, planting ourselves immovably on the principles of the Wilmot Proviso, "if we fall, we shall fall like the strong man—we will embrace the pillars of State, and pull down the Constitution along with us."

An Anonymous Report: "The Wilmot Proviso"

Newspapers regularly exchanged copies during the antebellum period, especially with likeminded editors. This selection from Boston's Daily Atlas *comes from two other papers that supported the Proviso, the New York* Evening Post *and the Kennebec, Maine,* Journal.

Daily Atlas (Boston, Massachusetts), 25 August 1847

The cause espoused by the Washington Union is hostile to the interests of every freeman in the Northern States—it is hostile to views of the citizens of Delaware, and probably of Western Virginia, of Kentucky, Missouri, a portion of Tennessee and North Carolina, and to the unbiased sentiments of thousands of voters in the slaveholding States, who have no interest in that peculiar kind of property.

It is painful to witness this advocacy of a mere local institution, in which not more than a million of the citizens of this republic have any pecuniary interest, at the expense of the welfare and prosperity of the nineteen millions who have no such interest; but vastly more painful is it to witness a print which holds the leadership of a party, the most glorious distinction of which is, that it defends the rights of man, and pledges to their development and security its very existence, advocates the extension of human oppression, and the sacrifice of human rights. Loyalty to the principles which are so dear to every democratic citizen, and which, after so many thousand years of conflict with injustice, have as yet acquired only a limited influence in the world, should burn with the purest flame in every democratic bosom.

Whatever the differences of opinion there may be on the Presidential question, which is to occur next year, one thing is clear enough, and that is, that Congress is the body in which the North must exert its power. The free States can elect men enough who are sound on this pint, if they, will, and if they do this, nothing farther is needed. This is the assailable point. It is the one where our strength should be turned, and not scattered upon others. Let no man be elected to Congress who can be induced to vote for the extension of slavery, or the admission of a foot of slave territory into the Union. A President, to be elected, must have the votes of the South and West, as well as the North: but the North and West can elect their members of Congress without the South. And now (not next year) is the time to look to this in the election of four members from Maine.

An Anonymous Report: "To the Point"

National Era *editor Gamaliel Bailey picked up as many articles as possible from all regions of the nation that dealt with the Wilmot Proviso and ran them in his newspaper. Bailey, an abolitionist, ran hundreds of clipped articles on the Proviso from 1847 through 1850. One of the South's principal arguments for not allowing passage of the Wilmot Proviso dealt with its unconstitutionality. This article, from the Washington* Patriot, *addresses that line of thinking.*

National Era **(Washington, D.C.), 18 November 1847**

One of the most powerful arguments which Anti-Wilmot Proviso men make, which they deem a clincher, is, that we have no just right to deny to the settlers in any territory the privilege of making laws for themselves; that when they shall form a government of their own, it is their business, not the business of the nation, to say whether they shall have slaves or not. Well, supposing a majority of the settlers came from Europe, and prefer a monarchical government to a democracy: they have a right, then, if this reasoning be correct, to make themselves a king, and claim the protection of this Government in so doing. Has Congress any more right to sanction the making of a slave than the making of a king? We should find, if monarchy were to be built up by the voice of the people in the territory under the jurisdiction of the United States, that the army of the nation would be set to pulling it down. *Washington Patriot.*

An Anonymous Report: "Rebuked"

Being able to prove that the South was not united in its opposition to the Wilmot Proviso was one way that Gamaliel Bailey of the National Era *could prove the South's stand on it was not valid. In a lengthy article, the editor presented numerous selections from Southern papers that tended to support the Proviso. A story from the Louisville, Kentucky,* Journal *notes that just as the nation had a right to limit slavery through the Northwest Ordinance and the Missouri Compromise, it has the same right now with the Wilmot Proviso.*

National Era (Washington, D.C.), 16 December 1847

The Wilmot Proviso, whether a just or unjust measure, is not a matter of such great practical importance that it should set the Union, or even so small a portion of it as is comprised within the limits of South Carolina, in an uproar. The Wilmot Proviso is simply a measure which it is proposed to apply to any future territory that may be brought into our Confederacy, leaving all the present States and Territories as they are. The authors of it say that it is strictly within the competency of Congress to pass such a proviso, as Congress has on several occasions exerted such power, and that, as the slaveholding States were strengthened by, and had the exclusive benefit of, the annexation of Texas, it is but justice that the free States shall have the benefit of the next extension of our boundaries.

The Wilmot Proviso proposes to accomplish nothing more nor less than was accomplished by the celebrated ordinance of 1787, which forever prohibited the existence of slavery or involuntary servitude, save as a punishment for crime, in all the vast Northwestern Territory. In the case of the Missouri Compromise, which declared that slavery should never be permitted to exist north of 36 deg. 30 min., Congress resolved that it had the power to limit the institution of slavery within certain bounds; and it is quite as competent in Congress now to declare that it should never have an existence in any territory north of the line of the Missouri Compromise.

Opposition to the Proviso

John E. Carew: "The Wilmot Proviso—The Ruin and Injustice of Its Operation"

No matter the editor of the Mercury, *this South Carolina paper was the champion of Southern rights from the 1820s through the secession of South Carolina. In this editorial, the first in a series by the same title, John Carew discusses the constitutional rights of slavery and how the Wilmot Proviso usurps them.*

Mercury (Charleston), 14 August 1847

"The citizens of each State shall be entitled to all privileges and immunities of citizens in the several States."—*Constitution United States, art. 4, sec. 2.*

If we were to look through the whole of the Constitution, designed as it was to afford equal security and confer equal privileges on the States of this Union, in no part will there be found the proof of more wanton aggression than arises from the comparison of this section with the Wilmot Proviso.

Whence is the territory derived on which the Wilmot Proviso is to operate? If it comes by purchase, do not the Slaveholding States contribute their full proportion to the Federal Treasury from which the price is paid? If it comes by conquest, is not the blood of the South poured out as freely on the battle-field as that of the North and East? If it comes by treaty, are not the Slaveholding States integral parts of the Government, by which, and for which, the treaty is made? In whatever way acquired, is not the new territory common property? And if it is so, (and that it is so who will doubt, if truth is valuable?) where is the authority for saying, that the principle which regulates *its enjoyment* is different from that which regulates *its acquisition?* Is the right to populate it common to all? Whence then the authority to say that the citizen of one part of the country shall go there as he pleases, but the citizen of another part shall not? Yet this is the Wilmot Proviso?...

Point us not to the part of the Constitution which gives a right to the citizen of New York or Pennsylvania to settle in newly acquired territory with whatever property he may choose, but withholds the same right from the citizen of a Slaveholding State? The citizen of New York puts his capital in whatever he pleases, and goes into the new territory. The citizen of Carolina or Georgia, who has his capital in negroes, is prohibited from placing his capital there. He must either sell his negroes, if he persists in removing, or if he determine to retain his capital in its present form, he must abandon the idea of a removal. This is the equalizing principle of the Wilmot Proviso! This is the way in which the citizen of a Slaveholding State enjoys an equality of privilege and immunity with the citizen of New York or Pennsylvania!

But there are other consequences, which, if omitted, would serve but to leave undeveloped all the ruinous and unjust consequences of this proposed invasion of our rights. The Wilmot Proviso *draws a line of social and political demarcation around the Slave States.* In so doing, it affects the value of the slave, because it limits the field within which his labor shall be productive. It is the great blow at the value of the labor of the slave, and in this will be, *if not promptly resisted, a sure blow at the institution itself.* In confining the space within which Slavery shall be allowed, it induces the evil of a redundant population, without an outlet. In confining and limiting the area in which this labor is to be exercised, it must have the effect of gradually diminishing the return of each year's labor, by the gradual wearing out of the land. These propositions, we think, must engage the assent of all who live in the Slaveholding portion of the United States: we should hope of the candid and just also in every part of the Union....

We have said that the Wilmot Proviso shows the uselessness of concession. Where is not the Missouri Compromise? Where is the line there laid down? Did not the Slaveholding States then concede? And what has been gained? Does the Slaveholding portion of the Union call for a fresh understanding? . . .But how terribly true has been the prophetic language of one of the most zealous opponents of that Compromise, when in the debate he uttered the following language: "*The people of this country have hitherto felt a complete security in the enjoyment of rights built on the laws, the faith of the nation. You now tell them these are revocable; held only at your pleasure.* The doctrines advocated, the reasoning urged to support this amendment, will alone be remembered—*the disclaimer of their application to the old States will be forgotten or discarded* . . . . This amendment becomes a new Constitution; as *a new source of power*, it will be construed, refined, and stretched, to justify *any usurpation* on the people of the States" . . .insulting the pride, injuring the property, and trampling even the Constitutional rights of the Slaveholding States.

James De Bow: "The Wilmot Proviso's Exclusion"

The South may have had no stronger advocate for slavery than James De Bow of New Orleans. De Bow believed that the Wilmot Proviso was the greatest threat to the Southern way of life of any legislation pertaining to slavery in that century. Here he calls for Congress to come to the protection of Southern rights.

Commercial Review of the South and West **(New Orleans), December 1847**

The South has, with just indignation, and with one voice, condemned the nefarious scheme in its very bud, which threatens in all future time to reduce her to a subordinate position in the Union; without any other rights than those that may be graciously conceded by a sovereign and hostile majority upon the floor of Congress; nothing, perhaps, for half a century has produced deeper excitement among us, and we look with the greatest anxiety to the meeting of Congress this month to determine the results. Everything depends upon them. If abolition and disorganization are but narrow sects at the North, of the ignorant and the deluded, let the members of Congress from this section speak out. We must and will insist upon knowing who are our friends; or rather—for we ask not friendship—*who have respect for our rights!*

It behoves [*sic*] the South to be firm in this crisis, and preserve its temper in every respect. From a want of discrimination we have often offended good and firm friends in the midst of abolition regions. There are thousands and hundreds of thousands of leading citizens in every part of the North and East, who deprecate all interference with us and our institutions, and who incur the hostility of their neighbors by an advocacy of our rights. Let us respect these men, and remember them always when we dispute. In our summer excursions at the North it surprised and delighted us to find so many. In fact, what is a little remarkable, we scarcely found a man willing to admit, in conversation with us, that he was an abolitionist in every sense of the term. There was always some one worse than himself. In fact, we often found that "abolitionist" was, in many sections, a kind of taint. We know, indeed, that the Democratic Convention of New York have rejected the Wilmot Proviso, and this is, without doubt, the sentiment of that State. . . .

John C. Calhoun: "Mr. Calhoun's Resolutions in the Senate"

John C. Calhoun was the South's most powerful and persuasive orator in the Senate. Using the Bill of Rights as his foundation, the South Carolinian introduced the "Calhoun Resolutions" in February 1847 as a counter to the Wilmot Proviso. The logic that Calhoun used to create his resolutions became the standard argument on which Southerners based their right to slavery for the next decade.

Commercial Review of the South and West **(New Orleans), December 1847**

Resolved, That the territories of the United States belong to the several States composing this Union, and are held by them as their joint and common property.

Resolved, that Congress, as the joint agent and representative of the States of this Union, has no right to make any law, or do any act whatever, that shall directly, or by its effects, make any discrimination between the States of this Union, by which any of them shall be deprived of its full and equal right in any territory of the United States, acquired or to be acquired.

Resolved, That the enactment of any law which should directly, or by its effects, deprive the citizens of any of the States of this Union from emigrating with their property into any of the territories of the United States, will make such discrimination, and would, therefore, be a violation of the Constitution, and the rights of the States from which such citizens emigrated, and in derogation of that perfect equality which belongs to them as members of this Union, and would tend directly to subvert the Union itself.

Resolved, That, as a fundamental principle in our political creed, a people in forming a Constitution have the unconditional right to form and adopt the government which they may think best calculated to secure their liberty, prosperity, and happiness, and that in conformity thereto, no other condition is imposed by the Federal Constitution on a State in order to be admitted into the Union, except that its Constitution shall be strictly republican; and that the imposition of any other by Congress would not only be in violation of the Constitution, but in direct conflict with the principle on which our political system rests.

Thomas Prentice Kettell : "The Wilmot Proviso"

To many Americans, slavery was repulsive, but the Wilmot Proviso was even more offensive because, they believed, it violated the Constitution. Just as John C. Calhoun used the Constitution to fight the Proviso in the Senate, Thomas Prentice Kettell, editor of the New-York based United States Democratic Review *attacked the Proviso in the pages of his publication. The Proviso, he said, potentially threatened the rights of all Americans and had to be eradicated from any legislation.*

United States Democratic Review (New York), September 1848

Of all the questions that have agitated the United States of America since the adoption of the Constitution, there are none that have ever been fraught with so deep and terrible an interest as that contained in the principles of the Wilmot Proviso. The effects and consequences of a National Bank, a Sub-Treasury, a high Tariff, the distribution of the proceeds arising from the sale of the Public Lands, Internal Improvements, and the questions of Peace or War, all sink into insignificance when compared to the results that *must* and *will* follow the carrying into effect the principles involved in that proviso. And these results will be the dissolution of the Union; the bursting asunder those bonds of unity that have preserved the empire, and made us what we are; the annihilation of our power and influence; the destruction of the Constitution, that sacred instrument of our common faith. And, not alone to America would its effects be confined, but they would pass the bounds of this continent and extend beyond the Atlantic, to rivet the fetters of millions yet unborn. But its first and most dangerous tendency, and the one from whence all its greatest evils will spring, is the arraying of the Northern portion of our country against the Southern, and, if not immediately producing civil war, creating and engendering a bitter and undying hate, a hate that may forever destroy the unanimity of our councils, and thus enervate the energy of our government. The moment there is a want of energy and power in the legislature of a nation, internal dissensions spring up and internal dissensions have been the cause of the downfall not only of republics, but of all states that have risen, flourished, and passed away; and internal dissensions alone, if this nation is ever dismembered, will be the cause of that dismemberment. Yet, with dissolution staring them in the face, and all the lamentable consequences that must necessarily follow such an event presented to their view, there are a set of men "who, (as it has been said of a class precisely similar,) so far from comprehending the great movement of empire, are not fit to turn a wheel in the machine." These men, composed as they are of broken down politicians and disappointed office-seekers, banded together for an unholy purpose, are endeavoring to enforce that principle by declamatory appeals to the passions of the multitude, and, unless counteracted by the sound sense of the sober and reflecting part of the community, will light the torch of civil war, and extinguish for ever the spirit of liberty upon American soil. Will men of judgment and patriotism give their countenance and support to a cause like this! And are they willing to cultivate and water the tree of discord, already rooted, until their country is sunk on a level with that upon our southern border? No! no! The warning voice that comes from the annals of the past—the voice of him sleeping among the dead at Mount Vernon, with its deep and solemn tones telling us to beware of internal dissensions, *will* have its effect upon all those who have any regard for exalted wisdom and acknowledged worth. We know that such men as we have mentioned will disregard this, for they are regardless of every thing that will not fill their pockets with dollars, or give them a lucrative office. They would sell their country's rights, barter her honor, and betray her liberties, for a far less sum than that which was the price of Arnold's treason. . . .

These are the men who urge upon our legislature the passage of an act, not only unjust and dangerous, but, according to all international law, illegal—an act that also violates our Constitution, and the rights guarantied to the citizens by that instrument. It is an act which, however potent and mighty for evil, is weak and powerless for good; and by a careful examination of the principle involved, it will appear that these assertions are well founded. That principle is the confining of slavery within its present limits; the exclusion of that institution, by the enactment of stringent laws, from all territories belonging to the nation. Now, territory is a part of the public wealth. It is property belonging to the whole. It is that in which all have a common interest, if purchased, it has been purchased by money taken from the public treasury: if conquered, it has been conquered by the united arms of the whole nation. Every individual, therefore, as composing a part of the nation, the whole, or the body politic, has an interest in that territory; he is entitled to that property as a tenant in joint tenancy; and, as such, he has a legal right to use and enjoy that interest under the law by which it was acquired, which right cannot be taken from him without his consent. This is the fundamental condition of the social compact as regards property. . . .

But, say the advocates of the Wilmot Proviso, we do not intend to exclude from the territories the slave-holder; we only *define* in what manner he shall enjoy his rights—we only *mean* to exclude slavery. NOW, slavery may be an evil. We go further, and say we believe it to be an evil whose lamentable effects, are to blight and wither every thing with which it comes in contact; yet it is an institution guarantied by the Constitution, and its principles recognized as forming a part of our system of government, and it cannot be excluded from the territory of the nation. Over this question Congress can have no power. The rights of the institution are derived from, and protected by, the Constitution; and the South might with the same propriety, and act [*sic*] in accordance with the law as much as the North, demand the prohibition of the manufactures of the northern states as an evil, and a system of labor calculated to injure the nation. It matters not whether this is true, or whether the facts will or will not warrant the conclusion. *They* arrogate to themselves the right to judge; and, judging that it is an evil, and having a majority in Congress, thus the power is in their possession.... Here, an institution that is protected by the Constitution, and recognized as a part of the system of government, is to be subverted and overturned by the fickle opinions of a crowd, actuated and moved by strong passions and intense excitement.

Now, this movement is directed against the peculiar institutions of the South; to-morrow, it may be against those of the North. Thus the very foundations of government would be upheaved and overthrown....

But that the power claimed by those who favor the adoption of the Wilmot Proviso, does not exist, we have to thank those profound and wise statesmen who were the authors of our noble institutions, and the founders of our free and just government. And to suppose that these great and sagacious men, (as the result of their labors proved them to have been,) would have constructed an instrument so faulty as those who favor the proviso consider it to be, is unreasonable. It is claimed that Congress has the power to pass all laws for the government of territories, and that this power is derived from the Constitution. The Constitution grants no such unlimited powers, nor is there a single section in that instrument that warrants the assertion. It is contrary to its genius and spirit. Territories, as well as states, have the right of local government.... The Constitution recognized slavery as a part of the system of our government, and by that act it must have necessarily recognized all its rights, immediate and collateral, and also guarantied the exercise of those rights wherever it was not in violation of the sovereignty of the states.... Now, if Congress has exclusive jurisdiction over the territories, and the power to exclude those rights and privileges that the Constitution guarantied to every citizen, it may establish in our territories a monarchical form of government—abolish the right of trial by jury, and prohibit the exercise of the rights of religious worship—curb and control the freedom of the press—destroy the liberties of the people, and rob them of those rights that they have been taught to consider as inalienable. The law and the Constitution to them are no protection, for Congress is above all law, and higher than the Constitution. They are the law; the sovereign power is in them.... This is what that proviso claims the Constitution has done—conferred on Congress the power it never possessed itself; and to support this monstrous doctrine, they say that the founders of the Constitution, being the best interpreters of their own acts, have sanctioned this view of the case by passing the ordinance of 87, and allowing that ordinance to stand after the adoption of the Constitution.

That the founders of our institutions were the best judges of their principles, we are prepared to admit; but that the Wilmot Proviso contains principles similar to those of the ordinance of 87, we are just as well prepared to deny. That ordinance was constructed on the same foundations as that on which that glorious monument of wisdom, the Constitution, was reared. The same spirit breathes through them both. It is that spirit which has given all the life and efficacy to our institutions, and permanency to our government.... That ordinance admits that slavery has a right to a part of the territories by its silence as it regards the existence of that institution south of the line designated by that act. The Wilmot Proviso, on the contrary, denies the existence of this right to a part, and extends its own claims to the whole.... There can be no greater evil done society than such violation. It is trampling upon the conditions of the social compact—undermining the foundations of government, and sapping the vital interest of society; it is disregarding the rules of action that have been laid down and sanctioned by the wisdom of ages.... With these remarks, let us, leaving the dry and dusty track of legal argument, ascend to a higher—more elevated and extended view of the subject, to see, the principles of the Wilmot Proviso being legal, if they would have the effect to undermine the power of slavery, and ultimately destroy an institution more baneful in its effects than any that has ever cursed mankind; and from wherever it has an existence, and lives and flourishes, energy, industry and enterprise are driven, to make room for indolence and idleness. The whole land seems as if a fire had rolled its desolating flood over it, consuming everything that was valuable as a means of wealth and power, while the institution remains dark and lowering, brooding over the destruction it has caused. We would use all legal and constitutional means for its extermination; yet, if it is one of the pillars on which the foundations of our government rest, we would not endanger the permanency of that government to secure even the annihilation of that institution, and hence arises our opposition to the Wilmot Proviso....

Questions

1. Southern apologists for slavery were skillful polemicists. Look carefully at Calhoun's resolutions. Based on what he tells you of the Constitution,

does his argument seem logical? Explain. Apply the same question to Thomas Prentice Kettell's editorial.
2. If Congress could limit slavery through the Northwest Ordinance and the Missouri Compromise, why did the South find the Wilmot Proviso so repulsive?
3. From the articles supporting the Wilmot Proviso, what do you think were the underlying reasons for support of the provision, other than issues of morality?

Notes

1. Discussion of the Wilmot Proviso is taken from Chaplain W. Morrison, *Democratic Politics and Sectionalism: The Wilmot Proviso Controversy* (Chapel Hill: University of North Carolina Press, 1967); and David M. Potter, *The Impending Crisis, 1848–1861* (New York: Harper & Row, 1976).

2. The Northwest Ordinance was legislation approved under the Articles of Confederation. When the Constitution was approved and established American law, its tenets were reaffirmed by Congress in August 1789.

3. *Congressional Globe,* 29 Cong., 1 sess., 1217; cited in Morrison, *Democratic Politics and Sectionalism,* 18; and Potter, *The Impending Crisis,* 21.

4. Potter, *The Impending Crisis,* 22.

5. *Whig* (Boston), 15 August 1846.

6. Quoted in George Brown Tindall, *America: A Narrative History,* 2 vols. (New York: W.W. Norton, 1984), 1:591.

CHAPTER 21

Seneca Falls and Women's Rights, 1848

When Elizabeth Cady Stanton returned to America from the first World Anti-Slavery Convention held in June 1840, in London, she was furious. She and other women delegates to the convention were partitioned off from the male delegates and required to sit behind a screen. Stanton, who was born to the wealthy New York family of Judge Daniel Cady and wife Margaret, had not run into such obstacles before. Her father allowed her to study law books in his Johnstown office, approved her study of other subjects, and permitted her to do activities that were normally set aside for boys only. So her treatment in London was not something she easily accepted. But the convention opened Stanton to a new purpose and a new friend. There, she met fellow delegate Lucretia Mott, and they formed a bond and a new common aim—the rights of women.[1] After the day's humiliating events, the two promised "to hold a convention . . . and form a society to advocate the rights of women" as soon as they returned to America.[2]

Eight years later, at Seneca Falls, New York, the two sponsored a conference on women's rights. There, about one hundred delegates met and agreed to a Declaration of Sentiments. That declaration, based on the Declaration of Independence began:

> When, in the course of human events, it becomes necessary for one portion of the family of man to assume among the people of the earth a position different from that which they have hitherto occupied, but one to which the laws of nature and of nature's God entitle them, a decent respect to the opinions of mankind requires that they should declare the causes that impel them to such a course.

The next line of the women's statement said, "We hold these truths to be self-evident: that all men and women are created equal." After outlining the injustices against women, the document closed by stating, "Now, in view of this entire disfranchisement of one-half the people of this country . . . we insist that they have immediate admission to all the rights and privileges which belong to them as citizens of the United States.[3]

YE MAY SESSION OF YE WOMAN'S RIGHTS CONVENTION—YE ORATOR OF YE DAY DENOUNCING YE LORDS OF CREATION.

Women's Rights Convention. *In 1848, at Seneca Falls, New York, America's first women's convention met to call for women's rights. Elizabeth Cady Stanton and Lucretia Mott, who met at an abolitionist meeting in London, spearheaded the movement, which called for suffrage for women. This illustration appeared in* Harper's Weekly *on June 11, 1859. Notice the jeering men in the balcony and the haughty looks of the women that the engraver supplied.*

The next major meeting to address women's rights and suffrage took place in Worcester, Massachusetts, in 1850. Much better organized and publicized than the Seneca Falls meeting, more than one thousand people came to the first national women's convention that began on October 23. Though Stanton did not attend because she was pregnant, the delegates followed her Seneca Falls lead and made suffrage the convention's principal issue. Representatives agreed to spread petitions through eight states in attempts to gain women the right to vote.[4]

The ideas that came out of the women's conventions for equality of women and men ran counter to the traditional American role of domesticity for women, especially Stanton's notion that there were not separate spheres of existence for men and women. Most Americans and most newspapers and magazines subscribed to the Cult of True Womanhood. Under the rubrics of this guideline for the ideal woman, women were to concern themselves only with domestic affairs and were to remain "a hostage of the home." Women took care of the domestic needs of husband and children. A woman was seen as the moral compass of family and society. Men operated in the business world and in the political arena.[5] The idea, then, that women should be allowed to be doctors, lawyers, and politicians, and should be able to vote was anathema to the traditional American view. Indeed, it would not be until 1919 that suffrage was granted to women for national elections with the ratification of the nineteenth amendment to the Constitution in August 1920.

The readings in this chapter focus on the Seneca Falls women's rights meeting and the first national meeting on women's rights held in 1850 in Worcester, Massachusetts. The first section, in support of women's rights, begins with a pair of articles from two papers named *National Reformer* that praise the efforts of the women at Seneca Falls. They are followed by Elizabeth Cady Stanton's reply to negative newspaper articles on the convention. The next entry comes from the *Massachusetts Spy* of Worcester announcing the women's conference there. It is followed by Horace Greeley's reply to an anonymous letter writer to the New York *Tribune* who attacks the Worcester Convention and then asks Greeley's opinion of the women's demands.

The section that opposes what took place at the conventions begins with commentary from Oneida, New York, on the deplorable demands of the women at Seneca Falls. It is followed by an editorial that says most women will feel ashamed of what has happened in New York. The next two entries are editorials by James Gordon Bennett. Bennett opposed what took place in Worcester as much because he detested Horace Greeley—who supported the women's movement—as he found the women's movement foolish and repulsive. Bennett's language is demeaning and belittling. The next reading is a letter to the *Tribune,* which is answered by Greeley in the first set of readings. The final reading deals with concepts of domesticity and the Cult of True Womanhood. Though it does not mention the meeting in Worcester, it ran concurrently with reports that were appearing in newspapers about the meeting there and its call for female suffrage.

Support for Women's Rights

E. W. Capron: "Women's Rights Convention"

The National Reformer *was a publication that supported abolition and other reform movements. Here, editor E. W. Capron praises the Seneca Falls convention for boldly taking a stand and presenting its arguments in a strong fashion.*

National Reformer (Auburn, New York), 3 August 1848

On Wednesday and Thursday week, one of the most interesting conventions of this conventional age, was held at Seneca Falls, for the discussion of the social, civil and political rights of women. During the day on Wednesday, the meeting was attended exclusively by women, (the only unwise move during the convention, in our opinion,) to enable them, in a preliminary meeting, to draw up a declaration of sentiments and prepare an address, uninfluenced and unembarrassed by the presence of men. Both of these documents would do honor to any deliberative body that assembled in this country.... The declaration was read and adopted. A series of resolutions were then read, on which a spirited discussion arose ...and they were finally adopted nearly as they were originally drawn up by the preliminary convention of women. Some hundred persons or more attached their names to the declaration, which, bold and ultra as some evidently regarded it, failed to call out any opposition, except in a neighboring BAR-ROOM. Not even lawyers, who were known to be opposed to the equal rights of women, and who were present, chose to contest the question with what they were wont to call the "weaker vessels." The whole convention was well attended and animated; and when that declaration and address is published ...they will carry a weight of argument which the cobwebs of misinterpreted authority and special pleadings of those who only wish for equal rights for one half of creation, can never answer. They may ridicule, but not reason away the *facts* and arguments there set forth....

George G. Cooper: "Woman's Rights Convention"

The National Register *of Rochester supported the work by Elizabeth Cady Stanton, Lucretia Mott, and the other women at Seneca Falls. In this edito-*

rial, Cooper announces the publication of the Declaration of Sentiments. In the introduction to the Sentiments, which is included here, Cooper says all should listen with open ears to what the women have to say.

National Reformer **(Rochester, New York), 10 August 1848**

We publish this week the proceedings of the Woman's rights Convention held in this city on the 2nd of August. The attendance was large, and many of our citizens who were spectators through curiosity have acknowledged that good will result from gatherings of this kind. There is a class of men (and many of them connected with the press) who stand ready to condemn, or what is worse, ridicule every movement of this character, simply because propositions are made to change certain usages with which they are familiar and which have long existed. They argue that if they were not right they would not have existed so long without an effort to change them. The absurd argument that "age sanctifies a wrong," will soon be obsolete. We think it the duty of every candid person to hear every proposal for the elevation of our race, and if they fall, let it be from want of argument to substantiate, not from the assaults of fulsome wit or vulgar sarcasm, which too often constitutue [*sic*] the weapons of those men who think lightly of the efforts of female philanthropists. . . .

Elizabeth Cady Stanton: "Mrs. Stanton's reply"

A number of disparaging newspaper reports appeared following the Seneca Falls convention. Elizabeth Cady Stanton wrote this letter to reply to some of the attacks. She criticizes the concept of separate spheres for females and males.

National Reformer **(Rochester, New York), 14 September 1848**

There is no danger of this question dying for want of notice. Every paper you take up has something to say about it, and just in proportion to the refinement and intelligence of the editor, has this movement been favorably noticed. But one might suppose from the articles that you find in some papers, that there were editors so ignorant as to believe that the chief object of these recent Conventions was to seat every lord at the head of a cradle, and to clothe every woman in her lord's attire. . . . For those who do not yet understand the real objects of our recent Conventions at Rochester and Seneca Falls, I would state that we did not meet to discuss fashions, customs, or dress, the rights or duties of man, nor the propriety of the sexes changing positions, but simply our own inalienable rights, our duties, our true sphere. If God has assigned a sphere to man and one to woman, we claim the right to judge ourselves of His design in reference to us, and we accord to man the same privilege. We think a man has quite enough in this life to find out his own individual calling, without being taxed to decide where every woman belongs; and the fact that so many men fail in the business they undertake, calls loudly for their concentrating more thought on their own faculties, capabilities, and sphere of action. We have all seen a man making a jackass of himself in the pulpit, at the bar, or in our legislative halls, when he might have shone as a captain of a canal boat, or as a tailor on his bench. Now, is it to be wondered at that woman has some doubts about the present position assigned her being the true one, when her every-day experience shows her that man makes such fatal mistakes in regard to himself?

There is no such thing as a sphere for a sex. Every man has a different sphere, and one in which he may shine, and it is the same with every woman; and the same woman may have a different sphere at different times. . . .

John Milton Earle: "The Convention"

On the day the Worcester Convention opened, John Milton Earle ran this announcement in his Massachusetts Spy. *His support of the convention meant support of his wife, who was instrumental in organizing the second meeting for women's rights.*

Massachusetts Spy **(Worcester), 23 October 1850**

A Convention will be held , today and tomorrow, at Brinley Hall, "to consider the question of WOMAN'S RIGHTS, DUTIES, and RELATIONS," a subject as important at least, as any other that claims the attention of the public, and one in which the welfare of society is most deeply involved.

Thoughtless persons may laugh this subject off, as many have done and do with a sneer, but a sneer proves nothing, and in our opinion is poorly applied in such a case as this. To suppose that the laws and customs of the community, as they now exist, in relation to the relative and reciprocal rights, duties, and relations of the sexes, are not susceptible of improvement, is not wise or philosophical. And surely that system, the operation of which subjects THIRTY THOUSAND females in the city of New York alone, to lives of hopeless infamy, and adds, annually not less than *five thousand* fresh victims to the number—that system which dooms still more thousands in the same city to lives of the most abject toil, both by day and night, for a pittance scarcely sufficient to keep soul and body together—that system must be susceptible of improvement. If it is not, it must surely be able to stand the test of the freest and fullest discussion.

We are not among those, therefore, who would meet such a movement as this with either opposition or ridicule. We pity those who would. We wish those engaged in it a hearty Godspeed in the work, knowing it can do no harm, and hoping it may do much good. Ultraisms may be broached in the Convention–it would be strange if they were not, for every movement that is worth anything has them as a matter of course; but where reason is free to meet them, and discussion open to combat them, they do no harm, and tend to elicit truth. We hope, therefore, that our citizens will attend the Convention and give a patient hearing to the discussions.

Horace Greeley: "Remarks to 'A'"

Horace Greeley published the proceedings of the Worcester Convention in the Tribune. *As seen below, James Gordon Bennett poked considerable fun at what Greeley printed. The selection below is Greeley's reply to an anonymous writer–A.–who wrote to the* Tribune *concerning one of those reports, "The Mothers of our Republic," requesting Greeley provide his opinion of the convention. A's letter is included in the second set of readings in this chapter.*

Daily Tribune **(New York), 2 November 1850**

That there is great injustice and evil in the present circumscriptions of Woman's sphere, we firmly believe: that the Worcester Convention indicated precisely the right *remedies* . . . . That the full and equal enjoyment of Political Franchises would improve the lot of Woman, may be doubtful; but we are willing to give the Democratic theory a full and fair trial. Whenever so many Women shall petition for the Right of Suffrage as to indicate that a majority of the sex virtually concur in the demand, then we shall insist that the Franchise shall be extended to them. Being a disciple of the faith which holds that 'all just government is founded on the *consent* of the *governed*,' we could do not less, even though we knew that the Women would make a bad use of the power thus accorded them. Right first; Expediency afterward.

As to our correspondent's fear that buttered toast will run short, and children's faces get crusted over, in case the Political Rights of Women are recognized as equal to and identical with those of Men, we do not share it. We know people who supposed that, when Slavery was abolished, there could be no more boots blacked, no wood chopped, bacon fried, et cetera. But we see that all needful operations go on, though Slavery *is* abolished throughout this region. We see not why it may not be so in case the slavery of Woman should in like manner be abolished. We do not see how an enlargement of her liberties and duties is to make a mother neglect her children or her household. She now performs her maternal duties because she delights in so doing, and not because man requires it.

Our friend's delightful picture of the home presided over by an exemplary wife and mother we appreciate, but all women are not wives and mothers. Marriage is indeed 'honorable in all,' when it *is* marriage; but accepting a husband for the sake of a position, a home and a support, is not marriage. . . . Now one radical vice of our present system is that it morally *constrains* women to take husbands (not to say, fish for them) without the least impulse of genuine affection. Ninety-nine of every hundred young women are destitute of an independent income adequate to their comfortable support; they must work or marry for a living. But in Industry, Woman's sphere is exceedingly circumscribed, and her reward, as compared with the recompense of masculine effort, very inadequate. Except as household drudges, it is very difficult for seven single women out of eight to earn a comfortable, reputable, independent livelihood in this country, and it is generally much worse in others. Hence false marriages and degradations more scandalous if not more intrinsically vicious.

What Woman imminently needs is a far wider sphere of action, larger opportunities for the employment of her faculties, and a juster reward for her labor. It is a shame, for example, that there should be several thousand male Clerks in our City dealing out dry goods mainly to women; these Clerks should have more masculine employments, and their places should be filled by women. The teachers in our schools should nearly all be women; the number should be doubled and the compensation largely increased. Watchmaking, tailoring, and many other branches of manufacturing industry, should in good part be relinquished to women. Women's work should command in the average two-thirds to three-fourths that of men; the present rates range from one-third to one-half.

Political franchises are but a means to an end, which end is the securing of social and personal rights. Other classes have found the Elective Franchise serviceable toward the attainment of these rights, and we see not why it would lose its efficacy in the hands of Women. And as to the exposure of Women to insult and outrage in the Town or Ward Meeting, or at the Election, we trust the effect would be just opposite to that anticipated—namely, that men would be constrained by the presence of ladies to keep sober and behave themselves. The presence of Woman has this effect ever in those public assemblages honored by her presence; and we trust its virtue is far from having been exhausted.

As to Women having to fight and knock down to maintain their Rights if once conceded, we don't believe a word of it. Knock down whom? Certainly not those who cheerfully concede them all they ask; and if there are any of the other sort, such brutes as choose to commence the game of knocking down, would be very sure to get enough of it before coming to the Women. But there would be no knocking down in the premises.

We heartily rejoice that the Women's Rights Convention was held, and trust it will be followed by others. Our correspondent admits that Woman endures great wrongs which cry aloud for redress, but thinks the Worcester Convention misunderstood both the disease and the remedy. Very well; let the discussion go on, until wiser heads shall be interested and safer counsels prevail. For our part, we are well satisfied with the general scope and bearing of the Worcester discussions, and trust they will be followed up.

Opposition to Women's Rights

An Anonymous Report: "Bolting Among the Ladies"

This account of the Seneca Falls Convention includes excepts from the Declaration of Sentiments, but it calls them "the most shocking and unnatural incident ever recorded in the history of womanity."

Oneida (N. Y.) Whig, 1 August 1848

A Woman's Rights Convention was held at Seneca Falls on the 19th and 20th inst., at which the opposers of *female* slavery adopted a declaration of sentiments, declaring that these truths are self-evident–that all men *and women* are created equal, &c., &c. and that when a long train of abuses and usurpations, pursuing invariably the same object, evinces a design to reduce then *under absolute despotism*, it is their right, it is their duty, to throw off such government . . . but the Woman's Rights Convention glory in the publicity of such an exchange. They have let the facts be submitted to a candid world:

"He has never permitted to exercise her alienable right to the elective franchise.
He has compelled her to submit to laws in the formation of which she has had no voice."

Was there ever such a dreadful revolt?–They set aside the statute, "wives submit yourselves unto your husbands." . . . This bolt is the most shocking and unnatural incident ever recorded in the history of womanity. If our ladies will insist on voting and legislating, where, gentlemen, will be our dinners and our elbows? where our domestic firesides and the holes in our stockings?

Here is another shot:

"Having deprived her of this first right of a citizen, the elective franchise, thereby leaving her without representation in the halls of legislation, he has oppressed her on all sides.
"He has made her, if married, in the eye of the law, civilly dead.
"He has taken from her all right in property, even to the wages she earns." . . .

This is the age of reform. . . . *They* used to speak,
"Not as desiring more,
But rather wishing a more strict restraint
Upon the sisterhood;"

but the bolters are too wise, too witty and too wilful to endure such a state of bondage, and the lords of creation will hardly escape the "predestined scratched face." They should recollect however, the illustrious member of their bolting sisterhood who had not long worn the nether garments before she found it in her heart to disgrace her man's apparel and to cry like a woman. The lion's skin in *history* was not large enough to hide the timidity of the peaceful animal who thought to swagger. . . .

John Tanner: "Women out of Their Latitude"

A number of newspapers published the Declaration of Sentiments agreed on by the delegates at the Seneca Falls Convention. The Mechanic's Advocate *of Albany belittled the gathering, saying the women were overlooking their "womenly duties" to attend this meeting. Tanner placed the article under a general headline "Female Department."*

Mechanic's Advocate **(Albany), 12 August 1848**

We are sorry to see that the women, in several parts of this State, are holding what they call "Woman's Rights Conventions," and setting forth a formidable list of those Rights, in a parody upon the Declaration of American Independence.

The papers of the day contain extended notices of these Conventions. Some of them fall in with their objects, and praise their meetings highly; but the majority either deprecate or ridicule them.

The women who attend these meetings, no doubt at the expense of their more appropriate duties, act as committees, write resolutions and addresses, hold much correspondence, make speeches, etc. etc. They affirm, as among their rights, that of unrestricted franchise, and assert that it is wrong to deprive them of the privilege to become legislators, lawyers, doctors, divines, etc. etc.; and they are holding conventions and making an agitatory movement, with the object in view of revolutionising public opinion and the laws of the land, and changing their relative position in society in such a way as to divide with the male sex the labors and responsibilities of active life, in every branch of arts, science, trades and professions!

Now it requires no argument to prove that this is all wrong. Every true-hearted female will instantly feel that it is unwomanly, and that to be practically carried out, the males must change their position in society. . . .

James Gordon Bennett: "Woman's Rights Convention"

This editorial by Bennett shows how some could find no credibility in anything discussed at the second women's convention held in Worcester, Massachusetts. Notice the terminology and derogation of those present at the convention. Bennett refers to Jenny Lind in the editorial. Lind was a famous Swedish singer brought to America by P. T. Barnum. She would have been considered a superstar by today's standards.

Herald (New York), 28 October 1850

Their Platform, and the Closing Scenes of the Gathering–Progress of the Pie-Bald Fanatics of the North.

That motley gathering of fanatical mongrels, of old grannies, male and female, of fugitive slaves and fugitive lunatics, called the Woman's Rights Convention, after two day's discussion of the most horrible trash, has put forth its platform and adjourned. The sentiments and doctrines avowed, and the social revolution projected, involve all the most monstrous and disgusting principles of socialism, abolition, amalgamation, and infidelity. The full consummation of their diabolical projects would reduce society to the most beastly and promiscuous confusion–the most disgusting barbarism that could be devised; and the most revolting familiarities of equality and licentiousness between whites and blacks, of both sexes, that lunatics and demons could invent. Doctrines like these contemplating the overthrow of society, law, religion, and decency, might occasion some alarm, but for the notoriously vagabond character of the leaders in the movement; and the fanatical and crazy mongrels, in breeches and petticoats, who make up the rank and file. Aided and abetted, however, as they are, by their special organ, Horace Greeley, whose identity with all the fag ends of all the insane and infidel factions of the day, constitutes his claim as a moral teacher, supported, as these creatures, are by their leading organ of this city, they are entitled to a passing notice, if it were only to throw off the paltry disguises with which their fiendish designs are concealed.

Now let us see what all this balderdash, clap-trap, moonshine, rant, cant, fanaticism, and blasphemy, means. One of their poetesses, worthy to have been appropriate for the $200 Jenny Lind song says . . .

> "A Woman's Rights Convention.
> Ring out the word on high;
> If my brother man will help me,
> To help myself I'll try." . . .

And they recommend all womankind to put on the breeches–to refuse obedience, and to do just whatever they like. It will refine, improve, and elevate society.

And they declare their disbelief in the Bible, their contempt of St. Paul and the Apostles, a savage and vindictive agency in the doctrines of abolition, amalgamation and disunion; a desire for civil war, promiscuous intercourse of sexes and colors, and the reign of the goddess of reason. There is not a lunatic asylum in the country, wherein, if the inmates were called together to sit in convention, they would not exhibit more sense, reason, decency and delicacy, and less of lunacy, blasphemy, and horrible sentiments, than this hybrid, mongrel, pie-bald, crack-brained, pitiful, disgusting and ridiculous assemblage. And there we drop them, and may God have mercy on their miserable souls. Amen.

James Gordon Bennett: "The Worcester Fanatics"

James Gordon Bennett disliked his rival Horace Greeley intensely. Greeley believed in the social movements of the day; Bennett supported slavery and continually poked fun at the women's movement. Here, Bennett claims that the Worcester Convention is another crazy scheme of reformers. In the first paragraph, Bennett refers to Charles Fourier, the Frenchman who advocated utopian socialism, and Arthur Brisbane, who wrote Social Destiny of Man, *which built on Fourier's ideas. All were considered frivolous by Bennett. Abby Kelly was one of the leaders of the Worcester Convention.*

***Herald* (New York), 29 October 1850**

Progress of Socialism, Abolition, and Infidelity. It has been known ever since Fourier, Brisbane, and Greeley first promulgated their social theories, that society is all wrong. It is known also that their attempts to reform it have signally failed. . . .

Grubby Greeley answers Abby Kelly at Worcester, with "Eureka." We have got it. Got what? The philosopher's stone—the key to the millennium—the one thing needful—the schedule of the final reformation. The Lord be praised.

It is the philosopher's omnibus bill—it is the putting all in a lump the several experiments of reform of the *Tribune* reformers, with a good deal of new matter, new principles, and fundamental ideas, as put forth on the platform of the Woman's Rights Convention, recently held in Worcester. Let the world rejoice. Lucretia Mott, Abby Kelly, Garrison, Phillips, Mrs. Rose, Fred. Douglas, Sojourner Truth, and the Widow Mercy, sitting in council day and night, backed up, heart and soul, by our glorious Greeley, have solved the problem of the age. They have squared the circle of society, and resolved the arcana of its perpetual motion. From our published reports of the proceedings, the speeches, the declarations, and the resolutions of the Worcester Convention, it will be seen that their platform is made up of all the timbers of all the philosophers and spiritual advisers of the *Tribune,* founded upon the strong pillars of abolition, socialism, amalgamation and infidelity, compassing all the discoveries in heaven and earth. The new dispensation of Lucretia Mott and the philosophers, proposes:

1. To dispense with Christianity and the Bible. After an experiment of nineteen centuries, they declare the system to be a humbug.

2. To abolish the existing political and social system of society as part of the false machinery of the age.

3. To put all races, sexes and colors upon a footing of perfect equality. The convention having proved by phrenology and biology that, the sexes are equal in point of intellect, and that color is a mere difference of complexion, it is proposed to abolish the only distinction of sex by a universal adoption of breeches.

Most assuredly, this grand reformation involves, as incidentals, the abolition of slavery, black and white, the doctrine of amalgamation to its fullest extent, fun and refinement, as was never dreamed of . . . from the inspiration of bran bread and turnips.

The philosophers of the *Tribune* have, therefore, published the Worcester platform in the capacity of the official organ of this tremendous reformation. Old things are to be done away with, and all things are to become new. Seward is to be sustained, and Fillmore is only to be tolerated till the advent of the new dispensation, when Lucretia Mott, Abby Kelly, Douglas, Greeley and Sojourner Truth are to rule the roost. Then, and not till then, shall we realise the jubilee of the Devil and his angels.

A.: "Women's Rights and Duties—The Worcester Convention"

Horace Greeley supported the women's rights movement. This letter by the anonymous A. was written to the Tribune *complaining of what was happening at the Worcester Convention. Greeley published the letter and did what the writer requested—gave his opinion of the convention. Greeley's reply is included in the first section of readings in this chapter.*

Daily Tribune **(New York), 2 November 1850**

H. Greeley, Esq.—Dear Sir: I notice that in publishing the proceedings of "the Mothers of our Republic," you refrain from all comment or remarks. I enjoy hearing your opinion, and am particularly anxious to know what you really think of this late movement in favor of "Woman's Rights."

Now, *I* am at a loss to what the Women of the Worcester Convention are aiming at. It is clear that, if we are going to live, or have any private comforts, there must be dinners cooked, children's faces must be washed, and there must be a home—a home to which the mind of the weary husband will turn to bear him up and urge him on in his toils for the inmates of that sanctuary—a home where he can for a time forget, in his wife's and children's society, the toils and troubles of this weary world—a home which he can never leave without carrying with him a new grace, a new strength, drawn from Woman's influence, to enable him victoriously and manfully to withstand the trials and temptations of the world. Now, if Women are given the right to vote, to electioneer, to become stateswomen, why it is an incontrovertible fact (that is, if they attend properly to politics) that the dinners must go *un*-cooked, the children's faces *un*washed, and home be forgotten—unless, indeed, the men exchange duties with them, as was proposed at the Convention, and stay at home and help their wives cook and wash the dishes.

So far from thinking Women "slaves," I do not see how it can appear in such a light to any thinking mind, any true-hearted woman. There is something so superior about Woman that would make one shrink as from profanation at the idea of her mingling in public with "the sterner and *worser* sex"—a spiritualization that raises her far above the intrigues of politicians and the vulgarity of rowdies—a superiority which, if not acknowledged in words, is confessed in actions, even by men who, however degraded they may be, refrain from the slightest word or action that could be comment upon, in the presence of a woman.

The Women of the Worcester Convention seem to have entirely overlooked the immense power given to women in the form of Home Influence. What power can be greater than a mother's holy and elevated example, which has given to the world so many shining lights? than a mother's gentle but impressive remonstrance to a straying son, or a wife's earnest pleadings to a wayward husband? all of which would be of no avail the moment a woman condescended to become a rowdy Senator or intriguing Politician. For my part, I look on Women as missionary angels, sent among men to remind them of their high calling and high duties. It is not because men think that women have no intellect, et cetera that they consider it inexpedient for them to vote. No, it is common sense directs them to this judgment. They know that there are two great duties to be performed in the world, *public* and *domestic* duties; and as no one can deny but that men are stronger than women, the former generally choose the more laborious and inferior duties.

We must also remember, that if women gained these absurd "rights," they would be obliged to maintain them; and this they have not the strength to do; for which of the women at the Worcester Convention could knock a man down if he chose to stand up? and what man would come forward to protect a woman as long as she claimed to herself the right of self-protection? It would be well enough for the ladies to endeavor to protect themselves, if it were practicable; but what rowdy, if he met Miss Dr. So &;So out on a sick call at 12 o'clock at night, would stand to listen to her explanations of "Woman's Rights"? . . .

Truly, we of the Nineteenth Century are wondrous wise, or either, I fear, *we* are imbibing some of the infidelity and self conceit of this same wonderful age. There can be no fault found with Miss Lucy Stone's desire not to have it placed on her grave-stone that she was "relict of somebody," as she can easily avoid being the "relict" of anybody.

I am sorry, dear Sir, to have trespassed so long upon your valuable time, but as I knew that on any subject you are always willing to give both sides a chance, as we Yankees say, I could not refrain from the above remarks.

Yours sincerely, A.

An Anonymous Report: "Home and Women"

As reports about the Worcester Convention were appearing in newspapers, so, too, were articles about the proper place of women in American life. The domestic role of women was considered paramount in the antebellum period as a way to keep home and family safe and strong. The Recorder, *just as most religious prints of the antebellum period, looked like its secular counterparts and competed successfully with them for readers. Religious newspapers contained news of the day that one would find in the secular press plus information specific to the denomination that sponsored it. In this article, the author believes that the new ideas of the day will tear society from its foundations, which are in the home. And, in the home, the woman is the cornerstone of all.*

Biblical Recorder (Raleigh), 2 November 1850

. . .Our homes, what is their cornerstone but the virtue of woman, and on what does social well-being rest but our homes? Must we not trace all other blessings of civilized life to the doors of our private dwellings? Are not our hearth-stones guarded by the holy forms of conjugal, filial, and paternal love, the cornerstones of Church and State; more sacred than either, more necessary than both? Let our temples crumble, and our academies decay; let every public edifice, our halls of justice, and our capitals of state, be levelled with the dust; but spare our homes. Let no socialist invade them with his wild plans of community. Man did not invent, and he cannot improve or abrogate them. A private shelter to cover two hearts dearer to each other than all the world . . .high walls exclude the profane eyes of every human being; seclusion enough for children to feel that mother is a holy and a peculiar name—this is home; and here is the birth-place of every virtuous impulse, of every sacred thought. Here the Church and the State must come for their origin and their support. Oh, spare our homes! . . .

Questions

1. Read the arguments against women's rights. What seem to be the main points against what the women want?
2. What are the spheres of men and women to which Elizabeth Cady Stanton refers? Is there any validity to this concept? What about in terms of nineteenth-century life?

Notes

1. Elisabeth Griffith, *In Her Own Right: The Life of Elizabeth Cady Stanton* (New York: Oxford University Press, 1984), 8–9, 36–37.

2. Elizabeth Cady Stanton, *Eighty Years and More: Reminiscences, 1815–1897* (New York: T. Fisher Unwin, 1898), 82; quoted in Griffith, *In Her Own Right,* 39.

3. Elizabeth Cady Stanton, *A History of Woman Suffrage,* 2 vols. (Rochester, N.Y.: Fowler and Wells, 1889), 1:70–71.

4. Griffith, *In Her Own Right,* 65.

5. Barbara Welter, *Dimity Convictions. The American Woman in the Nineteenth Century* (Athens: Ohio University Press, 1976), 21–30; Barbara Welter, "The Cult of True Womanhood," in *Our American Sisters: Women in American Thought and Life,* ed. Jane E. Friedman and William G. Shade (Boston: Allyn and Bacon, 1973). See also Jeanne Boydston, "The Pastorialization of Housework," in *Women's America,* ed. Linda K. Kerber and Jane Sherron De Hart, 3rd ed. (New York: Oxford University Press, 1991), 150–151; Mary P. Ryan, *Cradle of the Middle Class. The Family in Oneida County, New York, 1790–1865* (Cambridge: Cambridge University Press, 1981), 238.

CHAPTER 22

The California Gold Rush, 1848

In the fall of 1847, John Sutter was in a hurry to complete his four-stone flour mill in Brighton. However, the German immigrant who settled in the Sacramento Valley of Mexican-controlled California after coming to America in 1834, needed lumber to complete the flour mill. Since there was no lumber mill nearby, Sutter hired James W. Marshall, a contractor and builder, to construct a sawmill in Coloma to provide lumber for the grinding mill. Most people in the town of Yerba Buena—which would soon be called San Francisco—considered both mills to be "another folly of Sutter's," since he consistently sought to develop the wilderness rather than acquire property that already showed promise for financial gain.[1] On January 24, 1848, work on both of Sutter's mills stopped. Marshall spied some shiny flakes of metal in the tailrace, which would send water to turn the mill's wheel. The contractor picked up the material and announced to his workers, "Boys, by God I believe I have found a gold mine."[2]

A few days later, Marshall entered Sutter's office, demanded the door be locked, and pulled the yellow metal out of his pocket. Sutter ran tests on the metal and determined it was gold. The next day, Sutter headed for the mill site, which was more than fifty miles from San Francisco. He and Marshall, along with the other workers, found more gold. "I told them that I would consider it as a great favor if they would keep this discovery secret only for six weeks, so that I could finish my large flour mill at Brighton," Sutter recalled later. Although the workers promised to keep the gold secret, the word soon spread, mostly through a store owner near the mill site named Samuel Brannan. As prospectors arrived at Coloma, the workers quit constructing the mill and joined the hunt for gold. By summer, prospecting captured the focus of California. "It was the work of but a few weeks to bring almost the entire population of the territory together to pick up pieces of precious metal," the San Francisco *Californian* reported on August 14. "The result has been, that in less than four months, total revolution has been effected in the prospects and fate of Alta California."

The evening star. Godey's Lady's Book *was one of America's most popular antebellum magazines. Its target audience was, of course, women. This plate, which appeared in color in the magazine's November 1850 issue, started with a parody of "Twinkle, Twinkle, little star," but it also made reference to "California gold." The California Gold Rush of 1849 found its way into American life in many ways, including poetry.*

The newspaper's assessment of what was happening in California was correct. The government requested an official report since America had just recently gained control of California through the Treaty of Guadeloupe-Hidalgo that closed the Mexican War (see Chapter 19). Richard Mason, the territory's military governor, sent confirmation to Washington in August.[3] By September, amazing claims for gold slowly began to appear in Eastern newspapers. "Your streams have fish and ours are paved with gold," one California letter writer declared.[4] In December, President James K. Polk verified the discovery of gold in California in his annual message to Congress. Papers across America responded. The *Daily Dispatch* of Pittsburgh predicted, "An emigration will immediately commence for which we venture to say no parallel can be formed in history."[5] Within weeks, the gold rush was on.

Americans from all regions joined the flood of 49ers heading to California, but news of the discovery did not stop at the shores of the Atlantic or Pacific oceans. People seeking riches came to California from England, France, and Ireland, as well as from Australia, Hawaii, China, and Mexico. Native Americans who lived in California joined in the search, too, as did people from Latin America and South America. The territory's population grew by more than 600 percent from the beginning of 1848 until the end of 1849, growing from less than 14,000 to about 100,000. A year later, California's population had doubled, and the territory became America's thirty-first state in September 1850.[6]

Three basic routes led to the gold fields. Two required the 49ers to board a ship. The third used the overland trails that crossed the Great Plains and Rocky Mountains. One sea route sailed around Cape Horn at the southern tip of South America. The other dropped passengers off on the Atlantic coast of Panama. They trekked across the isthmus and boarded another ship on the Pacific side. Those who decided to travel by land generally left from Missouri in May to avoid the bad winter weather of the mountains and plains. The cheapest and most popular way to reach California was via the land route. Those who went in search of gold left the Eastern United States with high hopes. Many adapted popular music of the day into songs of the Gold Rush, such as this stanza, sung to Stephen Foster's "Oh, Susannah":

> I soon shall be in Frisco.
> And there I'll look around,
> And when I see the Gold lumps there
> I'll pick them off the ground.
> I'll scrape the mountains clean, my boys,
> I'll drain the rivers dry,
> A pocketful of rocks bring home–
> So brothers don't you cry.[7]

Most of the adventurers who headed to California were males, and not all of them sought their fortune from the gold fields. Miners needed supplies, and they needed a way to relax. Mercantiles and saloons were prevalent throughout the gold region, and they, just like the mining camps, were often mobile. Miners rarely established a permanent dwelling, opting instead for a wooden frame with canvas covering, and they sometimes moved from a place as quickly as they descended upon it. Women and children came to California, too, but they accounted for less than 5 percent of the massive 1849–1850 influx. Women's work—cooking, sewing, and washing—was in high demand, and women ran boarding houses, as well. By far the most profitable and popular profession for women during the gold rush, however, was prostitution. About 20 percent of all women who emigrated to California worked as prostitutes.[8]

At the height of 49er activity, miners could be found along a 150-mile stretch of the Sierra Nevada Mountains. Initially, the 49ers used picks, shovels, and placer mining—which allowed rushing water to remove dirt and other light particles to expose the heavier gold that could then be picked up. As the large pieces of gold became more scarce, miners began panning for gold—taking up pans of silt and sifting through it for bits of gold. By 1851, mining companies increasingly took over the search for gold. Mines were dug into the bedrock in search of veins of gold. Many of the 49ers who had once sought riches for themselves, now worked for a company for a salary. Others gave up the hunt for gold and found jobs in San Francisco or other large areas of population. Some moved on in search of gold in other places, and a few returned to their homes.

Some miners made $300 to $400 a day in the first days of the gold rush, but most of the 49ers found little gold. That did not stop many, however, from searching for California gold throughout the 1850s. As more sophisticated and expensive methods of mining for ore were introduced by mining companies, California's gold production rose. In fact, it consistently produced about $45 million annually in the 1850s, money that helped increase America's wealth and helped finance the nation's industrial bent following the Civil War.[9]

This chapter looks at the reaction to the California Gold Rush in the press. Despite the fact that gold offered opportunities for wealth for both individuals and the nation, not all Americans saw the exodus to California as something positive. Many people who lived along the Atlantic seaboard believed the wholesale migration of young men would be detrimental and said so in newspapers. That section of the chapter offers reports opposing the Gold Rush. The chapter begins with articles supporting the Gold Rush and starts with the initial report of gold discovery in the *Californian,* a San Francisco weekly.

Support for the Gold Rush

B.R. Buckelew: "Gold Mine Found"

The Californian *was California's first newspaper, printed initially in 1846, half in English and half in Spanish. Buckelew published the first story of gold nearly two months after its discovery. Eastern newspapers depended on the reports by the* Californian *and its rival, the* California Star, *for their reports of gold in California. In this article, Buckelew makes it sound as if discovering gold is a sure thing. He may, however, have been seeking more readers for his paper since San Francisco had fewer than 400 residents at the time. As many other California businessmen did with their companies, Buckelew folded his newspaper in the summer of 1848. He gave it to the editor of the* California Star, *which had folded earlier when its workers headed to the gold fields.*

Californian **(San Francisco), 15 March 1848**

In the newly made raceway of the Saw Mill recently erected by Captain Sutter, on the American Fork, gold had been found in considerable quantities. One person brought thirty dollars worth to New Helvetia, gathered there in a short time. California, no doubt is rich in mineral wealth, great chances here for scientific capitalists. Gold has been found in almost every part of the country.

An Anonymous Report: "California Gold"

Even before President James Polk officially informed the nation of the discovery of gold in California, news of it appeared in newspapers along the Atlantic seaboard. This article, from Horace Greeley's Daily Tribune, *makes it sound as if prosperity comes to any who go to California, be they digging for gold or working in some other enterprise. The article also recalls Greek mythology by referring to gold as "golden fleece" and to those who seek the gold as "modern Jasons."*

Daily Tribune **(New York), 30 November 1848**

We understand that interesting dispatches have been received at the War Department from Col. Mason, the present commanding officer in California, respecting the astonishing fertility of the gold mines in our new acquisition. It exceeds calculation, and almost reminds us of the treasures of Aladdin. These documents will probably accompany the report of the Secretary of War to Congress. The accounts are said to be wonderful. Sixteen whalers are reported as having been deserted by their crews. The smallest article of merchandise that happens to be in requisition, is said to command a great value in exchange for gold. The quantities daily dug up are very large.

We presume one of the first duties which Congress will be called upon to discharge, will be the preservation of the valuable public property which is thus attracting so many adventurous spirits, to gather the golden fleece of the modern Jasons.

An Anonymous Report: "The Gold Fever"

The day after President James Polk delivered his State of the Union address to Congress, the Hartford Courant *reported on "the gold fever." The paper referred to America's newly acquired territory as El Dorado—the mythical city of gold long sought by North America's early explorers. Even though the report is generally positive about going to California to search for gold, it does offer a good New England moral invective against those seeking out the riches of the world by calling gold "the condiment of their diseased minds."*

Courant (Hartford), 6 December 1848

The California gold fever is approaching its crisis. We are told that the new region that has just become a part of our possessions, is El Dorado after all. . . . By a sudden and accidental discovery, the ground is represented to be one vast gold mine.—Gold is picked up in pure lumps, twenty-four carats fine. Soldiers are deserting their ranks, sailors their ships, and every body their employment, to speed to the regions of the gold mines. In a moment, as it were, a desert country, that never deserved much notice from the world, has become the center of universal attraction. Everybody, by the accounts, is getting money at a rate that puts all past experience in that line fare in the shade. The stories are evidently thickening in interest, as do the arithmetical calculations connected with them in importance. Fifteen millions have already come into the possession of *somebody,* and all creation is going out there to fill their pockets with the great condiment of their diseased minds.

An Anonymous Report: "Gold! Gold!"

President James Polk sent an agent to California to scope out the rumors of gold in the summer of 1848. This article includes the agent's letter, which painted a picture of wealth in California.

Weekly Raleigh Register, and North Carolina Gazette, 31 January 1849

The latest news from California officially communicated by the Government, by Mr. Larkin and Com. Jones, confirms the most extravagant accounts that have heretofore come to hand. The following extract from Mr. Larkin's letter, is all that we have room for at present. Com. Jones represents the country in almost a state of anarchy. It is impossible to keep the sailors or soldiers in a state of subordination, in consequence of the strong temptation to be desert.

Extract of a letter from Thomas O. Larkin, Esq., late Consul and now Navy Agent of the United States, to the Secretary of State, dated at Monterey, November 16th 1848, and received in this city on Friday evening last.

"The digging and washing for gold continues to increase on the Sacramento placer, so far as regards the number of persons engaged in the business and the size and quantity of the metal daily obtained. I have had in my hands several pieces of gold, about twenty-three carats fine, weighing from one to two pounds, and have it from good authority that pieces have been found weighing sixteen pounds. Indeed, I have heard of specimens that weighed twenty-five pounds. There are many men at the placer, who in June last had not one hundred dollars, now in possession of from five to twenty thousand, which they made by digging gold and trading with the Indians. Several, I believe, have more. . . .

"Could you know the value of the California placer as I know it, you would think you had been instrumental in obtaining a most splendid purchase for our country, to put no other construction on the late treaty.

"The placer is known to be two or three hundred miles long; and as discoveries are constantly being made, it may prove 1,000 miles in length—in fact it is not counting the intermediate miles yet unexplored. From five to ten millions of gold must be our export this and next year. How many years this state of things will continue, I cannot say. You may wonder why I continue my correspondence. I answer from habit, and your many remarks of the interest you take in my letters."

Opposition to the Gold Rush

Edward Kemble: "The Excitement and Enthusiasm of Gold Washing Still Continues—Increases"

The weekly California Star *began publication in January 1847. New Yorker Edward Kemble assumed editorship of the paper, which was begun by Sam Brannan, in 1848. Initially scooped on the discovery of gold by its rival, the* Californian, *Kemble's paper published a series of stories calling the gold rush "a sham." In this account, Kemble discusses the damage the gold rush may do to California. He also points out basic facts about the worth of gold found to date. Four days after this issue, the* California Star *ceased publication, its workers headed to the gold fields to seek their own fortunes. Kemble did the same but soon returned and bought the defunct paper from Brannan. The* Californian *quit publication next, and its owners left the paper to Kemble. Eventually, Kemble's paper became a success, with new partners, under the name* Alta California.[10]

California Star (San Francisco), 10 June 1848

Many of our countrymen are not disposed to do us justice as regards the opinion we have at different times expressed of the employment in which over two thirds of the white population of the country are engaged. There appears to have gone abroad a belief that we should raise our voices against what some one has denominated an "infatuation." We are very far from it, and would invite a calm recapitulation of our articles touching the matter, as in themselves amply satisfactory. We shall continue to report the progress of the work, to speak within bounds, and to approve, admonish, or openly censure whatever, in our opinion, may require it at our hands.

It is quite unnecessary to remind our readers of the "prospects of California" at this time, as the effects of this gold washing enthusiasm, upon the country, through every branch of business are unmistakably apparent to every one. Suffice it that there is no abatement, and that active measures will probably be taken to prevent really serious and alarming consequences.

Every seaport as far south as San Diego, and every interior town, and nearly every rancho from the base of the mountains in which the gold has been found, to the Mission of San Luis, south, has become suddenly drained of human beings. Americans, Californians, Indians and Sandwich Islanders, men, women and children, indiscriminately. Should there be that success which has repaid the efforts of those employed for the last month, during the present and next, as many are sanguine in their expectations, and we confess to unhesitatingly believe probably, not only will we witness the depopulation of every town, the desertion of every rancho, and the desolation of the once promising crops of the country, but it will also draw largely upon adjacent territories—awake Sonora, and call down upon us, despite her Indian battles, a great many of the good people of Oregon. There are at this time over one thousand souls busied in washing gold, and the yield per diem may be safely estimated at from fifteen to twenty dollars, each individual.—

We have by every launch from the embarcadera of New Helvetia, returns of enthusiastic gold seekers—heads of families, to effect transportation of their households to the scene of their successful labors, or others, merely returned to more fully equip themselves for a protracted, or perhaps permanent stay.—

Spades, shovels, picks, wooden bowls, Indian baskets (for washing), etc., find ready purchase, and are very frequently disposed of at extortionate prices.

The gold region, so called, thus far explored, is about one hundred miles in length and twenty in width. These imperfect explorations contribute to establish the certainty of the placera extending much further south, probably three or four hundred miles, as we have before stated, while it is believed to terminate about a league north of the point at which first discovered. The probable amount taken from these mountains since the first of May last, we are informed is $100,000, and which is at this time principally in the hands of the mechanical, agricultural and laboring classes.

There is an area explored, within which a body of 50,000 men can advantageously labor. Without maliciously interfering with each other, then, there need be no cause for contention and discord, where as yet, we are gratified to know, there is harmony and good feeling existing. We really hope no unpleasant occurrences will grow out of this enthusiasm, and that our apprehensions may be quieted by continued patience and good will among the washers.

An Anonymous Report: "Ho! For California"

In the months after the president's "official" announcement of the discovery of gold, thousands of men left their homes to head for California. John S. Saywood, the editor of the Bangor Daily Whig and Courier, *realized that such a migration was dangerous for families. As a result, his newspaper published a number of letters from California on the deplorable conditions of the 49ers and this "special report" for the* Whig and Courier.

Bangor (Me.) Daily Whig and Courier, 29 January 1849

All who date back a couple of hundred years, will recollect that other magnificent schemes of enriching all concerned in them, have been presented to the people, as flattering as are now the prospects in California. . . .

Who does not remember the *Land* speculation of 1835; and Bangor as the scene of its operation? If lumps of gold were not found, were not fortunes made before breakfast? after breakfast? and during the whole 24 hours? . . .

These remarks are for those who are now balancing in their minds the idea of going, and have in one scale, large lumps of gold. Let a *thought* or two fall into the other and then see which of them will kick the beam! . . .

Gold is very convenient as a means, in procuring for yourselves and families comfortable positions. But as happiness does not increase in proportion to the increase of your gold, it may be well to fix a standard.

Nature *has* fixed a standard.

"A competence is all we can enjoy–
O be content, for heaven can give no more." . . .

A man who leaves his family, and goes to California, must be a loser if he *loves* his family. He will not pretend, that he enjoys himself so well as he should at home,—and his family enjoy *less* during his absence.

Good husbands are very convenient in families; and if ever they are really needed—it is in directing boys, and protecting girls as they first mingle in society. But the father is gone—the boy takes advantage—he is too big to mind his mother, and he sets up for himself. The chance is, that in steering his own bark, he will splite on the rock where thousands have perished! He may thus so unfit himself for society that gold may be his greatest curse; and in mercy to him, it may be your dying request to some friend to keep it from him.

Without looking to the desolation that may be caused in a family, or the anguish of a mother seeing her hopes blasted, it may well be doubted if any amount of gold would pay for such a sacrifice. You may give your family gold, but have robbed them of what is richer than the finest gold.

J.B.: "Letters from the Gold Region"

The Whig and Courier *printed a number of letters describing the bad conditions in the California gold fields. This one from the unknown J.B. describes those conditions and speaks of the likelihood that prospectors will not find gold.*

***Bangor (Me.) Daily Whig and Courier*, 29 January 1849**

MONTERREY, (Cal.) Nov. 17, 1848

Nothing that you have heard can give you an adequate idea of the horrible state of this country. In this, according to the old proverb, money, or the thirst for it is 'the root of all evil.' . . .

In regard to the wonderful gold country of California, the American papers are incorrect in speaking of gold mines. Here they are called "Gold Washings" which give a better idea of their true character. The region where they are found is very great; extending along the Sacramento and San Joaquin rivers and tributaries. The distance of the washings from San Francisco varies from 150 to 200 miles.—The country around them is for the most part a desolate and dreary waste, not fit for agriculture of any kind. . . .

There has been a vast amount of sickness and misery among the gold hunters; owing in a great measure to exposure, imprudence in dressing and improper food. . . .

Dazzling as the prospect of the country may seem to those at a distance, it is impossible for any one on the spot to believe that it will lead to the advancement of the territory in any of the elements of genuine prosperity.

Already the vicious and the outcasts of all lands are pouring into the country. The absence of all government and law gives them full license, and vice and immorality seem likely to hold full sway in El Dorado for a long time to come.

Very truly yours, J.B.

Rev. James Davis: "The Gold Pestilence"

The rush to California left many communities void of young people who had deserted home and family to seek the prospects of fortune in the Sierra Nevadas. Davis, a Congregational minister, warned his parishioners that the lust for gold was a disease like cholera and a threat to survival like war and famine.

Patriot **(Woonsocket, R.I.), 16 Feb. 1849**

This excitement is become truly appalling, and reaching not our cities alone, but our villages and towns and shaking every family. There never has been any excitement equal to it within the remembrance of our oldest citizens.—War, Pestilence, Famine, the most astonishing discoveries in the arts and sciences . . . the advancement of civilization and Christianity in the subjugation of heathen lands—all these have never filled our land and minds of our young men with such intense excitement. . . . the gold pestilancewhich is more terrific than the cholera, threatens to depopulate our land of those whom we had looked upon as the morning stars and bright hopes of future times.

Park Benjamin: "The California Gold-Seeker to His Mistress"

One of the most popular magazines at mid-century, Godey's Lady's Book, *offered a wealth of miscellany for women. Rarely did the publication delve into the political and social issues of the day, but it did offer several poems on the Gold Rush. As with this poem, most dwelt on the negative impact that the westward migration for gold had on relationships. Park Benjamin was a New York newspaper editor and a poet.*

Godey's Lady's Book **(Philadelphia), April 1849**

"I hear a voice thou canst not hear
That bids me not delay;
I see a hand thou canst not see
That beckons me away!"
FAREWELL, dear heart, awhile farewell!
I go o'er land and sea;

For wealth I brave the billows' swell
Afar from love and thee.
The vessel waits the gathered crew,
With hope and vigor bold,
Impatient long for regions new
That teem and burn with gold.
Unclasp thy arms; I must depart,
And leave these friendly skies;
I must forsake thy loving heart,
To tempt a dangerous prize.
What though from ease and pleasure here
I hasten wildly on
Ah, who but thee will shed a tear
To think that I am gone?
Yet weep not, sweet, for I will toil
Beneath the blazing sun,
Nor faint upon the sickly soil
Before my task is done.
Deep will I delve for gleaming ore
The Californian mine,
Though poor will seem the precious store
Till I have made it thine. . . .
The vessel waits, the wind is fair,
The streamers float on high,
There is no winter in the air,
No cloud upon the sky.
For gold I banish doubt and fear,
And thoughts of home dispel;
I must depart, the hour is near
Farewell awhile, farewell!

Questions

1. Why might ministers and town leaders in the East consider the Gold Rush to be "the gold pestilence"? What sorts of hardships did going to California create in relation to traditional life?
2. Why might California newspapers both support and attack the Gold Rush?
3. Almost all the news coming east concerning gold was based on hearsay. Why do you think people believed that they could gain a fortune in California?

Notes

1. John Sutter's account of the discovery of gold, which is the source of much of the material in the first paragraphs of this chapter, was published in *Hutchings' California Magazine,* November 1857.

2. Malcolm J. Rohrbough, *Days of Gold: The California Gold Rush and the American Nation* (Berkeley: University of California Press, 1997), 7.

3. See R.B. Mason to Brigadier-General R. Jones (17 August 1848), San Francisco Museum, http://www.sfmuseum.org/hist6/masonrpt.html.

4. *North American* (Philadelphia), 14 September 1848.

5. *Daily Dispatch* (Pittsburgh, Pa.), 12 December 1848.

6. James West Davidson, et al., *Nation of Nations,* 2 vols. (New York: McGraw-Hill, 1990), 1:509.

7. Richard A. Dwyer and Richard E. Longenfelter, eds., *The Gold Songs of the Gold Rush* (Berkeley: University of California Press, 1965), 15.

8. Davidson, *Nation of Nations,* 1:510.

9. Rohrbough, *Days of Gold,* 267.

10. Sidney Kobre, *Development of American Journalism* (Dubuque, Iowa: Wm. C. Brown, 1969), 308–10.

CHAPTER 23

The Compromise of 1850 and the Fugitive Slave Act, 1850

The national situation in 1850 was as precarious as it had ever been. Congressional bickering over the Wilmot Proviso (see Chapter 20) had raged since 1846. Pennsylvania's David Wilmot, as the House discussed ways to end the Mexican crisis and what to do with the territory the United States would gain, declared that "neither slavery nor involuntary servitude shall ever exist in any part of said territory."[1] Now, in 1850, the Wilmot Proviso threatened to end the Union, while Congress considered admitting California as a state, creating the New Mexico and Utah territories, forbidding slavery in the District of Columbia, and accepting or rejecting Texas' claim to portions of the New Mexico territory. While all of the above were important, Congress could not deal with legislation surrounding these issues because of the impending Wilmot Proviso. If the Proviso ever passed Congress, President Zachary Taylor was sure to sign it because he advocated no slavery in the territories. No new territory would ever be slaveholding if this happened, a fact that was certain to cause the secession of many Southern states and an end to the Union.

The situation appeared to be a stalemate. Neither side could muster the votes to accept or reject the Proviso, and this left the above issues unsettled. So, as he had done since 1820 when he introduced the Missouri Compromise, Kentucky's Henry Clay came forward with a plan to negotiate the nation through the impasse. Clay, who was now in his early seventies, proposed an Omnibus Bill—eight smaller measures that had to be voted on together. Clay's solution was as follows: 1. Admit California as a free state; 2. Organize the remainder of the territories of the Southwest with no slave restrictions; 3. Deny Texas' claim to New Mexico territory; 4. Pay off any Texas debt as compensation for denying that claim; 5. Keep slavery in the District of Columbia; 6. Abolish the slave trade in the District; 7. Adopt a better fugitive slave act; and 8. Deny congressional authority to impede interstate slave trade.[2] This time, however, Clay could not pull off the compromise, even though he combined forces with another Senate powerhouse, Daniel Webster of Massachusetts, who agreed to Clay's terms to the horror of the abolitionists he represented.

Although Clay and Webster failed to pass the compromise, another Senator succeeded. Stephen A. Douglas of Illinois carefully formed alliances with parties both North and South on various aspects of Clay's compromise. In addition, Taylor—who opposed much of the compromise and would have vetoed it—died, making Millard Fillmore, who was more accepting of slavery, president. Fillmore was amenable to the compromise, and it became law in the summer of 1850. Clay, Webster, Douglas, and many others breathed a sigh of relief. The Wilmot Proviso was dead, and the Union would remain intact. California immediately became a free state, and the territories of New Mexico and Utah formed. Whether they would become slave or free states remained to be seen. Texas was given $10 million to give up its land claims.

The biggest issue to arise from the compromise was the Fugitive Slave Act. Under the act, federal marshals were under mandate to return runaways, and all Americans were to assist in returning them to their rightful owners. Those who violated this act could be fined up to $1,000 and jailed. Fugitives under the law did not have the right to a jury trial, and they were to be tried by a specially appointed commissioner. If the commissioner returned the runaway to the claimant, he was paid $10. If the runaway was set free, the commissioner made $5. The law did not apply solely to slaves who were running away; it was retroactive, meaning it could apply to any slave who may have successfully run away years before. As a result, many blacks who had lived as free citizens for years or who had been born free were captured, tried, and returned to or cast into slavery. In the case of the latter, many free blacks were turned into slaves, and this could only be avoided if the slaveowner admitted that the person had never been a slave.[3] As a result, the Fugitive Slave Act became the most discussed element of the Compromise of 1850, and its repercussions continued well past that date. Still, the Compromise of 1850 helped avert schism in the nation for another ten years, but it could not erase the bitterness that the Wilmot Proviso had caused.

The readings in opposition to the Compromise begin with one by a former slave who speaks of the evil of the Fugitive Slave Act. The next discusses the Massachusetts abolitionist Senator Charles Sumner. The third reading is a description from Horace Greeley's newspaper of the triumph of a slavecatcher, and the last article discusses "slave power," a belief that the South wielded disproportionate power in federal government in relation to its population.

The readings that support the Compromise begin with a letter that says the South should use the time provided by the Compromise to ready itself to leave the Union. The second tells how the Fugitive Slave Act is already aiding Southerners. The final piece is a lengthy essay by an anonymous

Georgian written to a Northern publication that lays before readers the critical situation faced by the nation.

Opposition to the Acts

W.P. Newman: "The Climax of Infernal Wickedness"

African Americans reacted with great negativity to the Fugitive Slave Act. Newman, a former slave who was now a minister and antislavery advocate in Ohio,[4] *wrote this untitled letter to Frederick Douglass, who printed it in the* North Star. *In the letter, Newman attacks President Millard Fillmore for signing the act into law, advocates its repeal, and promises to "exterminate tyrants" who keep people in bondage. It is typical of African American's responses to the act.*

North Star (Rochester, New York), 24 October 1850

Frederick Douglass:

On arriving here, I find no little excitement about the "Fugitive Slave Bill." Since President Fillmore "has unchained the tiger," by the use of his pen . . . I have felt an ardent desire to have some religious-political watchman "tell us what the signs of promise are," for the world is expressing its opinion freely respecting that enlightened and Christian enactment called the "Fugitive Slave Bill," the sentiment of which is doubtless the result of the inspiring influence of his Satanic Majesty, the climax of his infernal wickedness.

It seems to me that the world has misunderstood, till the sitting of the last United States Congress, what the real and true mission of that government is. Is it not a mission of bonds and death? . . .

It may properly be asked, would not the Devil do well to *rent out hell* and move to the United States, and rival, if possible, President Fillmore and his political followers? *If* he can beat them at the game of SIN, the change will be well. . . .

Fillmore's heartless position, indecision of character, and the want of a virtuous soul, have rendered him despicable in the eyes of the good, and contemptible in the just opinion of the bad. In seeking to please tyrants, he has lost the favor of all, and alas, the true church of Christ can no longer pray for the success of his truckling administration. It has given their souls to the oppressor, and their bodies to the prison, if they dare do their duty in obedience to Christ. IN view of such facts, it is my candid conviction that the record of the infernal regions can exhibit no blacker deeds than the American archives, and the accursed Fugitive Slave Bill. Upright humanity cannot uphold the hand that signed that bill of abominations, unless it first does violence to its own nature. God is against the man who owns the hand. He is weighed in the balance, and found wanting. Such men as do him honor,

> The Devil fears,
> And slaves hate.

The truth will be exemplified, I believe, in certain parts of the country, in the attempts to take back to slavery and to death—yes, in the American hell itself—the dejected, poor, and panting fugitives. In honor of humanity, I am proud to say that Patrick Henry's motto is mine—"Give me Liberty or give me Death." I am frank to declare that it is my fixed and changeless purpose to kill any so-called man who attempts to enslave me or mine, if possible, though it be Millard Fillmore himself. To do this, in defence of personal liberty, to my mind, would be an act of the highest virtue, and white Americans must be real hypocrites if they say not to it—amen!

Do they not *saint* the spirits of '76 for their noble defence of their inalienable rights? Why then damn me for doing the same? 'Tis the 4th of July. Hark! What means that cannon's roar? 'Tis the joyful voice of a free people, eulogizing the man who exterminated tyrants, and gave to the American colonies freedom. Why, on a public day, those oratoric sounds, falling from human oracles—those words that burn—words mingled with eloquence divine—words that raise the dead? They are because for deeds done by our country's fathers, when they were oppressed and wronged. Such words tell how they obtained their earthly heritage, and independence for ourselves, pleasure for our families, and liberty forever for our hopeful posterity. Who that is oppressed himself, is not ready to do the like deeds for his race to come? Life is naught to lose. I am ready, willing, and should rejoice to die; and I glory in the fact that so many of my brethren in tribulation are of the same mind, and feel determined to be sacrificed rather than be enslaved. God grant that their number may be increased a thousand fold. Then shall tyrants know,

> Thrice armed is he
> Who hath his quarrel just. . . .

It is your duty to let the word "repeal! *repeal!!* REPEAL!!!" go forth, backed up by the Christian's motto, "resistance to tyrants is obedience to God."

And you, my brethren, the objects of hate and the victims of oppression, can you and will you allow yourselves to be made the dupes of despots and the slaves of tyrants, without resisting even to death? I hope not. Disgrace not your nature. Be not recreant to your God. Allow not posterity to curse thy memory and disown thy name for a base submission to avaricious knaves.

That you may "show yourself a man," is the constant and ardent prayer of
Your brother in bonds,

W.P. NEWMAN

X. Y.: "Mr. Sumner and the Fugitive Slave Law"

Senator Charles Sumner of Massachusetts was one of Congress' most outspoken opponents of slavery. His verbal attacks on slavery led to a physical attack on him in 1856 (see Chapter 26). In this report by the unnamed X. Y. in the New-York Daily Times, *Sumner promises retribution against those who have passed the Fugitive Slave Act.*

New-York Daily Times, 28 August 1852

The day has been chiefly occupied in the Senate by Mr. SUMNER, who is still on the floor speaking against the Fugitive Slave act. His main object has been to show that it cannot be executed, and that it is repugnant to the sentiment of the community. The fires created by the Stamp Act would be, according to him, dimmed by the flame which this act is to create. His summary of the Fugitive cases was very strongly drawn; and it is undoubtedly true that the act has not been executed except at the risk of tumult and bloodshed. In one case the slave was shot, and in another the slave-owner was shot. Who will speak—what many, Says Mr. SUMNER, will sing for Slavery? A hundred thousand copies of "Uncle Tom's Cabin" have been very greedily taken up by enemies of Slavery, and it has directed public vengeance against the slave-holders and slave-hunters. He promised that the sword which is exhibited in a northern European City, as a trophy of liberty,—a sword with which was decapitated the German Baron, who had violated its privileges by pursuing into it and capturing a fugitive slave;—he promised that that sword should yet hang in the free Cities and States of the North, whose rights have been insulted by the recapture of slaves in their limits.

Mr. SUMNER'S speech shows what every one knew—that the free discussion of Slavery must and will be tolerated, in spite of Platforms and Compromises. . . .

I do not know that, at this late day in the session, any of the agitators, on the Southern side of the question, will undertake to reply to Mr. SUMNER, and dispute his proposition that the Fugitive law is contrary to Divine law, and cannot be executed. Judge BUTLER declared, when the law was made, that it would never be executed except by the sword. X. Y.

Horace Greeley: "Slave-Catcher's Triumph"

No editor of a non-abolitionist newspaper opposed slavery more than Horace Greeley. When an escaped slave named Anthony Burns was captured in Boston and ordered to be returned to his owner in the South, Greeley wrote about the event. He predicted that slavery would eventually lead to war.

Tribune (New York), 3 June 1854

The fugitive Burns is delivered into slavery. A man as much entitled to his freedom as any other man on the soil of Massachusetts has been seized in that State by other men, manacled, and consigned to hopeless bondage. . . . Burns was not torn from the soil of freedom and consigned to slavery by any ordinary methods of imprisoning malefactors. He was not taken by a constable or sheriff, or even a whole police force of a great city. All these were insufficient. It took all the police of Boston, three companies of United States troops, one company of cavalry, and an entire battalion of militia, together with several pieces of artillery, to secure the capture of this citizen and remand him to slavery. It is said that this was an experimental case of slave-catching, got up especially for the purpose of showing how readily the North would acquiesce in the Nebraska bill, and succumb to the aggressions of the slave power. We trust the managers of the performance are satisfied. What do they think of the prospect of performing the same feat over again? . . .

It may be that they cannot see that through all this Burns trial the public peace has been slumbering upon the edge of a volcano. If they cannot, perhaps they had better devote themselves to a closer scrutiny of the existing state of the popular pulse.

There has been the most imminent danger of a violent and armed outbreak during this late tragedy. And suppose it had taken place? Who would have quelled it? Who would have restored the public peace when once broken? Burns has been taken away, but let us tell the slave power that nothing has been accomplished by that capture but to deepen the resolution that slaves shall not be taken on the soil of the Free States. Nothing has been accomplished by it but to arouse the Northern mind to a determination to resistance to such scenes in the future. This time men have been unarmed. Another time it may be otherwise. We are but at the beginning of the resistance to the arrogant domination of the slave power. Things are but in the bud, in the gristle. Nothing has been done in this case but to declare against the proceeding. Not an arrangement to rescue the fugitive has been made. Nothing which savored of earnest resistance has been attempted. But it will not be so always. Some such even as a forcible rescue will yet take place, and when that takes place in Massachusetts, the fugitive will not be sent to Canada. He will be held upon her soil, and a note of defiance sounded to let them come and take him who dare.

The future is big with events such as these unless something is done to allay the public excitement produced by the proceedings of the slave power, backed by our rulers. The fugitive slave law, as it now stands, can no longer be enforced without jeopardizing the public tranquillity to an alarming extent. We again call upon Congress to give their earnest and immediate attention to this grave subject. If there can be no repeal of the law at this session, which we think is quite certain, let us at least have the trial by jury. A modification of this sort is absolutely demanded unless the country is to be precipitated upon insurrection, and perchance civil war.

J.C.W.: "Liberty Versus Slavery"

The anonymous J.C.W., like many other Americans, believed that the South wielded an unfair amount of power in Washington in all branches of government. He referred to this as "Slave Power" and said that the Compromise of 1850 and the Fugitive Slave Act turned all Americans into slave-catchers.

National Era (Washington, D.C.), 7 September 1854

For the National Era.

Now that the so-called Representatives of the people have betrayed their constituents, it becomes the people themselves to take the matter in hand, and redeem our country from the foul curse of Slavery and Slave Despotism. It is one of the strangest anomalies of modern times, that a people professing the pure principles of republicanism and democracy, and holding themselves up as a model to all nations, should become the advocates of one of the foulest systems of oppression that ever cursed humanity. Our Government is nominally democratic, while it is virtually and practically aristocratic; or, what is worse, the nation is ruled by a petty Slave Oligarchy. Theoretically, all power emanates from the people; while virtually and practically, a political faction at Washington is the source. Equality of rights and privileges is the great and fundamental principle of the democratic creed; while, in the practical operations of the Government, this principle is annulled. Almost the entire power and patronage of the Government is prostituted to the Slave Power, and made tributary to its perpetuation; the national funds are squandered in the prosecution of expensive and destructive wars and the negotiation of treaties for the acquisition of more slave territory. Not content with the passage of the Compromise of 1850, by which we were made a nation of slave-catchers, it has at length succeeded, through the aid of Northern doughfaces, in effecting the double evil of extending slavery into free territory, and also in abrogating a solemn compact by which slavery was forever prohibited in said territory. As was anticipated, the passage of the Compromise of 1850 but prepared the way for fresh demands. The long and contemptible subserviency of the North has taught the South that her demands, however insolent, will be complied with.

Talk no more to me of African Slavery. Behold! are we not a nation of slaves? We are required, under pain of fines and imprisonment, to become slave-catchers for the South, and our hearts revolt!

We must not, and by the grace of God we will not, submit to such degradation. We are in the midst of a revolution, which, if not speedily effected at the ballot-box, will be effected by physical force. If our fathers were justified in resisting British despotism, certainly their posterity are justified in resisting the worst system of oppression upon which the sun ever shone. Is it true that the great doctrine of "Equality of rights and privileges" is a lie? Did our fathers flee from British despotism, only to establish in America another? Is slavery, then, the genius of our institutions—the sole object of their foundation? No; in the language of Patrick Henry, the great American orator, "Give me liberty, or give me death."

If ever any doubts have existed in the minds of Anti-Slavery men as to the designs of the Slave Power, recent events must have sufficed to remove them. From henceforth, Anti-Slavery men must not be satisfied with merely defensive measures—their movements must be aggressive in their character. For myself, I am satisfied that nothing short of the entire abolition of slavery throughout the nation ought to be attempted. Does any one say this is attempting too much? Not if we would have justice done to the slave, or secure peace to the nation. Does any one say, the Constitution guaranties to the South the right to hold slaves? This remains to be proved. (The framers of the Constitution, it is plain, could never grant rights and powers they never possessed.) But, even admitting this to be true, I deny the right of our fathers to enter into a league with Satan, and bind their posterity and all future generations to its observance. Moreover, the days of compromise are ended. Recent events have shown that there can be no peace to the nation while slavery is permitted to live. The doctrine of mere non-extension of slavery, as a means of curing the evil, has proved altogether inadequate.

Slavery is, and must be, from its very nature, aggressive. It will be satisfied with nothing short of universal dominion. As an evidence of this, look at the efforts which are being made by the Slave Power to acquire the West Indies, Central America, Mexico; also the proposed coalition with the Brazilian Government, for the purpose of extending slavery and the reestablishment of the African slave trade. In a word, it is evidently the design of the Slave Power to acquire all that joins them, for the purpose of extending over it the benign influences of slavery. We repeat, nothing short of the entire abolition of slavery will remedy the evil, or save our country from ruin; and what we do, must be done quickly. A few more conquests by the Slave Power, and it will be too late. We, as a nation, will have filled up the measure of our iniquities, and, as there is a God in heaven, ours is the oppressor's doom. Friends of Freedom, to the rescue! Let preachers, lawyers, doctors, farmers, mechanics, merchants, and men of every stripe—forgetting party names and party ties—to a man, unite for liberty, and, for once, let us have a "Government by the people."

J.C.W.

Whiteford, Mich., June 20, 1854.

Our correspondent expresses himself strongly, and he has reason. But, let us not forget that State Rights, in our system, are the best safeguard against Federal tyranny. Our business is, to redeem the Federal Government from vassalage to the Slave Power, and all responsibility for Slavery, and, through its constitutional exercise, foster a sentiment of Liberty in the slave States, as it has been made an instrument of encouraging Free Slavery sentiments in the free States.—Ed. Era.

Support for the Acts

An Anonymous Report: "The Duty of the South"

By 1850, some Americans believed disunion was inevitable. In this editorial originally printed in the Richmond Republican, *the Compromise of 1850 is seen as a temporary respite in the battle over slavery. The South should, the article says, use the time to build up its industry, schools, railroads, and the like so that it may declare its independence.*

Weekly Raleigh Register and North Carolina Gazette, 11 September 1850

The South will generally rejoice at the almost certain prospect of a pacification by Congress of the existing difficulties of the country. It will rejoice that, notwithstanding all the grievances it has suffered are not redressed and all its just demands are not conceded, the Union is preserved, and the firebrands of agitation and excitement quenched at least for a time. . . .

There are those who contend that the legislation of Congress, especially in regard to fugitive slaves, will prove nugatory, and that the abduction of slaves is an evil whose roots deeply embedded in Northern anti-slavery sentiment, cannot be eradicated by any legislation. Suppose we admit all this. Suppose that the anticipated settlement of our sectional difficulties will give the South security and repose but for a few years.

Yet, in those few years, she may obtain breathing time which will enable her to pass successfully through any future conflict. . . . The South, even a temporary settlement of difficulties, will have achieved a great point, if she but avail herself of her advantage. Hitherto, by purchasing entirely of the

North, she has fattened that section upon her own life-blood, and made the North strong at the expense of her own weakness, while she has looked to Congress for relief which it was in her own power to employ. She is now beginning to see her error. Let her correct that error, and she is safe now and forever.

What , then, is the duty of the South? It is to fling out at once the banner of UNION and INDEPENDENCE! It is to seize these *few years* of respite, and employ every moment of these in building up Southern Commerce, Southern Railroads, Southern Colleges and schools, Southern industry in every department of human enterprise. This should be considered a duty second only in importance to the most sacred duties of Religion. We should like to see Home Associations formed with these objects, and the whole force of Southern sentiment concentrated, organized and brought to bear in solid column in their behalf. We trust that the whole Southern People will not only transact their business, but seek their amusements within their own borders. Let this course be pursued, and the South in a short time, will be able to meet any adversaries, and inscribe upon her banner MIGHT as well as RIGHT.—*Richmond Republican.*

Seaton Gales: "The Fugitive Slave Bill"

As the troubles of the nation that centered on slavery grew, the nation became increasingly divided. This editorial from Raleigh, North Carolina, proclaims that the Fugitive Slave Act is already working to the benefit of the South.

Weekly Raleigh Register and North Carolina Gazette, 5 October 1850

The beneficial operations of this Bill have already begun to manifest themselves, as will be seen by reference to the cases of recapture and recovery mentioned in another column. Some idea of the efficacy of the law, may be formed from the fact, that, in the case of the fugitive taken in New York, the arrest was made, the examination held, and the prisoner on his way to Baltimore, within three hours, and that the expenses of the proceedings (defrayed by the United States Treasury,) only amounted to $71.

We see by late accounts, that in some of the towns and boroughs of Massachusetts, where occasions of excitement are rare that the least pretext for getting up one is greedily caught at, there seems to be a disposition to disregard the stringent provisions of this law. But, we take it for granted, that, when a fugitive slave can be successfully arrested in the great city of New York under the law where there are so many of the . . .appliances of Abolitionists constantly contending to inflame the passions of the populace, and where resistance on the part of the slave would have been seconded by a mob, the blustering of these busy borough fanatics may be taken as so much innocent bravado. But we shall see.

Georgia: "Plain Words for the North"

The Compromise of 1850 brought clearly into view for many Americans the tenuous state of the nation. Southerners increasingly turned to the Constitution to protect slavery. Northern abolitionists increasingly ignored that document's slave provisions or deemed that they needed to be changed. The anonymous writer to the American Whig Review *understood the seriousness of America's situation perfectly and sent this essay to the New York publication. In it he argues that if the constitutionality of slavery is not upheld, the South will no doubt leave the Union. Likewise, if certain segments of the North cannot live in confederation with the slave states, they will probably leave the Union. So, both sides must allow this compromise to work.*

American Whig Review (New York), December 1850

WE have fallen upon times of profound and startling interest. In our day the crisis of trial to our free government has approached imminently near. In the minds of those wise and great men who planned our government no little apprehension seems to have mingled with the hope which they felt of success. . . . Effort after effort has been made to set aside the Constitution, because it was too stringent a bridle upon selfish prejudice and ambition. But its inherent strength, grounded upon the good sense and sound principle of our people, has so far repelled triumphantly such insidious assaults. In our time these assaults have been directed from a position peculiarly dangerous. . . . We have seen the Congress of the United States spending month after month in the most vituperative and inflammatory debate upon this all-absorbing theme. . . .

In a government where sectional interests and feelings may come into conflict, the sole security for permanence and peace is to be found in a Constitution whose provisions are inviolable. . . . every State, before entering into that compact, stood in a position of independence. Ere yielding that independence, it was only proper that provision should be made to protect the interests of those which would inevitably be the weaker in that confederacy. In a portion of those independent States a peculiar and most important institution had grown up. It had entwined its tendrils around every interest of the country where it existed,—had become essential to its prosperity. With the foundation of the institution the ancestors of those now warmest to denounce it were identified. Southrons saw that its abolition, nay, even its modification by other hands than their own, might plunge them into all the horrors of a new and more terrible "servile war." While cognizant of all this, they could see the vast interest which posterity might have in this matter; how the North would grow daily in numerical superiority over the South; how slaves would become in process of time the chief source of the wealth of their descendants, and how complex and important would be their relations to society. They also saw how the seeds of fanaticism would grow, how sectional jealousy would increase, how these germs would ripen into animosity.... Those Northern men who at that day represented their States could not only perceive how reasonable it was that slavery at the South should be guaranteed in the new government, but also its immense advantages to their own constituency.... They acted wisely, and embodied in the Constitution all that the South could ask. But two Constitutional provisions are necessary to secure Southern rights upon this important question,—*the recognition of slavery where the people choose it, and the remedy for fugitive slaves*.... We hold that the Constitution of the Union does recognize slavery where it exists. But with the progress of time a spirit has arisen and grown strong, which refuses to make this recognition.... A large portion of our States have adopted and allow slavery. The entire country becomes possessed of new territory, to the acquisition of which these slave States contribute mainly. The South admits the right of this new territory to choose for itself whether slavery shall or shall not exist there. But the North insists, that while the territory was partly acquired by Southern men, is partly owned by Southern men, that they shall be excluded from its soil,—that they shall not carry their property into their own land—land which is theirs by the right of purchase. Thus it is rendered, if these views are carried out, simply impossible for any new State representing the Southern interest ever to come into the Union. The equilibrium which alone can preserve the Constitution is utterly destroyed....

During the last session of Congress it became evident that no further inroads upon the constitutional rights of the South could be permitted. Then, when the Union was endangered, statesmen of enlarged sentiments came forward to preserve it.... The conflict was severe; for against the Constitution were leagued the enthusiasts of the North and the ultras of the South. But there is sometimes a principle of strength in governments as in men, which is only developed by circumstances of danger and trial. So in our government has been found to exist a tenacity heretofore sufficient to resist all forces striving to draw it asunder.... So now, after every effort to warp and pervert its principles, the Constitution prevailed. The Congress acknowledged *both* the great sanctions which are essential to cement together the Union. It admitted, in the Utah and New-Mexico bills, that it had not the right to exclude slaves from territory common to the whole country, but that its adoption or prohibition depended solely upon the will of the people; and it provided a stringent and effective law for the recapture of fugitive slaves. The action of Congress in both these particulars was based on true principle—a determination to abide by the Constitution. The question now simply is, Will this action be sustained? For the South we answer unhesitatingly, Yes! . . .

The question is, Will the North remain content with the so-called Compromise Bills, or will her people persist in attempts to violate the Constitution? The issue must be fought north of the Potomac. And upon its results depends the existence of the Union. . . . The people at the North have now a fair, clear field for the contest. It is not ours to interfere. Themselves must decide whether they prefer Disunion to a confederacy with slave States. They have before them every aid to arrive at a decision. But that decision must be made, and will in all probability be final. If a majority of the people of the North shall see fit to deny us the privileges with which we came into the Union, it will remain for us to seek our rights in independence. . . .

Our Union is but the symbol of Constitutional freedom. Like all symbols which are sanctified by time-hallowed memories, it is dear in itself. The South will be the last to forget the sacred recollections which are entwined alike around the hearts of the inhabitants of every portion of this wide country. . . . But it can never be presumed that the cause of freedom would be advanced by the yielding of one section of the Union to the tyranny of another. . . . The Union, without a living, vital Constitution, is but a vain and empty name. Nay, more, it is but a body powerless for good, strong for evil.

Its destruction is inevitable unless the original guarantees are respected and maintained. Of its consequences to the cause of human freedom, of the frightful intestine wars which must follow, of the hatred which will be sown between brethren, of the terrible effects of a people combating against enemies abroad and a race in bondage at home, it is not our purpose to speak. . . .

With this matter we of the South have but little more to do. Some of us are, as has been already said, ready for the utmost. Others, we fondly believe a majority, are willing to forget the wrongs of the past and to hope for the future. But let the North refuse to abide by our rights, and the cry, which will go up from the hearts of the whole Southern people, will be, "Let us go out from among them." Meanwhile the battle rages at the North. The din of the conflict is borne to our ears. How it will end we may not know. We can but offer up heart-felt prayers for the success of those who battle for the Union and the Constitution. GEORGIA.

Questions

1. Why would the Fugitive Slave Act infuriate Northerners? Use the articles from the *Tribune* and *Raleigh Register* to formulate your answer.
2. From the readings, what do Northerners think of the Compromise? What do Southerners think?
3. The essay by Georgia lays out the situation in 1850. What does he believe must happen in order to preserve the Union?

Notes

1. *Congressional Globe,* 29 Cong., 1 Sess., 1217.

2. George Brown Tindall, *American: A Narrative History,* 2 vols. (New York: W.W. Norton, 1984), 1:579–80.

3. David M. Potter, *The Impending Crisis, 1848–1861* (New York: Harper & Row, 1976), 131–32.

4. C. Peter Ripley, ed., *The Black Abolitionist Papers,* 5 vols. (Chapel Hill: University of North Carolina Press, 1991), 4:66.

CHAPTER 24

Uncle Tom's Cabin, 1852

In 1851, the abolitionist newspaper *National Era* printed the first installment of a serial novel. Serials were not new to newspapers and magazines. This one, however, was different. It told the story of a gentle and kind slave named Tom and the pain, hardship, and eventual death inflicted upon him by the cruel and evil slave overseer Simon Legree. By the time the serial finished its run, its title, *Uncle Tom's Cabin, or Life Among the Lowly,* was known to most Americans. The ten-issue serial appeared as a book in March 1852. Quickly, *Uncle Tom's Cabin* became the best-selling novel of its time. About 50,000 copies were sold in eight weeks, and 300,000 in a year. *Uncle Tom's Cabin* went on to become one of the top-selling novels ever, with sales reaching 3 million in the United States and 3.5 million worldwide.[1]

Uncle Tom's Cabin was, no doubt, the most powerful polemic ever written against slavery in America, and that is exactly what its author, Harriet Beecher Stowe, had wanted. Stowe was the daughter of New England preacher Lyman Beecher and the sister of abolitionist minister Henry Ward Beecher. She vowed to write something profound against the evils of slavery following the passage of the Fugitive Slave Act, which increased the power of Southern slave-catchers to return runaways (see Chapter 23). Stowe was successful. The praise and condemnation of *Uncle Tom's Cabin* began almost immediately after its appearance in print. Hundreds of thousands were appalled at the treatment of slaves by evil masters as Stowe described it. Equally appalled were those familiar with slavery who decried Stowe's depictions as baseless, emotion-grabbing exaggerations and outright lies.

Gamaliel Bailey, editor of the *National Era,* said "that in writing 'Uncle Tom's Cabin,' Mrs. Harriet Beecher Stowe has done more to diffuse real knowledge of the facts and workings of American Slavery, and to arouse the sluggish nation to shake off the curse, and abate the wrong, than has been accomplished by all the orations, and anniversaries, and arguments, and documents, which the last ten years have been the witness of."[2] A reviewer

Uncle Tom's Cabin. *In 1851, the* National Era *in Washington, D.C., began running installments of a new book,* Uncle Tom's Cabin, or Life Among the Lowly, *by Harriet Beecher Stowe. The next year the entire book was released. Abraham Lincoln credited Beecher's book with starting the Civil War. This image is from the illustrated edition published in 1853.*

of the book from St. Louis, however, said, "As a collection of false facts and possible untruths it is unrivalled."[3]

Whether *Uncle Tom's Cabin* was a accurate portrayal or the imagined visions of slavery by an ardent abolitionist really did not matter. The book helped further galvanize both sides of the slavery issue. So great was its effect that when President Abraham Lincoln met Mrs. Stowe during the Civil War, he said, "So this is the little lady who wrote the book that made this great war."[4]

The readings in this chapter look at press reaction to Stowe's book. They begin with those that supported *Uncle Tom's Cabin.* The first comes from William Lloyd Garrison, the most prominent abolition editor in America. It is followed by an anonymous review of the book from the *National Era* in which the author says Stowe's words were God inspired. The next reading originally appeared in the *Times* of London but was reprinted in the *New-York Daily Times* to show the impact of the book elsewhere.

The chapter section that attacks *Uncle Tom's Cabin* begins with an article from a New York paper calling it fiction in every word. The next two works come from two of the South's most prominent literary publications. The first points out all the inaccuracies in the book in reference to the Southern system of slavery. The second uses the book as a way to discuss how the writer feels that Southern slaves are better off than free Northern whites.

Support for *Uncle Tom's Cabin*

William Lloyd Garrison: "Mrs. Stowe Awakens the Utmost Abhorrence of Slavery"

William Lloyd Garrison was the best known of American abolitionist editors. He found Uncle Tom's Cabin *to be exactly what the movement needed, and he was right. Many Northerners had been ambivalent about the evils of slavery before Stowe's work appeared, first in serial form and then as a book. Most were no longer on the fence after reading it.*

Liberator **(Boston), 26 March 1852**

In the execution of her very difficult task, Mrs. Stowe has displayed rare descriptive powers, a familiar acquaintance with slavery under its best and its worst phases, uncommon moral and philosophical acumen, great facility of thought and expression, and feelings and emotions of the strongest character. Intimate as we have been, for a score of years, with the features and operations of the slave system, and often as we have listened to the recitals of its horrors from the lips of the poor hunted fugitives, we confess to the frequent moistening of our eyes, the making of our hearts grow liquid as water, and the trembling of every nerve within us, in the perusal of the incidents and scenes so vividly depicted in her pages. The effect of such a work upon all intelligent and humane minds coming in contact with it, and especially upon the rising generation in its plastic condition, to awaken the strongest compassion for the oppressed and the utmost abhorrence of the system which grinds them to dust, cannot be estimated; it must be prodigious, and therefore eminently serviceable in the tremendous conflict now waged for the immediate and entire suppression of slavery upon American soil.

The appalling liabilities which constantly impend over such slaves as have "kind and indulgent masters," are thrillingly illustrated in various personal narratives; especially in that of "Uncle Tom," over whose fate every reader will drop the scalding tear, and for whose character the highest reverence will be felt. No insult, no outrage, no suffering, could ruffle the Christlike meekness of his spirit, or shake the steadfastness of his faith. Towards his merciless oppressors he cherished no animosity, and breathed nothing of retaliation. Like his Lord and Master, he was willing to be "led as a lamb to the slaughter," returning blessing for cursing and anxious only for the salvation of his enemies. His character is sketched with great power and rare religious perception. It triumphantly exemplifies the nature, tendency, and results of Christian non-resistance. . . .

An Anonymous Report: "*Uncle Tom's Cabin*"

The National Era *first introduced the world to* Uncle Tom's Cabin, *and this unsigned review, which may have been written by the paper's editor, Gamaliel Bailey, praises Stowe's effort. Calling upon biblical analogy, the paper compares Stowe's work with that of the Madonna, calling the author blessed among women.*

National Era (Washington, D.C.), 22 April 1852

We have not here the space in which to say all we think and feel regarding this wonderful work. It was a noble effort–it is a splendid success. The God of Freedom inspired the thought–the spirit of his love and wisdom guided the pen of the writer, so her words shall sink into the softened and repentant heart of the wrong-doer, and spring up into a harvest of good, for the poor and the oppressed.

This beautiful new evangel of freedom–for so the book seems to us–does not suddenly flash the intolerable light of God's truth upon souls benighted in error, but softly drops veil after veil till they stand in mid-day brightness, wondering and remorseful.

There are two characters in this work which will live as long as our literature– *Tom* and little *Eva*–the ebony statue of Christlike patience–the rose of love blossoming with immortal sweetness at its base. No human heart can receive these two visitants, and none can refuse them when they come, without taking in with them the pleading, sorrowing Spirit of humanity, and the stern Angel of justice.

We have undertaken nothing like a critique of this book; but we must be allowed to say, even in this circumscribed notice, that the work to us gives evidence of greater power, of deeper and more various resources, than any other novel of the time. It displays rare dramatic genius, its characters are strongly drawn, refreshingly peculiar and original, yet wondrously true to nature and to many a reader's experience of life. It abounds alike with quaint, delicious humor, and the most heart-searching pathos; with the vividest word-painting, in the way of description, with argument, philosophy, eloquence, and poetry. And straight and pure through all—through characterization, conversation, description, and narrative, sweeps the continuous moral—the one deep thought, flowing ceaselessly from the soul of the writer, and fed by "under-springs of silent deity."

So great and good a thing has Mrs. Stowe here accomplished for humanity, for freedom, for God, that we cannot refrain from applying to her sacred words, and exclaiming, "Blessed art thou among women!"

An Anonymous Report: "American Slavery"

Uncle Tom's Cabin *made an impact wherever it was read. This* Times *review of the book appeared first in the* London Times *on September 3. The article speaks of the pervasiveness of the book in England and then turns its attention to the book's fight against slavery.*

***New-York Daily Times,* 18 September 1852**

Twenty thousand copies of this book, according to its title-page, are circulating among the American people, but three times as many thousands more has probably been issued from the American press since the title page was written. According to the Boston *Traveller,* the authoress has already received from her publishers the sum of "$10,300 as her copyright premium on three month's sales of the work—we believe the largest sum of money ever received by any author, either American or European, from the sale of a single work in so short a period of time." Uncle Tom's Cabin is at every railway book-stall in England, and in every third traveller's hand. The book is a decided hit. It takes its place with "Pickwick," with Louis Napoleon, with the mendicant who suddenly discovers himself heir to £30,000 a year. . . . It is impossible not to feel respect for Uncle Tom's Cabin.

The object of the work is revealed in the pictorial frontispiece. Mrs. HARRIET BEECHER STOWE is an abolitionist, and her book is a vehement and unrestrained argument in favor of her creed. . . .

Perhaps there is, after all, but one method of carrying on a crusade, and that unscrupulous fighting is the rightful warfare of the crusader. Mrs. STOWE having made up her mind that slavery is an abomination in the sight of God and man, thinks of nothing but the annihilation of the pernicious system. From the first page of her narrative to the last this idea is paramount in her mind, and colors all her drawing. That she will secure precisely too we take for granted; for it is in the nature of enthusiasm to inoculate with passionate zeal the strong-hearted as well as the feeble-minded. . . .

Opposition to *Uncle Tom's Cabin*

An Anonymous Report: "*Uncle Tom's Cabin*"

Attacks on Uncle Tom's Cabin *did not come solely from the slaveholding regions of America. This anonymous letter in the* Courier and Enquirer *of New York City forcefully attacks Stowe's book by pointing out its errors concerning punishment by death of slaves and the charge that religion was intentionally kept from slaves.*

Courier and Enquirer (New York), 21 October 1852

In the comments we have given upon the controversy in question, we of course shall not be suspected of sympathy with the authoress of "Uncle Tom's Cabin." She manifestly has borne false witness against her neighbor. . . .

"Uncle Tom's Cabin" is a fiction in every sense of the word. It is not only untrue, but it is untruthful. It conveys erroneous impressions, it introduces false conclusions. It is not, as it purports to be, a picture of slavery as it is. All of the two hundred thousand Englishmen, and no small number of the one hundred thousand Americans, who now have it in their hands, are duped men. It is not one individual alone against whom Mrs. Stowe has borne false witness; she has slandered hundreds of thousand of her own countrymen. She has done it by attaching to them as slaveholders, in the eyes of the world, the guilt of the abuses of an institution, of which they are absolutely guiltless. Her story is so devised as to present slavery in three dark aspects—first, the cruel treatment of the slaves, second, the separation of families, and third, their want of religious instruction.

To show the first she causes a reward to be offered for the recovery of a runaway slave "dead or alive," when it has been decided over and over again in Southern courts that "a slave who is merely flying away cannot be killed." . . .

And yet in the face of such laws and decisions as these, Mrs. Stowe winds up a long series of cruelties upon her other black personages, by causing her faultless hero Tom to be literally whipped to death in Louisiana, by his master Legree; and these acts, which the laws make criminal and punish as such, she sets forth in the most repulsive colors to illustrate the institutions of slavery!

So too in reference to the separation of children from their parents. A considerable part of the plot is made to hinge upon the selling in Louisiana of the "child Eliza eight or nine years old" away from her mother, when had its inventor looked in the statute book of Louisiana she would have found the following language:—

"Every person is expressly prohibited from selling separately from their mothers, the children who shall not have attained the full age of ten years." . . .

The privation of religious instruction as represented by Mrs. Stowe, is utterly unfounded in fact. The largest churches in the Union consist entirely of slaves. The first African Church in Louisville which numbers 1,200, and the first African Church in Augusta which numbers 1,300 are specimens. On multitudes of the large plantations in the different parts of the South, the ordinances of the Gospel are as regularly maintained by competent ministers, as in any other communities, North or South. . . .

The peculiar falsity of this whole book consists in making exceptional or impossible cases the representatives of the system. . . . The Uncle Tom of the authoress is a perfect angel, and her blacks generally are half-angels; her Simon Legree is a perfect demon, and her whites generally are half-demons. She has quite a peculiar spite against the clergy; and, of the many she introduces at different times into the scenes, all save an insignificant exception are Pharisees or hypocrites. One who would know nothing of the United States and its people except by what he might gather from this book, would judge that it was some region just on the confines of the infernal world. We do not say that Mrs. Stowe was actuated by wrong motives in the preparation of this work, but we do say that she has done a wrong which no ignorance can excuse and no penance can expiate.

Jonathan R. Thompson: *"Uncle Tom's Cabin; or Life Among the Lowly"*

The Southern Literary Messenger *was one of numerous magazines in America that devoted itself to various literary issues and opened its pages to contemporary authors, Edgar Allan Poe serving as its editor for a brief time. In this review, editor and owner Jonathan R. Thompson spends seven full pages discussing* Uncle Tom's Cabin. *Much of the review points out inaccuracies in the novel as it discusses slavery and Southern life. In the portions included here, Thompson attacks Stowe on a number of fronts, referring to her and other women who delve into the sphere of politics as "diaper diplomatists and wet-nurse politicians." Thompson also quotes from the Bible to make his points.*

Southern Literary Messenger **(Richmond), October 1852**

Mrs. Stowe—to whose work of "Uncle Tom's Cabin" we now propose to devote ourselves—is . . .not a Joan of Arc. . . . Yet with all her cultivation she has placed herself without the pale of kindly treatment at the hands of Southern criticism. . . . She has volunteered officiously to intermeddle with things which concern her not—to libel and vilify a people from among whom have gone forth some of the noblest men that have adorned the race—to foment heartburnings and unappeasable hatred between brethren of a common country, the joint heirs of that country's glory to sow, in this blooming garden of freedom, the seeds of strife and violence and all direful contentions. Perhaps, indeed, she might declare that such was not her design—that she wished, by the work now under consideration, to *persuade* us of the horrible guilt of Slavery, and with the kindest feelings for us as brethren, to teach us that our constitution and laws are repugnant to every sentiment of humanity. We know that among other novel doctrines in vogue in the land of Mrs. Stowe's nativity—the pleasant land of New England—which we are old-fashioned enough to condemn, is one which would place woman on a footing of political equality with man, and causing her to look beyond the office for which she was created—the high and holy office of maternity—would engage her in the administration of public affairs; thus handing over the State to the perilous protection of diaper diplomatists and wet-nurse politicians. Mrs. Stowe, we believe, belongs to this school of Woman's Rights, and on this ground she may assert her prerogative to teach us how wicked are we ourselves and the Constitution under which we live. But such a claim is in direct conflict with the letter of scripture, as we find it recorded in the second chapter of the First Epistle to Timothy—

> "Let the woman learn in silence with all subjection.
>
> *"But I suffer not a woman to teach, not to usurp authority over the man, but to be in silence."*. . .

The reader will observe that two charges against the South are involved in this precious discourse—one, that it is the habit of Southern master to offer a reward with the alternative of "dead or alive," for their fugitive slaves, and the other, that it is usual for pursuers to shoot them. Indeed, we are led to infer that as the shooting is the easier mode of obtaining the reward, it is the more frequently employed in such cases. . . . Mrs. Stowe will not find many readers weak enough to believe it, even in New England. What man of Vermont, having an ox or an ass that had gone astray, would forthwith offer half the full value of the animal, not for the carcass which might be turned to some useful purpose, but the unavailing satisfaction of its head? . . .

Mrs. Stowe seeks to bring into contempt the entire communion of the Southern States. We have no words to express our scorn of such an effort, and therefore we proceed to say that this pious widow sets at naught her husband's already-begun proceedings with regard to Uncle Tom and sells him—conduct of which not one Southern lady of a thousand would be guilty. . . .

There are some who will think we have taken upon ourselves an unnecessary trouble in exposing the inconsistencies and false assertions of "Uncle

Tom's Cabin." . . .Let it be recollected, too, that the importance Mrs. Stowe will derive from Southern criticism will be one of infamy. Indeed she is only entitled to criticism at all, as the mouthpiece of a large and dangerous faction which if we do not put down with the pen, we may be compelled one day (God grant that day may never come!) to repel with the bayonet. There are questions that underlie the story of "Uncle Tom's Cabin" of far deeper significance than any mere false coloring of Southern society, and our readers will probably see the work discussed in other points of view, in the next number of the Messenger, by a far abler and more scholar-like hand than our own. Our editorial task is now ended and in dismissing the disagreeable subject, we beg to make a single suggestion to Mrs. Stowe—that, as she is fond of referring to the bible, she will turn over, before writing her next work of fiction, to the twentieth chapter of Exodus and there read these words—"THOU SHALT NOT BEAR FALSE WITNESS AGAINST THY NEIGHBOUR."

An Anonymous Author: "Southern Slaves Are Better Off Than Whites"

An anonymous female writer to De Bow's Review *sent her opinion to the New Orleans publication following the success of* Uncle Tom's Cabin. *James DeBow was one of the leading editors in the defense of slavery, and this letter—as did other apologies for slavery that appeared in the* Review—*defended slavery with a moral argument.*

***De Bow's Review* (New Orleans), March 1853**

It is useless for us to tell the benevolent ladies and gentlemen who have undertaken to instruct us in our catechism of humanity that they are entirely ignorant of the condition of the negro. "Uncle Tom's Cabin" tells them differently. It is useless for us to tell them that our slaves are not "interdicted education in the truths of the gospel and the ordinances of Christianity"; it is useless for us to repeat that their family ties and social affections are respected and indulged in a greater degree than those of any laboring class in the world. "Uncle Tom's Cabin" says differently; and the negrophilists have very nearly reached the point of pronouncing sentence of excommunication, on the ground of infidelity, against all who dispute the authenticity of so high an authority. It is useless for us to point to the comparative census of the nations of the earth; it is useless for us to show that in none are the tables of crime, of deformity, and insanity so low as in our slave population. Mrs. Stowe and Uncle Tom! Mrs. Stowe and Uncle Tom! Mrs. Stowe and Uncle Tom! ding, ding, dong. What is the use of reasoning, what is the use of facts, when those who should hear us deafen themselves with this eternal "ding, dong" of superstitious prejudice and pharisaical cant? As regards the condition of our slaves, compared with that of the white population of our own free States (than which, avowedly, no population in the world enjoys greater advantages), ten minutes' investigation of our late census returns, with about so much arithmetical knowledge as any boy of ten years old can command, will suffice to show that, for every insane slave, there are from eight to ten insane whites; and that this is not an exception resulting from any physical peculiarity of the negro, is proved by the fact that among the *free* blacks the proportion of insane is, within a very small fraction, equal to that among the whites. This fact alone speaks volumes. The number of deaf mutes and of blind, though the disproportion is not so great, shows largely in favor of the slave, and are worth dwelling upon as indicating the comforts of his position; but, would men consent to open their eyes and hearts to the truth, volumes of argument and cartloads of Uncle Tom's Cabins would not weigh a feather against the indisputable fact which we have just noted. . . .

Questions

1. Many people condemned *Uncle Tom's Cabin* as a work of pure fiction. Do you think it is acceptable to "stretch" the truth in order to stop a practice that is considered immoral? Explain.
2. The writer in *De Bow's Review* said that free blacks in America were worse off than Southern slaves. How, according to the writer, could this be possible?
3. Why, according to the readings, did abolitionists find *Uncle Tom's Cabin* so valuable?

Notes

1. Jan Whitt, "Uncle Tom's Cabin," in *The Media in America,* ed. Wm. David Sloan, 5th ed. (Northport, Ala.: Vision Press, 2002), 148; David M. Potter, *The Impending Crisis 1848–1861* (New York: Harper & Row, 1976), 140.

2. *National Era* (Washington, D.C.), 15 April 1852.

3. *Western Journal and Civilian Review* (St. Louis, Missouri), November 1852.

4. Quoted in "Harriet Beecher Stowe (1811–1896)," http://www.kirjasto.sci.fi/hbstowe.htm.

CHAPTER 25

The Kansas–Nebraska Act, 1854

For nearly thirty-five years, the United States had operated under an agreement known as the Missouri Compromise (see Chapter 1). Under the outline of the Compromise, slavery was limited in the territory west of the Mississippi River to land below the 36 degree 30 minute parallel with the exception of Missouri. The compact created a relative balance of power in the United States between free and slave states. Now, in 1854, a new proposal had been presented that appeared ready to undo the Missouri Compromise and open all United States territory to slavery.

By 1850, the United States stretched from the Atlantic to the Pacific oceans. The discovery of gold in California in 1848 quickly led to statehood (see Chapter 22). All land east of the Mississippi River was divided into states and, especially in the South, states pushed past the Mississippi toward California. Connecting California with the rest of the United States via the railroad became an American imperative. But even here, Americans could not agree on the best route. A southern route that ran through Texas and territory newly acquired from Mexico represented the route of least resistance because it did not run through Indian territory, and it bypassed the harsh weather of the Great Plains. Some Americans favored St. Louis as the departure point for the railway to California. Illinois Senator Stephen A. Douglas, however, wanted Chicago to be the rail center, but his proposal stood little chance of passage since it would require the railway to run through sparsely settled and unorganized territory that had been reserved for Native Americans.

Douglas came up with a plan. However, it meant that the Missouri Compromise would have to be altered or even repealed. Douglas proposed, as chair of the Committee on the Territories, the Nebraska Bill. It provided that the territory west of Missouri, Iowa, and the Minnesota territory—the unorganized remnant of the 1803 Louisiana Purchase—be settled under the policy of popular sovereignty. Popular sovereignty, according to Douglas's bill, said that "all questions pertaining to slavery in the Territories, and in the new states to be formed therefrom are to be left to the people residing therein, through their appropriate representatives."[1] With his new proposal for settlement, Douglas divided the Nebraska Territory into two territories, one called Kansas and the other, Nebraska. Douglas would now no doubt be able to count on Southern votes because the residents of the new territories would be able to choose for themselves whether they wanted to allow slavery or not when they joined the Union as states.

What Douglas had started as a means to secure a northern rail route quickly became a battle over slavery. President Franklin Pierce supported the Kansas–Nebraska Act, but it still faced stiff opposition, especially in the House of Representatives. Despite objections from many Northerners, Douglas's bill made it through Congress and was signed into law on May 30.

According to one scholar, "Few events have swung American history away from its charted course so suddenly or so sharply as the Kansas–Nebraska Act."[2] The political fallout was almost immediate. The Democratic party split and lost more than two-thirds of its seats from Northern states in the November elections. The Whig party, whose Northern members opposed the act while its Southern members supported it, faded into smaller factions as it died. A coalition of Northern Democrats, Free-Soilers (those who opposed expansion of slavery into the territories), and Whigs joined together and created a new party, the Republican Party, which took its name from the republican ideals of Thomas Jefferson. Within a year, Americans referred to Kansas as "bleeding Kansas," as pro- and antislavery advocates attempted to establish governments. By the end of 1856, nearly 200 people had been killed and about $2 million in property destroyed there.[3] Slavery, which had been tearing America apart slowly, increased the speed of its divisiveness.

This chapter looks at the reactions in America to the Kansas–Nebraska Act as it was being discussed in Congress and after its passage. It begins with readings that support the Kansas–Nebraska Act. The first comes from the *Free Press* of Detroit that discusses both the Missouri Compromise and the Wilmot Proviso. The next entry urges Southerners to keep vigilant because the attack on slavery will not end. Popular sovereignty was an integral part of the debate surrounding the Kansas–Nebraska Act and is the subject of the next editorial from the Cincinnati *Enquirer*.

The readings in opposition to the Act begin with one by Horace Greeley. Greeley, just as the writer of the first editorial in the support section, refers often to the Wilmot Proviso. Many Americans believed that the Kansas–Nebraska Act was the beginning of the end for the Union, and this entry from the Hartford, Connecticut, *Daily Courant* states that. The final reading comes from the Raleigh *Register*. Though most Southern newspapers supported the Kansas–Nebraska Act, the *Register* saw this Act as the end of the

Missouri Compromise, and its editor, Seaton Gales, believed it had served the nation well since 1820.

Support for the Kansas–Nebraska Act

An Anonymous Report: "New Territories"

Many Democratic newspapers supported the efforts of Douglas to pass the Kansas–Nebraska Act. The Free Press *of Detroit was one of these. In its discussion of the Act, the paper mentions the Wilmot Proviso, a proposal following the Mexican War to prohibit slavery in the territory acquired from Mexico. Although the House approved the Proviso, the Senate never did. It was, however, a consistent source of conversation as the nation divided over slavery.*

Free Press (Detroit), 6 January 1854

We see it stated that the Committee on Territories in the Senate will probably report bills for the organization of three new territories, to be formed out of the territory lying between the western boundaries of Arkansas, Missouri, Iowa and Minnesota, and the Rocky Mountains, and extending north and south between the 34th and 42d parallels of north latitude. The names of these new territories, it is further reported, will be Nebraska, Kansas, and Cherokee.

It is very probable that an attempt will be made by the abolitionists in Congress to revive the slavery prohibition question, by urging the embodiment of the Wilmot proviso in the bills for the organization of these new territories; and it may be that indiscreet southern men will seek the adoption of the Missouri compromise line in the same bills.

There is but one way to get along with the question, and that is to exclude both the Wilmot proviso and the Missouri compromise from all territorial bills. The public mind of the country, we apprehend, is settled in respect to this thing. . . . It is no part of the business of Congress to legislate for the territories. All Congress has to do with these embryo States is, to set the machinery of their governments in motion, and the people inhabiting them will take care of the rest. If they want slavery they will have it, and vice versa, and Congress cannot help it, on the same principle that Congress could not help it should the people of Michigan determine that slavery might exist within their borders.

We trust there will be found majorities in both houses of Congress who will promptly, and without debate, vote down all propositions, as connected with these territorial bills, relating to slavery.—That is the only safe, it is the only democratic, disposition that can be made of them. If they are entertained, they will lead to interminable discussion, the event of which will be in no respect propitious.

John M. Daniel: "The Duty of the South"

In the 1850s, the Richmond Enquirer *was one of the South's most important newspapers. In this editorial, Daniel warns Southerners that they cannot remain inactive in the battle over the Kansas–Nebraska Act because antislavery forces are actively at work attempting to defeat the bill.*

Enquirer **(Richmond), 16 February 1854**

This is no time for inaction. If the people of the South mean to insist on the recognition of their rights under the constitution, they must prepare for such a demonstration of their will and strength as must enforce a repeal of the unjust and odious restriction of 1820. There has never been before and perhaps there will never occur again, a conjuncture of circumstances so favorable for the re-conquest of the position which the South has lost by successive compromises of its rights. On our side we have the whole power of the Federal government and the moral support of a sound public sentiment; and we may exult in the assurance of harmony and zeal among our own people. With these advantages, there is no claim of right and justice which the South may not enforce by a fearless fidelity to its interests. But inaction will not do. A languid expression of public opinion is not all that is essential to the successful support of our rights. We must learn wisdom from our foe, and must counteract the effect of his vigorous blows by an equally energetic and imposing demonstration of our strength.

The North is not idle. Whatever hostility exists there to the repeal of the Missouri restriction, will be brought out with the utmost emphasis and power of expression. The opponents of the Nebraska bill have set in motion every engine of popular agitation. The public press, popular meetings, the pulpit and the State Legislatures have been employed as means for kindling the passions of the mob and coercing the action of Congress.

While the Abolitionists are thus inflaming the zeal of their followers, and marshalling the ranks of their forces, does it become the South to await the onset with apathy and indifference? Is it good policy to neglect the ordinary and necessary means of success, while our adversary is displaying the utmost energy in all his preparations for the contest? It seems to us, that we should give them the support of a firm declaration of our rights, and an emphatic expression of our feelings. Can we expect zeal and courage of them if we manifest indifference and timidity in our own cause? If the Southern

States stand as idle spectators of the struggle, may not the impression prevail that they feel no concern about the issue?

That there may be no doubt or misapprehension of the position of the South on this Nebraska question, we suggest that the Southern States should speak out their feeling and purpose. New York and Rhode Island, through their Legislatures, have pronounced against the repeal of the Missouri restriction, and doubtless other States in the North will follow their example. Let Virginia and the States of the South, in the same solemn and imposing mode, make a declaration of their rights under the constitution—not in the tone of complaint or of menace, but of calm resolution and earnest remonstrance. Let them make a demand for an equal position in the confederacy, and a just participation in the benefits of the Union. Let them protest against any violation of the great principle of *non-intervention* in regard to slavery, which the Compromise of 1850 established and guaranteed. The South is strong in a just cause, and its voice will be heard and respected.

James J. Faran: "Glorious News from Washington—Passage of the Nebraska Bill"

The Daily Enquirer *rejoiced for any number of reasons at the passage of the Kansas–Nebraska Act. First, this Democratic newspaper, whose editor James J. Faran probably wrote this editorial, believed that popular sovereignty—the right of citizens of a territory to choose whether or not to allow slavery—was constitutionally important. The fact that the railway to the Pacific might run through the territory—Douglas's original intention for the bill—was also important. The paper struck out at abolitionists in this report and said that Northern Democrats who supported the bill would be rewarded. The* Enquirer *was wrong on the last count since more than two-thirds of Northern Democrats were defeated in the fall elections.*

Daily Enquirer **(Cincinnati), 24 May 1854**

Our telegraphic column, this morning, contains the announcement that the Nebraska Bill has passed the house by thirteen majority. . . . It will go back to the Senate, which will doubtless concur with the House in its action, be signed by the President, and soon become the law of the land. The minority in the House used the most unscrupulous parliamentary action to kill the bill, but it was ineffectual. The struggle upon its passage was vehement and severe, the House being in session nearly all of Monday night.

We need not say that the success of the bill is to us a subject of peculiar gratification. We advocated it from its introduction, the principle in it—that of leaving the question of slavery to be decided by the people of the Territories themselves, which was so fiercely controverted—being right in our judgment, and worthy of the support of all patriotic citizens who desire the perpetuity of our Federal Union. Those who desire to keep the disturbing and distracting subject of slavery in Congress, as an eternal bone of contention between the North and the South, instead of referring its decision to those to whom it legitimately belongs, will, of course, send up a howl of rage over the result, which, to them, is so calamitous. But it is a great and glorious triumph to every one who believes in the doctrine of popular sovereignty and the right of every State and Territory to do its local legislation.

The success of the Bill, we expect, be made the occasion for a fresh outburst of indignation upon the part of the fanatical disunionists and traitors of the North, who have threatened to do terrible things in that event; but in a few days we shall hear no more of it. Greeley and Garrison, Fred. Douglas, Sumner and Chase, may fret and foam, but it will have little effect upon the great body of the American people, who do not sympathize with them in their unpatriotic views. . . .

We rejoice over its passage for other reasons than the provision which is in it respecting slavery—a territorial organization being sadly needed in Nebraska and Kansas, to render comfortable the great tide of overland emigration to California and Oregon. To the West, especially, it is very important. We cannot conclude our notice of its passage without a word of commendation of the noble band of Democrats from the North and West, more than forty in number. . . . They will have their reward, not only in the approval of their own consciences, but in the future good opinion of their countrymen.

Opposition to the Kansas–Nebraska Act

An Anonymous Report: "Nebraska"

Horace Greeley's newspaper strongly supported antislave causes. Some people thought that it would be impossible for the Nebraska territory to ever become slave-holding because it would not support the plantation system, but this article explains that, if any territory is opened to slavery, there is always the possibility that it will become a slave state. The article, just as one above from Detroit, speaks often of the Wilmot Proviso.

Tribune **(New York), 10 January 1854**

The special organ of the Administration backs up Douglas's Nebraska Bill. This is natural. In fact it is a godsend to The Union to have a subject on which it can denounce the Free-Soilers and pledge itself anew to lick the feet of the Slaveholders. Its Hunker friends have been crowding it hard lately for its devotion to the Softs, and the Abolition proclivities which they charge upon it.

We hear from Washington that Douglas's Bill is likely to be supported by some Northern Whigs. We shall not be surprised at any turn affairs may take at Washington. It takes pluck to resist a strong adverse current in political affairs. And this is too much to expect of a good many gentlemen who find their way to Washington. It is vastly easier to go with the tide always than to stem it. But why Northern men who have steadily sustained the doctrine of the Wilmot Proviso should now abandon it, is past our art to discover. . . .

There was a solemn compact made between North and South, on the admission of Missouri, that there should never be a Slave State north of the 36*30'. It was clearly and unequivocally agreed that Slavery should never pollute the great North-west Territory, and up to this time, the idea of departing a hair's breadth from this explicit stipulation and compact, would have been scouted by the entire North and by every honorable man in the South. . . . But what do we now hear? That Northern men and Northern Whigs even, are conspiring to abandon the only consistent, honorable and manly ground, when the compact of which we speak is basely and treacherously assailed. We shall believe it when we see the votes. . . .

It is said that Douglas's Bill will not make Nebraska a Slave State? How do we know that? If Congress avows its purpose in advance to disregard a solemn obligation, designed to forever exclude Slavery from that Territory, and coquettes with the stipulations of a sacred compact, instead of resolutely enforcing it, we may expect to see this inebriated political morality taken advantage of, and desperate efforts made to reconquer for Slavery a Territory whose defenses have been deliberately torn down to invite invasion and subjection to remorseless servitude. But, on the other hand, it is safe to insist upon the doctrine of discountenancing and excluding Slavery therefrom. The moral force of the application of the Proviso to the Territorial Government of Nebraska will make assurance doubly sure that when it is created into a State, it will be a Free State. We cannot conceive how intelligent and conscientious men, who possess a real regard for the great doctrines of human freedom, can excuse themselves for such an abandonment as that which we have been apprised is in contemplation. We shall not believe such desertion possible till we are called upon to record the abject capitulation.

An Anonymous Report: "Compromises"

Compromises are necessary to the proper functioning of a government, this article says, but the compromise that the Kansas–Nebraska Act requires will be the "the beginning of the end" for the nation. This report offers a good history of the slave compromises from 1820 forward.

Daily Courant (Hartford), 16 May 1854

As their name implies, compromises are settlements of difficulties by mutual concessions. Each side gives up to the other something upon which it had insisted, often with much zeal. Of course no compromise is entirely acceptable to those who form it. Neither side has obtained that for which it had been contending, having mutually given away on some points, and therefore neither side feels satisfied at first. . . .

But as time goes on, especially where equal and mutual concessions have been made, the compromise, as first only acquiesced in, becomes a part of the policy of the nation and is considered every year as more sacred, until practice under it makes it to be considered as a permanent and unalterable agreement.

Such was the feeling of the Whig party at the North at the Compromise Measures of 1850.—Many of the concessions which they made to the South were exceedingly distasteful to them. They opposed them bitterly at first, but finally acquiesced in them because they were *Compromises,* dependent on mutual concessions. . . . —The Whigs of the North are as much opposed to the extension of the area of slavery, as any other set of men. But they are a party of principles, not of a principle, and they feel that other things are to be contended for in consulting the good of the whole country. On this account, they submitted to the compromises of 1850.

Such was the feeling of the North at the Compromise of 1820. A concession had been made. —Many of them were opposed to it. But, being a concession on their side, and having received what was considered an equivalent concession on the part of the South, their opposition soon died away and they acquiesced in it and proceeded to act in good faith under it.

Such was the feeling of the whole nation at that greatest Compromise Measure of all—the Constitution of the United States—here, mutual concessions and mutual forbearance were necessary and were practised, and the nation prospered under them.

No Confederacy can exist without Compromises and concessions. . . . Under those compromises between the North and South, on that point on which they are antagonistic, the nation has prospered and *has been kept united.*

A dark spot now arises in the history of our country. The South, having elected a Northern President devoted to their interests who is supported by a section of the North equally devoted to their interests, have stept over the boundary of the Compromises and insist upon the abrogation of that of 1820, by which a violent contest was pacifically settled. . . .

The consequences arising from this movement are, that the whole slavery agitation has been reopened by the South themselves and what the end will be no one can predict; that the North are aroused up to a more determinate resistance to the extension of the area of slavery, than they have ever before been, being chained down by what appeared to them was a sacred compact; that no future Compromise can ever be made between the two antagonistic parties, for the North can never place confidence in the declarations or agreements of men who would uphold the violation of the Missouri Compromise; and that there is danger not only of the loss of the Compromise measures of 1850, but of the still greater Compromise of the Constitution. The voluntary destruction of one of these compacts by the South will weaken the obligatory force of the rest on the minds of the North. We fear lest the vote on the Nebraska bill will prove "the beginning of the end" of the permanency of the American confederation.

Seaton Gales: "A Cunning Game!"

The region of the nation in which a newspaper was located did not necessarily determine its position on issues. The Raleigh Register, *a Southern Whig newspaper, felt repeal of the Missouri Compromise would be disastrous to Southern interests. Gales felt that since the closest states to the Kansas and Nebraska territories were free states, both areas would likely become free, not slave states. He felt the South was better served with the existing agreement of the 1820 Compromise.*

Register (Raleigh), 17 May 1854

It is rumored that the leading friends of the Administration in Congress—those who are determined "to rule or ruin"—are playing a deep game in politics. They see that the Nebraska-Kansas Bill cannot pass without striking out the Clayton amendment, by which move every worthless foreigner, having no knowledge of our institutions, and less attachment for some of them, will be admitted to the ballot box in those territories, thereby excluding most effectually all Southern slaveholders. They also see, that, allowing such men to vote in those territories, the Homestead Bill is a stumbling block, at least with the members of the old States, in the way of the passage of the Nebraska Bill, and therefore they have agreed to "sing low" and play "possum" on the Homestead, until the Nebraska is through. *Then,* is any man fool enough to suppose, that Douglas will suffer it to rest? Is any man so blind as not to see that it is the settled purpose of the President to approve that bill? If he does, it will be the most ruinous to the South. Hear what the "*Washington Union,*" the organ of the Administration, says on this subject. It deserves the most serious attention of every man who does not wish the South made, most effectually, the "hewer of wood and drawer of water" to the North. Hear the "*Union*":

"To our mind it is rash to declare, *that because the President cannot approve a bill appropriating land for a purely eleemosynary purpose, he cannot approve one which grants his homestead to the hardy pioneer, or one which grants alternate sections of land for the construction of a railroad.*"

Can such language as this be mistaken?—Does it not show, most conclusively, what are the views and purposes of the President,—that he is resolved to approve the Homestead Bill? Will the people of the old States, on whom this measure will fall most ruinously, suffer themselves to be humbugged by the basely cunning and false representations of the lackeys of the Administration? Let them look to it before it is too late to remedy the evil!

Questions

1. Compromises are often necessary in a democracy. Why are compromises that deal with moral issues such as slavery so difficult?
2. Why might people oppose the nullification of the Missouri Compromise of 1820?
3. A number of newspapers called the Kansas–Nebraska Act "the beginning of the end." Based on the readings, what was their rationale for this statement?

Notes

1. Quoted in George Brown Tindall, *America: A Narrative History,* 2 vols. (New York: W.W. Norton, 1984), 1:591.

2. David M. Potter, *The Impending Crisis, 1848–1861* (New York: Harper & Row, 1976), 167.

3. Tindall, *America,* 1:595.

CHAPTER 26

The Caning of Charles Sumner, 1856

In 1854, Congress passed the Kansas–Nebraska Act, which said that the people residing in a territory could decide for themselves whether slavery would be allowed within a territory once it became a state (see Chapter 25). Popular sovereignty, as this concept of selection was called, did not solve problems; it made things worse in the Kansas and Nebraska territories and in the United States, as the argument over slavery intensified. By now it was apparent to most Americans that no compromise on slavery would ever be reached. Kansans set up separate governments, one headed by free-soilers, who opposed slavery, and a second, established by the proslavery movement. Their confrontations took place in print and in public debate. They also led to violence. In May, a proslavery mob marched into Lawrence—a free-state town—and destroyed property, including the residence of the free-state governor. One free-soiler was killed, and the violence escalated, spurred on by a free-state advocate named John Brown (see Chapter 29). Kansas became known as "bleeding Kansas" because by the end of the year, nearly 200 people had been killed and about $2 million in property destroyed.[1]

The angry confrontations over popular sovereignty in Kansas did not stop at the territory's border. They spilled over into all regions of the United States, and even into Congress. In the midst of the escalating violence in Kansas, Charles Sumner, a Massachusetts Senator and staunch antislavery proponent, addressed the Senate with a speech titled "On the Crime Against Kansas." Sumner described what was happening in Kansas as "the rape of a virgin Territory, compelling it to the hateful embrace of Slavery." The Republican Senator then turned his diatribe on several Senators, especially Andrew P. Butler of South Carolina who was not present for the speech. "Of course he has chosen a mistress to whom he has made his vows, and who, though ugly to others, is always lovely to him; though polluted in the sight of the world, is chaste in his sight. I mean the harlot, Slavery," Sumner said of Butler. Sumner continued to accost the absent South Carolina

Senator, saying, "the chivalric Senator will conduct the State of South Carolina out of the Union! Heroic knight ! Exalted Senator! A second Moses come for a second exodus!" That, to Sumner, was no great loss, however. As he continued, he noted that if South Carolina's history were blotted out, civilization would lose nothing.[2]

Though Butler was not present to hear what was said about him and his state, his relative, Congressman Preston Brooks, was in Washington, and he was irate at what he considered to be a libelous attack on a family member, his home state, and the South in general. On May 22, Brooks entered the Senate chamber after adjournment and announced that Sumner had, indeed, libeled the South Carolina Senator. Sumner was working at his desk. Without warning, Brooks began to beat Sumner on the head with what Horace Greeley called "a loaded cane."[3] The stunned Massachusetts Senator attempted to stand but could not. Brooks continued to beat Sumner on the head with the cane. Finally, Sumner pulled his desk from the bolts that attached it to the floor and staggered forward. Brooks did not stop hitting Sumner, though. At last, another Congressman halted Brooks, and Sumner fell unconscious to the floor.

The reaction to the caning of Sumner was immediate and showed just how galvanized the nation had become over the issue of slavery. Most Northern newspapers—especially those who supported Sumner's Republican party—viewed Brooks's attack as an accurate portrayal of what proslavery forces would do to promote the peculiar institution in America. Brooks, on the other hand, was seen as a hero by many newspapers for his chivalrous defense of a gentleman's and a region's honor. Brooks even received a plethora of canes from well-wishers. Bleeding Kansas was not overlooked, either. The Republican party, which had been pointing to Kansas as a barometer of the intentions of America's proslave forces, now had the proof it needed to support its contentions. The caning of Charles Sumner helped strengthen the party.

This chapter looks at the reactions in the press to Sumner's caning. While many newspapers chastised Sumner for his brutish remarks, they found them to be no excuse for Brooks's actions. Editors did not miss the implications of the caning for the United States. It seemed, they reasoned, that America was growing into two nations, and the United States might not be able to continue united. The readings begin with those that support Sumner and antislavery. The first, by Horace Greeley, refers to Brooks's actions as "Southern cowardice." It is followed by another Boston report, an anonymous letter, claiming the actions of Brooks were typical for Southerners. The next entry comes from the *New-York Times.* It asks readers to read all the facts of the incident but does say Sumner did nothing to provoke the attack. The final selection in this section comes from Horace Greeley's *Tribune.* It praises Sumner.

The second set of readings support Brooks and the proslavery faction. They begin with an anonymous letter that appeared in Charleston, South Carolina, claiming Sumner was "elegantly whipped." The next article comes from Illinois. Though Sumner's beating is regrettable, it says, the attack was justified. The *Federal Union* of Georgia, the source of the final press account, regretted that the beating took place in the Senate and suggested that Brooks should have, justifiably, made the attack elsewhere.

Support for Sumner

Horace Greeley: "Southern Cowardice"

Abolitionist editor Horace Greeley gave no title to his initial comments on the caning of Charles Sumner, but he saw Brooks's actions as typical of Southern cowardice. He also believed, "We are either to have Liberty or Slavery." Brooks's actions proved this.

Tribune (New York), 23 May 1856)

By the news from Washington it will be seen that Senator Sumner has been savagely and brutally assaulted, while sitting in his seat in the Senate chamber, by the Hon. Mr. Brooks of South Carolina, the reason assigned therefore being that the Senator's remarks on Mr. Butler of South Carolina, who is uncle to the man who made the attack. The particulars show that Mr. Sumner was struck unawares over the head by a loaded cane and stunned, and then the ruffianly attack was continued with many blows, the Hon. Mr. Keitt of South Carolina keeping any of those around, who might be so disposed, from attempting a rescue. No meaner exhibition of Southern cowardice–generally miscalled Southern chivalry–was ever witnessed. It is not in the least a cause for wonder that a member of the national House of Representatives, assisted by another as a fender-off, should attack a member of the national Senate, because, in the course of a constitutional argument, the last had uttered words which the first chose to consider distasteful. The reasons for the absence of collision between North and South–collision of sentiment and person–which existed a few years back, have ceased; and as the South has taken the oligarchic ground that Slavery ought to exist, irrespective of color–that there must be a governing class and a class governed–that Democracy is a delusion and a lie–we must expect that Northern men in Washington, whether members or not, will be assaulted, wounded or killed, as the case may be, so long as the North will bear it. The acts of violence during this session–including one murder–are simply overtures to the drama of which the persecutions, murders, robberies and war upon the Free-State men in Kansas, constitute the first act. We are either to have Liberty or Slavery. Failing to silence the North by threats, notwithstanding the doughfaced creatures who so long misrepresented the spirit of the Republic and of the age, the South now resorts to actual violence. It is reduced to a question whether there is to be any more liberty of speech south of Mason and Dixon's line, even in the ten miles square of the District of Columbia. South of that, liberty has long since departed; but whether the common ground where the national representatives meet is to be turned into a slave plantation where Northern members act under the lash, the bowie-knife and the pistol, is a question to be settled. That Congress will take any action in view of this new event, we shall not be rash enough to surmise; but if the Northern people are not generally the poltroons they are taken for by the hostile slavebreeders and slavedrivers of the South, they will be heard from. As a beginning, they should express their sentiments upon this brutal and dastardly outrage in their popular assemblies. The Pulpit should not be silent.

If, indeed, we go on quietly to submit to such outrages, we deserve to have our names flattened, our skins blacked, and to be placed at work under task-masters; for we have lost the noblest attributes of freemen, and are virtually slaves.

An Anonymous Report: "A Brutal Assault"

The Atlas *gave no title to its report on the caning of one of its senators, but the newspaper said such actions are what should be expected from Southerners. Northerners, therefore, should be prepared.*

Atlas **(Boston), 23 May 1856**

Hon. Charles Sumner, one of the Senators of Massachusetts, was yesterday brutally assaulted by a ruffian named Brooks, who represents South Carolina in the lower House. Those who know Mr. Sumner will readily believe that nothing in his conduct or conversation could have provoked the outrage, and that it must be attributed to the bold and vigorous demonstration of the Kansas inequity, which he has just uttered in the Senate. The reign of terror, then, is to be transferred to Washington, and the mouths of the representatives of the North are to be closed by the use of bowie-knives, bludgeons, and revolvers. Very well; the sooner we understand this the better. If violence must come, we shall know how to defend ourselves. We hope, for the credit of the State, that every man in it will feel this outrage upon Mr. Sumner as a personal indignity, no less than an insult to the Commonwealth of Massachusetts, and that there will be such a general and spontaneous expression of opinion, as will fully manifest our deep disinclination to submit to any repetition of the contumely.

An Anonymous Report: "No Just Provocation"

The New-York Daily Times *said little about the caning of Sumner in its initial, untitled report of the incident. Instead, the paper advised its constituency to read Sumner's speech. Even though the paper seemed to want readers to make up their own minds, the article intimated that Sumner said nothing that was provocative, except his comments about Stephen Douglas, a Senator from Illinois. In fact, the article said, there was no "provocation for the brutal outrage of Brooks."*

New-York Daily Times, 23 May 1856

We publish in a Supplement to this morning's *TIMES* the speech recently made by Mr. Sumner in the Senate of the United States upon the affairs of Kansas,–together with the debate which followed between him and Senators Cass, Douglas and Mason. Mr. Sumner's speech is one of the ablest ever made in the body of which he is a useful and honorable member. It presents the whole case of Kansas, especially so far as it is connected with the action of the Federal Government, more clearly and strongly than has been done in any other document. Its tone is sharp and controversial;–and Mr. S. certainly does not shrink from speaking of those, in the Senate and elsewhere, who have urged opposite sentiments and advised or defended the acts of the Pro-Slavery propaganda in regard to Kansas, in very decisive and emphatic terms. But he does not in any instance,–except in his rejoinder to Mr. Douglas,–transcend the limits of Parliamentary propriety or afford any ground whatever for the imputations of personality which have been so freely lavished upon him by the Pro-Slavery press. The most fastidious reader will search in vain for anything which could give the slightest color of just provocation for the brutal outrage of Brooks. We are confident the debate will be read with general interest.

Horace Greeley: "The Assault on Senator Sumner"

Two days after the attack on Sumner, Horace Greeley released an untitled editorial praising the Massachusetts Senator. He also said that the nation would never solve its problems if blows had to be exchanged.

Tribune (New York), 24 May 1856

The assault on Senator Sumner reverberates through the land, causing throughout the Free States the intensest excitement and indignation. Other men have been as causelessly assailed, and as wantonly, if not as savagely, beaten; but the knocking-down and beating to bloody blindness and unconsciousness of an American Senator while writing at his desk in the Senate Chamber is a novel illustration of the ferocious Southern spirit. It carries home to myriads of understandings a more vivid, if not a wholly original perception, of the degradation in which the Free States have consented for years to exist. The degradation was as real years ago, but never before so palpable as now. . . .

There is no man now living who within the last five years has rendered the American People greater service or won for himself a nobler fame than Charles Sumner.

It is high time that this People should take a stand not only against the immediate perpetrators of ruffian assaults but against their confederates and apologists in public life and in the Press. As long as words sincerely spoken can be pleaded as an apology for blows, we shall be regarded by impartial observers as barbarians—and justly so regarded. So long as our truly civilized and refined communities succumb to the rule of the barbarian elements in our political system, we must be judged by the character and conduct of our accepted masters. The youth trained to knock down his human chattels for "insolence"—that is, for any sort of resistance to his good pleasure—will thereafter knock down and beat other human beings who thwart his wishes—no matter whether they be Irish waiters or New England Senators. Once admit the idea of the predominance of brute force—of the right of individual appeal from words to blows—and human society becomes a state of war, diversified by interludes of fitful and hollow truce. And they who, as legislators, editors, public speakers, or in whatever capacity, suggest apologies for ruffian assaults, or intimate that words can excuse them, make themselves partners in the crime and the infamy.

Support for Brooks

Palmetto: "Elegantly Whipped"

The author of this letter to the Mercury *used a pseudonym, and the paper gave the letter no title. However, it is obvious that the writer, who was in Washington and wrote two days after the caning, saw the actions of Brooks as a defense of the South.*

Mercury (Charleston), 28 May 1856

MESSRS. EDITORS: There is high excitement in Washington. You will have heard, through telegraphic reports, that Col. BROOKS, of your State, punished Mr. SUMNER, of Massachusetts, on last Thursday, for a libel on South Carolina and a slander against Judge BUTLER.

SUMNER, on Monday and Tuesday, delivered a coarse and malignant Abolition speech, in which he assailed South Carolina and Judge BUTLER with great bitterness. The speech was so coarse and insulting, that even his own faction condemned it, and the Southern men freely said he should be chastised. His peculiar friends tauntingly declared that he was armed during its delivery, and that he was prepared for all responsibility. Col. BROOKS, who is a relative of Judge BUTLER, and from his immediate district, deemed it his duty to chastise Mr. SUMNER for his insolence, and his slanders against Judge BUTLER and the State. He sought Mr. SUMNER on Wednesday, but could not find him except in the Senate Chamber. He had determined to postpone the punishment no longer, and therefore he remained in the Senate until it adjourned.

After the adjournment, a number of ladies came into the Senate Hall, and loitered there for some time. Col. BROOKS waited about an hour after the adjournment, until all the ladies had left, Mr. SUMNER having remained in his seat, engaged in franking off his speech. As soon as the last lady had left the hall, Col. BROOKS went up to Mr. SUMNER, and facing him, said: "Mr. SUMNER, I have read your speech with great care, and all the impartiality in my power, and I have come to tell you that you have libelled my State, and slandered my relative, who is old and absent, and I deem it my duty to punish you, which I shall now proceed to do." Col. BROOKS thereupon struck Mr. SUMNER, who was rising, across the face with a gutta percha cane. He continued repeating the blows until Mr. SUMNER fell upon the floor, crying out for help. Col. BROOKS then desisted voluntarily, saying, "I did not wish to hurt him much, but only punish him."

SUMNER was well and elegantly whipped, and he richly deserved it. Senator TOOMBS, of Georgia, who was in the midst of it, said, "BROOKS, you have done the right thing, and in the right place." Gallant old Governor FITZPATRICK, of Alabama, who was in the midst of it, warmly sustained BROOKS also.

The Black Republicans have shingled the occurrence all over with falsehood. They charge Mr. EDMUNDSON, of Virginia, and Mr. KEITT, of South Carolina, with sharing in the attack. It is false. Mr. EDMUNDSON was not in the Senate Chamber when the caning took place, and Mr. KEITT was at the remotest corner of the room, with the President's desk intervening; so he did not even see the beginning of the attack. Hearing the blows of the cane and the cries of SUMNER, he hurried to the spot, and found Senator FOSTER, of Connecticut, and an officer of the Senate, attempting to grasp BROOKS, when he threw himself between them, and ordered them back at their personal risk. They immediately desisted, and BROOKS flogged SUMNER without any interference.

Sumner is much the largest and most athletic man, and, had he resisted, might have defended himself; at least that is my opinion. BROOKS was immediately afterwards arrested. The magistrate could not fix the amount of bail, as he did not know the extent of SUMNER'S injuries, so he has fixed four o'clock this evening for taking the bond.

The whole South sustains BROOKS, and a large part of the North also. All feel that it is time for freedom of speech and freedom of the cudgel to go together.

The Senate have appointed a Committee of Investigation. The House, in its super-serviceable Black Republican zeal, has done the same thing. Its action has been imbecile and contemptible. A Speaker elected by a sectional vote—a resolution against HERBERT supported by a sectional vote—and now one against BROOKS by a sectional vote.

Events are hurrying on. A despatch has just been received that Lawrence has been demolished, and lives lost. Next it will be a line of battle for two thousand miles!

PALMETTO.

An Anonymous Report: "Assault in the United States Senate Chamber"

A number of newspapers and editors in Ohio and Illinois tended to oppose the newly forming Republican party and its platform. Here, Sumner is referred to as a member of the "black guard," meaning those who made the rights of slaves and free blacks a top priority.

Illinois State Register (Springfield), 26 May 1856

A telegraphic dispatch of the 22d inst. states that immediately after the adjournment of congress on that day, Preston S. Brooks, of South Carolina, a member of the lower house, entered the senate chamber and approached the seat of Mr. Sumner, and struck him a powerful blow with a cane, at the same time accusing him of libelling South Carolina, and his gray-headed relative, Senator Butler. . . .

The assault on many accounts is to be regretted, but when we take into account the provocation, much may be said in palliation of it. All parties confess that Sumner's speech, surpassed in blackguardism anything ever delivered in the senate. Blinded by rage at being used up in debate by his political opponents, he commenced levelling his filth and slime at every senator opposed to him, among whom was the venerable Butler—who was not present. Sumner is a young man; professes to be a non-combatant; proclaims to the world that he does not profess to be a gentleman; claims the right to use just such language as he pleases in the senate and out of it, to old men as well as young, without holding himself answerable to any code of honor, or any recognised rules of etiquette, or senatorial courtesy. Pursuant to these assumptions he made a speech against Senator Butler which was never equalled by the lowest pot house slime. . . .

Such scenes are greatly to be regretted. They are disgraceful to the nation; but when such crawling, sneaking reptiles as Sumner assume the shield of non-combatancy in order to establish for themselves the executive privilege of violating every rule of decorum known among men, and every usage of parliamentary courtesy observed in deliberative bodies, there is certainly great allowance to be made for gentlemen who, momentarily losing their tempers, may mete out well-merited but possibly illegal punishment to the offenders. However much we may regret the act on account of the scandal it may bring upon the senate, we cannot but believe that the nation will say that Sumner got no more than he deserved. He is a base, lying, blackguard, a bully without courage, a peace man and a blusterer, a provoker of fights, and a non-resistant–in short a heterogeneous conglomeration of everything knavish, mean and cowardly.

An Anonymous Report: "The Brooks and Sumner Difficulty"

Newspapers throughout the South commended Brooks for defending the honor of family, state, and region. This report from the Federal Union *in Milledgeville, Georgia's capital, is similar to many others.*

Federal Union **(Milledgeville), 3 June 1856**

Our readers will find an account of the whipping which Mr. Brooks of South Carolina gave Mr. Sumner, of Massachusetts, in another place. We regret very much that Mr. Brooks had not selected some other place than the Senate Chamber in which to inflict that chastisement. We are well aware that the enemies of Republican institutions will seize upon this as a strong argument against our government and people. For Mr. Sumner we have not the least sympathy. When he delivered that compound of vulgarity, abuse and falsehood called a speech, he knew that he violated all the laws of decency, and deserved a severe corporeal castigation, but he relied upon his position as a Senator to protect him. We believe there are some kinds of slander and abuse, for the perpetration of which, no office or station should protect a man from deserved punishment. Whether Mr. Sumner's slander in the Senate was of this species we leave those to judge who heard it. All agree that this was one of the most malignant and indecent tirades ever uttered in the Senate Chamber, and in our opinion such a speech in the Senate of the U.S. is much more dishonorable to a nation, than the chastisement inflicted upon the perpetrator. Massachusetts has no right to complain, for she has for a long time been without the pale of the constitution and the laws of the Union by virtue of an act of her own legislature. Whilst she refuses to submit to the laws of the Union, she cannot claim the protection of those laws for her Senators, and whilst she chooses to be represented in the U.S. Senate by blackguards, she ought not to complain if they receive a blackguard's reward.

Questions

1. Why, do you think, some writers to newspapers could justify a physical attack on an unsuspecting person?
2. From these newspaper accounts, can you tell what people in the North and South thought of each other?
3. Some newspaper accounts maintained that Sumner said nothing that should have angered anyone. Others said he deserved the beating. Having read some of Sumner's speech, do you think he may have libeled Senator Butler, considering libel as a false and damaging attack on another person's character?

Notes

1. George Brown Tindall, *America: A Narrative History,* 2 vols. (New York: W.W. Norton, 1984), 1:595.

2. For in-depth scholarship on Charles Sumner, see David M. Potter, *The Impending Crisis: 1848–1861* (New York: Harper & Row, 1976); David Herbert Donald, *Charles Sumner and the Rights of Man* (New York: Alfred Knopf, 1970); David Herbert Donald, *Charles Sumner and the Coming of the Civil War* (Chicago: University of Chicago Press, 1960); George H. Haynes, *Charles Sumner* (Philadelphia: G.W. Jacobs, 1909); Moorfield Storey, *Charles Sumner* (Boston: Houghton Mifflin, 1900). Sumner's speech may be found in *Congressional Globe,* 34 Cong., 1 session, appendix, 529. The events of the caning are compiled from several news sources by the *Spartan* (Spartanburg, South Carolina), 29 May 1856.

3. *Tribune* (New York), 23 May 1856.

CHAPTER 27

The Dred Scott Decision, 1857

On March 6, 1857, the United States Supreme Court handed down its decision in the case *Dred Scott v. Sandford.* The Court's ruling shocked many Americans. At the same time, many people who lived in slave-holding states rejoiced. Scott, a slave, had sued for his freedom because he had lived in Illinois—a free state—and in Wisconsin—a free territory. The Court, in a 7–2 vote, denied that living in a free state or territory made Scott free. But the Court did not stop there, and its subsequent pronouncements in Scott's case further heightened tensions in the United States between free and slave states.

The Dred Scott case spent more than a decade in the judicial systems of Missouri and the nation, but the circumstances surrounding what happened stretched over more than two decades. Scott's original owner, Peter Blow, moved to Missouri from Virginia in 1830 and then sold Scott to John Emerson, an Army surgeon. During the next few years, Emerson moved first to Illinois and later to the Wisconsin territory, taking Scott with him. Emerson—with his slave—returned to Missouri in 1838. When Emerson died in 1843, Scott unsuccessfully attempted to buy his freedom. Instead, he became the property of John Sandford, Emerson's brother-in-law. Assisted by antislavery advocates, Scott brought suit in Missouri courts, claiming that he was a free man because he had lived in parts of the nation that disallowed slavery. He could not, according to Scott's argument, be a slave any longer. The lower court sided with Scott, but Sandford appealed. The Missouri Supreme Court reversed the decision; Scott appealed to the United States Supreme Court, which agreed to hear the case.[1]

The case, *Scott v. Sandford,* was highly complex. It challenged many of the laws in place in America that dealt with slavery in the territories and with the legal status of blacks both free and slave. The first question that the case posed was whether Scott even had the right to bring suit in the nation's courts. Could a black person—free or slave—be a citizen of America? Next, the case asked whether Scott, by virtue of living in regions of the nation that

FRANK LESLIE'S ILLUSTRATED NEWSPAPER

Entered according to Act of Congress, in the year 1857, by Frank Leslie, in the Clerk's Office of the District Court for the Southern District of New York. (Copyrighted June 27, 1857.)

No. 62.—VOL. IV.] NEW YORK, SATURDAY, JUNE 27, 1857. [Price 6 Cents.

TO TOURISTS AND TRAVELLERS.

We shall be happy to receive personal narratives, of land or sea, including adventures and incidents, from every person who pleases to correspond with our paper.

We take this opportunity of returning our thanks to our numerous artistic correspondents throughout the country, for the many sketches we are constantly receiving from them of the news of the day. We trust they will spare no pains to furnish us with drawings of events as they may occur. We would also remind them that it is necessary to send all sketches, if possible, by the earliest conveyance.

VISIT TO DRED SCOTT—HIS FAMILY—INCIDENTS OF HIS LIFE—DECISION OF THE SUPREME COURT.

While standing in the Fair grounds at St. Louis, and engaged in conversation with a prominent citizen of that enterprising city, he suddenly asked us if we would not like to be introduced to Dred Scott. Upon expressing a desire to be thus honored, the gentleman called to an old negro who was standing near by, and our wish was gratified. Dred made a rude obeisance to our recognition, and seemed to enjoy the notice we expended upon him. We found him on examination to be a pure-blooded African, perhaps fifty years of age, with a shrewd, intelligent, good-natured face, of rather light frame, being not more than five feet six inches high. After some general remarks we expressed a wish to get his portrait (we had made efforts before, through correspondents, and failed), and asked him if he would not go to Fitzgibbon's gallery and have it taken. The gentleman present explained to Dred that it was proper he should have his likeness in the "great illustrated paper of the country," overruled his many objections, which seemed to grow out of a superstitious feeling, and he promised to be at the gallery the next day. This appointment Dred did not keep. Determined not to be foiled, we sought an interview with Mr. Crane, Dred's lawyer, who promptly gave us a letter of introduction, explaining to Dred that it was to his advantage to have his picture taken to be engraved for our paper, and also directions where we could find his domicile. We found the place with difficulty, the streets in Dred's neighborhood being more clearly defined in the plan of the city than on the mother earth; we finally reached a wooden house, however, protected by a balcony that answered the description. Approaching the door, we saw a smart, tidy-looking negress, perhaps thirty years of age, who, with two female assistants, was busy ironing. To our question, "Is this where Dred Scott lives?" we received, rather hesitatingly, the answer, "Yes." Upon our asking if he was home, she said,

"What white man arter dad nigger for?—why don't white man 'tend to his own business, and let dat nigger 'lone? Some of dese days dey'll steal dat nigger—dat are a fact."

ELIZA AND LIZZIE, CHILDREN OF DRED SCOTT.

Dred Scott. *The Supreme Court case* Dred Scott v. Sandford *shocked many people when Chief Justice Roger Taney handed down his decision in 1857. Taney ruled that Scott, who had been a slave, had no rights.* Frank Leslie's Illustrated Newspaper *featured Scott and his family in its June 27, 1857, issue.*

prohibited slavery, was free by default. Indirectly, and perhaps of most importance to the nation, the Dred Scott case sought answers to whether slavery could be prohibited in any United States territory by an act of Congress, specifically the Missouri Compromise of 1820 (see Chapter 1).

Even though the Supreme Court ruled against Scott 7–2, the justices all had differing opinions as to why Scott could not bring suit and why he remained a slave. Each wrote a separate opinion, but that of Chief Justice Roger Taney of Maryland and a former slave owner became the majority opinion and the one that established legal precedent. As to Scott's status as a citizen capable of bringing suit in court, the chief justice denied the possibility. "The question before us is, whether the class of persons described in the plea in abatement compose a portion of this people, and are constituent members of this sovereignty?" Taney posed in his decision. His answer was, "We think they are not, and that they are not included, and were not intended to be included, under the word 'citizens' in the Constitution, and can therefore claim none of the rights and privileges which that instrument provides for and secures to citizens of the United States." Taney did not stop, however. He gave reasons for his ruling, saying blacks were "a subordinate and inferior class of beings, who had been subjugated by the dominant race, and, whether emancipated or not, yet remained subject to their authority, and had no rights or privileges but such as those who held the power and the Government might choose to grant them."[2]

On the issue of Scott's manumission by virtue of living in a free state or territory, Taney declared "that Scott and his family upon their return were not free, but were, by the laws of Missouri, the property of the defendant." They returned, Taney also noted, voluntarily to the slave state. Taney went on to explain that the Constitution never implied the denial of property rights to Americans. When Congress passed the Missouri Compromise that disallowed slavery in the territory of the Louisiana Purchase above the 36 degree 30 minute latitude line, therefore, it violated constitutional provisions:

> [I]t is the opinion of the court that the act of Congress which prohibited a citizen from holding and owning property of this kind in the territory of the United States north of the line therein mentioned, is not warranted by the Constitution, and is therefore void; and that neither Dred Scott himself, nor any of his family, were made free by being carried into this territory; even if they had been carried there by the owner, with the intention of becoming a permanent resident.[3]

Many Americans wondered what the decision would mean for the nation's future. If the decision stood, all United States territory would be reopened to slavery. The concept of popular sovereignty, which allowed territories to decide whether slavery would be allowed within its borders, was nullified. Taken to the extreme, slavery would once again become legal in those states that had outlawed it. Even more frightening to many was the idea that the government might have to protect the rights of slaveholders to own slaves no matter where they went in the nation. The Dred Scott decision further polarized America, and free blacks in New York vowed the ruling was "a foul and infamous lie which neither black men nor white men are bound to respect."[4] In the South, however, many viewed the ruling as "a *finality*, so far as the federal legislation on the institution of slavery is concerned."[5]

The readings in this chapter look at the reaction to the Dred Scott decision. While one would expect Southern publications to favor the decision, newspapers that supported the Democratic party nationwide tended to support the verdict, too. The reason for this may be because the Court's ruling essentially derailed the entire platform of the newly formed Republican party. Whatever the reason, newspapers in some free states—principally in the Midwest—supported the decision. The readings begin with those that supported the ruling. The second section contains readings that attack Taney's rationale.

Support for the Dred Scott Decision

James J. Faran: "The Important Decision of the Supreme Court of the United States on the Slavery Question"

Just because a newspaper was located in a state that disallowed slavery did not mean that the newspaper would automatically disagree with the Dred Scott decision. Support of the Democratic party, opposition to the Kansas–Nebraska Act, and distrust of the newly formed Republican party all played into the reaction of the Daily Enquirer *of Cincinnati in this editorial that was probably written by the paper's editor James J. Faran.*

Daily Enquirer (Cincinnati), 8 March 1857

The decision of the United States Supreme Court in the famous "Dred Scott" case . . . is an event of great political importance. The Court of last resort, which has jurisdiction over questions appertaining to the powers of the Federal Government, decided that Congress has no power under the Constitution to legislate upon slavery in the Territories, and that all such legislation as the so-called Missouri Compromise, which undertook to do so, is null and void. This is a complete vindication of the doctrine of the Nebraska Bill, which now, it is judicially determined, only swept an illegal and unconstitutional measure from the statute-book. To the friends of the "Wilmot

Proviso" and the Abolition legislation for the Territories this decision of the Supreme Court will be most crushing and annihilating. Hereafter they will have no pretense whatever for keeping Congress and the country in a turmoil on that subject, as it would be no use for Congress to pass laws on a subject which the Supreme Court would immediately annul, in accordance with this decision. The whole question of slavery, in its judicial aspects, has been argued by the best lawyers before the Court, which, after mature and long deliberation, have come to the conclusion announced above. The influence of their action upon the country must neccesarily be immense. The whole people, without distinction of party, have confidence in that august tribunal, the Supreme Court of the United States, which, by virtue of the age, eminent legal attainments of its members, their life tenure, which places them beyond the influence of party feeling, have no motive whatever in the world to bias and corrupt their decision.

Additional force will be given it when it is known that the bench, composed of Northern and Southern members, was nearly unanimous on the main point, there being but two dissenters out of the nine Justices who compose the Court. . . .

While thus anticipating a general acquiescence in the decision of the Supreme Court, it would be too much to expect that it will escape attack and censure from disappointed and embittered partisans, whose political capital and hope of office will wither before it. They will doubtless blackguard and assail the Court; but it will still further weaken their cause among sober and intelligent men, who will never countenance their foray upon an honest and intelligent Judiciary. The men who aided in the passage of the Nebraska Bill of 1854, and sustained it against an unreasoning and infatuated opposition, will, by this decision, be placed in an enviable attitude before the country, and will have a good position assigned them in history. Coming after the result of the late election and the new President's inaugural, it is the last of a series of triumphs, political and judicial, to which hereafter they will ever refer with pleasure and pride.

Robert Barnwell Rhett: "The Past and the Future"

The Charleston Mercury *was one of the South's leading proponents of slavery and states' rights, and its editor, Robert Barnwell Rhett, consistently used the columns of the paper to promote those causes. The newspaper had, since the late 1820s, urged that South Carolina not allow the federal government to usurp its rights as a state, and Rhett advocated dissolution of Union decades before South Carolina's secession. Here, Rhett gloats, after the Dred Scott decision, that he and other Secessionists have been properly interpreting the law all along.*

Mercury (Charleston), 17 March 1857

Our columns, for some time past, have teemed with a record of facts that it is impossible to review without feelings of strong indignation, and even of amazement—indignation at the humiliations that have been forced upon us, and amazement at the quiet submission that has marked our counsels and repressed our action.

The Supreme Court of the United States, in a recent case, has, by a decision of seven to two of the Judges, established as law what our Southern statesmen have been repeating daily for many years on the floors of Congress, that the whole action of this Government on the subject of slavery, for more than a quarter of a century, from the initiation of the Missouri Restriction in 1822, to the California Compromise in 1850, has been all beyond the limits of the Constitution; was without justifiable authority; and that the whole mass should be now proclaimed null and void, and that slavery is guaranteed by the constitutional compact.

In this decision of the Court there is certainly presented to the minds of all those anxious Union-savers south of MASON and DIXON'S line—the men who have been teaching us so anxiously lessons of peace, and forbearance, and self-sacrifice—a charming subject of contemplation and retrospection. It appears that we, Secessionists, have been all the while not disturbing the law, not intruding novelties upon the country, not seeking to break up established principles, but that we have been simply a step in advance of the highest tribunal in the country, in declaring what was the law of the land, and seeking honestly and faithfully to enforce it.

But it is a curious spectacle that the Southern people have presented to the world during this controversy. With a domain three times greater than that of the French Empire, with a population greater than that which FREDERICK of Prussia made the terror of Europe, with agricultural productions which govern the markets and freight the ships of the whole civilized world—a people independent in themselves, necessary to all others, compact in the position of their territory, warlike in their character, and with their whole vast internal strength easily at command—the South has, for a period of more than thirty years, allowed her public men to deal in windy boastings, and sometimes even to descend to servile entreaty, for the purpose of saving, from the abuse of demagogues and the persecution of traducers, those institutions which form her lifeblood, the sources of her prosperity, and the whole foundation of that social and industrial existence which makes her, more than any other people, the centre of civilization of the world. We have allowed ourselves to be assailed in our social, political, moral and legislative relations, and this by a people not distant or professedly hostile, but bound to us by the ties of a common Government—bound by every consideration of political brotherhood, social sympathy and commercial interest, to treat us not only with forbearance, but even to stand as our friend against all aggressors from without—by a people to whom we are indebted for no protection—who have hung for half a century, for the support of their industry, upon that Central Government which we have fed and nurtured into strength, and who have a thousand times proclaimed that their country would become a howling wilderness but for the exactions which have wrested from the South the best part of the profits of her industry. Now the highest tribunal in the country decides that every principle on which the North has assailed us and sought to repress us in the exercise of our rights as a part of the Confederacy, and to limit the spread of our institutions, to undermine their stability and to endanger their peace, is false in law, and that every enactment of Congress tending to carry out these principles is null and void.

Now, however, we may congratulate ourselves that the highest tribunal has at last interposed and given its sanction to principles that recognize distinctly the equality of the States, and condemn the interference of the Federal Government with affairs that are peculiarly under their jurisdiction, and for interfering with which there is no warrant in our common Constitution, we cannot help feeling a sense of mortification that there has been so little of consistent union, on the part of the South, in the maintenance of principles on which depend absolutely her power, her industrial prosperity, and even her very existence. We might have made a better, as we might have made a more successful, battle in favor of interests so great and so vital. When all was at stake, we ought to have risked all, for the settlement of this question. What was it to us that there was a President to be elected, a Cabinet to be appointed, and a squad of subordinate officers to be placed or displaced. The sea is whitened with the rich freightage of our commerce, and the great country of our home is teeming with the abundant products of our peaceful industry. These are mighty interests, compared with which the shuffling game of politics is pitiful in the extreme; and these are the interests which we have too much allowed our public men to forget, or at least to make secondary to considerations of personal interest.

William Butterfield: "The Question Settled.—Black Republicanism vs. the Constitution"

The Dred Scott decision allowed many newspapers the opportunity to attack the Republican party. Many Democratic-supporting newspapers referred to the new party as the "black republican" party. In this report, the Patriot *takes delight in what it considers the demise of "the whole black republican platform," which, it says, is directly in opposition to the Constitution.*

New Hampshire Patriot (Concord), 18 March 1857

We give in this paper an abstract of the decision of the U.S. Supreme Court in the Dred Scott case, in which it is solemnly adjudged and decided, by the highest judicial tribunal of the Union, that the Missouri Compromise was unconstitutional, and that Congress has no constitutional power or authority to legislate upon the subject of slavery in the Territories. It will be seen that other incidental questions were decided in this case, but this is the one of the most political importance, and interest. It utterly demolishes the whole black republican platform and stamps it as directly antagonistical to the constitution. This is the end of the matter, so far as argument and voting and legislation are concerned. The constitution is the supreme law; the Supreme Court is the authorized interpreter of the constitution; the construction which that tribunal puts upon that instrument is, for all practical purposes, the constitution itself, and therefore their decision must be fully and freely acquiesced in by all good citizens. That decision is now the supreme law of the land; it is practically the constitution itself, being the meaning and intent of that instrument as officially interpreted and declared by the tribunal authorized to interpret it, and from whose decision there is no appeal. Resistance to that decision is, therefore, resistance to the constitution—to the government—to the Union itself. It cannot be made legally, rightfully, peacefully, or with the least chance or hope of success. That decision must be carried into effect—that interpretation must be acquiesced in and acted upon, *or else it must be resisted by force.* There is no other alternative. It is the law, the constitution, and will be respected and acted upon by the constituted authorities, no matter to what party they belong nor what their private views may be in regard to it. It cannot be evaded; if Congress and the President should undertake to resist it, the effort would be futile. In a word, we repeat, nothing but force, open rebellion, can successfully oppose the practical application and enforcement of the decision of the court in this case.

But what is the course and talk of the black republican organs upon this subject? Why, one would suppose, from their talk, that the decision of the highest judicial tribunal of the Union is of no binding force! The N. Y. Tribune even declares that their decision in this case is entitled to "no more weight than would be the judgment of a majority in a Washington barroom," and other black papers declare the judges to be "scoundrels," and Benedict Arnolds, and the black press and pulpit unite in reviling the court and denouncing their decision!

Now this only goes to prove, what we have heretofore alleged, that the black republican creed and purposes are at war with the constitution, are treasonable, and contemplate the overthrow of the Union. It only goes to show that their leaders stand precisely upon Garrison's platform, and that the road to the attainment of their objects lies over the ruins of the constitution and the Union. There is no escape from this; they preach resistance to law, to the supreme law— resistance to what is authoritatively adjudged to be the constitution. Such resistance, if carried into practical effect, would be treason; and all who preach it, preach treason, and all who seek to make a practical thing of it, seek to overthrow the constitution. . . .

Whoever now seeks to revive sectionalism, arrays himself against the constitution, and consequently, against the Union. Of course, it is to be expected that fanaticism will rave and clamor against the decision of the Supreme Court. But fanaticism ceases to be a formidable enemy when it seeks to measure strength with the Union-loving spirit of the people, sustained and confirmed by the great arbiter of constitutional questions. Fanaticism becomes powerless against such a combination, and hence we may smile at the madness with which the organs of black republicanism assail the late decision of the Supreme Court. It is the last dying fit of fanatical sectionalism. It will have the effect of fixing public attention upon the reckless wickedness which has heretofore impelled the sectional agitators to force the republic to the very verge of disruption.

We feel, therefore, that the danger is for the present over; that sectionalism is virtually dead—that it has been crushed out by the popular verdict in the presidential election; and that the decision of the Supreme Court had left nothing vital in republicanism, and has placed the Democratic party beyond and above all competition as the constitutional, national, Union party of the country. Mr. Buchanan takes the helm under these auspicious circumstances, and his acts thus far give token of a successful and prosperous administration.

Opposition to the Dred Scott Decision

Thurlow Weed: "The Opinion of Chief Justice Taney"

Under Thurlow Weed, the Albany Evening Journal *had long been a political organ, first for the Whigs and now for the Republicans. Here, the* Evening Journal *reacts to the announcement of the Scott decision, comparing it to the work of Britain's Star Chamber, which functioned without a jury, met in private, and in the first third of the seventeenth century worked to suppress any opposition to the increasingly unpopular authority of James I and Charles I.*

Evening Journal (Albany), 10 March 1857

We print to-day a sophistical, dogmatic, muddy, and extreme Pro-Slavery document, which future historians will speak of as the present age speaks of the edicts of Jeffries and the Star Chamber. Unworthy of the Bench from which it was delivered, unworthy even of the previous reputation of the jurist who delivered it, unworthy of the American people, and of the nineteenth century, it will be a blot upon our National character abroad, and a long-remembered shame at home. It declares that the slaveholder may take his Slaves and hold them in any Territory under Federal control, and that neither Congress, nor the Territorial Government, nor the People, have the power now or hereafter to forbid him. It declares that the Constitution, though established "to secure Liberty," nowhere protects the existence of Freedom, and though it never mentions the word "Slave," everywhere legalizes Slavery! The monstrous absurdity of the argument, is only equalled by the astonishing revolution it seeks to effect in our jurisprudence. It falsifies the most reliable history, abrogates the most solemn Law, belies the dead and stultifies the living, in order to make what has heretofore been a local evil, hereafter a National institution!

Horace Greeley: "A Southern Sophism"

Horace Greeley gave no title to this editorial, but in it he attacked slavery as the fallacy of the Southern way of life that was now made legal for all of the United States. Since the nation's highest court had ruled that slavery was part of the Constitution, nothing was left to stop the reintroduction of the slave trade to New York City and elsewhere.

Tribune **(New York), 11 March 1857**

It is impossible to exaggerate the importance of the recent decision of the Supreme Court. The grounds and methods of that decision we have exposed elsewhere; and we now turn from them to contemplate the great fact which it establishes—the fact that *Slavery is National;* and that, until that remote period when different Judges, sitting in this same Court, shall reverse this wicked and false judgment, the Constitution of the United States is nothing better than the bulwark of inhumanity and oppression.

It is most true that this decision is bad law; that it is based on false historical premises and wrong interpretations of the Constitution; that it does not at all represent the legal or judicial opinion of the Nation; that it is merely a Southern sophism clothed with the dignity of our highest Court. Nevertheless there it is; the final action of the National Judiciary, established by the founders of the Republic to interpret the Constitution, and to embody the ultimate legal conclusions of the whole people—an action proclaiming that in the view of the Constitution *slaves are property.* The inference is plain. If slaves are recognized as property by the Constitution, of course no local or State law can either prevent property being carried through an individual State or Territory, or forbid its being sold as such wherever its owner may choose to hold it. This is all involved in the present decision; but let a single case draw from the Court an official judgment that slaves can be held and protected under National law, and we shall see men buying slaves for the New York market. There will be no legal power to prevent it. At this moment, indeed, any wealthy New York jobber connected with the Southern trade can put in his next orders: "Send me a negro cook, at the lowest market value! Buy me a waiter! Balance my account with two chambermaids and a truckman!" . . .

We have been accustomed to regard Slavery as a local matter for which we were in no wise responsible. As we have been used, to say, it belonged to the Southern States alone, and they must answer for it before the world. We can say this no more. Now, wherever the stars and stripes wave, they protect Slavery and represent Slavery. The black and cursed stain is thick on our hands also. From Maine to the Pacific, over all future conquests and annexations, wherever in the islands of western seas, or in the South American Continent, or in the Mexican Gulf, the flag of the Union, by just means or unjust, shall be planted, there it plants the curse, and tears, and blood, and unpaid toil of this "institution." The Star of Freedom and the stripes of bondage are henceforth one. American Republicanism and American Slavery are for the future synonymous. This, then, is the final fruit. In this all the labors of our statesmen, the blood of our heroes, the life-long cares and toils of our forefathers, the aspirations of our scholars, the prayers of good men, have finally ended! America the slavebreeder and slaveholder!

An Anonymous Report: "No Citizen, No Crime"

The Dred Scott decision stated that a person of "African descent" was not a citizen of the United States. That statement created a series of interesting court cases similar to this untitled one reported in the abolitionist paper the National Era. *An African American could not break a law that did not apply.*

National Era **(Washington, D.C.), 18 June 1857**

Judge Taney's Dred Scott decision continues to be used by the colored people in a way that the Judge did not probably contemplate. The Bangor Whig says: "David Sands vs. William L. Barronett, action of debt for $20, balance of account. The defendant being of 'African descent,' and 'having no rights which white men are bound to respect,' put in a special plea, that, under the late decision of the U.S. Supreme Court by Judge Taney, he is not a citizen of the United States, and therefore cannot sue in any court, nor be sued. The learned counsellor for the plaintiff, being a hunker of the most hunkerish stripe, immediately upon reading the plea, wilted, and allowed a non-suit. It is maliciously said, in groups where politicians do most congregate, that the counsellor had fears for his political standing, if he dared oppose the decision of Judge Taney, which is universally received by the Democratic press as a part of their party creed. The defendant, 'guilty of a skin not colored like our own,' departed from the awful presence of Judge Pratt with a smiling face and humming snatches of 'The De'il came fiddling through the town.'"

Henry Raymond: "The Dred Scott Decision"

Like many other newspapers that supported the Republican cause, Henry Raymond's New-York Times *lashed out at the Court's decision in* Scott v. Sandford. *In this editorial months after the decision, the* Times *claims the international reputation of the United States is diminished.*

***New-York Times*, 15 July 1857**

When the country was convulsed by the tidings that the Supreme Court, at Washington, in deciding upon the claims of the negro man, named DRED SCOTT, to the possession of his own person, had laid down the doctrine that, under the Constitution of the United States, no person of the African race could be a citizen of this Union, we declined pronouncing upon the merits of the case, for the good and sufficient reason that the news of this extraordinary result could not be accepted as authentic before its verification by the accurate publication of the Decision itself. . . .

Very serious damage to the reputation of the nation, as well as to the cause of good order, was done by these hasty proceedings. It has gone ahead on the wings of the wind over all the world, that the Supreme Court of the United States, in the middle of the nineteenth century, had put an interpretation upon the Constitution of the country, which, if it were to be sustained, would throw our national character back from its place in the vanguard of Christian civilization, to a level with that of Austria or Russia. At home the confidence of the people in the honesty of that branch of the Government, to which the reputation of spotless honesty is as essential as was the fame of virtue to the wife of CÆSAR, has been seriously shaken. . . .

Lloyd H. Brooks: "Resolutions"

The dismay that the Dred Scott decision produced in the United States was felt doubly by its free African American population. Lloyd H. Brooks was a black leader in New Bedford, Massachusetts. He and other African Ameri-

cans met at the Third Christian Church there to protest the decision. Abolitionist printer William Lloyd Garrison reprinted the resolutions in his newspaper, the Liberator. *Brooks uses rhetoric of the American Revolution in his resolutions when he borrows from the writings of Thomas Paine's* The American Crisis, *which first appeared in Dunlap's* Pennsylvania Packet *on 27 December 1776. He also uses Biblical references.*

Liberator (Boston), 9 July 1858

Whereas, For many years all of the Southern, and a majority of the Northern States, have by their legislation increased in acts of hostility and malignity towards the colored people of this country, as evinced by the repeated and continued passage of oppressive, disfranchising and expatriating laws. And

Whereas, The general government of these United States, the object of whose existence is declared to be to protect the weak, and to secure the blessings of liberty to the whole people, have not only from time to time sanctioned these flagitious outrages, but has itself become the patron of all these, and the perpetrators of the most highhanded injustice ever inflicted upon an unoffending and unprotected people. And . . .

Whereas, The colored people of this country have ever proved themselves worthy of the confidence and respect of their countrymen, by their daring bravery in behalf of the country at the times of her greatest peril, "that tried men's souls," and their loyalty to its interests and general welfare, in the time of peace as well as war, in all the aspects of life. Therefore,

Resolved, That the infamous "Dred Scott" decision is palpably vain, arrogant assumption, unsustained by history, justice, reason or common sense, and merits the execration of the world as a consummate villainy. . . .

Resolved, That we neither recognize nor respect any laws for slavery, whether from Moses, Paul, or Taney. We spurn and trample them all under our feet as in violation of the laws of God and the rights of men.

Resolved, That slavery does not exist as a right, and has no guarantee but in usurpation, might and brute force, the many and strong oppressing the few and weak; and were we equal in numbers, no attempt would be made to enslave us, nor deny us the respect due to our manhood. . . .

Resolved, That we will endeavor to use all honorable means to induce that interchange of harmonious action which is so indispensable to the promotion and establishment of our national rights as natives of the United States of America.

Resolved, That as no attempt for human freedom was ever successful unless perfect union existed in the ranks of the oppressed, we consider it a paramount duty for all *lovers of liberty* to join in waging a war of annihilation against every vestige of oppression under which we are now suffering. . . .

Questions

1. What were the principal reasons used by those who supported the Dred Scott decision to assume that the Court ruled correctly?
2. What were the principal reasons used by those who disagreed with the Dred Scot decision to say that the Court ruled incorrectly?
3. What else besides the case comes into play in the arguments on both sides of this issue?

Notes

1. For treatment of the Dred Scott case, see Don E. Fehrenbacher, *Slavery, Law, and Politics: The Dred Scott Case in Historical Perspective* (New York: Oxford University Press, 1981); Walter Ehrlich, *They Have No Rights: Dred Scott's Struggle for Freedom* (Westport, Conn.: Greenwood Press, 1979); Don E. Fehrenbacher, *The Dred Scott Case, Its Significance in American Law and Politics* (New York: Oxford University Press, 1978); Stanley I. Kutler, ed., *The Dred Scott Decision: Law or Politics?* (Boston: Houghton Mifflin, 1967).

2. *Dred Scott v. John F.A. Sandford,* 19 Howard, 393 (1857).

3. Ibid.

4. Quoted in C. Peter Ripley, ed., *The Black Abolitionist Papers,* 5 vols. (Chapel Hill: University of North Carolina Press, 1991), 4:391.

5. *Enquirer* (Richmond, Va.), 13 March 1857.

CHAPTER 28

The Lincoln–Douglas Debates, 1858

In the summer of 1858, two senatorial hopefuls hit the campaign trail in Illinois. In the midst of their regular campaign stops, the two agreed to a series of seven debates in various parts of the state. The incumbent, Stephen A. Douglas, returned to Washington, but his challenger, Abraham Lincoln, gained national exposure and added support from the new and growing Republican party. In 1860, that party would nominate Lincoln to run for president, and he would win.

The Lincoln–Douglas debates[1] followed a series of powerful speeches by Douglas and Lincoln, made as the two prepared to begin their campaigns. Lincoln, however, veered from the normal and invited Douglas to join him in a series of campaign appearances to be held throughout Illinois. "Will it be agreeable to you," Lincoln wrote in July, "to make an arrangement for you and myself to divide time, and address the same audiences during the present canvass?"[2] Douglas consented, but he told Lincoln they would only be able to share the stage at certain times since he and the Democratic party had already set dates for party rallies with other candidates. Lincoln agreed.

The major issue surrounding the two candidates was slavery. The Kansas–Nebraska Act, which Douglas successfully steered through Congress (see Chapter 25) and the Dred Scott decision (see Chapter 27) were two of the prime issues both candidates addressed as they discussed their views on slavery. The rights of black Americans played a crucial role, too, with Douglas consistently maintaining that the white race was superior to all others and that the Constitution and the Declaration of Independence applied only to whites. Lincoln never came out and said that black and white were equal racially, but he did say that the words "All men are created equal" had to apply comparatively.

The elections of the time differed from today. In 1858, states chose legislators who, in turn, selected the state's United States senators. The candidates who supported Lincoln polled the most votes statewide; they did not

HON. STEPHEN A. DOUGLAS, UNITED STATES SENATOR FROM ILLINOIS.—[PHOTOGRAPHED BY WHITEHURST, WASHINGTON, D. C.]

The Little Giant. *Stephen A. Douglas of Illinois played a vital role in the activities of the nation. He guided the Kansas–Nebraska Act through Congress in 1854 to help establish the national policy of popular sovereignty. He debated with Abraham Lincoln as the two vied for an Illinois Senate seat in 1858. Known as "the Little Giant" because of his small size but great oratory ability, Douglas won his contest against Lincoln, but Lincoln went on to be elected president in 1860. This image of Douglas and a story about him appeared in the December 26, 1857, issue of* Harper's Weekly.

win enough elections to win a majority of representatives. As a result, Douglas was re-elected. Though Douglas won the battle, that is, the Senate seat, Lincoln won the war, and one can see that his understandings of the issues would ultimately become law in the United States.

The readings in this chapter include those from Lincoln and Douglas that outline their political platforms. These are the speeches that spurred the debate. The speeches allow readers to see the differences that divided the candidates and the nation concerning slavery. Each section also includes a report that attacks the opposition. The "Support for Lincoln" section includes an attack on Douglas; the "Support for Douglas" section contains an assault on Lincoln.

Support for Lincoln

Abraham Lincoln: "Speech of Hon. Abraham Lincoln"

On June 16, Lincoln opened his candidacy for Illinois senator with what has come to be known as the "House Divided" speech. The state Republican convention nominated Lincoln to run against Douglas, the state's incumbent senator, and the following is Lincoln's acceptance speech. He attacks the Kansas–Nebraska Act, which Douglas guided to passage and Lincoln believed opened all free territory to slavery, along with the 1857 Dred Scott decision.

Illinois State Journal **(Springfield), 18 June 1858**

If we could first know where we are, and *whither* we are tending, we could better judge *what* to do, and *how* to do it.

We are now far into the *fifth* year since a policy was initiated with the *avowed* object and *confident* promise of putting an end to slavery agitation.

Under the operation of that policy, that agitation has not only *not ceased,* but has *constantly augmented.*

In *my* opinion, it will not cease until a *crisis* shall have been reached and passed.

"A house divided against itself cannot stand."

I believe this government cannot endure permanently half *slave* and half *free.*

I do not expect the Union to be *dissolved*; I do not expect the house to *fall*–but I *do* expect it will cease to be divided.

It will become *all* one thing, or all the other.

Either the *opponents* of slavery will arrest the further spread of it, and place it where the public mind shall rest in the belief that it is in the course of ultimate extinction, or its *advocates* will push it forward till it shall become alike lawful in all the States, old as well as *new—North* as well as *South.*

Have we no *tendency* to the latter condition?

Let any one who doubts, carefully contemplate that now almost complete legal combination—piece of *machinery,* so to speak—compounded of the Nebraska doctrine and the Dred Scott decision. Let him consider, not only *what work* the machinery is adapted to do, and *how well* adapted, but also let him study the *history* of its construction, and trace, if he can, or rather *fail,* if he can, to trace the evidences of design, and concert of action, among its chief architects, from the beginning.

The new year of 1854 found slavery excluded from more than half the States by State Constitutions, and from most of the National territory by Congressional prohibition.

Four days later, commenced the struggle which ended in repealing that Congressional prohibition. This opened all the National territory to slavery. . . .

While the Nebraska bill was passing through Congress, a *law case* involving the question of a negroe's freedom, by reason of his owner having voluntarily taken him first into a free State and then into a Territory covered by the Congressional prohibition, and held him as a slave for a long time in each, was passing through the United States Circuit Court. . . . The negroe's name was "Dred Scott," which name now designates the decision finally made in the case. . . .

The reputed author of the Nebraska bill finds an early occasion to make a speech at this capital indorsing the Dred Scott decision [see Chapter 27], and vehemently denouncing all opposition to it. . . .

Such a decision is all that slavery now lacks of being alike lawful in all the States.

Welcome, or unwelcome, such a decision is probably coming, and will soon be upon us, unless the power of the present political dynasty shall be met and overthrown.

We shall *lie down* pleasantly dreaming that the people of *Missouri* are on the verge of making their State *free,* and we shall *awake* to the *reality* instead that the *Supreme* Court has made Illinois a *Slave* State.

To meet and overthrow the power of that dynasty, is the work now before all those who would prevent that consummation. That is what we have to do. How can we best do it? . . .

Senator Douglas holds, we know, that a man may rightfully be *wiser today* than he was *yesterday*—that he may rightfully change when he finds himself wrong.

But can we, for that reason, run ahead, and *infer* that he *will* make any particular change, of which he himself has given no intimation? Can we *safely* base *our* action upon any such vague inference?

Now, as ever, I wish not to misrepresent Judge Douglas's position, question his *motives,* or do aught that can be personally offensive to him.

Whenever, *if ever,* he and we can come together on *principle* so that *our great cause* may have assistance from his great ability, I hope to have interposed no adventitious obstacle. . . .

Our cause, then, must be intrusted to, and conducted by, its own undoubted friends—those whose hands are free, whose hearts are in the work, who do care for the result. . . .

The result is not doubtful. We shall not fail; if we stand firm, we shall not fail.

Wise councils may *accelerate,* or *mistakes* delay it, but sooner or later, the victory is *sure* to come.

Abraham Lincoln: "Reply to Senator Douglas"

Lincoln wasted no time in replying to Douglas's speech upon returning to Illinois. He spoke the next night—July 10—in Chicago. He repeated some points from his June 9 speech and then rebutted Douglas's remarks.

Daily Democrat (Chicago), 13 July 1858

My Fellow-Citizens:—On yesterday evening, upon the occasion of the reception given to Senator Douglas, I was furnished with a seat very convenient for hearing him, and was otherwise very courteously treated by him and his friends, and for which I thank him and them. During the course of his remarks my name was mentioned in such a way as, I suppose, renders it at least not improper that I should make some sort of reply to him. I shall not attempt to follow him in the precise order in which he addressed the assembled multitude upon that occasion, though I shall perhaps do so in the main. . . .

Popular sovereignty! everlasting popular sovereignty! Let us for a moment inquire into this vast matter of popular sovereignty. What is popular sovereignty? We recollect that at an early period in the history of this struggle there was another name for the same thing—"Squatter Sovereignty." . . .

To-day it has been decided—no more than a year ago it was decided by the Supreme Court of the United States, and is insisted upon to-day—that the people of a Territory have no right to exclude slavery from a Territory; that if any one man chooses to take slaves into a Territory, all the rest of the people have no right to keep them out. This being so, and this decision being made one of the points that the Judge approved, and one in the approval of which he says he means to keep me down—put me down I should not say, for I have never been up. He says he is in favor of it, and sticks to it, and expects to win his battle on that decision, which says that there is no such thing as Squatter Sovereignty, but that any one man may take slaves into a Territory, and all the other men in the Territory may be opposed to it, and yet by reason of the Constitution they cannot prohibit it. When that is so, how much is left of this vast matter of Squatter Sovereignty I should like to know? . . .

Judge Douglas made two points upon my recent speech at Springfield. He says they are to be the issues of this campaign. The first one . . .I believe I can quote correctly from memory. I said there that "we are now far into the fifth year since a policy was instituted for the avowed object, and with the confident promise, of putting an end to slavery agitation; under the operation of that policy, that agitation had not only not ceased, but had constantly augmented. I believe it will not cease until a crisis shall have been reached and passed. 'A house divided against itself cannot stand.' I believe this Government cannot endure permanently, half slave and half free. I do not expect the Union to be dissolved"—I am quoting from my speech—"I do not expect the house to fall, but I do expect it will cease to be divided. It will become all one thing or the other. Either the opponents of slavery will arrest the spread of it and place it where the public mind shall rest, in the belief that it is in the course of ultimate extinction, or its advocates will push it forward until it shall become alike lawful in all the States, North as well as South." . . .

I want your attention particularly to what he has inferred from it. He says I am in favor of making all the States of this Union uniform in all their internal regulations; that in all their domestic concerns I am in favor of making them entirely uniform. He draws this inference from the language I have quoted to you. He says that I am in favor of making war by the North upon the South for the extinction of slavery . . .I did not even say that I desired that slavery should be put in course of ultimate extinction. I do say so now, however, so there need be no longer any difficulty about that. It may be written down in the great speech. . . .

I have said a hundred times, and I have now no inclination to take it back, that I believe there is no right, and ought to be no inclination in the people of the free States to enter into the slave States, and interfere with the question of slavery at all. I have said that always; Judge Douglas has heard me say it—if not quite a hundred times, at least as good as a hundred times; and when it is said that I am in favor of interfering with slavery where it exists, I know it is unwarranted by anything I have ever intended, and, as I believe, by anything I have ever said. If, by any means, I have ever used language which could fairly be so construed. . . .

A little now on the other point—the Dred Scott decision. Another of the issues he says that is to be made with me, is upon his devotion to the Dred Scott decision, and my opposition to it. . . .

If I were in Congress, and a vote should come up on a question whether slavery should be prohibited in a new Territory, in spite of the Dred Scott decision, I would vote that it should. . . .

We were often—more than once at least—in the course of Judge Douglas's speech last night, reminded that this government was made for white men; that he believed it was made for white men. Well, that is putting it into a shape in which no one wants to deny it; but the Judge then goes into his passion for drawing inferences that are not warranted. I protest, now and forever, against that counterfeit logic which presumes that because I did not want a negro woman for a slave, I do necessarily want her for a wife. My understanding is that I need not have her for either, but, as, God made us separate, we can leave one another alone, and do one another much good thereby. There are white men enough to marry all the white women, and enough black men to marry all the black women; and in God's name let them be so married. The Judge regales us with the terrible enormities that take place by the mixture of races; that the inferior race bears the superior down. Why, Judge, if we do not let them get together in the Territories they won't mix there. . . .

We have . . . descended by blood from our ancestors . . . those old men say that "We hold these truths to be self-evident, that all men are created equal." . . . That is the electric cord in that Declaration that links the hearts of patriotic and liberty-loving men together, that will link those patriotic hearts as long as the love of freedom exists in the minds of men throughout the world. . . .

An Anonymous Report: "The Pro-Slavery Ringleader"

The partisan nature of the press led to reports that portrayed a paper's candidate in a positive light. At the same time, the candidate's adversary was attacked. Here, the Press and Tribune *assails Douglas the day before the first debate, getting to the heart of the controversy surrounding the 1858 election—slavery.*

Press and Tribune **(Chicago), 20 August 1858**

The Pro-Slavery Ringleader of the North-West has visited us and made a speech, which has cruelly disappointed his friends, and lost him a hundred votes in Mason County, at the very least. A considerable majority of these new-created enemies will vote the Republican ticket this fall. . . . Mr. Douglas can do noting so *certain* to elect Abe Lincoln to the Senate, as to deliver the speech which he gave us today, in every county seat in the State. . . .

A curious and unexpected feature of Douglas' speech to-day is that he spent almost the whole of his time in *defending himself*. . . .

In the "attacking" part of the speech I heard nothing but negro equality and amalgamation—amalgamation and negro equality—with a slight tincture of blackguardism against the Declaration of Independence. These themes he pursued till his audience was wholly nauseated. . . .

When Douglas had finished, there was a dead silence for about two minutes, when a man with a mottled face came forward and proposed three cheers for Stephen A. Douglas. They were responded to by about thirty men near the platform. And so ended one of the rankest humbugs that ever visited the old County of Mason.

Support for Douglas

Stephen Douglas: "Speech of Senator Douglas"

On July 9, Douglas spoke to a large gathering in Chicago. The senator had just returned from Washington and used the occasion to respond to Lincoln's June speech, "A House Divided." Lincoln attended the speech, and Douglas acknowledged this by giving his opponent a special seat. Douglas plainly presented his views on popular sovereignty, and he pointed out the differences between himself and Lincoln. Note Douglas's views of African Americans, Native Americans, Chinese Americans, and any other "nonwhite" group.

Times **(Chicago), 11 July 1858**

I can find no language which can adequately express my profound gratitude for the magnificent welcome which you have extended to me on this occasion. . . .

I regard the great principle of popular sovereignty as having been vindicated and made triumphant in this land as a permanent rule of public policy in the organization of Territories and the admission of new States. Illinois took her position upon this principle many years ago. . . . I saw no reason why the same principle should not be extended to all of the Territories of the United States. . . .

Hence what was my duty, in 1854, when it became necessary to bring forward a bill for the organization of the Territories of Kansas and Nebraska? Was it not my duty, in obedience to the Illinois platform . . . to incorporate in that bill the great principle of self-government, declaring that it was "the true intent and meaning of the Act not to legislate slavery into any

State or Territory, or to exclude it therefrom, but to leave the people thereof perfectly free to form and regulate their domestic institutions in their own way, subject only to the Constitution of the United States?" . . .

I will be entirely frank with you. My object was to secure the right of the people of each State and of each Territory, North or South, to decide the question for themselves, to have slavery or not, just as they chose. . . . I deny the right of Congress to force a slaveholding State upon an unwilling people. I deny their right to force a Free State upon an unwilling people. I deny their right to force a good thing upon a people who are unwilling to receive it. The great principle is the right of every community to judge and decide for itself whether a thing is right or wrong. . . . Whenever you put a limitation upon this right of any people to decide what laws they want, you have destroyed the fundamental principle of self-government. . . .

Mr. Lincoln made a speech before that Republican Convention . . .in which he states the basis upon which he proposes to carry on the campaign during this summer. In it he lays down two distinct propositions which I shall notice, and upon which I shall take a direct and bold issue with him.

His first and main proposition I will give in his own language, scripture quotations and all . . .I give his exact language: "'A house divided against itself cannot stand.' I believe this government cannot endure, permanently, half *slave* and half *free*. I do not expect the Union to be *dissolved*; I do not expect the house to *fall*; but I do expect it to cease to be divided. It will become *all* one thing or *all* the other."

In other words, Mr. Lincoln asserts, as a fundamental principle of this government, that there must be uniformity in the local laws and domestic institutions of each and all the States of the Union; and he therefore invites all the non-slaveholding States to band together, organize as one body, and make war upon slavery in Kentucky, upon slavery in Virginia, upon the Carolinas, upon slavery in all of the slaveholding States in this Union. . . . In other words, Mr. Lincoln advocates boldly and clearly a war of sections, a war of the North against the South, of the Free States against the Slave States,—a war of extermination,—to be continued relentlessly until the one or the other shall be subdued, and all the States shall either become free or become slave.

Now, my friends, I must say to you frankly that I take bold, unqualified issue with him upon that principle. I assert that it is neither desirable nor possible that there should be uniformity in the local institutions and domestic regulations of the different States of this Union. The framers of our government never contemplated uniformity in its internal concerns. The fathers of the Revolution and the sages who made the Constitution well understood that the laws and domestic institutions which would suit the granite hills of New Hampshire would be totally unfit for the rice plantations of South Carolina. . . .

The framers of the Constitution well understood that each locality, having separate and distinct interests, required separate and distinct laws. . . . I therefore conceive that my friend, Mr. Lincoln, has totally misapprehended the great principles upon which our government rests. Uniformity in local and domestic affairs would be destructive of State rights, of State sovereignty, of personal liberty and personal freedom. Uniformity is the parent of despotism the world over, not only in politics, but in religion. Wherever the doctrine of uniformity is proclaimed, that all the States must be free or all slave . . .you have destroyed the greatest safeguard which our institutions have thrown around the rights of the citizen.

How could this uniformity be accomplished, if it was desirable and possible? There is but one mode in which it could be obtained, and that must be by abolishing the State Legislatures, blotting out State sovereignty, merging the rights and sovereignty of the States in one consolidated empire, and vesting Congress with the plenary power to make all the police regulations, domestic and local laws, uniform throughout the limits of the Republic. . . .

From this view of the case, my friends, I am driven irresistibly to the conclusion that diversity, dissimilarity, variety, in all our local and domestic institutions, is the great safeguard of our liberties. . . .

The other proposition discussed by Mr. Lincoln in his speech consists in a crusade against the Supreme Court of the United States on account of the Dred Scott decision. . . .

I am . . .to say that the reason assigned by Mr. Lincoln for resisting the decision of the Supreme Court in the Dred Scott case does not in itself meet my approbation. He objects to it because that decision declared that a negro descended from African parents, who were brought here and sold as slaves, is not, and cannot be, a citizen of the United States. He says it is wrong, because it deprives the negro of the benefits of that clause of the Constitution which says that citizens of one State shall enjoy all the privileges and immunities of citizens of the several States; in other words, he thinks it wrong because it deprives the negro of the privileges, immunities and rights of citizenship, which pertain, according to that decision, only to the white man. I am free to say to you that in my opinion this government of ours is founded on the white basis. It was made by the white man, for the benefit of the white man, to be administered by white men, in such manner as they should determine. It is also true that a negro, an Indian, or any other man of inferior race to a white man, should be permitted to enjoy, and humanity requires that he should have, all the rights, privileges and immunities which he is capable of exercising consistent with the safety of society. I would give him every right and every privilege which his capacity would enable him to enjoy, consistent with the good of the society in which he lived. But you may ask me, what are these rights and these privileges? My answer is, that each

State must decide for itself the nature and extent of these rights. Illinois has decided for herself. We have decided that the negro shall not be a slave, and we have at the same time decided that he shall not vote, or serve on juries, or enjoy political privileges. I am content with that system of policy which we have adopted for ourselves. . . .

I do not acknowledge that the negro must have civil and political rights everywhere or nowhere. I do not acknowledge that the Chinese must have the same rights in California that we would confer upon him here. I do not acknowledge that the cooley imported into this country must necessarily be put upon an equality with the white race. I do not acknowledge any of these doctrines of uniformity in the local and domestic regulations in the different States.

Thus you see, my fellow-citizens, that the issues between Mr. Lincoln and myself, as respective candidates for the United States Senate, as made up, are direct, unequivocal, and irreconcilable. He goes for uniformity in our domestic institutions, for a war of sections, until one or the other shall be subdued. I go for the great principle of the Kansas–Nebraska bill,—the right of the people to decide for themselves. . . .

He objects to the Dred Scott decision because it does not put the negro in the possession of the rights of citizenship on an equality with the white man. I am opposed to negro equality. I repeat that this nation is a white people,—a people composed of European descendants; a people that have established this government for themselves and their posterity,—and I am in favor of preserving not only the purity of the blood, but the purity of the government from any mixture or amalgamation with inferior races. . . .

I am opposed to taking any step that recognizes the negro man or the Indian as the equal of the white man. I am opposed to giving him a voice in the administration of the government. I would extend to the negro and the Indian and to all dependent races every right, every privilege, and every immunity consistent with the safety and welfare of the white races; but equality they never should have, either political or social, or in any other respect whatever.

My friends, you see that the issues are distinctly drawn. I stand by the same platform that I have so often proclaimed to you and to the people of Illinois heretofore. I stand by the Democratic organization, yield obedience to its usages, and support its regular nominations. . . .

An Anonymous Report: "Failing Rapidly"

Though the Times *supported Douglas, it used every chance it got to berate Lincoln. This story covers Lincoln's arrival and visit to Havana and appeared on the day before the first debate.*

Times (Chicago), 20 August 1858

Our little city, which has been in a state of unusual political excitement since the commencement of the Senatorial contest, was in a vortex of excitement yesterday when Senator Douglas, addressed the people, which has not yet entirely subsided, Mr. Lincoln being here today. . . .

As Lincoln was about leaving the boat, the American flag was run up on board, but, as if indignant at being raised in honor of such a man, it displayed itself at mast head Union Jack down, and this little circumstance, together with his forgetting his carpet bag and umbrella, and being obliged to go back for them seemed to affect Lincoln so much that it was with difficulty that the committee could convey him ashore over the plank, which in fact they did not succeed in doing until a gentleman relieved him of his umbrella, which he manifested a determination to carry between his legs, and which it was with the greatest difficulty he could be extricated from. . . .

Lincoln is failing rapidly, but he has lost none of his awkwardness. He is all legs and arms, and his constant efforts to hide the extreme length of these members by keeping them twisted up when not in use, makes his movements very kinky and uncertain. His gestures when speaking, are positively painful, and while listening to him we are constantly uncomfortable, because you cannot divest yourself of the idea that he is suffering from an attack brought on by an imprudent indulgence in unripe fruit. . . . He confessed that the negro was the subject of his thoughts by day, and that the Declaration of Independence having declared their equality, he was at a loss to know what to do with them, that they might exercise it. He admitted that they were not physically equal to the white race, but thought they were equal under the law. . . .

Did you ever see a sick dog, with his tail between his legs, and looking as mournful as if he had no friends to mourn for him after his death, and was obliged to act a part of the funeral ceremony himself before giving up life, well that is just the appearance of Abe Lincoln. . . .

Questions

1. What exactly is popular sovereignty, and what was Lincoln's opinion of it? Elaborate.
2. What was Douglas's opinion of African Americans in relation to whites? What statements did he make to support his views? Do you think most white Americans agreed with Douglas in the 1850s? Why, or why not?
3. What did the writer for the *Times* attack most about Lincoln? Why do you think he did this?

Notes

1. Numerous sources are available that discuss Lincoln, Douglas, and the debates. For full coverage of the debates, see Paul M. Angle, ed., *Created Equal? The Complete Lincoln–Douglas Debates of 1858* (Chicago: University of Chicago Press, 1958). Other sources include Saul Sigelschiffer, *The American Conscience: The Drama of the Lincoln–Douglas Debates* (New York: Horizon Press, 1973); Harry V. Jaffa, *Crisis of the House Divided: An Interpretation of the Issues in the Lincoln–Douglas Debates* (Garden City, N.Y.: Doubleday, 1959); Robert W. Johannsen, *Stephen A. Douglas* (New York: Oxford University Press,1973); Don E. Fehrenbacher, *Prelude to Greatness: Lincoln in the 1850's* (Stanford, Calif.: Stanford University Press, 1962); William H. Herndon and Jesse W. Wirk, *Abraham Lincoln: The True Story of a Great Life* (New York: D. Appleton, 1892); and H.M. Flint, *Life of Stephen A. Douglas* (Philadelphia: John E. Potter, 1863).

2. Quoted in Angle, *Created Equal? The Complete Lincoln–Douglas Debates,* 83.

CHAPTER 29

John Brown's Raid, 1859

On December 3, 1859, the *New-York Times* noted that Lewis Tappan, the famous abolitionist, called the execution of John Brown the death of "a Christian martyr at the hands of an infuriated mob." Nearly five hundred miles away in Cincinnati, Ohio, an editor called Brown "a murderer of innocent persons" who "attempted one of the greatest crimes against society."[1] That is how America reacted to Virginia's hanging of the man many referred to as "Old Brown of Osawatomie," or "madman," depending upon their perceptions of what Brown and his followers had done at Harper's Ferry, Virginia, or in Kansas a few years earlier.

By 1859, the Connecticut-born Brown had made a name for himself as a slavery fighter in the Kansas territory, though he had failed at being a farmer, cattleman, land speculator, and at nearly all other occupations he tried. Early in the 1850s, pro- and antislavery forces drew a line in the Kansas dirt. Whether the territory would eventually enter the Union as a free or slave state became a cause for both sides. In 1854, Congress passed the Kansas–Nebraska Act (see Chapter 25). The Act divided the Nebraska territory into two parts, Kansas and Nebraska, and accepted popular sovereignty as the basis for establishing government. This meant that the residents of the territories would decide on whether the territory would allow or ban slavery. Immediately both factions established governments, and just as quickly both sides began to use intimidation and violence as political tools. By the end of 1856, nearly 200 people had been killed and about $2 million in property destroyed in what the nation referred to as "bleeding Kansas."[2]

John Brown moved to Kansas in 1855, along with his sons, all of whom immediately took up the free-state cause. Brown cemented his reputation as a fighter against slavery in 1856. Retaliating against the burning of the antislavery capital Lawrence, Brown led four of his sons and some other men on a raid of a proslavery settlement of Pottawatomie. There, Brown murdered a father and two of his sons along with two other men. Four months later,

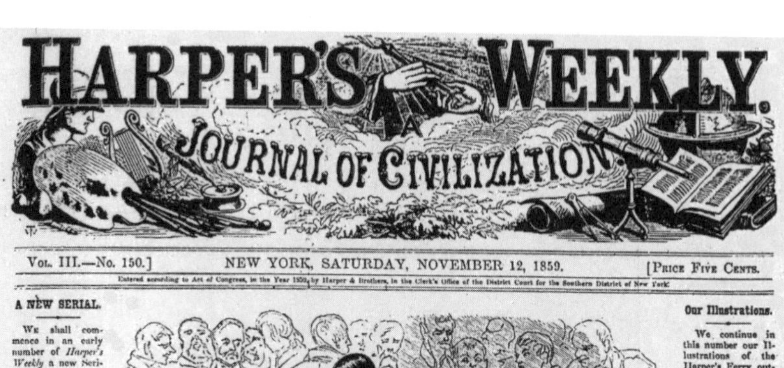

Vol. III.—No. 150.] NEW YORK, SATURDAY, NOVEMBER 12, 1859. [Price Five Cents.

Entered according to Act of Congress, in the Year 1859, by Harper & Brothers, in the Clerk's Office of the District Court for the Southern District of New York.

A NEW SERIAL.

We shall commence in an early number of *Harper's Weekly* a new Serial Tale by Wilkie Collins, Esq., of which we have purchased the advance proof-sheets from the author. This Tale will be continued through the *Weekly* till it is completed.

In reply to several inquiries, we beg to say that Mr. Dickens's new Serial, "A Tale of Two Cities," was commenced in *Harper's Weekly* on May 7, and Mr. Curtis's delicious Story of American Society, entitled "Trumps," on April 9. We can send back numbers from those dates, or from the beginning of the year, to any person who remits the money.

We print from 80,000 to 93,000 copies per week.

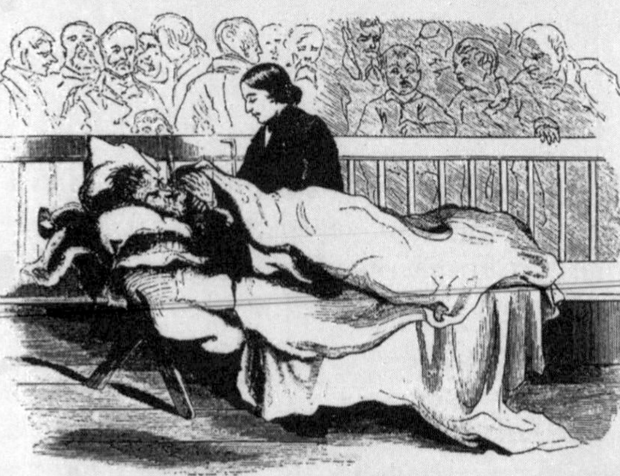

THE PRISONER BROWN AND HIS BOSTON COUNSEL, MR. HOYT.—Drawn by Porte Crayon.—[See Page 729.]

Our Illustrations.

We continue in this number our Illustrations of the Harper's Ferry outbreak, drawn by our special artist, Porte Crayon. We have now published the following Illustrations of this memorable event:

1. Harper's Ferry.
2. Another view of the same, showing the Armory, etc., etc.
3. The attack on the Engine-house by the U. S. Marines.
4. The Guard-room, with the wounded prisoners.
5. Brown, wounded and a prisoner, during his examination by Governor Wise.
6. Body of Brown's son.
7. The trial of Brown at Charlestown.
8. The arraignment.
9. Brown and his counsel, Mr. Hoyt.
10. Portrait of Colonel Washington.
11. Brown's arms—swivel gun and pike.
12. The school-house in the mountain, used by Brown as an arsenal.

THE ARRAIGNMENT.—Drawn by Porte Crayon.—[See Page 729.]

The trial of John Brown. *The amount of coverage that John Brown's raid on Harper's Ferry and the subsequent trial received was as great as for any other event in the antebellum period.* Harper's Weekly *ran a multipage spread about the trial, including numerous illustrations. On this page, one sees Brown on a cot and accompanied by his lawyer. Below it is an image of Brown's co-conspirators at their arraignment.*

Brown defended the antislavery town of Osawatomie; people throughout America now knew of John Brown.[3] Brown spent the next three years traveling through the North, raising money for his cause. In 1858, he told Frederick Douglass, America's leading African American and a newspaper printer, about his plans to lead a raid and rebellion against a slaveholding state.[4] Soon he revealed his plan to his major investors in the North, and that raid on Harper's Ferry would make Brown's name one known to generations of Americans.

On the night of October 16, 1859, Brown left Maryland with nineteen accomplices, crossed over into Virginia, and captured the arsenal. He cut the telegraph lines on his way into town, which kept news of his activities out but surely drew some attention, too. Brown believed that the slaves in the area would join him in revolt, but that never happened. Instead, militia surrounded the magazine house. Late on the evening of October 17, the United States Cavalry, led by Robert E. Lee, joined the militiamen. The next day, after offering Brown and his men the chance to surrender, the troops attacked. Ten of Brown's men died, and he was wounded and taken into custody.

Though still not recovered from his wounds, the Commonwealth of Virginia quickly put Brown on trial for treason. The one-week-long trial ended in a guilty verdict and a sentence of death by hanging. At his sentencing, Brown explained that he had led the raid on Harper's Ferry for the same reasons he had done other things—for the benefit of those held in bondage. He said,

> I believe that I interfered as I have done, as I have always freely admitted I have done, in behalf of His despised poor, is no wrong, but right. Now, if it is deemed necessary that I should forfeit my life for the furtherance of the ends of justice, and mingle my blood further with the blood of my children and with the blood of millions in this slave country whose rights are disregarded by wicked, cruel, and unjust enactments, I say, let it be done.[5]

Bells in Northern churches tolled for Brown after his death. In the South, many had believed before Harper's Ferry that remaining in the Union was necessary for the region to prosper. Now the North seemed to be more of a threat and enemy than a different region of the same country. Southerners quickly came to believe that Brown's raid was financed by a large number of Northerners, who, the Richmond *Enquirer* charged, "have aided and abetted this treasonable invasion of a Southern state." And South Carolina Governor William H. Gist declared that the South must "now unite for her defense."[6] For more than forty years—and really since the forming of the United States under the Constitution—Americans had bickered over the practice of slavery. The pace of events had quickened in the 1850s. In November 1860, the nation elected a new president, Abraham Lincoln—the candidate of the "black Republicans"—as many in the South called Lincoln's party. Six weeks later, South Carolina—which had been threatening to do so for more than thirty years—seceded from the Union. It would be only a matter of time before that for which the antebellum period was named—war—would divide the nation. John Brown would have approved.

This chapter looks at press reaction to Brown's raid and Virginia's response to it. The readings begin with those supporting Brown. The first comes from the Pittsburgh *Gazette,* which disapproved of Brown's violence. It this editorial, David N. White says that such is to be expected, however, whenever people are willing to act on the conviction that slavery is wrong and must be abolished. The next, from Boston abolitionist Wendell Phillips, praises Brown for his Puritan approach to slavery—putting belief into action. He also compares Brown's death—in terms of what the nation has lost—to that of George Washington. The next, by William Lloyd Garrison, says that "John Brown was right."

Readings attacking Brown begin with an editorial by Robert Barnwell Rhett of the Charleston *Mercury.* A longtime advocate of Southern rights, Rhett saw the Harper's Ferry raid as a direct attack on the Southern way of life, not just slavery. The next, by John G. Polhill of the *Federal Union* of Milledgeville, Georgia, assails Brown's raid as an attack on the Union. Polhill and Rhett take opposing views here. Polhill believes that the Union will remain intact, while Rhett advocates immediate disunion. John Syme of North Carolina, in the next report, says that Brown's raid will be the watermark to determine American unity. He also boldly claims that no Northern troops could ever hold any Southern territory in the event of war. The next report, from Savannah, Georgia, shows how volatile the times were, as a Savannah man is tarred and feathered for reading accounts of Brown's trial to slaves. The next reading comes from Cincinnati, Ohio, where the *Enquirer*'s editor rejoices at Brown's lynching. The last writing, from the *New-York Times,* says Brown's raid marks the end of the Union.

Support for Brown

David N. White: "Daring to Act on Conviction"

In this untitled editorial, the editor of the Pittsburgh Gazette *sees the actions of John Brown as a necessity. Though White believes Brown to have been insane, he nonetheless thinks selfless acts such as Brown's are what will be needed to end slavery.*

***Gazette* (Pittsburgh), 3 December 1859**

The immolation of John Brown was, in short, in accordance with the philosophy of slavery—*a necessity.* He had dared to act on the conviction of his life, and these settled principles of his were the only ones which such a man could entertain. He was too brave to have thought differently from what he did, and the same noble impulses which inculcated a love of Freedom and Right, impelled him constantly and irresistibly to the practical development of his theory. He has failed, according to the popular mode of calculating failure and success; but that his life and tragic death must of necessity constitute a failure, is a point too broad and high to be disposed of in this summary manner. We cannot but disapprove his mad and folly-stricken act, but the unselfishness of the deed; his moderation, when victorious, over the town which he captured; his spartan courage in defending himself and his fellows, and his sublime contempt of death while overborne and made the manacled tenant of a prison; his stern integrity in scorning the technicalities of the law, and his manliness *in all things*, will not be quickly forgotten; but rather a contemplation of this heroic old man's character will irresistibly compel thinking men to ask themselves whether it is John Brown, of Ossawatomie, or the system of slavery which has failed in this conflict.

The execution of the old man at Charlestown yesterday, was a plain admission on the part of Slavery that they dare not spare a brave man's life, and that magnanimity is impossible to a system based on wrong and upheld by violence. History will do justice to the institution of Slavery and its uncompromising foe alike, when both are gone; and, in the meantime, the comparison which this affair provokes between the two, which none can clearly foresee, but enough of which is now plainly visible to change the popular judgment. Slavery in all the plenitude of its triumph and power is a failure; and old John Brown of Ossawatomie has succeeded—Sampson-like—in dragging down the pillars of Slavery in his fall, and his victory is complete! While millions of prayers went up for the old martyr yesterday, so millions of curses were uttered against the hellish system which so mercilessly and ferociously cried out for his blood. Every heart in which a free spirit throbbed gave utterance to its pent-up agony in contemplating the enormities of this bloody institution—this sum of all villainies—in the dispensations of its power and the exactions of its bloody code.

Wendell Phillips: "The Puritan Principle and John Brown"

Boston's Wendell Phillips had been fighting against slavery since the 1830s. He had long been a supporter of Garrison's Liberator *and contributed articles to it regularly. He also often spoke at public gatherings on the evils of slavery and attacked the Constitution because it protected slavery. In this editorial, Phillips praises Brown for putting rhetoric into action.*

The last paragraph is by Garrison, who tells readers that the Liberator *has received hundreds of letters in support of Brown.*

Liberator (Boston), 23 December 1859

What has John Brown done for us? The world doubted, over the horrid word "insurrection," whether the victim had a right to arrest the course of his master, and even at any expense of blood, to vindicate his rights; and Brown said to his neighbors in the old school-house at North Elba, sitting among the snow,—where nothing grows but men—wheat freezes—"I can go South and show the world that he has a right to rise, and can rise." He went, girded about by his household, carrying his sons with him. Proof of a life devoted to an idea! Not a single, spasmodic act of greatness, coming out with no back-ground, but the flowering of sixty years. The proof of it, that every thing around him grouped itself harmoniously, like the planets around the central sun. He went down to Virginia, took possession of a town, and held it. He says—"You thought this was strength; I demonstrate it is weakness. You thought this was civil society; I show you it is a den of pirates." Then he turned around in his sublimity, with his Puritan devotional heart, and said to the millions, "Learn!" And God lifted a million hearts to his gibbet, as the Roman cross lifted a million hearts to it, in that divine sacrifice of two thousand years ago. To-day, more than a statesman could have taught in seventy years, one act of a week has taught these eighteen millions of people. That is the Puritan principle. . . .

It is utterly impossible for us to chronicle in our columns a hundredth part of what is transpiring on the all-exciting question of slavery in the country. To do this, we need to publish a daily *Liberator*, of twice its present size. We have on hand the proceedings of scores of commemorative meetings held in different parts of the country on the day of the execution of John Brown, all of which we should be glad to publish if it were practicable. No such popular demonstration of sympathy and exalted appreciation has been witnessed at the North since the death of George Washington. Well may the South tremble! . . .

William Lloyd Garrison: "John Brown Was Right"

Not all of those who opposed slavery felt the way William Lloyd Garrison did. In this piece, the Liberator*'s editor of thirty years said Brown was right in what he did at Harper's Ferry, just as those before him who stood up to tyranny were right in the violent actions to which they were forced. This editorial dealt in part with gubernatorial elections in Massachusetts. Garrison supported John A. Andrew, who had financed, in a small way,*

Brown's trip to Harper's Ferry. Garrison attacked another Boston paper for supporting anyone who might disagree with what Brown did or who might support slavery in the South.

***Liberator* (Boston), 7 September 1860**

John Brown was right, because he faithfully 'remembered those in bonds as bound with them,' and did for them what he would have had them do for him in like circumstances.

John Brown was right, because he abhorred the practice of reducing to chains and slavery those whom God created 'but a little lower than the angels.'

John Brown was right, because he denied the validity of unrighteous and tyrannical enactments, and maintained the supremacy and binding obligation of the 'Higher Law.'

John Brown was right in all that he did–in his spirit and object, in his measures and warlike instruments, in taking the Arsenal and capturing Col. Washington, in killing 'Mr. Beckham, the Mayor, and Mr. Boerly, the grocer'–if Washington and Hancock and Warren were right–if Putnam, and Prescott, and the soldiers under them, on Bunker Hill, were right–if the Revolutionary struggle was right–if Wallace, and Tell, and Wrinkel-reid, and Leonidas were right, in resisting tyranny unto blood! Only John Brown was before them all, and nobler than any of them, inasmuch as he gave his life to free others of a different race from a horrible bondage, with a spirit more than patriotic, because deeply religious and profoundly reverent toward God.

The Courier is politically foolish and morally demented in supposing that any party capital is to be made in the old Bay State, or out of it, in stabbing the memory and insulting the grave of John Brown, whom Christendom has already apotheosised as one of the bravest and noblest of those who have fallen martyrs to a great idea. It may rant and rave, give its sympathies to the traffickers in human flesh, and advocate the right to hunt slaves on Massachusetts soil, but it cannot stop the march of Freedom.

OPPOSITION TO BROWN

Robert Barnwell Rhett: "The Plan of Insurrection"

Robert Barnwell Rhett may have been the most outspoken of all Southern editors on the cause of the South. His paper, the Mercury, *had been the champion of South Carolina versus the nation since the tariff issues of the 1820s. In this editorial, Rhett tells readers of a conspiracy to begin slave insurrections in the South, John Brown's raid being the first of a series of attempts. And, just as the* Mercury *had done during the nullification crisis (see Chapter 10), its editor suggested a separation from the United States.*

Mercury (Charleston), 1 November 1859

Although BROWN'S effort at an insurrection has been silly and abortive, the developments are rapidly showing that a wide-spread scheme was maturing at the North for insurrections throughout the South. A carefully concocted plan is published in the New York *Herald*, republished in the Richmond *Whig*, and incorporated into the address of the Democratic Committee of the City of New York in an address to the people of New York, by which slavery was to be overthrown in the South with the aid of military force from the North. We forbear laying this scheme before our readers on account of its incendiary nature, but we advise our readers to get it and read it for themselves. It will give them a clearer insight into the true relations they occupy in the Union, and the "priceless value" of its continuance to them, than any other document which has yet seen the light. It is no answer to say that the diabolical incendiaries who can in cold blood get up such a scheme for our destruction, are comparatively few in numbers in the North. It is enough for us to know that, few or many, they have, by the Constitution of the United States, the right to come among us—to live among us—and in their good time carry out their purposes; and even if their purposes should fail again and again, and scaffold after scaffold shall drip with their gore, the elements of mischief and trouble may survive them, and give new impulse to future adventurers and fanatics. The great source of the evil is, that we are under one government with these people—that by the constitution they deem themselves responsible for the institution of slavery, and, therefore, they seek to overthrow it. They do not plot insurrections for Cuba or Brazil. If we had a separate government of our own, the post office, all the avenues of intercourse, the police and military of the country, would be under our executive control. Abolitionism would die out at the North, or its adherents would have to operate in the South as foreign emissaries, in a country armed and prepared to exclude their intercourse or arrest their designs, and punish their intervention. As it is, the "irrepressible conflict" of SEWARD is destined to go on, although it may be checked and suppressed by repeated failures, until one of two things shall take place—the Union shall be dissolved, or slavery shall be abolished. The experience of the last twenty-five years, of ignominious toleration and concession by the South, with the lights of the present reflected on them, show to the most bigoted Unionist that there is no peace for the South in the Union, from the forbearance or respect of the North. The South must control her own destinies or perish.

John G. Polhill: "The Abolition Insurrection at Harper's Ferry"

For the nearly thirty years of its existence, the Federal Union *in Milledgeville—Georgia's capital—supported the belief that Georgia and other Southern states were better off as part of the Union. Here, Polhill says that Brown's raid was an obvious attempt to overthrow the federal government. He says abolitionists encouraged the "fanatics" to act, but he also says that it will take more than this to overthrow government.*

Federal Union **(Milledgeville), 1 November 1859**

In our columns this week will be found further particulars concerning the insurrection at Harper's Ferry. There can no longer be any doubt but what this was a regularly concocted, and premeditated attempt of Abolition Fanatics to overthrow the Government, and emancipate the slaves. The form of a provisional government has been found among the papers of the prisoners, and the officers of the new Government are there named. Without such positive proof, it would be difficult to believe that such fools could be found running at large in the United States. To think that about twenty men should deliberately attempt to overthrow the Government, and commence their operations in a thickly settled portion of the country, surrounded by the chivalry of Virginia and Maryland, shows a degree of ignorance and infatuation among these fanatics never before dreamed of. If they have received direct encouragement, and have been promised assistance from any of the leaders of the Black Republican Party, it is to be hoped all these facts will come to the light. We know they have received indirect encouragement from William H. Seward, Joshua Giddings, Horace Greeley, and other Republican leaders, who, by their speeches and writings, have encouraged fanatics to such deeds as this.

Perhaps the sudden and dreadful retribution that has overtaken their fanatical followers will cause these arch traitors to pause in their career. Upon their heads rests the direful responsibility of the blood that has been shed at Harper's Ferry. Will not honest and conscientious men at the north now see the necessity of putting down a party whose principles, if carried out, can lead only to civil war, murder, and rapine? The discovery and sudden overthrow of the conspiracy before it could produce much damage, shows that our country is still under the guardianship of Divine Providence. No weapon forged against our Government, whether by enemies without or traitors within has ever prospered, and we believe they never will prosper so long as the great mass of the people shall be worthy of liberty; or capable of self-government.

John Syme: "Execution of the Four Conspirators"

John Syme bought the Register *in 1856 and turned it away from the more moderate stance of editor Seaton Gales. Syme predicted that the way in which the nation reacted to the Harper's Ferry raid would determine whether the Union could continue. He also boldly announced that no Northern troops could ever hold a piece of the South for more than forty-eight hours.*

Register (Raleigh), 21 November 1859

We give to-day a full account of the scenes at Charlestown on the 15th and 16th insts. The other two conspirators will in all probability pay the penalty of their crimes on the gallows, and then the curtain will fall upon the tragedy of Harper's Ferry, unless the investigation under Mr. Mason's resolution fastens complicity in the foray on persons at the North and West and brings them to trial.

The affair at Harper's Ferry marks a new and most important era in our country's history. It will bring to an immediate solution the question as to whether the Union can be preserved, and the right of the South to hold property in slaves be maintained. This is the issue to be tried now. The trial can no longer be deferred. The issue has been forced upon the South, and let the result be what it may, her skirts will be clear of all responsibility.

There has been one gratifying fact developed by the Harper's Ferry raid. The promptness and ease with which large numbers of troops were brought together from different quarters of Virginia, and the alacrity with which the call to arms was obeyed, will prove to the Abolitionists at the North that although they make an occasional foray into a Southern State, and commit a few murders and arsons, they can never maintain a foothold on Southern soil for more than forty-eight hours. Virginia has showed conspicuously that she was able to take care of herself. Had she not been, had she stood in need of aid from her sister States of the South, she would have received it to an amount more than equal to her necessities, as the prompt tender of aid from all quarters of the South most abundantly proves.

An Anonymous Report: "Tarred and Feathered"

John Brown's raid brought increased vigilance in the South to stop abolitionist activity. In this report, a Savannah man is tarred and feathered for, among other things, reading accounts of John Brown's trial to slaves.

Republican (Savannah), 2 December 1859

Sewall H. Fisk, a dealer in boots and shoes, on Market-square, of several years standing, has been the object of suspicion for some time, in consequence of his known Abolition proclivities, which he has taken, as we are informed, some trouble to make known to our slave population. His latest acts are, enticing negroes into his cellar at night, and reading them all sorts of Abolition documents, and last Sunday night was devoted especially to the history of the trial of John Brown, and a general exhortation upon the institution of Slavery and the advantages of freedom. These facts, as we hear, were sworn to before a Justice of the Peace by his nephew and his clerk; and coming to the ears of some parties who have constituted themselves a quasi-vigilance Committee, Mr. Fisk's store, over or in which he sleeps, was visited, *and he was called out and gagged before he could make either noise of resistance.* He was then placed in a carriage, and driven a short distance from the city, *and the application made to his nude person.* He was then left to find his way back, as best he could. His first appearance in the limits was near the hospital, where he came in sight of a watchman, who was so alarmed at the sight that he gave a spasmodic jerk to his rattle and took to his heels, not willing to face so dreadful an apparition. A reinforcement, however, was brave enough to approach him, when he was conducted home, the most pitiable object it is possible to imagine. Not a spot of his skin was visible, and his hair was trimmed close to his head.

James Faran: "Our Harper's Ferry and Charlestown News"

Virginia hanged John Brown on December 2, and papers everywhere carried that report the next day, courtesy of the telegraph. The Cincinnati Enquirer *had long been sympathetic to Southern causes and states' rights. In this editorial, James Faran rejoices that Brown is dead.*

Enquirer **(Cincinnati), 3 December 1859**

Elsewhere we publish a letter and dispatch from our special reporter at Harper's Ferry and Charlestown. They disclose a great state of excitement in Virginia. The arrest of those three merchants on the cars is evidence of the extent to which the authorities of Virginia have deemed it necessary to go for the public safety. But what a great wrong has been inflicted on Virginia by her brethren of the North, that compels her to resort to such extreme measures for her safety. She has done nothing to merit such treatment.

She is now as she was in the days of the Revolution, at the adoption of the Constitution, and has done nothing since to demand worse treatment from the people of the free States than she merited at these periods from those with whom she was laboring for the liberties of the people and the establishment of a National Government. She was slave then; she is no more so now. And the people of the free States have entered into a compact with her not to interfere in her internal domestic affairs, and if any of her slave property escapes, to interpose no obstacle to its return. Why, then, should her peace be threatened, the lives and property of her citizens jeopardized by citizens of the free States?

We rejoice that old BROWN has been hung. He was not only a murderer of innocent persons, but he attempted one of the greatest crimes against society—the stirring up of a servile and civil war. He has paid the penalty for his crimes, and we hope his fate may be a warning to all who might have felt inclined to imitate his aggressive conduct.

An Anonymous Report: "The South and John Brown. Agitation Unabated"

For the most part, Northern newspaper editors may have sympathized with those who opposed slavery, but they did not think that the actions of John Brown were correct, nor did they think that Brown should not be punished for his actions. In this anonymous letter from Washington, D.C., the writer—as did many people both North and South—feels that Brown's actions signaled an end to both regions living under one government, a more pessimistic view than that of John Polhill in the Milledgeville Federal Union *above. The writer recalls the nullification controversy of 1832, in which many Southerners opposed such an act, but says that now every Southern state will respond to a call for the dissolution of the Union if given a reason.*

New-York Times, 7 December 1859

GLOOMY PICTURE OF THE POLITICAL CONDITION OF AFFAIRS. . . .

In all our previous troubles I never had a shadow of a fear as to the Union—my nerves are not easily moved; on the contrary, I am hopeful and always disposed to look on the favorable side. But now I acknowledge that my fears amount almost to *conviction* that we on the 5th see the *last Congress* of the present Union assemble. . . .

It is all idle talk to say this Union can be maintained by *force* and *conquest.* The first drop of blood shed in that way, would of itself be fatal. In 1832, when South Carolina took the bit in her mouth, when Gen. JACKSON had his whole party to support him—when the Whig Party rallied also to his support, and when South Carolina had no support or even sympathy from her Southern friends within her own limits, and a very strong Union party in her own bosom,—even under all these circumstances, had there been a collision of arms, the Union would then have perished. Now, not a Southern State that would not bound up to the cry dissolution, and I really fear the evil is gone too far to be corrected.

Still, we must all do what we can; and, as the head of a leading influential Press, you have a great responsibility upon you. I think the duty of the Northern Press is certainly to denounce the course of the ultras: to repress all feelings of sympathy for, and all attempts to make BROWN a martyr—to try and pour oil on the troubled waters—to soothe the irritated feelings which have sprung up at the South, and to try and convince them that the North are not hostile—that the number are but very limited who preach the doctrine of blood and ire at the South—that the Phillipses, Smiths, Giddingses and Garrisons have no extensive influence, and, in short, to do all that will tend to restore good and friendly feelings between the two sections. The atrocious and cold-blooded course of BROWN in Kansas debars him from all consideration of feeling towards him, and it is really surprising that one individual can have a particle of feeling for such a miscreant, entirely independent of the affair at Harper's Ferry. I wish you could spend next week here, and I think you would be convinced that my views and fears are not unfounded. I have letters from some of the most sober-minded, conservative, old-line Whigs at the South—all of the most gloomy kind, and all uniting in the belief that the event is inevitable. I pray it may be otherwise!

QUESTIONS

1. In the reports supporting John Brown, the writers say violence is sometimes necessary to support a cause or to end injustice. Support or refute this idea, using the American situation as it existed at the time of the Harper's Ferry raid and at other times of crisis for the nation.
2. The Southern argument for slavery included the concept that it was legal according to the Constitution. How might you argue to support or refute this position?
3. Why do you think the South felt so threatened by John Brown's raid?

NOTES

1. *Enquirer* (Cincinnati, Ohio), 3 December 1859.

2. George Brown Tindall, *America: A Narrative History,* 2 vols. (New York: W.W. Norton, 1984), 1:595.

3. A number of sources discuss John Brown, his exploits in Kansas, the Harper's Ferry raid, and Brown's trial. See Jules Abels, *Man on Fire: John Brown and the Cause of Liberty* (New York: Macmillan, 1971); Stephen B. Oates, *To Purge This Land with Blood: A Biography of John Brown* (New York: Harper & Row, 1970); James C. Malin,

John Brown and the Legend of the Fifty-Six (Philadelphia, 1942; reprint, New York: Haskell House, 1970). David M. Potter, *The Impending Crisis, 1848–1861* (New York: Harper & Row, 1976) contains a condensed but good recounting of Brown and his activities.

4. Frederick Douglass, *Life and Times of Frederick Douglass, Written by Himself* (Hartford, Conn.: Park Publishing, 1881), 315–20.

5. *Herald* (New York), 3 November 1859.

6. Richmond *Enquirer*, and William H. Gist, quoted in Potter, *The Impending Crisis*, 383.

Selected Bibliography

Angle, Paul M., ed., *Created Equal: The Complete Lincoln–Douglas Debates of 1858.* Chicago: University of Chicago Press, 1958.

Arrington, Leonard J. and Davis Bitton. *The Mormon Experience: A History of the Latter-day Saints.* New York: Vantage Books, 1980.

"Avalon Project at Yale Law School." http://www.yale.edu/lawweb/avalon/19th.htm.

Benson, T. Lloyd. "Secession Editorials Project." http://history.furman.edu/~benson/docs/index.htm.

Blocker, Jack S. *American Temperance Movements: Cycles of Reform.* Boston: Twayne Publishers, 1989.

Boucher, Chauncy Samuel. *The Nullification Controversy in South Carolina.* Chicago: University of Chicago Press, 1916.

Broadhurst, Dale. "Readings in Early Mormon History." http://www.lavazone2.com/dbroadhu/index.htm.

Brown, Richard D. *Knowledge Is Power: The Diffusion of Power in Early America, 1700–1865.* New York: Oxford University Press, 1989.

Coward, John M. *The Newspaper Indian: Native American Identity in the Press, 1820–1860.* Urbana: University of Illinois Press, 1999.

Cremin, Lawrence A. *American Education: The American Experience, 1783–1876.* New York: Harper & Row, 1980.

Ehrlich, Walter. *They Have No Rights: Dred Scott's Struggle for Freedom.* Westport, Conn.: Greenwood Press, 1979.

Ellis, Richard E. *The Union at Risk: Jacksonian Democracy, States' Rights, and the Nullification Crisis.* New York: Oxford University Press, 1987.

Evarts, Jeremiah. *Cherokee Removal: The "William Penn" Essays and Other Writings,* ed. Francis Paul Prucha. Knoxville: University of Tennessee Press, 1981.

Fehrenbacher, Don E. *The Dred Scott Case, Its Significance in American Law and Politics.* New York: Oxford University Press, 1978.

——.*Prelude to Greatness: Lincoln in the 1850's.* Stanford, Calif.: Stanford University Press, 1962.

——.*Slavery, Law, and Politics: The Dred Scott Case in Historical Perspective.* New York: Oxford University Press, 1981.

Flint, H.M. *Life of Stephen A. Douglas.* Philadelphia: John E. Potter, 1863.

Foreman, Grant. *Indian Removal: The Emigration of the Five Civilized Tribes of Indians.* Norman: University of Oklahoma Press, 1932.

Fraser, James W. *The School in the United States.* Boston: McGraw-Hill, 2001.

Freehling, William W. *Prelude to Civil War: The Nullification Controversy in South Carolina 1816–1836.* New York: Harper & Row, 1966.

Govan, T.P. *Nicholas Biddle: Nationalist and Public Banker.* Chicago: University of Chicago Press, 1959.

Griffith, Elisabeth. *In Her Own Right: The Life of Elizabeth Cady Stanton.* New York: Oxford University Press, 1984.

Hammond, Bray. *Banks and Politics in America from the Revolution to the Civil War.* Princeton, N.J.: Princeton University Press, 1957.

Herndon, William H. and Jesse W. Wirk. *Abraham Lincoln: The True Story of a Great Life.* New York: D. Appleton, 1892.

Hoover, Merle M. *Park Benjamin: Poet & Editor.* New York: Columbia University Press, 1948.

Humphrey, Carol Sue. *The Press of the Young Republic, 1783–1833.* Westport, Conn.: Greenwood Press, 1996.

Huntzicker, William E. *The Popular Press, 1833–1865.* Westport, Conn.: Greenwood Press, 1999.

Jaffa, Harry V. *Crisis of the House Divided: An Interpretation of the Issues in the Lincoln–Douglas Debates.* Garden City, N.Y.: Doubleday, 1959.

Johannsen, Robert W. *Stephen A. Douglas.* New York: Oxford University Press, 1973.

Jones, Howard. *To the Webster–Ashburton Treaty: A Study in Anglo-American Relations, 1783–1843.* Chapel Hill: University of North Carolina Press, 1977.

Kutler, Stanley I., ed. *The Dred Scott Decision: Law or Politics?* Boston: Houghton Mifflin, 1967.

"Making of America." http://moa.umdl.umich.edu.

May, Ernest R. *The Making of the Monroe Doctrine.* Cambridge: Harvard University Press, 1975.

McFaul, John M. *The Politics of Jacksonian Finance.* Ithaca, N.Y.: Cornell University Press, 1972.

Merk, Frederick. *Manifest Destiny and Mission in American History.* New York: Alfred A. Knopf, 1963.

——. *Slavery and the Annexation of Texas.* New York: Alfred A. Knopf, 1972.

Moore, Glover. *The Missouri Controversy 1819–1821.* Lexington: University of Kentucky Press, 1966.

Morrison, Chaplain W. *Democratic Politics and Sectionalism: The Wilmot Proviso Controversy.* Chapel Hill: University of North Carolina Press, 1967.

O'Brien, Frank M. *The Story of* The Sun. New York: D. Appleton, 1928; reprint, New York: Greenwood Press, 1968.

Osagie, Iyunolu Folayan. *The* Amistad *Revolt.* Athens: University of Georgia Press, 2000.

Perdue, Theda, ed. *Cherokee Editor: The Writings of Elias Boudinot.* Knoxville: University of Tennessee Press, 1983.

Perdue, Theda and Michael D. Green, eds. *The Cherokee Removal: A Brief History with Documents.* Boston: Bedford Books, 1995.

Perkins, Dexter. *A History of the Monroe Doctrine.* Boston: Little, Brown and Company, 1941.

Peterson, Merrill D. *Olive Branch and Sword: The Compromise of 1833.* Baton Rouge: Louisiana State University Press, 1982.

Railton, Stephen. Uncle Tom's Cabin *and American Culture.* http://www.iath.virginia.edu/utc.

Remini, Robert V. *Andrew Jackson and the Course of American Freedom, 1822–1832.* New York: Harper & Row, 1981.

Ripley, C. Peter, ed. *The Black Abolitionist Papers.* 5 Vols. Chapel Hill: University of North Carolina Press, 1991.

Rohrbough, Malcolm J. *Days of Gold: The California Gold Rush and the American Nation.* Berkeley: University of California Press, 1997.

Satz, Ronald N. *American Indian Policy in the Jacksonian Era.* Lincoln: University of Nebraska Press, 1975.

Sigelschiffer, Saul. *The American Conscience: The Drama of the Lincoln–Douglas Debates.* New York: Horizon Press, 1973.

Smith, Culver H. *The Press, Politics, and Patronage: The American Government's Use of Newspapers 1789–1875.* Athens: University of Georgia Press, 1977.

Smith, W.B. *Economic Aspects of the Second Bank of the United States.* Cambridge: Harvard University Press, 1953.

Staudenraus, P.J. *The African Colonization Movement, 1816–1865.* New York: Columbia University Press, 1961.

Sydnor, Charles S. *The Development of Southern Sectionalism, 1819–1848.* Baton Rouge: Louisiana State University Press, 1948.

Thomas, John L. *The Liberator: William Lloyd Garrison.* Boston: Little, Brown and Company, 1963.

Tucher, Andie. *Froth and Scum: Truth, Beauty, Goodness, and the Ax Murder in America's First Mass Medium.* Chapel Hill: University of North Carolina Press, 1994.

Tyrrell, Ian R. *Sobering Up: From Temperance to Prohibition in Antebellum America, 1800–1860.* Westport, Conn.: Greenwood Press, 1979.

Index

About the Author

DAVID A. COPELAND is the A. J. Fletcher Professor of Communication at Elon University. He is the author of *Debating the Issues in Colonial Newspapers* (Greenwood, 2000), *Colonial Newspapers: Character and Content* (1997), and *Benjamin Keach and the Development of Baptist Traditions in Seventeenth-Century England* (2001). A past president of the American Journalism Historians Association, he was named Carnegie Foundation for the Advancement of Teaching Virginia Professor of the Year in 1998.